Philosopher on Dover Beach

Philosopher on Dover Beach
Essays

Roger Scruton

St. Augustine's Press
South Bend, Indiana

Manufactured in the United States of America.

Cataloging in Publication Data

Scruton, Roger.
    Philosopher on Dover Beach : essays / Roger Scruton.
        p.   cm.
    Includes bibliographical references (p.   ) and index.
    ISBN 1-890318-60-4 (alk. paper)
        1. Philosophy and culture. 2. Europe—Civilization—Philosophy.   I. Title.
    B59.S37 1998
    824'.914—dc21   97-37676
                                                                      CIP

∞The paper used in this publication meets the minimum requirements of the American
National Standard for Information Sciences—Permanence of Paper for Printed Materials,
ANSI Z39.48-1984.

CONTENTS

Contents

PREFACE

The culture of Europe, and the civilization that has sprung from it, are not yet dead. The opportunity remains to give our best to them, and to receive, in reward, the experience of belonging. For a century or more, Western man has listened to prophecies of his own decline, has been schooled in guilt and self-abnegation, and has doubted the civilizing force of his beliefs, his institutions and his way of life. Since nothing has ever been put in the place of those good things, save tinsel illusions and lawless power, the result of this self-repudiation has been a kind of active nihilism – a nihilism not of the mind and the soul only, but of the forms of social life and the structures of political power.

It is unfashionable to say that Western civilization still lives, that it is nobler, better and more worthy of survival than its rivals, and that we ought to cease our childish lamentations and give ourselves to its defence. Nevertheless, I hope that these essays offer some partial vindication of the culture of Europe, and of the moral sense that speaks through it. And I hope that some of my readers will take heart, recognizing that there is a way out of the barrenness of modernism, and that it is a way not forwards into the unknown, but backwards into the familiar. These essays and reviews, written over a decade, form a sequel to an earlier collection, *The Politics of Culture*. Three categories have been excluded from this collection: those of ephemeral interest; those on architecture, which will appear in another volume; and those addressed to the readers of learned journals. The learned journal is an important institution, and some of my arguments here are taken further in pieces submitted to academic editors. Nevertheless, the language of scholarship has been corrupted. The constraints of the modern university lead to a style of thought that is both intellectually timorous and asleep to the sensory world. I have therefore tried to distance myself from academic philosophy. Here and there – as in the essay on Masaryk and Patočka – I suggest other tasks for philosophy than those favoured by the schools. I also try to revive the concern for culture, as the neglected purpose of intellectual life. And everywhere I endeavour to combine subjects which, while belonging to separate academic compartments, belong together in the spiritual life of modern man.

Some of these essays appear for the first time; others are reprinted, or adapted from material already published. I am grateful to the various editors for permission to use them again.

London, September 1989

PART I
PHILOSOPHY AND
CULTURE

1

THE PHILOSOPHER ON DOVER BEACH

In *The Critique of Pure Reason*, Kant struck such a blow against the traditional arguments of theology as to leave that science in a condition of self-doubt from which it has never recovered. Nevertheless religion survived; it was Kant's declared hope, indeed, that, by destroying the claims of Reason, he had made room for those of Faith. It may not be possible to deduce the existence of a necessary being from the premiss of the world's contingency; yet a true understanding of the world and of our place as free beings within it opens the way, he thought, to a religious experience that is all the more secure through being independent of theology. Through the moral law, and the act of obedience which it compels from us, we are presented with so vivid an intimation of transcendence, as to want nothing that is needed for the worship of God.

In *The Critique of Practical Reason*, Kant went further, arguing that practical reason, which is the foundation of morality, could provide a substitute for theology, a new science of the divine which would uphold the very system of beliefs that traditional theology had sought in vain to justify. We need not follow Kant into these difficult regions in order to feel some sympathy for the idea which originally inspired him: the idea that morality, far from depending on the belief in God, provides a unique and vivid support for it. So persuaded was Kant, however, by the view that morality is the ground rather than the consequent of religion, that he allowed himself to describe the moral life in terms borrowed directly from liturgical tradition. The worship due to God became a kind of 'reverence' for the moral law. The faith which transcends belief became the certainty of practical reason, which surpasses understanding. The object of esteem was not the Supreme Being, but the supreme attribute of Reason.

The moral order was the 'realm of grace', the actual community of rational beings the 'mystical body' in the world of nature, and the Kingdom of God to which mortals aspire became the Kingdom of Ends which they make real through their self-legislation.

Thus, in providing a moral basis for religious doctrine, Kant presented a thoroughly 'theologized' morality, one which preserved, in transfigured form, the basic conceptions of Christian doctrine. It is not surprising, therefore, if Nietzsche, in his persona as Antichrist, should have sought to undo the work of this 'catastrophic spider'. The web of sophistication which Kant had spun around the Christian religion was torn to shreds. Nietzsche was one of the officious housemaids who savaged it; the other was Marx. Both wished to destroy the authority of Christian doctrine by providing a naturalistic explanation – a 'genealogy' – of our belief in it. For Nietzsche, Christianity, and the Kantian morality which now sits bareheaded upon the grave thereof, are illusions of the resentful, distorting mirrors in which the strong are crumpled and the cripples stand tall. For Marx, religion was the controlling ideology of the powerful, which translates the artifice of power into a natural order and a gift of God. For both of them, the inherited religion of the West is not just an untruth, but a sophisticated *lie*.

The Nietzschean and Marxian explanations of Christian belief are incompatible. It is therefore somewhat surprising that the two philosophies are not more fervently at loggerheads, that Marxists do not devote pages to the refutation of the Nietzschean theory of *ressentiment*, and Nietzscheans pages to the refutation of the Marxist theories of ideology and class. A Marxist, wishing to increase the power of the powerless, seeks to destroy religion; if a Nietzschean joins with him in the work of destruction, however, it is because he seeks to take away from the powerless the little power that they have. Nevertheless, both Marxists and Nietzscheans rest secure in the belief that either of their explanations will undermine the credibility of the thing explained. This 'undermining of belief' is the real source of the appeal of both philosophies – the sense that the world is being rid of faith, mystery and illusion; that we are coming face to face with a 'bare reality', and also with ourselves as part of that reality, the disillusioned centre of an ungoverned world.

From that disenchanted vision of the cosmos flow two rival moralities: the aesthetic one of self-affirmation, and the political one of Utopian justice. Perhaps nothing is more remarkable, in these moralities of unbelief, than the ease with which they may be conjoined in a single soul – the ease with which a person may believe that the cause of self-affirmation and the cause of Utopia are one and the same, and that whatever is right according to the one standard will also be right according to the other. Such is the state of mind conveyed in his later writings by Sartre, for whom the absolute lawlessness and unanswerability of the existentialist anti-hero were identical with the selfless pursuit of a revolutionary justice. The mental labour whereby Sartre accomplished this synthesis was perhaps not so great as that involved in writing, let alone reading, the *Critique de la raison dialectique*. A pattern of thought that is reiterated by every articulate terrorist cannot derive from the opaque justification which Sartre provided for it. Sartre's *Critique* should perhaps be seen as an attempt at theology: a presentation of arcane reasons for an independently existing emotional tendency. Whether in its theological or in its spontaneous form, however, this tendency shows the extraordinary ease with which disenchantment and the love of self can be combined into a revolutionary purpose. The point is perhaps familiar from the writings of Turgenev and Conrad. Nevertheless, it is worth returning to: the gap between nihilism and revolutionary commitment remains as narrow today as it was a century ago, and the sparks which fly across it are as inflammatory now as then.

Judged as 'genealogy', the Nietzschean and Marxian theories of Christian belief are far from satisfactory. Nietzsche's theory is incompatible with the manifest truth that Christianity has provided such psychological space for the strong and the dominant as to allow them to establish empires throughout the world. Marx's theory of religion – like his theory of so much else – is trivial, amounting to little more than the indisputable claim that religion survives because it is not dysfunctional.

I doubt that any serious believer would be very much disturbed by the general possibility of a naturalistic explanation of religion. If the claims of faith are true, then it follows that no scientific explanation of our belief could involve a commitment to God's existence, since God is transcendental. That religious belief is to be explained naturalistically is precisely what a true believer must expect. Debunking explanations of religion can therefore hardly give us any new reason for rejecting it – any reason that was not already contained in Kant's attack on natural theology. Their interest lies rather in their moral character.

Some insight into this character can be obtained from the archetype of naturalism: Ludwig Feuerbach's *Essence of Christianity*, in which the traditional conceptions of Christian theology were explained in terms of a brilliant theory of psychological projection. Religion in general, Feuerbach argued, and Christianity in particular, can be seen as elaborate devices whereby man frees himself from the arduous task of self-improvement, by personifying his virtues and his communal life, and setting them up outside himself, in a transcendental realm, all possibility of access to which is barred to him. The evil of religion consists precisely in its ability to sever man from his possibilities, to alienate him from his fulfilment in 'species being', and to maintain him in a condition of slavery and subjection, the victim of his transcendental illusions.

The success of Feuerbach's book – which influenced, in language, thought and outlook, the entire history of German nineteenth-century social thinking – is again to be seen, not in the fact that it explained the belief in God without also evincing it, but in the fact that the explanation served to focus a profound hostility to religion, and to represent faith as the root cause of the very evil for which it had always been offered as a remedy – the evil of guilt, or 'original sin'. At the same time, the theory seems to preserve one of the fundamental components of religious thinking. It offers us redemption, in a new and 'disenchanted' form. Feuerbach, like Nietzsche and Marx, saw the Christian religion as a barrier to man's fulfilment, and man as containing within himself the possibility of his own salvation. Religion, far from being the palliative to original sin, is in fact the cause of man's fall. Thus the theory continues to see man's destiny as Christianity sees it, as a transition from innocence to fault to final redemption.

Feuerbach's theory not only displaces God from the explanation of religion; it also makes God redundant, by placing his redemptive capacity in the hands of man. A Muslim might say that this final negation of the religious urge is the price we have paid for the idea of incarnation. In fact, however, the secular faiths of our time constitute precisely a reversal of the doctrine of an incarnate God. They regard God as deriving his nature and purpose from our own activity. It is not that God incarnates himself in man, but that man spiritualizes – and so enfeebles – himself in God.

Secular survivals of the belief in redemption provide significant testimony to man's religious need. Religion does not provide the obstacle to the 'species being' that was of such concern to Feuerbach. Rather, it *stems* from species being, and is the clearest sign, in our daily business, that we are creatures who need to be joined not only to each other, but to our forebears and our progeny, and who are called to sacrifice ourselves for the sake of collective survival. By worship of the transcendental we give form and content to our need for renunciation – a renunciation which is in the long-term interest of the tribe. If you like naturalistic explanations of religion, then this one is surely the most intuitively plausible: that religion is the voice of the species, which becomes articulate in us, in order that we should more willingly obey it. The need for individual salvation is also the need to be reconciled with the community; the need to overcome the reluctance to sacrifice; the need to be accepted back into the realm of love – love of mate, family, ancestors and progeny, love in particular of what has yet to be. (If you ask yourself why marriage is a sacrament and a vow before God, then you will instantly see the plausibility of such an explanation, as well as the real contribution made by religion to the happiness of man.)

If you point to the actual unhappiness of modern man under the rule of secular doctrine; if you mention the Holocaust, the Gulag and the self-expanding system of enslavement which has been built from the new morality of Marx and Lenin; if you say that here, for everyone to see, is the proof of original sin, and the evidence that man is after all not sufficient for his own redemption, failing most dismally in emancipating himself precisely when he seeks to free himself from God: if you say such things, a thousand excuses are offered, and a thousand accusations made against the old transcendental faith. And it is indeed right to insist that all human institutions – religion included – are contaminated by man's vanity and imperfection. Nevertheless, rather than dismiss the accusations that are made against the Marxian and the Nietzschean religions, we should look more closely, I believe, at what is peculiar about the cruelties that have been perpetrated in the name of them – apart from the obvious fact of their astonishing scale.

It seems to me that the morally decisive feature of the death camp – and of the totalitarian system which engenders it – is its impersonal, cynical and scientific approach to the victims. Systematic torture and murder become a bureaucratic task, for which no one is liable, and for which no one is particularly to blame. Hannah Arendt wrote, in this connection, of a 'banalization' of evil. It would be more appropriate to speak of a 'depersonalization', a severance of evil from the network of personal responsibility. The totalitarian system, and the extermination camp, which is its most sublime expression, are without the marks of individual care. In such a system, human life is driven underground, and the precious ideas of freedom and responsibility – ideas without which our picture of man as a moral subject disintegrates entirely – have no public recognition, and no place in the administrative process. If it is so easy to destroy people in such a system, it is because human life enters the public world already severed from its value.

I do not offer to prove, what nevertheless has been vividly impressed on me by my own study and experience, that this impersonal (and therefore ungovernable) evil is the true legacy of the naturalistic view of man. Those very philosophies which enjoin us to place man upon the throne from which God was taken away for burial, have been most influential in creating the new image of man as an accident of nature, to whom nothing is either forbidden or permitted by any power beyond himself. God, they tell us, is an illusion; so too is the divine spark in man. Human freedom is nothing but an appearance on the face of nature; beneath it rides the same implacable causality, the same sovereign indifference, which prepares death equally and unconcernedly for all of us, and which tells us that beyond death there is nothing. This vision – whose moral temper was captured so perfectly by Leopardi – is present, in some form or other, in almost all truly modern literature and art. It rises to brief and threatening glory in the revolutionary consciousness of Lenin. But, even though it may clothe itself in Utopian ambitions, the very adoption of a 'morality of goals' serves further to fuel its inner nihilism. The machine which is established for the efficient production of Utopia has total licence to kill. Nothing is sacred, and its killings are not murders (for which human individuals alone are liable) but 'liquidations'. Such is the liturgical language of the religion of Antichrist, the religion which puts man in God's place, and yet which sees in man only the mortal organism, the slowly evaporating gobbet of flesh.

It is misleading, however, to describe the disenchanted faiths of the Marxist and the Nietzschean simply as religions. Rather they are superstitions; for they direct towards what is merely contingent the absolute submission which is due to God. They also recall only one half – and the less vital half – of religious thinking. They preserve, in doctrinal form, the quest for man's redemption, while scorning the sacred as a sign of man's incompetence. From this, I believe, stems the profoundly destructive character of these secular superstitions.

The naturalistic explanations which threaten our sense of the sacred, threaten also the impulse of piety, upon which community and morality are founded. This is what Matthew Arnold foresaw on that 'darkling plain': the loss of piety, the loss of respect for what is holy and untouchable; and in place of them a presumptuous ignorance, fortified by science. We should ask ourselves, therefore, whether we really are constrained, by our scientific realism, to dismiss the sacred from our view of things. Perhaps we might yet be able to find in our lives some intimation of a transcendence that we can neither explain nor describe, but to which we must address ourselves through symbols.

Kant argued that, while there is no place for the free being in the world described by science, our own self-awareness, without which no description of the world makes sense to us, forces upon us the idea that we are free. We live with two seemingly incompatible views of ourselves, and neither can be rejected without losing all title to objective knowledge. To see the world as scientifically explicable is to understand the object of knowledge; to see ourselves as free is to understand the subject. Subject and object exist in mutual interdependence, and each is nothing without the other.

Kant's answer to the problem of freedom was not so much a solution as a suspension of the question. The mystery, he argued, could never be comprehended. All we can do by way of reconciling the perspective of freedom with the perspective of science is to suggest that they open on to a single reality. That which, to scientific explanation, appears lawlike and caused, to the moral life seems free; and neither appearance is delusory. The perspective of freedom asks questions that are never asked by science. The 'Why?' of the free being seeks meanings, not causes. And from this search for meanings all value is derived. Freedom is the mysterious lining of the human organism, the subjective reality which gives sense and direction to our lives. Yet the free being is incarnate, and to see the human life as a vehicle for freedom – to see a face where the scientist sees flesh and bone – is to recognize that this, at least, is sacred, that this small piece of earthly matter is not to be treated as a means to our purposes, but as an end in itself.

Kant's theory of freedom shows us how we might understand the sacred and the miraculous. Our understanding of the miraculous is like our understanding of the person. When we see another's smile we see human flesh moving in obedience to impulses in the nerves. No law of nature is suspended in this process: we smile not in spite of, but because of, nature. Nevertheless, we understand a smile in quite another way: not as flesh, but as spirit, freely revealed. A smile is always more than flesh for us, even if it is only flesh.

A miraculous event is one which wears, for us, a personal expression. We may not notice this expression, just as someone may stare at a portrait, see all the lines and colours which compose it, and fail to see the face. Similarly, a sacred place is one in which personality and freedom shine forth from what is contingent, dependent and commonplace – from a piece of stone, a tree, or a patch of water. Here we approach a thought that Kant expressed rather differently, in *The Critique of Judgment*. There is an attitude that we direct to the human person, and which leads us to see, in the human form, a perspective on the world that reaches from a point outside it. We may direct this very attitude, on occasion, to the whole of nature, and in particular to those places, things, events and artefacts where freedom has been real. The experience of the sacred is the sudden encounter with freedom; it is the recognition of personality and purposefulness in that which contains no human will. In a place of martyrdom, where the utmost personal freedom has been exercised in a final renunciation, the sense of the sacred is distilled, becoming the common property of all who have it in themselves to worship there.

Religion is inseparable, in the end, from our sense of holiness – from our recognition that the meaning that we find in the human person exists also, in heightened and more awesome form, outside us, in places, times and artefacts: in a shrine, a gathering, a place of pilgrimage or prayer. Nothing in the scientific view of things forbids the experience of the sacred: science tells us only that this experience has a natural cause. Those who seek for meanings are indifferent to causes, and those who communicate with God through prayer should be no more cut off from him by the knowledge that the world does not contain him, than they are cut off from those they love by the knowledge that words, smiles and gestures are nothing but movements of flesh.

It is difficult, however, to retain the sense of the sacred without the collective ritual which compels us to listen to the voice of the species. For the modern intellectual, who stands outside the crowd, the memory of enchantment may be awakened more easily by art than by prayer. Yet art, properly understood, is a kind of prayer: it is an attempt to call the timeless and the transcendental to the scene of some human incident. Hence Rilke's vision of the new, almost private religion through which the reign of the machine may be negated:

> But being is still enchanted for us; in a hundred
> Places it remains a source, a play of pure
> Forces which touches no one who does not kneel and wonder.

> Words still go softly out towards the unsayable.
> And music, always new, from palpitating stones
> Builds in useless space its godly home.

As Rilke showed in his life and poetry, and Eliot in his, the restoration of the sacred is no easy task. The point of intersection of the timeless with time may not be an occupation for the saint; but for those who are not in some measure saintly, it demands the willing co-operation of a whole community. And without the sacred, man lives in a depersonalized world: a world where all is permitted, and where nothing has absolute value. That, I believe, is the principal lesson of modern history, and if we tremble before it, it is because it contains a judgment on us. The hubris which leads us to believe that science has the answer to all our questions, that we are nothing but dying animals and that the meaning of life is merely self-affirmation, or at best the pursuit of some collective, all-embracing and all-too-human goal – this reckless superstition contains already the punishment of those who succumb to it.

From: *The Times Literary Supplement*, 23 May 1986.

2
SPENGLER'S
DECLINE OF THE WEST

Like many Englishmen of my generation, I entered grammar school with the sense that I was taking my first step toward a scientific career. Neither I nor my parents had a clear notion of what this involved, but it had been established in our minds that the future lay with science. Accordingly, I was set to work at differential calculus, the theory of heat, light, and sound, and the chemistry of carbon. Everything was settled and no questions asked.

One day I came across a volume of Rilke's letters. I read them with a feeling of astonished recognition, a sense of being myself the author of the words before me. I was dumbfounded, my senses alert as though in the presence of an unknown danger. I had been granted a vision. I had no words for it, except that it concerned a knowledge beyond science, beyond calculation, beyond our attempts to gain mastery over the future. The very concept of the future had no place in this other knowledge. Yet its mysterious content was such as to justify every effort on the part of the one who pursues it, as Rilke had pursued it through the written word, and Rodin, through those restless, titanic forms that illustrated the book. This knowledge also came, I conjectured, through music and through the asceticism that sets itself apart from things, and knows them through the Word alone.

That day saw a change in my plans, I continued with my studies, but with a sense that it was only some dead and dutiful part of me that engaged in them. The real me existed in those hours when literature and philosophy passed through my hands uncomprehended. And because I understood nothing, every word was invested with enormous power – a power of destiny, as though my life now ran in channels marked out for it by

12

authors long since dead. An air of holiness, a reckless disregard for the world and its requirements, seemed to radiate from those mysterious pages. They referred me to a place where justification was no longer needed and where it was sufficient just to be.

At the same time, a sadness grew in me, a sense that something was wrong with the world. Science and progress and money had prevented people from observing this thing; I too had been blind to its existence, so lost had I been in the world's concerns. But my feeling testified to its reality. Sadness looked out at me from art and literature, like the pitying face of a painted saint. I encountered it in the words of Eliot, I saw it in the mad paintings of Van Gogh, and I heard it in the infinite, still spaces of Beethoven's last quartets – spaces made through sound, in which, however, there reigns a greater silence than can be heard in any desert.

When I was sixteen, a second decisive experience occurred. I discovered that my school contained others like myself – boys who had stumbled across the world of art and philosophy, or who (not being confined as I was to the science laboratories) had been gently guided there by some enlightened master. Friendships sprang up; we exchanged notes, books, and arguments. I even ventured to express the feeling that had weighed on me: the feeling of catastrophe, of a falling away from some never-to-be recovered state of serenity. The boy who received my confidence was younger than I and had the reputation of being a kind of genius – which he was, by our standards, for he could play the Bartók piano sonata (the object of all our ambitions) and could also recite from memory pages of German verse. His response to my confusion was to look at me intently through thick spectacles and command me, in his treble voice, not to read *The Decline of the West*. As long as I kept away from that book, I might still be saved. But if I so much as touched it, he warned, I was doomed forever.

I went straight to the public library and found the volume. (My friend, I discovered later, had his own tattered copy, which he pored over nightly.) The title alone was intoxicating. Indeed, for several days I did not advance very far beyond it. Those five words told me that the sense of decline that troubled me was no personal foible but the sign of a cosmic tragedy that was playing itself out in me. It linked my own paltry emotions to the destiny of civilization itself. I had been caught up in a drama of untold proportions and, just as the heart of the worshipper leaps to discover God's personal interest in him; just as the psychoanalytic patient feels a renewed will to live on learning that his petty suffering conforms to some universal archetype; so did I become happy in my mournful emotions, knowing that it was not I, but culture itself, that was alive in them, and also dying there. I became more fully wedded to despair, in the very act of discovering that the despair was not mine. And when, a few days later, my mischievous friend forbade me to read another of his favourite books – Erich Heller's *Disinherited Mind* – I was able to add a second sloganizing title to the one that had first impressed me. I felt that I possessed, at last, the secret of my *Weltschmerz*. I was disinherited, like all my generation, from the culture to which my soul was owed.

Culture was the name for that knowledge beyond science which had been promised to me in Rilke's letters. Culture, I thought, was a kind of self-sufficient knowledge, not tainted like science by the separation of the knower from the known. It lives in us, and us in it; and what is living must also die. Its concern is not being but becoming; not mechanism, cause, and experiment, but life, history, and destiny. Those ideas came to me by a kind of osmosis from Spengler, who also told me that I had already been initiated into culture, since it was this that had made me sad. My experience of art came to me with a sense of loss, a knowledge that I was among the last to whom it would be offered, and that, with the passing of my generation, the light of civilization would be extinguished forever and all meaning gone from the world. Unlike the cheerful scientific view of things that I learned in my formal classes – the view of a constantly accumulating store of knowledge, whose application would ensure the mental and physical progress of mankind – the image that I acquired from Spengler was of an inheritance more easily lost than won, and never more easily than through the heedless pursuit of objective science: 'One day the last portrait of Rembrandt and the last bar of Mozart will have ceased to be – though possibly a coloured canvas and a sheet of notes may remain – because the last eye and the last ear accessible to their message will have gone' (vol. 1, p. 168). When I first came across those words, I knew so little about Western culture (although the thesis of its decline was already an immovable part of my mental equipment) that I could hardly be said to have believed them. Nevertheless, I greeted them with enthusiasm. Like Pound, whose poems I was reading at the time, I was a 'barbarian let loose in a library', who took from what he read just so much as was necessary to satisfy his own emotions.

From Spengler I took two further things, besides the view of culture to which I have alluded. First, the cyclical theory of history, and second, the idea that such a theory could not be established by scientific argument. This second idea, far from being a refutation of Spengler's theory, struck me as a refutation of science: a proof that the real truths, those which we understand and accept in the life-process itself, are inaccessible to scientific method. How impressive indeed, was the opening chapter of *The Decline of the West*, in which mathematics is thrown from its pedestal. The theory that had been offered to me as a paradigm of objective certainty and the heart of scientific knowledge was placed beside the 'Magian' mathematics of Arabia and the 'Apollinian' mathematics of Euclid. It was shown (by reasoning which only later did I see to be entirely fraudulent) to be of no greater and no lesser validity than they, and to derive its value not from its status as objective science but from its ability to give form and expression to the Faustian spirit that lives and thrives in all the great creations of our culture, and whose death-pangs had been foretold in me. Spengler offered not a science of history but a philosophy – and the philosophy of history, he claimed, was the only possible philosophy for our times. Accordingly, when I went at last to university, I changed the direction of my studies from natural science (the price of my admission) to philosophy – a subject that, I supposed, counted Nietzsche and Spengler among its greatest masters.

The university I attended was Cambridge, and the philosophy I studied was that bequeathed by Russell, Wittgenstein, and Moore. I learned that neither Spengler nor Nietzsche was a philosopher in anything but a metaphorical sense; that both had an extremely weak grasp of the logical principles my teachers were impressing on me; and that in neither thinker's theories was truth accorded a position comparable to that occupied by empty rhetoric. I resisted such conclusions, of course, but with a dwindling self-confidence and a sense of defeat. Little by little, thanks in part to my own scientific training, whose preconceptions were now fortified by the truths of logical analysis (truths that are denied only by those who do not understand them), I gave in to analytical philosophy; and when, at the end of my first year of studies, I returned to the book which had first set me on the path of them, I found in it nothing more than megalomaniac fantasies, implausible analogies, and false distinctions founded neither in logic nor in fact.

However, the new philosophy I studied proved no more satisfactory to me than the science it had replaced. Still, it seemed to me, there was another and more important way of seeing things, a view onto the world for which the word 'culture' remained the most appropriate description. And still there was contained, in this other perspective, an experience of human value, together with the painful recognition of its mortality. It was never given to me to be a progressive, nor was I to acquire that cheerful 'clairantism' (as J. L. Austin called it) of the positivists and their successors: the belief that the mystery of things is our own creation, and that it wants only the effort of removing it for science to deliver the full and final truth about our condition. And if I have retained those traces of an *Urverdunkelung*, of an obstinate resistance to enlightenment and a belief in the necessity of culture and in the fact of its decline, it is as much the work of Spengler as of any of the more powerful thinkers who replaced him in my pantheon.

Looking back on *The Decline of the West*, I find one of the strangest creations of the human spirit, monstrous as a Grünenwald crucifixion, equally full of exaggerated feeling and a strange, exalted beauty. History is there, but reshaped in the telling of it, moulded into artistic forms, and painted over with a passionate chiaroscuro. Art is there too: the prime object of Spengler's reflections and the guiding principle of his argument, which moves with the urgency of poetry and in a style that speaks straight to the heart. Nothing is mentioned that is not touched with the writer's feeling, gathered into the *Sturm und Drang* of an inner drama. The writing is compelling because it is compelled, governed from first to last by a force of emotional necessity. To gain an objective view of such work is difficult, perhaps impossible. For to what category does it belong? Should we read it as historiography, as philosophy, as poetry, or as prophecy? In fact, Spengler answers a profound need of our culture: the need to bring philosophy, historiography, and art together in a form of speculation that will synthesize their insights and justify the title 'humane'. It is for this reason, I think, that we should still pay attention to his masterpiece. In this assessment I shall be unable to do justice to a gift of synthesis without which, I believe, there can be no such thing as serious writing in the humanities.

The thesis of the book is deceptively simple:

I hope to show that without exception all great creations and forms in religion, art, politics, social life, economy and science appear, fulfil themselves, and lie down *contemporaneously* in all the Cultures; that the inner structure of one corresponds strictly with that of all the others; that there is not a single phenomenon of deep physiognomic importance in the record of one for which we could not find a counterpart in the record of every other; and that this counterpart is to be found under a characteristic form and in a perfectly definite chronological position. (vol. 1, p. 122)

Deceptively simple, as I say, but also magical in its appeal, engaging at once with the inner emotions of anyone who has felt death in his body and longing in his heart – anyone for whom the religious urge is still a lived reality. And there is no denying the poetic insight that Spengler was able to bring to this idea. Here, for example, is a fragment of his discussion of the *Stabreim* (alliterative verse) of the Icelandic sagas:

> The accents of the Homeric hexameter are the soft rustle of a leaf in the midday sun, the rhythm of *matter*; but the Stabreim, like 'potential energy' in the world-pictures of modern physics, creates a tense restraint in the void without limits, distant night-storms over the highest peaks. In its swaying indefiniteness all words and things dissolve themselves – it is the dynamics, not the statics, of language. The same applies to the grave rhythm of *Media vita in morte sumus*. Here is heralded the colour of Rembrandt and the instrumentation of Beethoven – *here infinite solitude is felt as the home of the Faustian soul*. (vol. 1, p. 186)

And here is part of the astonishing description of the city in volume 2 – one of those sustained deliberations that form the high points of Spengler's vision and his most lasting contribution to our understanding of what we are:

> And then begins the gigantic megalopolis, the *city-as-world*, which suffers nothing beside itself and sets about *annihilating* the country picture. The town that once upon a time humbly accommodated itself to that picture now insists that it shall be the same as itself. *Extra muros*, chaussées and woods and pastures become a park, mountains become tourists' viewpoints; and *intra muros* arises an imitation of Nature, fountains in lieu of springs, flower-beds, formal pools, and clipped hedges in lieu of meadows and ponds and bushes. In a village the thatched roof is still hill-like and the street is of the same nature as the baulk of earth between fields. But here the picture is of deep, long gorges between high, stony houses filled with coloured dust and strange uproar, and men dwell in these houses, the like of which no nature-being has ever conceived. Costumes, even faces, are adjusted to a background of stone. By day there is a street traffic of strange colours and tones, and by night a new light that outshines the moon. And the yokel stands helpless on the pavement, understanding nothing and understood by nobody, tolerated as a useful type in farce and provider of this world's daily bread. (vol. 2, pp. 94–5)

And here is the beginning of one of those analogies that form the heart of Spengler's thinking, his literary greatness, and also – in their reckless disregard for real distinctions – the source of his intellectual failure:

In a rock-stratum are embedded crystals of a mineral. Clefts and cracks occur, water filters in, and the crystals are gradually washed out so that in due course only their hollow mould remains. Then come volcanic outbursts which explode the mountain; molten masses pour in, stiffen and crystallize out in their turn. But these are not free to do so in their own special forms. They must fill up the spaces that they find available. Thus there arise distorted forms, crystals whose inner structure contradicts their external shape, stones of one kind presenting the appearance of stones of another kind. The mineralogists call this phenomenon *Pseudomorphosis*.

By the term 'historical pseudomorphosis' I propose to designate those cases in which an older alien Culture lies so massively over the land that a young Culture, born in this land, cannot get its breath and fails not only to achieve pure and specific expression-forms, but even to develop fully its own self-consciousness. All that wells up from the depths of the young soul is cast in the old moulds, young feelings stiffen in senile works, and instead of rearing itself up in its own creative power, it can only hate the distant power with a hate that grows to be monstrous. (vol. 2, p. 189)

As I remarked, Spengler described *The Decline of the West* as a work of philosophy: a study of history which is at the same time the development of a philosophical idea. He believed that historiography could deliver philosophical conclusions, truths about man and his condition that would rival, in their comprehensiveness and authority, the conclusions of a Kant or a Plato – indeed, which would, by setting the works of other philosophers in their historical context, remove from them all claim to absolute validity, showing them to be, at best, only the manifestation of a particular human spirit at a particular stage of its inherent life.

The project was not new. A version of it had been put forward by Hegel. But there is an important difference. Unlike Spengler, Hegel was a real philosopher, capable of entering the stream of ideas above which he believed himself to stand in all-surveying majesty. He contributed arguments of his own to those of Aristotle, Leibniz, and Kant. In Spengler there is nothing similar – only a sly relativism, a way of standing apart from others' arguments in the belief that they can express no truth transcendent of the conditions of their production. If every culture is self-sufficient – containing both the way of knowing and the object known – then all expressions of a culture are also descriptions of it. Their truth is not universal, but extinguished, like life itself, in the flux of historical becoming.

Spengler set himself against scientific method. Science, he claims, uses causality as its principal category; its object of study must therefore be dead, immovable, without history. His historical philosophy replaces causality by destiny, which describes the principle of living things – of 'things becoming' and 'things become'. Perhaps the first step in disillusionment with Hegel, and with all the philosophy that has stemmed from Hegel, is the recognition that such contrasts are, in the last analysis, spurious. Causality governs the movement of living things as it governs the sun and the stars; becoming is not a separate condition, distinguishable from being and obedient to different laws; destiny, far from being the denial of causality, is simply another name for its final triumph. If Spengler has a meaning for us, it is not because of his attachment to those dichotomies – which in themselves have no authority – but because he uses them to present a vision that is not just unscientific, but *anti*-scientific, and which relates history to our present perception in a way that no science can.

Spengler stands in obvious and significant contrast to Marx, for whom the authority of science was absolute. Marx's science of history was to be materialistic: that is, it was to subsume history under the laws of motion that govern matter. At the same time, Marx believed, history has a direction, and this direction is precisely that of scientific progress. The Marxists have never reconciled their desire for a materialist theory of history with a progressivism that is so manifestly inspired by an image of mental, rather than material, accumulation. Rather than endeavour – as Buckle did in his *History of Civilization in England* – to show how the movement of history itself obeys the movement of intellectual advance, the Marxists have tried to reverse the causal order, always without success. In some sense, perhaps, mental processes are physical: but only in a sense that trivializes the Marxist theory of history and undermines the vulgar materialism that inspired it.

Marxism is not a scientific, but a *scientistic* theory: a metaphysic, decked out with the signs and symbols of science, and at the same time deprived of explanatory conceptions. It ended life as it began, as an alchemy of history, used not to explain the world but magically to transform it. The nature of a spell is to persuade the object of desire to yield itself, to become inevitable in reality, as it already is in thought. Marxism has, for the average believer, the consoling function once possessed by the Books of Thoth and Uriel: it describes what is impossible in the language of necessity, and by force of incantation seeks to overcome the obstinacy of the world.

Set beside Marxism, Spengler's *Decline of the West* can only win our sympathy. Here is another alchemy of history, but one that frankly admits itself to be such, that lays aside all claims to science and applies to the human world in its entirety and, with the daring of a Paracelsus or a Faust, the categories that describe the individual soul. The movement of history is a spiritual movement. Hegel had described it as a kind of logic: the triumphant march of the dialectic toward the goal of absolute truth. For Spengler, however, history is not a process of thought, but a process of life. Life, unlike thought, is not progressive; it contains the seeds of its own decline. Its movement is not linear but cyclic, and its destiny is not to triumph but to sink forever into nothingness and night.

Spengler belongs to the school of *Kulturgeschichte*, which grew up in the wake of Hegel and whose first major representative was Burckhardt. Out of this school arose the art history of Wölfflin, with its celebrated comparative method, and out of Wölfflin's work grew one of the most triumphant academic disciplines of the nineteenth century. We know this discipline as art history. In fact, however, its goal is not historical explanation but critical insight. Its historical judgments – true to the comparative method of Wölfflin – point always to aesthetic discrimination and are assessed accordingly. Categories like Romanesque, Gothic and Mannerist are not historical but aesthetic categories. The famous distinction between Renaissance and Baroque is not so much a distinction of period as of style, and the representatives of the two are united under each category by an aesthetic, rather than a temporal, conformity. This aesthetic conformity is, in turn, a sign of spiritual unity. In this way, the historical judgment whereby one work is assigned to the Renaissance, another to the Baroque, receives its justification entirely in aesthetic terms. This is not a way of dating works of art, but a way of understanding them.

At the same time, aesthetic judgment acquires a historical dimension. Art-historical criticism contributes to our understanding of works of art by casting light on the historical context that gave rise to them. For Wölfflin and his followers, not only did history become a way of understanding art – art became a way, perhaps even *the* way, of understanding history. It is only a small step from there to Spengler: to the vision of history as itself a kind of work of art, with the organic unity and consistency of spirit that are the marks of aesthetic imagination. History, like art, becomes an expression, to be understood in terms of the spirit that is embodied in it. In a nutshell, all history is cultural history, and all cultural history criticism.

Cultural history succeeds, therefore, only by contributing to the culture that it studies: by reorganizing it and transforming it in such a way that the reader is in tune with its inner life and meaning. That is precisely what Spengler did. He made Western culture a reality to Western man, by viewing it through the image of decline. Spengler's history is an exercise in the 'art of deliberate misunderstanding' by which (he suggests) cultures are appropriated by those who do not belong to them. (See vol. 2, p. 58.) The past can be brought back to life in the act of aesthetic judgment. But this judgment imperiously reorganizes its material, casts it in the form of present life, and finds its meaning through terms and conceptions that have nothing to do with the impulse from which it arose. Modern culture – the culture of man detached from his origins and beset by a consuming nostalgia – consists in a self-renewing sequence of such misappropriations, through which, nevertheless, we become aware of our spiritual proximity to the dead. This truth about our condition is one that can never be shown by science; it is, indeed, forever imperceivable to those who neglect the way of culture.

It seems to me that cultural history, conceived in Spengler's terms – as a history that is itself part of the culture it studies – still has something important to say to us. Spengler's method, however strange it may seem to the empirical historian, is one that we all use in our attempts to live historically and to experience the 'presence of the dead'. We use it whenever we read a work from the past, whenever we hear old music and are aware of its distance from us; whenever we study old buildings, walk in old streets, or participate in those religious ceremonies in which the voice of ages strives to speak to us. Spengler builds a theory of history on something that exists (and perhaps ought to exist) without theory: the historical consciousness of the cultivated man.

Can anything be salvaged from this theory? Or must it be regarded as nothing more than one man's sudden vision, as mortal as he? Along with much that is absurd, wild, or merely commonplace, *The Decline of the West* contains, it seems to me, thoughts that are genuinely illuminating. Consider, for example, the well-known theory of the Faustian spirit, which is allegedly distinctive of our culture. Faustian man, according to Spengler, reaches out with unassuageable ambition beyond his present spiritual possessions, demanding and creating room for himself in every realm of thought and action – in the entire dimension of becoming. This, for Spengler, explains the directional character of Western culture, as manifest in the Gothic cathedral (a favourite and all-too-obvious example), in the Protestant rebellion of the spirit, in *Sturm und Drang*, in Western science, and in the works of art, law, and religion characteristic of our way of life. It even explains, he suggests, the emphasis of Western politics on tolerance and individual rights, although Spengler's way of expressing the point has a sting in its tail: 'The Faustian instinct, active, strong-willed, as vertical in tendency as its own Gothic cathedrals, as upstanding as its own "ego habeo factum", looking into distance and Future, demands toleration – *that is, room, space* – for its proper activity, but only for that' (vol. 1, p. 343).

Such passages show not only the power of the idea, but also its greatest weakness: It is overextended. Like a bag into which everything one owns has been crammed, it comes apart at the seams; its contents, gathered into a temporary unity, promise soon to cascade in far worse disorder to the floor. For Spengler everything classical is also Apollinian, everything Western, Faustian. The manifest proximity of Western political thought to the *Politics* of Aristotle is therefore only a superficial characteristic; the Tempietto of Bramante is only superficially related to the Pantheon, and so on. The real spirit of the Tempietto is manifest also in the cathedral of Chartres, just as the real spirit of Locke manifests itself, in another guise, in the Spanish Inquisition.

It is obvious that a theory that endeavours to cover so much can attach itself only here and there to the matter it covers – only to those points of light that flash to each other across the sombre ocean of history. Thus the method that generates, for Spengler, the sole profundity that he recognizes – which gives, as he says, the *spirit* of a culture – is reached precisely by refusing to be profound, by resting on the surface, and by studying the products of a culture from what is, in the last analysis, a purely aesthetic point of view.

Far more successful, it seems to me, than either the theory of Western culture (so deeply inspired by Goethe's *Faust*) or the classical worldview (which Spengler took in large measure from Nietzsche) is the account of the Magian spirit – the spirit of the Judaeo-Christian and Islamic movements in the Middle East. Here Spengler is at his most illuminating and original, and his arguments can still be read with profit by those who hold no brief for the cyclical theory of history. Magian culture, he writes, involves an idea of community that has no developed parallel elsewhere. This idea is that of a 'creed-community', a collective and incorporeal person whose principle of unity is neither racial nor political, but religious. For such communities, law takes on a special form: it is not, because it cannot be, a collection of edicts expressive of a territorial sovereignty; instead, it derives its authority from the very act of obedience that generates the community itself – the act of faith. The result is a legal order in which tradition and consensus take precedence over explicit command, and in which the individual is considered only as, and in so far as, he is incorporated into the collective soul of his community. (The contrast that Spengler draws with the classical cult, in which deities are neither detachable from their shrines nor demanding in the matter of faith, is beautifully worked out and to a great extent persuasive.) From this pursuit of a collective soul results the mysticism and God-intoxication of the Middle Eastern sects. Spengler quotes from Horton words that, while describing Islam, duplicate much that we know of early Christianity:

> The mystic community of Islam extends from the here into the beyond; it reaches beyond the grave, in that it comprises the dead Muslims of earlier generations, nay, even the righteous of the times before Islam. The Muslim feels himself bound up in one unity with them all. They help him, and he, too, can in turn increase their beatitude by the application of his own merit. (vol. 2, p. 242–3)

The insight here should not be overlooked by those who seek to understand the Middle East. Even now, the communities of Lebanon enjoy their own separate private law (the *statut personel*, which concerns inheritance, marriage, and family, and which differs for Shiite, Sunni, Maronite, Orthodox, and Druze). The attempt to impose on the vestiges of this Magian order some version of the nation-state has failed to extinguish the traditional view of community. This fact (in Spenglerian terms, the conflict between late Magian and late Faustian ideas of legal order) lies at the root of regional instability.

The weaknesses of the theory become apparent, however, once we leave the realm of illuminating analogy and examine the nuts and bolts of history. Spengler fails to consider the Ottoman Empire, whose legal system nevertheless showed all the marks of the Magian order. (Each of the various nations – *milletler*, defined in Spenglerian terms as creed-communities – enjoyed its own domestic law, while every *millet* was bound also by the overarching law of Constantinople.) Here he would have found a civilization that could be fitted into neither the Magian nor the Faustian straitjacket, yet which left a mark on the world order that remains with us even now.

In those matters that he does consider, Spengler is given to bending the historical evidence, once he considers his favourite thesis has been demonstrated. It is worth pausing to see this process at work in his consideration of Magian culture, since here he is on strongest ground. According to Spengler, the Magian idea of community as a kind of collective soul is the real inspiration behind the Roman law doctrine of the corporate person. Hence we should not be surprised to find this doctrine emerge, transfigured, in the Pauline theory of the church, and in subsequent Hellenistic thinking concerning the nature of the Christian community. (Spengler even goes so far as to say that the doctrine is an invention of those who composed the Institutes and the Digest – men who were, of course, not of classical but of Aramaean, and therefore Magian, provenance!)

Two facts stand against that argument. First: the idea of corporate personality and the comparable English concept of the trust lie at the root of Western institution building, and have become cornerstones of law and politics throughout the Western world. Such concepts are among what is most distinctive of our civilization and constitute a prime explanation of its success. Second: the only developed legal system of the Magian order – the *Sharī'ah* of Islam – lacks the concept of corporate personality altogether, and has shown itself incompetent, as a result, to adjudicate the major conflicts of modern Muslim society. (The nearest equivalent to a trust in Islamic law – the charitable *waqf* – is, as its name implies [*waqafa*: to stop], property that is 'stopped' – that is, in which ownership has ceased – rather than property in the hands of a non-individual person, or entrusted to another.)

To point to such facts is not to quibble, for they are the stuff of true history and a sure indication that Spengler's aesthetic method will always misdescribe those institutions, such as law, that are designed to be understood in some other way than through aesthetic judgment. All the same, the original insight, though it was bought at a price, remains a genuine one: an insight into what the Magian order means to us.

The same can be said of another Spenglerian felicity: the dichotomy between a culture – in which the inner life of communities is experienced in all its vigour – and the civilization that is built upon its ruins, as ours has been built upon the ruins of Christianity, perpetuating its spirit in rigid, rational, and legalistic forms. (The thought here recalls Weber's account of the transition from traditional to legal-rational forms of authority.) Two passages will bring out the meaning of this dichotomy:

> Every soul has religion, which is only another word for its existence. All living forms in which it expresses itself – all arts, doctrines, customs, all metaphysical and mathematical form-worlds, all ornament, every column and verse and idea – are ultimately religious, and *must* be so. But from the setting in of Civilization they *cannot* be so any longer. As the essence of every Culture is religion, so – and *consequently* – the essence of every Civilization is irreligion – the two words are synonymous. He who cannot feel this in the creativeness of Manet as against Velasquez, of Wagner as against Haydn, of Lysippus as against Phidias, of Theocritus as against Pindar, knows not what the best means in art. (vol. 1, p. 358)

(Note the blatant use of the comparative method of the art historian in that passage – the reference to artists, composers, and poets is all the evidence that Spengler believes necessary!) And:

> As soon as life is fatigued, as soon as man is put on to the artificial soil of great cities – which are intellectual worlds to themselves – and needs a theory in which suitably to present life to himself, morality turns into a *problem*. Culture-morality is that which a man has, Civilization-morality is that which he looks for. The one is too deep to be exhaustible by logical means, the other is a *function* of logic. As late as Plato and as late as Kant ethics are still mere dialectics, a game with concepts, or the rounding-off of a metaphysical system, something that at bottom would not be thought really necessary. The Categorical Imperative is merely an abstract statement of what, for Kant, was not in question at all. But with Zeno and with Schopenhauer this is no longer so. It had become necessary to discover, to invent or to squeeze into form, as a rule of being, that which was no longer anchored in instinct; and at this point therefore begin the civilized ethics that are no longer the reflection of life but the reflection of knowledge upon life. One feels that there is something artificial, soulless, half-true in all these *considered* systems that fill the first centuries of all the Civilizations. They are not those profound and almost unearthly creations that are worthy to rank with the great arts. All metaphysic of the high style, all pure intuition, vanishes before the one need that has suddenly made itself felt, the need of a *practical* morality for the governance of a life that can no longer govern itself. (vol. 1, p. 354–5)

This, I think, is intellectual history at its best, giving a real insight into the transition from the Enlightenment to Romanticism and into the corresponding development of German philosophy. There is, moreover, a melancholy comment on the ambition of ethics in the modern world. Spengler reminds us that, precisely because morality had become a problem for us, something vital to human happiness has been lost. In one lucid paragraph he conveys a thought that occupies Alasdair MacIntyre through a whole book of hesitations.

Of course, much could be questioned in the historical details Spengler adds to his basic insight, and I shall return to this point in the conclusion of this article, since I believe that Spengler's negative view of the condition he called civilization is at the root of what is most objectionable in his outlook. Before turning to those criticisms, however, let me give one final instance of the striking observations that are scattered everywhere along Spengler's wild path through history: his account of the 'studio brown' of post-Renaissance painting and of the 'Magian gold' that forms the background of the Byzantine mosaic. This breathtaking section, which establishes the identity of brown as a 'historical colour', is a piece of art criticism to be set beside Fromentin and Ruskin. At the same time, its combination of sharp-eyed observation and poetic description, set within the force-field of a great idea, is unique to Spengler. Only he could write like this, and beside his achievement, the later attempts at such synthetic mastery (I think of the verbiage of George Steiner and Michel Foucault) pale into insignificance.

But now the reasons for resisting Spengler's charm. Most of my reasons are intellectual: however, I shall say something from the point of view of the moralist about that original seduction to which I, and no doubt many others on the threshold of adolescence, succumbed.

First, a flaw that arises from Spengler's method: attaching himself to an undefined idea of destiny, Spengler dresses up his conclusions, not in the loose apparel of contingency, but in the uniform of an inviolable necessity. We are doomed, it seems, to our period of Caesarism, just as we are henceforth doomed to express all our aspirations in the impoverished language of socialism. Such conclusions could be justified only by an explanatory theory of history, and explanation (as opposed to interpretation) is precisely what the method of *Kulturgeschichte* precludes. (The point is already obvious from Spengler's deliberate rejection, on the first page of his book, of the category of causality.) Just to take one point: suppose I were to ask why the Faustian spirit emerged when and where it did. To such a question Spengler has no answer. The Faustian spirit can be invoked in the explanation of its own manifestations; but the spirit itself, being the manifestation of nothing, remains unexplained. It steps into history as *causa sui*, self-created, godlike, demanding (and receiving) worship. The 'must' of Spengler's prose is a religious rather than a scientific modality.

It said that explanation is precisely what the method precludes. By this I mean that the categories of scientific explanation are transcultural. Science endeavours to see the world as it is, unmarked by the forms of human community. Its methods are, so to speak, transparent to truth, while all cultures (and the religions on which they are founded) are opaque – or at best translucent. Reality may shine through them, but always transfigured, domesticated, bearing the outline of a human community and a collective face. Spengler attempts to describe science as a part of culture. Thus we have not mathematics but Magian mathematics, not mechanics but Baroque mechanics, and so on.

But suppose Spengler could successfully defend those descriptions: suppose he could show, for example, that the mechanics of the seventeenth century were marked by the same desire for encrustation as was the architecture of the period. His argument would still concern only what is most superficial in the theory – its mode of presentation, so to speak – rather than its scientific content. Thus the differential calculus of the Baroque period is a true mathematical theory and the common property of everyone who seeks to know the world. And the same is true of modern physics. We may believe that there is no such thing outside mathematics as a conclusively established theory. Nevertheless (and Thomas Kuhn notwithstanding) we prefer scientific theories on the grounds of their truth, and the knowledge that Einstein's physics approximates more closely to the truth than Newton's is common to every scientist, whether his culture be that of a Zulu Christian, Japanese Shintoist, Palestinian Druze, or North American sceptic.

Spengler obscures such difficulties by describing the world of science as though it were not truly independent of the theory that explains it: as though the scientist creates nature, in something like the way the religious leader, the legislator, and the artist create the community of men. This falling away from the idea of objective reality is to be firmly resisted – whether here, in the writings of a declared alchemist, or in the thought of a Foucault, a Barthes, or a Derrida, all of whom provide similar nourishment to the fantasy that thought can make and unmake the world in accordance with its own requirements. This idea, the master premiss of every charlatan, is the sign of a lack of honest curiosity, or of an adulation of the intellectual life that is at the same time an abrogation of the intellect. No more than those lesser thinkers who followed him does Spengler avoid the charge of cheapness. To desire conclusions that are not wrested from an independent reality is to end up without any real intellectual possessions.

Although it was Spengler's anti-science that first drew me to him, it was the very same feature of his thinking that led me, in time, to think of him as an enemy, rather than a friend, of culture. The repudiation of objective truth and the relativistic view of the world end by putting science on the same level as culture, and therefore obscure what is distinctive in both. To defend culture is to reconcile its claims with those of science, but the claims of science enjoy a special privilege in the hierarchy of objectivity. The search for meaning and the search for explanation are two different enterprises, and while the first has its own truth and its own modality, it is incompetent to legislate among the truths delivered by the second. Only a more nuanced attitude than Spengler's, both toward science and toward culture, could therefore do justice to either. Only from the ground of such an attitude, it now seems to me, can the long and laborious task of defending culture against the inroads of the scientific worldview begin.

Besides that methodological weakness, three glaring deficiencies of observation and analysis stand out in Spengler's work. Spengler's three favourite cultures are defined so as to cross promiscuously the boundaries between religious faiths. Christianity, for example, has its Magian, its late classical, and its Faustian manifestations, and in all its manifestations it is the culture, rather than the religion, that takes precedence. Or rather, Christianity is, for Spengler, not one but three quite separate religions, which bear only a superficial resemblance to each other. This, it seems to me, is great nonsense. Christianity exists, of course, in many varieties. But everywhere it produces similar moral, social, and political expectations. This constancy is far more impressive a feature of the world than the infinite striving of the Faustian spirit. Nor does the weakness lie only in Spengler's account of Christianity. To see Islam simply as the late manifestation of a spirit whose flower and fruit are Judaism and the early church is to overlook not only the autonomous power of the Muslim faith, but also one of the most important deep divisions among modern cultures.

Spengler located the Faustian spirit exactly where Goethe had: in the Gothic communities of the Middle Ages, communities that already exhibited everything that most needs explaining about the social world of Europe. His history of the West is in fact a history of the European city. Consequently he neglects the greatest of all Faustian expansions, one in which the inhabitants of those cities cast their art and high culture aside and, taking with them what was to prove, in the end, of far greater use to them – their religion, commerce, and laws – established themselves in every corner of the earth.

For Spengler, the great event that brought Western culture to an end and launched it on the path of civilization was the French Revolution – the very same revolution whose image of turmoil had fascinated Marx. The American Revolution, which preceded the French and which inaugurated two hundred years of increasingly stable government, is not, so far as I can see, even noticed in *The Decline of the West*. This event was not drastic enough for Spengler, not sufficiently imbued with that air or catastrophe he and Marx affected to regard so neutrally, but which in fact seized their morbid imaginations far more firmly than they were seized by any human happiness. Hence Spengler is led to overlook the first of the decisive developments that led to the creation of the modern world: the transformation of the European rule of law into a constitutional democracy, implanted in a land that was both free from history and isolated from the high culture of the European city. Here was a triumph that was to fascinate the world and, in our own time, to inspire everywhere a bitter and destructive envy.

This brings me to another great weakness in Spengler's account of modernity: his inability to see that institutions have a life of their own, which is something other than the life of a culture. This fact is enshrined, indeed, in the concept of the corporate person that Spengler so adroitly misunderstood. It is manifest in the continuing vitality of our legal systems and in the universities, towns, and churches of our world, which continue to maintain a civilization that is elsewhere crumbling to dust.

And there is a penalty to pay for this misperception of institutions – this perception of them as mere forms, which have no independent part to play in the reproduction of social life. It is a penalty that Spengler paid, thereby destroying his credentials as a prophet. He could not distinguish those institutions which are truly dead from those which are vital and (in the Roman sense) personal. Hence he was unable to foresee the second major transformation of the modern world: the rise of totalitarianism. In the totalitarian state the life of institutions is extinguished forever and replaced by a machinelike control – by the 'administration of things' (as Saint-Simon and Engels foretold). Totalitarianism marks a complete break with every social and political expectation of our culture. Spengler foresaw the totalitarian state neither in the excesses of the French Revolution, nor in the Bolshevik power that was busy installing itself as he worked on his treatise. And if he had foreseen it, he would not have seen it correctly. He would not have seen that totalitarianism marks the end of our form of life.

Thus the two great facts of modern civilization – American democracy and the totalitarian socialism that has sought to destroy it – eluded Spengler's imagination. His mind remained focused on those captivating images in the evening sky of culture, in whose twilight forms the tragic destiny of mankind took on, for him, an air of melancholy dignity. Lost in sunset dreams, he could not see that hell was opening beneath his feet.

Every adolescent, feeling the imperious demands of life in his body, is prone to presentiments of death. The species erupts into his consciousness with all the terrifying force of a barbarian army, sweeping the glass menagerie from the table of the self. Religion tames this species-feeling, so that when it appears at the threshold of the adolescent soul, it is not a savage force but a quietly beckoning presence, an invitation to community, and a promise of initiation. Shorn of religion, the adolescent experiences his awakening as a kind of doom. He dwells on the idea of devastation and is led either to join some millennarian search or else to dignify his emotions with an image of cosmic decline.

Either way he turns away from the world, ceases to see its real importance and his own objective littleness. He loses sight of the real decisions that lie before him although they have yet to be made. Such an adolescent responds to Spengler for the same reason his contemporary responds to Marx: he finds himself in the presence of thinkers who are neither wiser nor more mature than he. Spengler and Marx are the archetypal adolescents of modern literature, thinkers whose vision remained locked in the trauma of puberty. In Spengler's case, this led to a morbid withdrawal from the world; in Marx's to a fierce desire to negate it.

Rather than overcoming loss by discovering a path for himself, rather than ceasing his lamentations for the sake of what might yet be saved, Spengler chose to contemplate the image of catastrophe and find his consolation there. He remained on the threshold of a world from which he withdrew in tragic self-contemplation, risking nothing, fathering nothing, and tenderly brooding on the fact of death. How right my young friend had been to warn me against him, but how rewarding it has been to wrestle with his influence and, finally, to cast him aside.

From: *The World and I*, September 1988.

3
UNDERSTANDING HEGEL

In recent years analytical philosophers have become increasingly self-conscious about their isolation from the mainstream of European culture. Their attempts to join hands with their contemporaries usually begin from a study of Hegel, who is now as much the subject of analytical commentary as is Kant or Wittgenstein. The task these philosophers have set themselves is, however, extremely hazardous. Hegel's philosophy is like a beautiful oasis around a treacherous pool of nonsense, and nowhere beneath the foliage is the ground really firm. The analytical commentator, stepping from the desert lands of logic on to this slimy surface, may immediately recoil, and thereafter do no more than touch it gingerly at the perimeter with the tip of an outstretched toe. Alternatively, he may step out boldly. Unable, however, to swing through the trees like Bradley and McTaggart (last survivors of a race of long-armed hominids), he then begins to skid ominously towards the slough of meaninglessness around which Hegel's philosophy grows, and from which it seems to take such inexplicable vitality.

As yet no analytical philosopher has been able to find a path of *terra firma* through this jungle. Charles Taylor, in the fullest and most impressive of recent commentaries (*Hegel*, 1975) succeeds in smashing his way through the Hegelian system only by constantly throwing himself forward into the swamp, and resolutely ignoring the steady change in his own appearance. The Charles Taylor who emerges from this experience is not the Charles Taylor who embarked on it. In particular, it cannot be said that his attachment to analytical philosophy has survived. Having failed to step on *terra firma* he rejects the normal use of his feet, reaching his destination instead by a process of creative stumbling, following a path which no observer can trace. What every

31

analytical philosopher was looking for – the safe map of the Hegelian territory – is still not available, and, while Taylor's reports of the wondrous flora surprise and tantalize his readers, his staring eyes and mud-bespattered features give little confidence that we could ever arrive – were we to enter the swamp behind him – at the same destination. To show us an argument, which leads by logical steps from truth to truth, and which ends at last at one of Hegel's ripe conclusions – *hoc opus, hic labor est.*

Naturally, therefore, every analytical philosopher will be interested to find a volume dedicated to Hegel in the so far extremely successful series of commentaries composed by members of the Anglo-Saxon establishment, and dedicated to 'The Arguments of the Philosophers'. Is this the long awaited chart of Hegeland? If it is, then we should forgive M. J. Inwood the otherwise inexcusable breach of wise editorial policy, that the commentaries should be short enough to justify the time taken to read them – time which might otherwise be spent with the philosophers themselves.

Unfortunately, after struggling with Inwood's commentary for several tortured days, I was forced to conclude that it is largely useless. Your average philosopher, asked to name the most important of Hegel's 'arguments', would probably refer to the passage in the *Phenomenology of Spirit* describing the conflict between master and slave. Here, in a few terse, beautiful pages, Hegel seems to condense an entire vision of man's social conditions, and to promise an answer to some of the most important questions of moral and political philosophy. Theories of freedom, of law, of institutions, of personal existence – all are suggested in a passage which has influenced every serious moral and political thinker who has made the effort to study it. My greatest shock on reading Inwood's book – containing 550 pages ostensibly devoted to Hegel's 'arguments' – was to find that this famous argument is not once so much as mentioned.

The path that Inwood traces is a long, irresolute meander on the desert fringes of the system, lacking the only virtue which it could conceivably possess – that of tracing the full circumference of the danger. Hegel's achievement as a philosopher lies not in his logic – which, for all its influence, deserves Russell's judgment, that the worse your logic, the more interesting its results – but in his profound description of man's spiritual condition. Philosophers ought to study Hegel not for his logic, but in spite of it. The important and lasting achievements of Hegel's system include the philosophy of the self, of its estrangement and restoration; the philosophy of the state (superior, in my view, to anything since Aristotle); the philosophy of art and culture (again without serious rival in the modern world); the brilliant re-creation of Christian theology, as an extended parable of man's spiritual pilgrimage. Only the last of these is considered by Inwood, and then in a desultory manner that ignores altogether the breathtaking moral perspective which Hegel opens to us, preferring to concentrate, instead, upon its flimsy frame of worm-eaten metaphysics.

Even as a guide to the logic and metaphysics, Inwood is at best erratic, staying constantly at a safe distance from thoughts which appear, in truth, scarcely to interest him. As he recognizes, 'Hegel . . . hardly ever criticizes a proof in respect of its validity, but rather the conclusion it establishes.' Nor is this surprising, for, with a few exceptions, the proofs given by Hegel are invalid, and anyone seriously concerned either to consign him to one dustheap or to rescue him from another, must concentrate on his conclusions, and endeavour to elicit in them a meaning that would both attract our interest, and also suggest how Hegel might have retained it, had he possessed the gift of logical argument. It seems that the method adopted by most sympathetic commentators has been the right one: namely to take Hegel's most important work, *The Phenomenology of Spirit*, to show that it contains a lasting insight into the human condition, and thereafter to consider the logic as an attempt to justify this insight by generalizing it, so as to see in the workings of self-awareness the intimation of an order exhibited by being as a whole. If the 'dialectic' is not thereby justified, at least it is made intelligible.

While one may respect Inwood's attempt to re-state the dialectic independently, and without Hegelian jargon, and to find in it principles of reasoning other than the impetuous idealism of Fichte or the self-serving rhetoric of Engels, the resulting picture is depressing in the extreme. Hegel appears in these pages as an enfeebled word-monger, seeking to base the most grandiose metaphysical claims on arguments which are seldom more than half-baked. Consider Hegel's 'proof' that the statement 'a plant is a plant', far from being logically true, is in fact a *contradiction*:

> The beginning, 'the plant is . . .', sets out to say *something*, to bring forth a further determination. But when it is just the same thing which returns, rather the opposite has happened, *nothing* has emerged. Such *identical* talk therefore *contradicts* itself.

To win over the reader to such reasoning is no easy task. The least that is required is a scrupulous explanation of the terms in which Hegel's 'proofs' are couched.

I would suggest that the analytical commentator on Hegel must perform at least the following tasks: (1) He must point out that the term 'logic' in Hegel is not used in the modern way. Rather, it is taken from the 'Transcendental Logic' of Kant's *Critique of Pure Reason*, where it means the study of the *a priori* conditions for the application of concepts: in other words, the basic moves in an anti-sceptical metaphysics. (2) He must explain the technical terms, which in the German frequently occur in inverted commas. Most important among these is the term 'moment' – as in 'moment of consciousness'. (It is significant that Marx thought that he could make his theory of history intelligible to German readers by describing the stages of historical development as 'moments'.) (3) He must show why Hegel thinks that argument must begin from what is most 'abstract', and advance, by a process of successive *Aufhebungen* to what is most 'determinate', and show why he believes that the 'abstract' is also 'immediate' (*unmittelbar*).

Inwood does none of those things. His references to Kant are sparse and ill-informed. He postpones all serious discussions of the 'temporal' character of Hegel's logic until page 433 (meanwhile allowing the term 'moment' to feature unexplained in crucial quotations). He gives no glossary of terms, and in particular avoids the question why Hegel should have thought 'the abstract' and 'the immediate' to be co-extensive. Inwood's expositions seem hardly to progress beyond the postulate that, for Hegel, 'truth' is a form of 'comprehensiveness', the contradictions into which reasoning entices us being always resolved by ascending to a more comprehensive point of view. (Such is the *journey* of 'Spirit' towards the absolute – a journey which never ends, since the 'absolute' point of view is related only asymptotically to our reasoning.)

But how are we to understand that idea? There are occasions in the critical examination of a philosopher when a little history of ideas is beneficial. One of these occasions is the study of Hegel, who self-consciously related himself to his predecessors and left unexplained what they had already expounded. In understanding the dialectic, it seems to me, it is extremely important to study Kant's 'Antinomies', and to recognize the relation between the Hegelian absolute, and the 'unconditioned' point of view to which Pure Reason is supposed to aspire. It is also useful to study Fichte, and in particular Fichte's idea – everywhere assumed by Hegel – that knowledge arises through the 'positing' (*setzen*) of its object, which then stands before the subject like a mirror. Inwood's only extended venture into the history of ideas consists in a peripheral discussion of Jacobi – an important influence, certainly, but one without the revolution-ary power over German philosophical thinking that had been wielded by Fichte and Kant. The neglect of those philosophers partly explains why Inwood fails to interest the analytical reader in the dialectic. To present the dialectic as a mode of *reasoning*, which 'approaches' the 'truth' by an *Aufhebung*, and which makes only *a priori* assumptions, and only logically valid moves: to do this is merely to invite scepticism. For better or for worse, analytical philosophy has taught us that such things *cannot* be true. By returning Hegel to his sources in Fichte and Kant, however, one may discern deeper metaphysical questions which are still very much alive for us, and to which Hegel, for all his cavalier logic, provided interesting answers: Can we separate the world from our perspective upon it? Can the object of know-ledge be understood independently of the subject? Where, in the world, *is* the subject? To all such questions Hegel gave answers which have been influential because they are also plausible.

It is fashionable to praise Hegel for having overthrown (it would be more accurate to say, dismissed) the claims of epis-temology, and replaced them with those of ontology (the theory of being). And Inwood repeats the praise. The true significance of this shift of focus is revealed, however, not in Hegel's metaphysics, but in his philosophy of mind, about which Inwood has little to say. Hegel recognized that the premiss of traditional (Cartesian) epistemology is the immediate know-ledge that I have of my 'subjective' states. The content of immediate awareness, the Cartesian tells us, is 'given': the rest must be deduced from it. But what does that mean? Under the influence of Fichte (and, more respectably, of Kant), Hegel argues that what is given to me *immediately* is precisely nothing. The immediacy of subjective awareness is an index of its empti-ness. Nothing can be deduced from the content of immediate awareness – for it has no content. *What* I am aware of remains to be 'determined'; hence I cannot deduce, from the surface glow of immediate awareness, any substantial conclusions concerning myself: not even the conclusion that I exist as an individual.

Hegel's statement of the argument is characteristic. My first-person awareness is immediate, he argues, because it is *abstract* (and he supports this claim with some surprisingly modern reflections on the 'indexicality' of such terms as 'I', 'now', 'here' and 'this'). That, indeed, is the character of all immediate know-ledge, which can gain its content only by a progressive removal of its abstraction, a progressive 'determination', whereby its 'immediacy' is 'mediated', and so overcome.

This process, which, for the subject, is a process of self-understanding, is mirrored objectively, in the development of the individual person. I repeat in my thinking the destiny which made thinking possible. I owe my self-conscious existence to a process (a *Bildung*) which I also re-enact within myself, in all my attempts at self-discovery. Only a certain kind of being can have the 'immediate awareness' from which epistemology begins. The task of philosophy is to deduce conclusions, not from the *content* of immediate awareness, but from the *fact* of it. What is given is not the object of immediate awareness, but the subject, and (to mimic Wittgenstein) to understand this given we must study the form of life in which it is created.

The great truth that Hegel dramatizes in all his philosophy can be glimpsed in that idea: the self is an artefact, dependent upon the process whereby it becomes an object of its own awareness (the process of *Selbtsbestimmung*). The self is created in society, through our dialectical resolution of conflict, and our emergence into custom, morality, and civil association: these constitute the immovable 'given' of the human condition, for without them there cannot be the self-conscious awareness that would enable us to question our existence. From such premises Hegel derives his masterly description of man's social essence, and of the inextricable ties which bind us to culture, institutions, morality and law. Nothing human is alien to this philosophy, since nothing human could be alien to it. Without the human element, however, the Hegelian ontology is an arid skeleton, loathsome in its suggestion of evaporated life, a *memento mori* lying beside the poisoned water-hole of dialectical abstraction. Such is the Hegel to whom Inwood eventually leads us.

Robert Solomon (*In the Spirit of Hegel*) is in many ways the opposite of Inwood. He has already made his reputation as a populist, in the vein of Walter Kaufman, concerned to restore the meaning to philosophy, and to return its frontiers to the territory that it formerly claimed. Solomon is well read, articulate, plausible, and accustomed to the positive approach. He takes us on an adventure into the Hegelian thicket, much as an American father would take his children on a camping holiday, well provided with the comforts of civilization, but with a didactic reverence for the wild. Solomon packs his equipment thoroughly. Nearly half the book is devoted to a survey of post-Kantian philosophy, of Hegel's development and self-opinion, and of the various important matters which we must bear in mind on our journey into the heart of darkness. Only at page 291 does the examination of Hegel's argument begin. Solomon then limits his attention almost entirely to the *Phenomenology*, upon which his book is a kind of homely commentary. He advances no further into

Hegel's system than is reached down the only path that modern philosophers have trodden into relative firmness. We are set down in the little clearing made by the parable of the master and the slave, and there we are given a picnic of liberal platitudes.

Solomon's Hegel is a humanist, a progressive, even an atheist of sorts, the kind of guy who, had he enjoyed the benefits of an East Coast education, would now be a regular contributor to the *New York Review of Books*, and a stalwart lobbier in the liberal interest. Occasionally, it is true, Solomon notices some dark shapes moving in the undergrowth, and, with touching solicitude, he announces the fact, in the tone of one who warns his children not to feed the bears. More often he directs our attention to the sunny tree-tops, to the great exposition of 'positive freedom', and to the wondrous presumption which led Hegel to envisage the whole world as obedient to the inner imperatives which governed his soul.

Solomon's exposition of the master and slave argument is clear, serious, and to a certain extent convincing. But the book's claim to be a commentary on the *Phenomenology* as a whole must be discounted. The remainder of Hegel's argument is given scant and often rather feeble treatment, and the interpretation is far from reliable. To take one example: Hegel's 'beautiful soul' – usually thought to refer to the swooning preciosity of Novalis – is interpreted (not for the first time) as a portrait of Jesus. But did Jesus die – as, according to Hegel, the 'beautiful soul' must die – of consumption? Nobody familiar with the Gospels could possibly see Jesus in this description:

> [The] activity [of the 'beautiful soul'] consists in yearning which merely loses itself in becoming an unsubstantial shadowy object, and rising above this loss and falling back on itself merely as lost . . . its light dims and dies within it, and it vanishes as a shapeless vapour dissolving into thin air.

Solomon's interpretation is part of a spirited, but rather philistine, attempt to represent Hegel's theology as nothing more than a metaphor, behind which a humanist atheism lies concealed. In supporting this interpretation Solomon presents a caricature of theology, and also of religious belief itself, which appears in his pages as mere superstition. Whether or not one accepts Hegel's theology, it is clear that he was a Christian. He also gave the deepest available exposition of the doctrine of the incarnation, and showed that if one is to believe in God, one must believe in incarnation too.

Solomon's writing is consciously laid back. He promises a

popular Hegel, for daily use; and to this end, provides a welcome glossary of Hegelian terms. However, his reluctance to pursue any argument beyond the point at which his favoured interpretation expires, curtails the discussion of underlying issues. Solomon's opposition to the 'reactionary' Hegel causes him to dismiss the defence of the family as little better than a rationalization of local, and superseded, social arrangements. In fact, however, Hegel's discussion of the family (extended further in *The Philosophy of Right*), provides one of the cornerstones of his philosophy. He defends, not the particular structure of the 'bourgeois family', but relations of 'natural piety' (to use Wordsworth's phrase) in general. 'Piety' denotes the unchosen obligation upon which social reality is founded. It is from this 'immediate' attachment that the human soul sets forth on its journey towards the free association of 'civil society', and to which it is restored, in fully 'realized', 'determinate' and self-knowing, form, in the bond of political obligation.

That movement – from immediate immersion in experience, through separation and estrangement, back to a self-conscious acceptance of a new and comprehended unity – is the basic movement of the Hegelian dialectic. Solomon perceives as much. At the same time he could never accept the political philosophy which Hegel here derives from it. The very idea of an obligation of piety – an obligation that is not freely chosen – is anathema to the liberal conscience. And to make of such obligations (however self-conscious) the foundation of our allegiance to the State is to alienate the progressive reader. Yet Hegel's reasoning is here at its most powerful. He provides, I believe, the true reason why 'social contract' theories cannot provide the ground of political obligation. As a backwoods liberal, Solomon refuses to acknowledge Hegel's meaning. But that only serves to discredit his favoured interpretation. Rather than cherish the image of Hegel as a liberal humanist, he would have done better, I believe, to contemplate the meaning of such passages as the following:

> Woman – the eternal irony in the heart of the community – changes by intrigue the universal end of government into a private end, transforms its universal activity into the work of a specific individual, and perverts the universal property of the State into a possession and ornament for the family. Thus she turns to ridicule the grave wisdom of maturity, which, being dead to mere particulars (pleasure, satisfaction and activity), attends only to what is universal; she makes this wisdom a laughing stock before the malice of wanton youth, as something unworthy of their enthusiasm. She holds up as princi-

pally valuable the strength of youth, – of the son, as lord of the mother who bore him, of the brother as the man who is equal to the sister, of the youth, through whom the daughter is freed from dependence, so as to find the satisfaction and dignity of wifehood.

Although Solomon's style is more agreeable than Inwood's, its long-term effect is somewhat deadening. What claims to be vitality is really a kind of jauntiness, and Solomon's much-travelled intellect has acquired a kind of guidebook patter whose cumulative effect is heavy and wearisome. Returning to the *Phenomenology* I was struck by the contrast. Hegel's prose is clear, mobile, propelled by an abundance of life. A student who learns to ignore its pretence at logic will gain more from reading it than from reading any of the commentaries. Both Inwood and Solomon tell us, however, that the *Phenomenology* was rapidly composed; and this, according to Solomon, is the explanation of its disorganized form and ill-written style. In opposition, I would suggest that there is no work of Hegel's that is better written than the *Phenomenology*, and that it shows the most meticulous attention to both structure and content.

Such a suggestion is borne out by H. S. Harris, in the second volume of his prodigious intellectual biography, which deals with the years in Jena preceding the writing of the *Phenomenology* (H. S. Harris, *Hegel's Development: Vol. 2, Night Thoughts*). Harris's first sentence is the most disheartening in the whole book: 'At midnight on 31 December 1800 the eighteenth century of the Christian era ended and the nineteenth dawned.' Had he said 'at 10.45 pm' or 'December 30th' the reader would have anxiously read on. As it is, one's first inclination is to close the book, imagining it to be from the same stable as Leon Edel's biography of Henry James. Once past the hurdle of the first sentence, however, everything changes. Harris's lengthy examination of five years of Hegel's life is justified by his sensible conviction that Hegel's life is in his writings, and that the interesting thing about the writings is what they *mean*. Harris therefore sets out on an extended examination of the Jena texts, many of which remain without commentary.

The result is extremely illuminating. Here – judiciously expounded by a writer with a real philosophical intellect, a deep sympathy for Hegel, and a formidable gift of scholarship – are all the conceptions of the *Phenomenology*. From Harris's study we learn that the material of the *Phenomenology*, far from being hastily thrown together in response to a publisher's demand, had been repeatedly worked over, during five years of intense creative labour. To see the *Phenomenology* not as the hasty effusion of a young man new to lengthy speculation, but as the inspired summary of patient investigations, is to recognize the indisputable claim of this work to be the most important text of nineteenth-century philosophy, and one that has yet to be provided with the commentary that it deserves.

From: *The Times Literary Supplement*, 21 September 1984.

4
HEGEL AS A CONSERVATIVE THINKER

The suspicion with which Hegel has been regarded by English writers generally, and by British and American conservatives in particular, is not wholly unfounded. This grandiose metaphysical system, which claims completely to embrace the actual and the possible, to unite them in a total vision of man's becoming, and to explain and justify everything that is, was and will be – such a system must inevitably awaken the scepticism of the empiricist philosopher, as well as the alarm and repugnance of the compromising politician. Nothing seems further from the pragmatic hesitation of Toryism than this supremely arrogant and supremely unified vision of the world, in which the sublime conceptions of theology are re-cast as a secular parable, and human history transformed into its own redeemer.

Yet no philosopher is more pertinent to our times, or to the intellectual task faced by modern conservatism, than is Hegel. It is precisely Hegel's recognition of modernity as a distinct spiritual condition, which gives to his analysis the depth and the authority that are missing from 'neo-conservative' thinking. Modern man is severed from history, from custom, from religious usage, and at the same time burdened with a conscious yearning for those things – a yearning from which he vainly attempts to rid himself by turning upon his inheritance the fires of a self-made animosity. If this spiritual condition is so often ignored or mis-described by conservative theory, it is at least in part because the lesson of Hegel has not been learned. Thanks to Sir Karl Popper, whose negative ideal of an 'open society' takes such scant notice of real human interests, neo-conservatives have forgotten the important task which Hegel set them: the task of providing to the spiritually homeless, a promise of their proper home.

But how is this task to be accomplished? To defend the unthinking prejudice of the normal active man was easy in an age when prejudice followed at once from the dogmas of revealed religion, or when social continuity ensured that those who rose to self-consciousness nevertheless departed only in the smallest items of belief from the happier mortals who were fated never to question what they knew. But already in Burke – the first modern conservative – the defence of custom and prejudice has assumed a distinctly paradoxical air: what is defended is precisely that which is destroyed by its own defence. Prejudice is discredited by self-discovery. It is because he recognized this fact, and sought to reconstitute the truths of prejudice at the level of reflection, that Hegel is, for us, the most substantial and authoritative of modern conservatives. He too doubted that the task was possible; he too doubted that conservative thought would ever be timely. For there is a sense in which the recovery of prejudice must always come too late: 'When philosophy paints its grey in grey, then has a form of life grown old. By philosophy's grey in grey it cannot be rejuvenated, but only understood. The owl of Minerva spreads its wings only with the gathering of the dusk,' (*The Philosophy of Right*, preface). At the same time, Hegel's philosophy points the way to a recovery of faith: faith in what is concrete, complete, and knowable. The modern man, to whom Hegel consciously addressed himself, is the man for whom all connection with an order greater than himself must be won through some effort of his own, and who will never be able to accept unquestioningly that which stems from his own imperfect labours. Such a man is discontented with every faith that may be offered to him. It is no defect in Hegel that he provides the faith which is most worthily adopted in a state of uncertainty, and praises the irony with which we must, in our unbelief, receive it.

One of the greatest problems for a radical conservatism is that of distinguishing the conservative from the liberal visions of society. How can we give to conservatism a plausibility that is something more than the reflected glory of the liberal idea? The philosophy of liberalism reposes all politics and morality in an idea of freedom, while providing, as a rule, no theory of human nature that will tell us what freedom is, or why we should value it. It isolates man from history, from culture, from all those unchosen aspects of himself which are in fact – according to the Hegelians – the preconditions of his true autonomy. When the modern liberal tries to make concrete the idea of freedom that he proposes, he finds himself always constrained to endorse (whether wittingly or not) the habits and predilections of a particular way of life – the way of life of the emancipated urban intellectual. Human nature survives in this philosophy only in a peculiar and attenuated form. Our fulfilment lies in the satisfaction of as many choices as short time allows. Such a philosophy presents no idea of the self, as an entity over and above the desires and beliefs which compose it. It therefore provides no idea of self-fulfilment other than the free satisfaction of desire. The problem of politics is reduced (as in J. S. Mill) to a problem of co-ordination: how to ensure that the satisfaction of one person's desire does not impede the satisfaction of another's?

Hegel was the first systematic thinker to attack the intellectual roots of liberalism. The liberal, he noticed, represents as 'chosen' every institution on which men have conferred legitimacy. However, men's sense of legitimacy stems precisely from their respect for themselves as beings formed, nurtured and amplified by institutions. It is not that men have desired and chosen their institutions, for without institutions there would have been no choice to make. Nor is it that they know how to draw back from every inherited arrangement and pronounce it legitimate by some act of will – any more than they can stand back from themselves and ask, 'Shall I, or shall I not, be this thing that I am?' The error of liberalism lies in the attempt to found a vision of society on the idea of rational choice alone – on an 'abstract' notion, as Hegel put it, of practical reason, which makes no reference to history, community and the flesh. Liberalism esteems choice above everything, and regards justice – the securing of rights – as the procedure whereby each person's freedom may be reconciled with the freedom of his neighbour. The concepts of freedom and justice thereby become intertwined: as they are intertwined in the liberal theory of John Rawls. The modern liberal goes further, arguing with Rawls that the idea of justice must be freed from every particular conception of the human good. No particular scheme of values, no particular historical community, no particular custom, circumstance or prejudice, can be incorporated into the abstract statement of our basic rights, which reflects only the fundamental requirement, that justice is the guarantee of freedom, and respect for freedom the ground of legitimate government.

Behind the abstract ideas of freedom and justice, Hegel argued, lies an equally abstract idea of the individual person. The liberal assumes (in the words of Rawls) that 'the self is prior to the ends that are affirmed by it'. Our values and aims are 'possessions' – variable circumstances which cannot be considered sacrosanct by any idea of justice that seeks to be universally imposed. To achieve such a universal standard, the liberal must abstract from all that distinguishes individuals one from another, so as to approach the hypothetical position (the position of the 'original contract') in which individuals have no other basis for their choice than choice alone. The self becomes, for the liberal, the 'transcendental subject' of Kant, a noumenal creature, divorced from 'empirical conditions', whose *principium individuationis* can never be defined.

Hegel accepted the Kantian idea of a 'transcendental subject', as the premiss of practical reasoning. But he disagreed with the liberal conception of society, arguing that the self is not prior to its history, to the community from which it derives, or to the historical values and customary morality which attach it to the world. The liberal self, and the liberal morality, are alike abstractions, which must be made real and concrete through the morality of custom – or *Sittlichkeit*. The liberal individualist, who identifies himself as outside the moral order, self-motivated and self-created, bestowing or withholding legitimacy through his own sovereign acts of will, is dependent upon the order of *Sittlichkeit* for his existence. The liberated self is a social artefact, made possible only by institutions whose authority transcends whatever may be bestowed on them by a liberated will. Autonomy, which is the highest gift of political existence, cannot be the ground of political order.

For Hegel, political philosophy is not a self-sufficient realm of enquiry, independent of logic, historiography and the philosophy of mind. We must understand the realm of institutions through the study of *Geist* (spirit). We must show the relation between outer and inner, between free institutions, and the free choice of the individual who is nurtured by them. To approach Hegel's political philosophy, therefore, we must pass through the complex argument of the *Phenomenology of Spirit*.

The premiss of traditional epistemology is the immediate knowledge that I have of my 'subjective' states. From the very same premiss the liberal individualist derives his peculiar vision of man, as constituted by his subjectivity, and fulfilled in the free choice which stems from it. The final recourse of Cartesian epistemology is the same as that of liberal political theory: the immediate knowledge of the self, as subject. The certainty 'I am' matches the equal certainty, 'I want'. We arrive at this certainty by abstraction from the material world (Descartes), or from the empirical conditions of agency (Kant). But what is given to me by this abstraction is precisely nothing – as Kant himself had recognized in his arguments against Descartes. The immediacy of subjective awareness is an index of its emptiness. The real self, for Hegel, is an artefact, which comes to reality through the process whereby it becomes an object of its own awareness and intention (the process of *Selbtsbestimmung*). The self is created in society, through our dialectical resolution of conflict, and our emergence into custom, morality and civil association. These constitute the immovable 'given' of the human condition, for without them there cannot be the self-conscious awareness that would enable us to question our existence.

This vision of man is given its first political resonance in the celebrated description of the relation between master and slave (*Phenomenology of Spirit*, ch. 4, part I). Enslavement, Hegel argues, is the first resolution of the 'life and death struggle' with the other. This struggle results from the self's need to affirm itself against others, and to compel their recognition of its freedom. Without this recognition the self is essentially incomplete, 'un-realized', without 'self-certainty' – without the assurance of its objective reality as an estimable agent in a public world. In resolving the life and death struggle by a trial of strength, one side wins the power to deprive the other of life. To kill the other, however, is to destroy the possibility of compelling the recognition that is sought – it is to forswear precisely the self-certainty that was the aim of the conflict. Hence the victor must content himself with enslaving the vanquished. By presenting him at every instance with the unanswerable demands of his master's will, the master compels the slave's acknowledgement.

This project, Hegel argues, is inherently paradoxical. Precisely in the act of enslaving, the master relinquishes the power to obtain what he desires. For what he desires is not bare power, but *freedom* in a 'positive' sense of the term, according to which freedom presupposes a certain kind of social existence. Freedom is not simply the ability to obtain what I desire: it is the ability to value what I can also obtain, and so to find confirmation of my significance. Not every social order can confer this freedom upon those who belong to it. Consider the 'freedom' enjoyed by the citizens of Aldous Huxley's *Brave New World*, who can obtain all that they desire, and differ from us only in this: that their desires, implanted in them by those who seek to control them, add no significance to their moral life. They cannot say whether it is worthy or unworthy, wise or foolish, to possess or fulfil their inclinations. In their desires, the self of the agent is not engaged: to satisfy them is not to express oneself in an act of self-realiza-tion, nor is it to exercise the freedom which is proper to our rational nature. The sense of oneself as present in and confirmed through one's desires requires a specific kind of social context –

one in which a sense of validity can form the ground of self-esteem.

The enslavement of the other renders him incompetent to provide this context. Precisely in being compelled to respect, the slave ceases to respect. The master, hungry for recognition, cries out for it tyrannically; without it, he has power but no authority, and the slave's servile obedience is no more than an irksome reminder of the moral emptiness which his power conceals. At the same time, released from the need to labour for his advantages, the master enjoys another kind of freedom: freedom from necessity. But this freedom is the freedom of the consumer, who seeks in vain for that which will assure him of the value of his actions, and whose gratification is always abolished in the moment of attaining it.

To understand the master's predicament, we must understand also the predicament of the slave. Hegel argues that we can do this only if we first understand two fundamental components of the human world: labour and the fear of death. It is the nature of rational activity to possess an end or purpose, and to seek to change the world so as to realize that purpose. The final end of every rational being is the building of the self – of a recognizable personal entity, which flourishes according to its own autonomous nature, in a world which it partly creates. The means to this end is labour, in the widest sense of that term: the transformation of the raw materials of reality into the living symbols of human intercourse. By engaging in this activity, man imprints on the world, in language and culture as well as in material products, the marks of his own will, and so comes to see himself reflected in the world, an object of contemplation, and not merely a subject whose existence is obscure to everyone including himself. Only in this process of 'imprinting' can man achieve self-consciousness. For only in becoming a publicly recognizable object (an object for others) does a man become an object of knowledge for himself. Only then can he begin to see his own existence as a source of value, for which he takes responsibility in his actions, and which creates the terms upon which he deals with others who are free like himself.

Hegel argues that the power of the master cannot amount to freedom, since it contains no active engagement with the world. The master has only a diminished sense of his own reality as a responsible agent. The slave, by contrast, does not lack that sense. On the contrary, he becomes increasingly aware of it, and aware, too, of the unjust usage which deprives him of the power to do for himself what he has the mental and physical resources both to undertake, and to value, on behalf of another. Of necessity, therefore, the slave must grow to resent his position, while the master must cease to find value in the dominion which he enjoys. The first acquires the desire to overthrow the power that oppresses him, the second loses the will to retain it. Their relation contains the seeds of its own collapse. And as it develops, the inner contradiction gradually bursts their unstable intercourse asunder, and places the slave in the master's shoes, and the master in the slave's.

The outcome of this 'dialectic' – this to-ing and fro-ing of power between master and slave – is, according to Hegel, the eventual 'overcoming' (*Aufhebung*) of the contradiction which binds them. The relation of master and slave is transcended into that of equals, in which the partners cease to treat each other as means, and begin instead to treat each other as ends in themselves. Then, at last, in the emergence of an 'ethical' relation, the contradiction is resolved. Each now has the whole of freedom: the power to exercise it, and the social recognition that makes its exercise worthwhile. The 'recognition' that led to the original conflict requires just this resolution: it is *this* – the acknowledgement of the personal autonomy and individual right of the other – that confers the true recognition that was sought. Thus Hegel argues for the thesis that the true freedom and true fulfilment necessitate obedience to the 'abstract right' of Kant; and in particular to the law which enjoins us to respect all persons, and to treat them, not as means only, but as ends in themselves.

Many thoughts are suggested by the parable of the master and slave – and conservatives have no monopoly over its interpretation. (The outlines of Hegel's argument survive, for example, in Marxist humanism, and even in the theory of history expounded in *Das Kapital*.) For the conservative Hegel's parable is important primarily as a challenge to the liberal conception of the self and society. If Hegel is right, then freedom is a social artefact, born out of conflict, submission and struggle. Moreover, the 'equality of respect' which liberals and socialists esteem as the foundation of civilized order comes into existence inherently tainted by conflict. Such equality is to be *won* out of inequality, and the ideal of an absolute equality, free from the marks of power, bondage and exploitation, is no more than a delusion. The history of freedom survives in the very quality of freedom, and it is a history of bondage. We must understand our social condition as emerging from an unequal struggle, the basis of which could never be finally destroyed or overcome. The freedom that Hegel ascribes to us is both political, and profoundly anti-utopian. Moreover, whatever equality exists in this stage of freedom is a negotiated equality, compatible with the greatest inequalities in advantage, wealth and power.

The encounter between master and slave represents what Hegel calls a 'moment' of consciousness – that is, an archaeological layer of our being, which is revealed in all that we say and do, and which can be separated from the fullness of rational activity only by such fictions and parables as those which Hegel relates to us. The parable depicts as a process what is in fact a structural component of the product. The 'dialectic' is a temporal representation of an unchanging spiritual condition. It is neither absurd nor unilluminating to represent the structure of human consciousness in this way. For time is the condition of our being, and consciousness involves the constant need to mythologize its own past, and to find within itself the fossilized remainders of a history that proceeded from elsewhere, and immemorially.

Represented as process, the dialectic involves a transition from immediacy, through separation and estrangement back to a self-conscious acceptance of a new and comprehended unity. The resolution of the life and death struggle in a purely abstract conception of right – the 'natural law' – leaves the subject's ethical experience still only partly 'determined'. *What* he should value, and to *what* he should submit: such questions are still without meaning for him, and gain sense only through his ensuing separation from others in the sphere of 'morality'. In this sphere we are governed by specific obligations, and are set at odds by the need to judge every action, every person, and every conflict, in terms of the individual history that renders it recalcitrant to principles. The opposition between abstract justice and concrete duty is overcome only in the ethical life – *Sittlichkeit* – in which customs, laws and institutions give reality to our moral scruples, and reconcile in us the contrasting demands of autonomy and community.

Sittlichkeit is the label which Hegel bestows on man's social and political condition. It too contains within it the structure of the dialectic. The individual moves, in this realm, between the immediate ties of love, marriage and child-bearing and the wide-ranging and open bond of competition and contract. The resulting tension between 'family' and 'civil society' (*bürgerliche Gesellschaft*) finds its resolution and realization in 'the State', as the highest of human institutions. In the State, man's 'immediate' attachment to his circumstance, which is alienated in the flux of the great society, is finally restored, 'realized' and 'determined', as a form of fulfilled self-certainty. Hegel cautions us, as always, against a literal reading of his temporal metaphors:

. . . In the ethical sphere we again start from an immediate, from the natural undeveloped shape possessed by the ethical mind in the *family*; then we come to the *splitting up* of the ethical substance in *civil society*; and finally in the State, attain the unity and truth of these two one-sided forms of the ethical spirit. But this course followed by our exposition does not in the least mean that we would make the ethical life (*Sittlichkeit*) *later in time* than right and morality, or would explain the family and civil society to be *antecedent* to the State in the *actual* world. On the contrary, we are well aware that the ethical life is the foundation of right and morality, as also that the family and civil society with their well-ordered distinctions already presuppose the existence of the State. In the *philosophical* development of the ethical sphere, however, we cannot begin with the State, since in this the ethical sphere has unfolded itself into its most concrete form, whereas the beginning is necessarily something abstract. (*Encyclopedia*, *Zusatz* to §408.)

By 'family' Hegel means, not the specific arrangements with which he himself was familiar, but all those relations of 'natural piety' which provide the individual with the core of moral identity and support from which his social nature develops. Piety is the ability to recognize and act upon obligations which were never contracted. Such obligations surround the individual at birth, forming his self-consciousness and invading his freedom, even before he has fully possessed himself of either. Such obligations belong to the household (and are symbolized, for Hegel, in the Roman *penates*). Disloyalty to the household is a form of disloyalty to the self, since it involves the rejection of the force without which freedom, will and reason would be empty gestures in a moral void. Hence it is an essential part of rationality to recognize these obligations which are not self-imposed. All the arguments for thinking that a rational being *must* (as the liberal argues) recognize a legitimacy in contractual rights, are therefore also arguments for saying that he must recognize legitimacy in something else. It is this something else which the conservative philosopher must describe and the conservative politician defend.

It is easy to see why Hegel rejected the liberal theory of legitimacy, as founded in a 'social contract'. For it is only in the condition of mutuality, when he recognizes himself as a social being, bound by a moral law which constrains him to recognize the selfhood of others, that the individual acquires (or 'realizes') his autonomy. By then society already exists. Society could not, therefore, have been based in a contract, since the individual autonomy, without which no genuine contract could be made, pre-supposes the very social order that is supposedly formed through it.

In place of the liberal idea, Hegel introduces a concept of legitimacy which transcends individual choice. This non-contractual legitimacy originates in the sphere of piety, concerning which Hegel has many interesting things to say. He argues that marriage, which originates in contract, cannot be understood as a contractual obligation. Rather, it is a *'substantial* tie', and the life involved in it is 'life in its totality – i.e. as the actuality of the race, and its life-process' (*Philosophy of Right*, §161). In such an arrangement the species lives in us, and the transcendent obligations which stretch from generation to generation become real and vivid in the immediate love between individuals. This union, which is a self-restriction, is also a liberation, since it endows the parties to it with a new consciousness and certainty of the validity of their common world (*The Philosophy of Right*, §162). Such relationships are inevitably endowed with a sacral character by those party to them, and the sense of political obligation can be seen as a recuperation at the highest level of the sense of the sacred, the orderly and the unquestionable that is first acquired through these ties of the flesh.

We may speak of civil society as the *sphere* of contract, for its principle or order (in its natural, realized form) is voluntary association. However, this 'sphere of contract' is not itself either founded on, or justified by, a contractual tie. Rather, it is the arena of spontaneous institution-building, in which obligations are undertaken and fulfilled, not to society as a whole, but to its members. Still less is it true to say that the *State* is founded on a social contract. Just as marriage cannot be construed in contractual terms, so is it

> equally far from the truth to ground the nature of the State on the contractual relation, whether the State is supposed to be a contract of one with all, or of all with the monarch and the government . . . the intrusion of this contractual relation, and of relationships concerning private property generally, into the relation between the individual and the State, has been productive of the greatest confusion in both constitutional law and public life. (*Philosophy of Right*, §75)

The contractual mode of thinking introduces an illusion of choice where there is no choice, erodes the habit of obedience, and leads us to treat in instrumental terms an arrangement – legal sovereignty – which can be understood or realized only as an end in itself.

The State is therefore an entity whose authority transcends anything that might have been conferred on it by contractual choice, much as its historical reality transcends the life of any historical subject. Taking a hint from Rousseau, and also from the Roman Law, Hegel goes on to argue that the State is in fact a person, not merely in the legal sense of possessing adjudicable rights and duties, but also in the moral sense. It has agency, will, answerability and identity through time. It forms plans, entertains reasons – which may be good or bad – and takes responsibility for its actions. (Or at least, that is its nature in its correct or 'realized' form.) This personal State is, in Hegel's words, 'the actuality of the ethical idea' (*Philosophy of Right*, §257). By this he means that it both embodies and upholds the ideal of free personal existence which is the *telos* of our endeavour. The great person of the State has rights that no individual human person can have (for example the right to put the individual criminal to death, or to demand the supreme sacrifice from those who fight in its defence). It also has duties which transcend the duties of individuals – such as the duty to uphold an impartial system of law, whereby all conflicts (including conflicts with itself) might be peacefully adjudicated. Like any person, the State must be treated not as a means only, but as an end in itself – in other words, its survival and its rights are non-negotiable.

It is because the State has this identity as an ethical person that it must be distinguished from civil society. Associated with the contractual theory of legitimacy, is the equally dangerous idea, that society and State are one and the same. Hegel gives a succinct and complex warning against what may reasonably be described as the ruling fallacy of Victorian liberalism (the fallacy that almost entirely vitiates J. S. Mill's argument in *On Liberty*):

> If the State is confused with civil society, and if its specific end is laid down as the security and protection of property and personal freedom, then the interest of the individuals as such becomes the ultimate end of their association, and it follows that membership of the State is something optional. (*Philosophy of Right*, §258.)

In other words, to confuse State and civil society is to take an instrumental view of government, and to loosen the tie of political obligation. It is to re-cast the ties of citizenship and sovereignty as relations of interest, defeasible and extinguishable in the manner of a business partnership. It is to neglect precisely that which makes obedience a habit, and civil association a profound ethical force: the transcendent authority of the political order.

Perhaps the most significant development in modern politics has been the emergence of political systems with the opposite vice to that criticized by Hegel: the vice not of dissolving the State in the provisional order of civil society, but of destroying civil society by means of a coercive State. The modern totalitarian polity – which ignorant Popperians like to blame on Hegel – is as much the antithesis of Hegel's ideal as is the disposable, take-away State of the liberal. For here too the distinction between State and civil society has been destroyed. The autonomous institutions (or 'corporations', as Hegel describes them) – which are the core of civil society – have all been subverted, and no association is permitted that is not a branch of the central system of control. Totalitarian government is, in the true sense, impersonal: subject to no corrective influence from civil society, it ceases to be answerable for its actions, and begins to stand above the law through which it endeavours to impose itself. Perhaps nothing vindicates as well as the history of totalitarian power the two major conceptions of Hegel's political theory: the theory that State and civil society can flourish only when not confounded, and the idea that the State, in its proper form, has the identity, authority and manners of a person.

This is not to say that the relation between State and society is either easy to characterize or easy to defend. Hegel's description of that relation in terms of the 'dialectic' adequately expresses the fact that what are here distinguished are also intimately conjoined. We should perhaps understand the relation between State and society, in the spirit of Hegel, by analogy with the human person. The human person is neither identical with his body nor distinct from it, but joined to it in a metaphysical knot that philosophers labour fruitlessly to untie. When treating someone as a person, we address ourselves to his rational and decision-making part: when treating him as a body (when he is ill or incapacitated) we study the anatomical functions which lie outside his will. Civil society is like the human body: it is the substance which composes the State, but whose movements and functions arise by an 'invisible hand' out of voluntary associations which in no way intend them. And the State is like the human person: it is the supreme forum of decision-making, in which reason and responsibility are the only authoritative guides. State and society are inseparable but nevertheless distinct, and the attempt to absorb the one into the other is the sure path to a stunted, crippled and pain-wracked body politic.

Hegel's development of the idea of a personal State is full of interesting asides, and has lost none of its urgency. Like de Maistre, he argues for the sanctity of constitutions.

> The constitution should not be regarded as something made, even though it has come into being in time. It must be treated rather as something simply existent in and by itself, as divine therefore, and constant, and so as exalted above the sphere of things that are made. (*Philosophy of Right*, §273.)

Hegel is here arguing for a truly conservative 'as if'. By seeing the constitution *as if* it were divine, we recognize the life of the State as beyond choice, a 'given', which is neither instrumental to our aims, nor without rights against us. It is in such a way that persons must be regarded. To lose the inherent respect for what is historically given is to embark on an endless sea of choice, upon which we float without guidance beneath nihilistic skies.

Again like de Maistre, Hegel recognized monarchy as the concrete embodiment and symbolic enactment of the individuality of the State. In the person of the monarch.

> the unity of the State is saved from the risk of being drawn down into the sphere of particularity and its caprices, ends and opinions, and saved too from the war of factions around the throne, and from the enfeeblement and overthrow of the power of the State. (*Philosophy of Right*, §281.)

Hegel goes on to argue for the stabilizing effect of a hereditary establishment, which conveys more cogently than any other mode of succession the historical contingency of the body politic, and the 'given-ness' of its loyalties. He adds, however, that it is always dangerous to give utilitarian arguments for an institution whose authority depends, in the last analysis, upon simple piety. To offer consequential reasons for hereditary monarchy is

> to drag down the majesty of the throne into the sphere of argumentation, to ignore its true character as ungrounded immediacy and ultimate inwardness, and to base it not on the idea of the State immanent within it, but on something external to itself, on some extraneous notion such as 'the welfare of the State' or 'the welfare of the people'. (*ibid.*)

In such passages one discerns the fertility of the dialectic, which enables Hegel to do justice not only to human institutions and the individual experiences which they engender, but also to our sense that political order, like life itself, contains a core which is sacred, unconditional, and central to all that we are.

The detail of Hegel's theory is immense and far-reaching. As well as providing plausible and imaginative defences of the basic civil institutions – of private property, law, civil rights and the freedom of contract – he deals subtly with the more delicate features of political order, such as education, ceremony, welfare and the division of powers. Hegel was not a democrat, although he advocated representative government in which parliament would balance and correct the executive power. He perceived that representation may be as much threatened by democracy as engendered by it, and that it could exist only when mediated by constitutional provisions of the utmost delicacy. The maintenance of these provisions requires active co-operation from the majority, and this co-operation would never be secured in a condition of need. Hegel therefore advocated the creation of a welfare state, and gave, for the first time, what is perhaps the most important argument for such an institution. The State, he suggested, cannot stand in a personal relation to its citizens and at the same time remain indifferent to their needs. Although their needs are not rights – it being one of the peculiar corruptions of socialism so to conceive them – they nevertheless define duties of the sovereign.

At the same time, the free market – as the core institution of civil society – is the necessary instrument for the transfer of wealth. Moreover, Hegel argued, there could be no security in the household, and no established order from generation to generation, without the accumulation of capital. Capitalism is therefore the inescapable consequence of the distinction between civil society and State, and the necessary instrument of social continuity. This surprising defence of the 'bourgeois order' presents an important challenge to the modern socialist: for it is a defence that refuses to see the 'economic structure' of capitalism as the fundamental or decisive feature of a personal body politic. On the contrary, it is a consequence, an epiphenomenon, made necessary by law and continuity. A similar consequence is the system of classes, which, in Hegel's eyes, has none of the cruelty or oppression upon which socialists so insistently dwell. In all these matters, Hegel implies, the socialist confuses what is accidental with what is essential, and directs his resentment to features of the human condition which are both unobjectionable in themselves, and also natural offshoots of an order which is uniquely suited to the development of human happiness.

If one were to express in a brief compass just why Hegel is so supremely important as a conservative thinker, one should say that it was because he rescued the human individual from the philosophy of individualism. By seeing institutions and individuals in their true inter-dependence, he overcame both the simplifications of liberalism, and the dangerous desire of the socialists for an end to politics – a final goal in which men will be equal, unconstrained and free, and in which power will no longer be exerted. An understanding of the human individual as a social artefact, shows inequality to be natural, power to be a good, and constraint to be a necessary ingredient in the only freedom that we can value. The *bürgerliche Gesellschaft* is neither historically transitory, nor morally corrupt: it is simply the highest form of ethical existence, in which man's enduring but imperfect nature is realized to the full. It is, as Hegel rightly said, the ethical reality upon which all our individual satisfactions depend, and without which we are disordered, alienated and unfree.

From: *The Salisbury Review*, Vol. 4, No. 4, July 1984.

5

GIERKE AND THE CORPORATE PERSON

The reputation of Otto Gierke once stood high. He found British disciples in F. W. Maitland and J. N. Figgis, the first a thinker of great subtlety, able to match and even to surpass the complexity and erudition of Gierke's argument; the second an able rhetorician who adapted Gierke's ideas to his own polemical purpose and made a brief but startling commotion in the world of ideas. Like Gierke, Maitland and Figgis were conservatives. However, the liberal constitutionalist Sir Ernest Barker also took an interest in the German jurist, translating (as Maitland had done) an extended section of *Das deutsche Genossenschaftsrecht*, to which he added his own elegant reflections in an effort to distance himself from what he feared to be the collectivist implications of Gierke's argument. Socialists too – G. D. H. Cole, Harold Laski, and S. G. Hobson – were influenced by Gierke's conceptions, Cole finding in them authority for the 'guild socialism' that he advocated as a remedy for the decline in social life.

Nor was it only in Britain that Gierke made his mark. His influence was felt in France in the liberal-socialist thought of Léon Duguit and Hugo Krabbe, and in the conservative theory of institutions developed by the jurist Maurice Hauriou. In his native Germany, Gierke was taken up by the nationalists and by the liberal constitutionalist Hugo Preuss.

Yet today Otto Gierke is all but forgotten. His great study of the law of associations – *Das deutsche Genossenschaftsrecht*, the fourth and last volume of which was published in 1913, when the author was seventy-two years old – is now long out of print, and has never been translated in its entirety. (We owe the two English fragments to Maitland and Barker, whose versions are also out of print.[1]) Gierke's followers are now few and far between, and his writings are seldom referred to, except ritualis-

56

tically and then only by either philosophers, historians, or juris-prudents. The German law whose principles he described has been transformed beyond recognition, and his conception of it was in any case based more on an ideal of history than on a record of judicial practice. Thanks to Nazism, Gierke has also had to bear a weight of accusations on account of a worldview that had only the shallowest relation to the national monarchism he espoused.

Gierke was born in Stettin in 1841 and devoted his life to the study of law. The controversy between the Romanists (followers of Savigny) and the Germanists (advocates of a distinctively German 'historical' jurisprudence, as opposed to the univer-salism of the 'civilians') had already begun, and was to exert a lifelong influence on Gierke's intellectual development. Gierke postulated a system of purely German law, arguing that such a system once existed, but had been overlaid by alien codes and practices, and then finally destroyed by the ascendancy of a 'natural law' that recognized no national character, no spatial or temporal boundaries, and no historical allegiance through which the peoples of the world were divided both in fact and in law. The German law, he hoped, would be revived; indeed, was already being revived, and would be truer to the national spirit and more worthy of obedience than the civilian statute books of Napoleonic Europe.

In a series of scholarly volumes, designed in part to justify the Prussian state of Bismarck and to plant the seeds of legality in the rich soil of archaeology, Gierke systematized and expounded the laws of the German *Volk*. These volumes – *Deutsches Privatrecht* (1895–1917), *Deutsches Personrecht* (1895), *Deutsches Sachenrecht* (1905), and *Deutsches Schuldrecht* (1917) – show in their very titles a break with the classical divisions of the subject, and a desire to fix the province of law within a national boundary and in accordance with a historical entitlement. Rather than distinguish the branches of law into the public and the private, he divided the individual from the social, and described both in terms of jurisprudential categories that were to a great extent his own invention.

It is not for these productions, however, that Gierke deserves to be remembered. His masterwork is *Das deutsche Genos-senschaftsrecht* (the German Law of Associations), in which his distinctive historical and philosophical vision is freed from the constraints of textbook law. In this immense work of scholarship, Gierke defends a 'German' conception of right, which had become, he thought, the dominant juridical idea in Europe. In defending his national feelings, Gierke also transcended them, producing an argument of universal significance in the study of human society.

Das deutsche Genossenschaftsrecht is a vast historical survey of philosophical and juridical ideas from the Dark Ages to the *Goethezeit* in Germany. Like Maitland in his *Constitutional History of England*, Gierke perceived an order in history that was to be understood primarily through legal conceptions, and through the social order that is achieved in the courts. Battles, kings, and conflicts of religion; economic power and military prowess – all these came second to the law in Gierke's understanding of the historical process. For law is the supreme instrument whereby men attempt to understand and regulate their social condition; it is the maker of history, precisely because it contains the truth of history, and the indelible record of a form of life. Law is man-made, and arises from the same spirit that creates the nation. It develops with a life of its own, and its interpretation of the world is intrinsically historical. Through law, therefore, we can understand the inner impulse of a society, and the force behind its institution-building.

The historical thesis of *Das deutsche Genossenschaftsrecht* can be simply expressed: the Germanic peoples of Europe had passed through four periods before 1806 (the point at which Gierke's investigations stop). The first period, ending in about AD 800, was one of free association, in which organization had a tribal character and law took the form of priestly edicts, or of customs sanctified by time. With the growing pressure toward defensive unions, the German peoples began to gather around their chieftains, who offered military protection in exchange for feudal services. Thus began the second period, that of lordly union (*herrschaftlicher Verband*), which, according to Gierke, lasted from 800 to 1200 and produced the first systems of sovereignty among the Germans. The beginning of the thirteenth century saw the birth of the *Genossenschaft* – the free union (*freie Vereinigung*, or *freie Einung*) among equals, which was the institution-building force of German medieval society. Thus arose the guilds, the towns, and the leagues, in a period when social life flowered in its many autonomous forms, each striving for and achieving personality, and each giving sense and direction to the individual lives that were comprised in it.

This period was brought to an end by the Reformation, by individualism, and by the modern conceptions of sovereignty. The blaze of the Enlightenment was soon to burn away the rich social undergrowth, removing shelter from communities and purpose from their members. From 1526 to 1806, the associations and institutions of civil society gave way to the new, all-embracing order of the state, which emerged as the 'supreme corporation', jealous of every rival and determined to control every competing power. The sovereign assumed the right to grant and withhold the legal identity of the institutions that were subject to his law; and eventually there was no institution that did not owe its existence, in some way, to a permission granted by the jealous crown.

As in all periodizations, Gierke's scheme reflects less the objective order of history than the interests of the historian. The four periods owe their contours and their boundaries to a narrative of ideas, and Gierke's real distinctions are not historical but conceptual. So long as we disregard his embryonic theory of history, however, we shall find in him one of the most serious and fruitful conservative philosophers of the nineteenth century. Through his partly fictive idea of the *Genossenschaft*, Gierke developed three themes of enduring importance to the theory and practice of politics:

1) The theme of the autonomous association, as an entity with will, right, responsibility, and personality, which is also an essential part of man's social fulfilment;

2) the theme of civil society, as an order distinct from that of the state, with its own institution-building powers; and

3) the theme of law as a source of authority, which grows from the power of association, without reference to the sovereign legislator.

British and American readers will approach these themes rather differently from Gierke's German contemporaries. Their ideal association is not the medieval guild, but the club, and they look upon civil society as an aspect of citizenship, a natural offshoot of common decency, rather than an ideal to be consciously pursued and justified. They see the customary law in terms of the common law: as a series of precedents, delivered by judges, with the tacit but distant approval of a presiding sovereign. Nevertheless, these distinctive marks of the Anglophone view of society do not alter the importance of Gierke for us. For Gierke's discussion, for all its superficial remoteness, does more to articulate the conservative vision of society than has almost any analysis since Burke's.

The subject of Gierke's study was the corporation and its claim to personality. In what sense are corporations persons? This question has been neglected by recent political philosophy, which tends to make no distinction between institutions with personality and those without it: Indeed, the distinction is strictly imperceptible to the current theories of collective choice, and plays no part in those competing theories of justice – put about by Rawls and Nozick – that have such appeal for American academic philosophers. Nor do the modern philosophers who notice the distinction have any real apprehension of its importance, or recognize the manifest catastrophe of a political order (such as that established and upheld by communism) in which corporate personality has been reduced to the mask or fiction that positivistic jurisprudence wrongly holds it to be.

For Gierke, however, as for his disciples Maitland and Figgis, the concept of the corporate person was as important as any other in the description of social life. Human individuals, he suggested, are by no means prior to the corporations that include them. On the contrary, we owe our personality in part to our experience of membership, and with the decline of that experience comes the decline of responsibility and, hence, the extinction of personal life.

Roman law recognizes two kinds of association: the *societas* and the *universitas*. A *societas* is constituted by a contractual relation between its members; its assets are owned by the members, subject to the terms of the contract that binds them. A *universitas* is a separate legal entity, which can hold property, and has rights and obligations distinct from those of its members. (An example is the *collegium*; perhaps the earliest form of corporation in law.) There is no decisive Roman authority for the view that the *universitas* is a person; nevertheless, the *universitas* is often taken as a paradigm instance of corporate personality – precisely because it is not reducible to a contractual relation between its parts. Legally speaking, the modern firm is like a *universitas*; morally speaking, however, it is a partnership for gain and in this resembles the *societas*; hence, firms have played only a minor role in the thinking of those who defend the personality of corporations.

Canon law described the corporate person as a *persona ficta*.[2] Its corporators stood in law as guardians of property that in fact belonged to no one, and guardianship, rather than agency, became the mark of legally competent association. In a parallel, but more subtle, development, English law began to speak of a trust, thereby deriving a law of trusts separate from the common law of the kingdom, by appeal to principles of equity that owed their authority in part to the canon law.

In *Das deutsche Genossenschaftsrecht*, Gierke made the bold suggestion that the canonist theory of the corporation – and all those views deriving from it – arises from the desire to safeguard natural law as the supreme source of right and obligation. The tendency of natural law is to confer rights and duties upon individuals, and to regard all legitimate groups as arising from, and reducible to, an agreement between their members. Even when the existence of noncontractual unions is recognized, the tendency is to see them not in terms of a will and personality of their own, but as the sign and product of some common purpose among their human parts – who are therefore the true agents in all corporate actions.

There is more than one thing wrong with the theory of corporations that Gierke attributes to the exponents of natural law. It is not true, for example, that all legitimate associations are reducible to contracts; nor is it true that all associations are directed to some purpose beyond themselves – even if that is true of the firm and the partnership. Gierke's *Genossenschaft* (fellowship) signified a kind of group friendship, whose purpose lay at least partly within itself.[3] Gierke's disciple, Figgis, took the church – and in particular the Nonconformist church – as his example.[4] And although he (wrongly) described the church as deriving from a contract between its members, he was clear that its purpose is bound up with its own existence, and that one does not join a church for the sake of a salvation that could be achieved in some other way.

If the church is a *means* to salvation, it is a unique means, whose purpose is inseparable from itself. As the communion of the church includes the communion of the saints, in joining it one participates in the sacred gifts, which have their being in the very act of association. Henri de Lubiac expresses the point in Jesuit idiom:

> The Church is either an historic institution or else she is the very city of God. In the first case, as a society founded by Christ for the salvation of men, she labours to bring them to it; she is then a means, and we can say with Pius IX: 'men were not made for the Church, but the Church was made for men: *propter nos homines et propter nostram salutem.*' A necessary means, a divine means, but provisional as means always are. Whereas in the second case, since the Bride is henceforward but one with the Bridegroom, she is that mysterious structure which will become fully a reality only at the end of time: no longer is she a means to unite humanity in God, but she is herself the end, that is to say, that union in its consummation.[5]

The question of whether the church is an end in itself is distinct from the question of whether it is constituted by a contract. The contractual theory was born, according to Gierke, among Calvinist sectarians in Holland, expounded by Voet,[6] and transported from that august source into Scottish Calvinism, whence Figgis derived it. The Roman Catholic Church seems to endorse the theory in its Tridentine liturgy, which refers to the church as a *compago spiritualis*. But this hardly does justice to Saint Paul's meaning when he describes the adherents of the church as 'members' one of another, or to the meaning of the *Book of Common Prayer*, when it refers to 'baptism, wherein I was made a member of Christ': certainly no contract to which the speaker was a party!

Gierke did not explore all the divisions that exist between corporations, and his failure to do so is a price paid for his historical method. A full conceptual investigation would distinguish among associations between the voluntary, the involuntary, and the nonvoluntary; between the contractual and the noncontractual, and, within the contractual, between those constituted by a contract *among* their members and those that contract *with* their members; between those with an independent purpose, those with an internal purpose (e.g., the Catholic Church), and those with no purpose at all; and, within all those, between the personal and the impersonal.

The club that really matters to its members is voluntary, and is joined for the sake of membership. The ruling purpose of such a club is the club itself. In the eyes of its members, it is not a means but an end: a bond in which each is at rest, as he is at rest beside his hearth. It is an object of respect and esteem, and no one who treats it as a mere instrument to his goals deserves the benefit of membership. In using the language of the Kantian imperative to describe such a club, I merely record the usual feelings of its members. It was with such an association in mind that nineteenth-century writers pleaded for the recognition of the moral personality of corporations.

All of the following can be true of corporations (whether clubs, churches, or firms):

they make decisions;

they act freely and responsibly;

they have both moral rights and duties;

they have both legal rights and duties;

they can make laws for themselves and their members, for the breach of which they are held responsible;

they are objects of praise and blame; of loyalty, pride, and affection; of anger, resentment, and hate;

they are historical beings, which flourish and decline according to the success of their undertakings;

they have habits of mind, including moral virtues and vices;

they stand in personal relations and can adopt many of the roles adopted by human persons. A corporation may even be the leading character in a drama (as in Wagner's *Die Meistersinger*).

How are we to interpret those statements? According to Pufendorf – whom Gierke vigorously criticizes – the corporation is a *persona moralis composita*, consisting in *homines per vinculum morale in unum systema connexi*.[7] For Wilhelm von Humboldt, such a composite person 'should be regarded as nothing more than the union of the members at a given time.'[8] Such has been the gut reaction of liberal thinkers ever since. However, von Humboldt's suggestion manifestly fails to do justice to the fact that the membership of corporations is in a state of flux. Those who are members at the time when a decision is executed may not have been members when the decision was made; while a wholly new membership may have replaced them before the legal and moral consequences of the decision are felt.

If we were to follow von Humboldt, then we should adjudicate the affairs of corporations by holding the present membership individually liable for the deeds of those to whom they have succeeded, and who may be already dead. This is both legally absurd and contrary to natural justice. Furthermore, the continuity of corporate agency is not explicable in terms of the continuity of individual plans. A corporation may even survive for periods, with all its rights and duties intact, despite having no members whatsoever. (For example, the vacant crown or any other 'corporation sole' currently without an occupant.)

It is true, as Maitland has demonstrated,[9] that the device of corporate personality is not strictly necessary for the protection and control of associations – the English law of trusts being a rival method, whose very existence might tempt us to the view that personality, like trust, is a mere creature of the law that discerns it, and not something that exists in itself. However, whenever the rights of beneficiaries are unknowable, trusts cannot safeguard their interests; and associations with no specifiable purposes, and no beneficial ownership of property, lie outside the domain of trusteeship altogether.

Furthermore, it seems that trusts arose precisely because the law has an inbuilt tendency to recognize personality, whether or not under that description. And this tendency persists, even in the face of parliamentary attempts to thwart it. It was already clear in the celebrated *Taff Vale* case that the endeavour to free trade unions from the burdens of personality was in tension with the English common law; and this tension has persisted to the present day, being the source of other, more tangible, conflicts, as those injured by the activities of unions seek a redress that is unjustly withheld from them.

Nevertheless, English jurisprudence tends to acknowledge the legal personality of corporations, while denying their moral personality. This desire reflects a suspicion of the German *genossenschaft*, with its Hegelian and Fichtean overtones. It is a small step, the English liberal supposes, from Gierke's *genossenschaft* to the corporate state. If Mussolini and Hitler were more inspired by socialist than conservative visions of society, this only serves to show the threat of collectivism lurking behind the noble conceptions of German jurisprudence, which found their application, at last, in totalitarian power.

Thus Sir Ernest Barker, distancing himself from Gierke, argues that no group can incur moral, as opposed to legal, liability: 'Moral responsibility falls only on the individual moral agent . . . and it is a dangerous doctrine which would avert it from him and make it fall on any transcendental being.'[10] So far as I can see, Barker offers two arguments for this position: first, he contends that we cannot attribute moral responsibility to a group without also attributing it to members of the group, and therefore that the responsibility of the members exhausts the content of corporate liability. Second, moral personality presupposes psychological personality – the 'power or capacity of self-consciousness'[11] – and this is resident only in the individual and never in the group.[12]

Barker's first argument is without force. Suppose it were true that we could attribute moral responsibility to a group only if we also attribute such responsibility to its members. This would give grounds for denying corporate liability only if the two responsibilities were exactly the same, so that the first attribution became redundant. But they need not be the same, either in content or in degree. Groups can commit crimes that lie beyond the capacity of any individual; they can plan and encompass actions no single human being could undertake. Thus, while it is true that the evil brought about by the National Socialist Party of Germany inculpates at least some of its members, and would not have been possible without their own evil intentions, these individuals are not, and could not be, blamed for all that the Nazi Party did.

Some organizations – the Communist Party, for instance – have committed crimes that defy the human imagination, using individuals who intended only to act for the good. While there is a temptation to attribute these crimes to individuals – to Lenin, Stalin, Mao, or Pol Pot – this shows an exaggerated estimate of the individual capacity for evil. Individuals are certainly inculpated in the murder of the Jews, the kulaks, and the Chinese and Cambodian 'bourgeoisie'. But no individual is guilty of the full extent of genocide that should be laid at the door of the Nazi and

Communist parties – not even Hitler or Stalin.

Nor does membership in those evil institutions automatically confer on the individual the responsibility that lies on the group personality as a whole. Barker's refusal to attribute this responsibility to the collective has a commendable cause: He wished to close the channel of easy excuses, to forbid the defence that says, 'It was not *I* who did it, but the party.' But his refusal blinds him to a real moral evil for which he can propose no remedy: namely, that there are groups which ought not to exist – groups like the Nazi and Communist parties, only the first of which has confronted its rightful destiny, in suffering judicial execution.

Barker's second argument is more interesting, since it suggests a metaphysical, rather than a moral, objection to the idea of corporate personality. It is undeniable that corporate persons lack subjective awareness and are subjects only in the technical sense of French and German law. It is true that they may have (and lack) self-knowledge: A corporation can deliberate in the first person plural, asking itself what we *really* want, believe, or stand for. And the overcoming of self-deception may be as important in corporate life as in the life of individuals. But self-knowledge must be distinguished from the self-awareness of the Kantian subject: the 'I think' that accompanies all my perceptions. I have immediate, incorrigible, and self-intimating awareness of my present thoughts and sensations; consequently, I am presented with a subjective realm, concerning which I can make no distinction between how things seem and how things are.

There is no such subjective realm in the life of corporations. Their mental processes are purely objective: as much the subject matter of doubt and speculation in the first-person-plural as in the third-person view of others. In this sense, there is no distinctive first-person view on the affairs of corporations, nor is there such a thing (in Thomas Nagel's phrase) as 'what it is like' to be a church or a firm.

However, it is not clear what follows from that. It is certainly possible for corporations to act freely and independently. And while individuals are always involved in their acts, and provide the vehicle for their projection and accomplishment, the acts of corporations are not necessarily identical with the acts of individuals, either in themselves or in their moral consequences. A company can commit a crime of which no individual is guilty – even, it seems, the crime of manslaughter.[13] It can confer benefits for which no individual can claim credit and harms for which no individual need be blamed. Why should its lack of self-awareness impede our natural tendencies to transfer our moral attitudes toward it and to summon it for judgment in the tribunal of personal life?

In an attempt to approximate corporate persons to their natural cousins, Gierke argued for the organic nature of the *Genossenschaft*, claiming that it has a life and a life-process, just as do you and I. Its moral personality consists in this life, which is the thing we ought to safeguard through the law of corporations. The idea is repeated forcefully by Figgis:

> It is, in a word, a real life and personality which those bodies are forced to claim, which we believe that they possess by the nature of the case, and not by the arbitrary grant of the sovereign. To deny this real life is to be false to the facts of social existence and is of the same nature as that denial of human personality which we call slavery, and is always in its nature unjust and tyrannical.[14]

Hauriou objected to this way of arguing, as giving a wrong conception of what he called the individuality of corporations. They have, he said, the individuality of institutions, not that of organisms.[15] The intuitive distinction here is not easy to render in precise terms. But it casts interesting light on the contrast between the natural and the corporate person. Hauriou saw institutions as characterized by procedures and roles that exist independently of those who make use of them; they have a longevity conferred by the principle of succession to office, and this longevity is something which, in the nature of things, is not shared by an organism.

Not every institution has personality, Hauriou claimed, although every institution has some measure of autonomy. 'Individual autonomy' corresponds to Spinoza's *conatus*: organisms have it, and so do institutions; stones, however, do not. It constitutes *l'état des choses immédiatement nécessaire pour l'acquisition de la personnalité*. Personality exists, according to Hauriou, only where there is a corporate will: that is, only where decisions are taken and responsibilities assumed, which are not the decisions or responsibilities of any single human being.

Hauriou therefore makes a distinction between those institutions that have no personality and which exist in the realm of things, and those that have personality and are subjects. Hauriou's way of drawing this distinction – in terms of the forces acting on and maintaining an institution – is highly questionable; the distinction, however, is not.

Moral personality is a matter of degree, and an institution might gain or lose some of its personal attributes during the course of its history. Thus there are institutions that make decisions but recognize neither legal nor moral liability for their errors (the Mafia, the Communist Party); there are those that confess their faults and make amends for them but are deprived of all lawmaking capacity and depend upon others to set limits to their conduct (the firm); there are those that impose their will on their members, and even conscript those members regardless of their own desires, but nevertheless acknowledge personal responsibility for their welfare (armies); there are those that, while possessing moral personality, endeavour to escape the legal burden of it, and constitute themselves accordingly (trade unions). I shall therefore draw a contrast between the most fully personal institution conceivable, and a 'thing' institution, and try to show what happens to the social world, when thing institutions displace corporate persons in regulating society.

Consider an institution with the following features:

1) It is a voluntary association, which has no penalties for those who withdraw from it.

2) Its primary benefit to its members is that of membership, and all that is intrinsically connected with membership.

3) It has no contract with its members and enshrines no contract between them. Its assets are its own and are held in trust for no one.

4) It is a deliberative body and its deliberations are conciliar, proceeding by rational discussion among its members. (The deliberative procedure may or may not be democratic; what is important for personality is that it be constitutional – that is, that there be a means to determine whether the procedure has been correctly followed and a means to correct irregularities.)

5) It is authoritative, so that its decisions may be binding on its members, with its officers empowered to impose their decisions. (This authority may be recognized, and made an object of reverence and enjoyment, through custom and ceremony.)

6) It is a lawmaking body, exerting jurisdiction over its members. The process of adjudication conforms to natural justice (as understood in English administrative law): the judge is independent, there is a right of hearing, laws are applied consistently and a right of appeal exists for irregularities.

7) It is open and answerable in all its workings. Records are kept of decisions, which can be publicly criticized and publicly justified. The corporation regards itself as being bound by its own law (if it has one) and as obliged to make amends for its transgressions.

8) It is obedient to the moral law and remorseful for its transgressions. Sins committed by the corporation are atoned for, once

acknowledged, and accomplices are held up to shame.
9) It is obedient to the positive law of the state within which it resides.
10) It has been accorded legal personality or the equivalent, so as to conduct its affairs as an independent legal entity, subject to due process.

It should be obvious that the least important of those features, from the point of view of moral personality, is the last: the external recognition granted by the law. If the first nine features are present, then the tenth is simply what Gierke said it is: the recognition by the sovereign of an independent moral reality. And if this recognition is withheld – as from the Roman Catholic Church in the Ukraine, from the trade union Solidarity in Poland, or from the jazz section of the Musicians' Union in Czechoslovakia (to take three notorious recent examples) – an injustice is done. To suppose that feature ten is capable in itself of creating any or all of features one to nine is to have but a rudimentary understanding of the forms of social life.

We can also see why Gierke was wary of the view that legal personality must be bestowed by the state if it is to exist at all, for this puts in the hands of the state the power to destroy associations. It is surely a marvellous device of English law that it has been able, through the concept of trust, to allow moral persons to create their own legal identity and to claim their proper recognition, while asking permission of no one other than their members. It is this development rather than any actual or implied Bill of Rights that has been the greatest source of English liberty. For the freedom to associate, and to protect associations from their natural predator, the sovereign, is the most precious of freedoms. It is the freedom whereby civil society exists in the first place, and is thus the most important of the forces that can delimit the state.

It should also be obvious that the institution that I have described approximates closely to the church, as this was understood by the canonists – or at least the church in its conciliar interpretation, the church of Nicholas of Cusa and Jan Hus. All that it lacks (although for the believer this is everything) is the gift of the Holy Spirit. For the most part, clubs, societies, and *Genossenschäften* make no such claim for themselves – and for that we should be grateful.

There are also corporations that, while possessing sufficiently many of the listed features to be accorded moral personality, do not possess the full personality of the institution I have envisaged. Firms, for example, possess features one, four, five (as a rule), seven, eight, nine, and ten (as a rule). And by comparing the various partial realizations of the above ideal, we should come to an understanding of the relative importance, for the idea of personality, of the features I have mentioned, and of the separate contribution that they make to the richness of social life.

Hostility to corporate persons – as sources of authority, bestowers of value, and supplicants to power – has been, according to Gierke, a regular concomitant of the political philosophies based in natural law. As it evolved into the modern theory of natural right, natural law theory came to employ an abstract (as we should say, Kantian, or Rawlsian) conception of the individual agent, who is presented as the sole possessor of rights and duties. The individual, according to Locke and other natural-right thinkers, derives these rights and duties from his faculty of choice and with the benefit of no institution. The institutions that surround him owe their legitimacy to his contract to maintain them and are ultimately subservient to the state – the supreme institution in which the sum of human contracts is inscribed and given personality, like the runes on Odin's spear.

The state tends to be seen as the only permissible corporate person; all others either derive from it or else remain suspect, usurpers of its power, and threats to the rights of individuals. Thus, according to Gierke:

> In the age of Enlightenment, the prestige of historical law increasingly paled before the splendour of the new ideal law, and the more it paled, the easier it was to advance from denying that corporations had a sanction in Natural Law to questioning whether they existed at all. Natural-law theory of this extreme order became a powerful ally of the practical policies which were directed to the destruction of the corporative system of Estates inherited from the Middle Ages. There were now two forces in the field – the State, with its passion for omnipotence; the Individual, with his desire for liberation.

Such a view was adopted by Hobbes, both in *De cive* and in *Leviathan*, and became part of the natural right tradition. Perhaps its earliest transfer into practice came with the French revolutionaries who, on 18 August 1792, decreed that 'a state that is truly free ought not to suffer within its bosom any corporation, not even such as, being dedicated to public instruction, have merited well of the *patrie*.'[18]

Writing before the Bolsheviks came to power, Auguste Cochin made a trenchant analysis of the French Revolution by studying the system of 'parallel structures' established in the Breton countryside.[19] He described the transformation as involving a move away from personal government (in which civil powers are also persons, sometimes individual, usually corporate) toward a new kind of 'impersonal government', which would be a true 'administration of things'. As Cochin shows, the exercise of power, once depersonalized, becomes unanswerable: decisions are taken for which no person is liable, and neither the rights nor the duties of associations are defined. Associations are regarded with suspicion, unless and until controlled by the central machine; and all, in the end, are subverted or destroyed.

The process of depersonalization was perfected by Lenin, through a brilliant invention that we might call, following Russian usage, the Potemkin institution. All associations were to be infiltrated by the party and made subservient to it. They could retain no autonomy, and any attempt to do so was visited with the harshest punishment. Particularly important were the churches: the paradigm *Genossenschäften*, whose personality is founded in a transcendent bond of membership. The Russian Orthodox Church was forced to become the servant of the party: Those churches that were not infiltrated were suppressed, and all corporate action by religious bodies other than the act of worship was forbidden.

Other institutions that had acquired moral personality – universities, schools, clubs, and societies – were also either destroyed or turned into Potemkin replicas, in which the semblance of autonomy was the thinnest mask for external control. Private charities were expropriated and then suppressed, and in place of the personal institutions of civil society were created the thing institutions of the communist state: the Komsomol, the unions of workers and artists, and the 'agitation centres' that were to serve as churches of the new belief. No thing institution had reality other than that conferred on it by the party, which was to possess the sum of institutional autonomy, united beneath a single corporate command. Thus was the Enlightenment vision of emancipation realized at last, as men were freed from the bonds of membership that had previously ensnared them, and conscripted to a purpose that was not their own.

It was as much the pursuit of depersonalization as the belief in cranky economic theories that dictated the policies of collectivization and a centralized economy. The farm and the firm are also corporate persons; they have the capacity for autonomous action and responsible choice. They can go bankrupt, commit crimes, offer benefits, and incur obligations. Such facts threaten the party's monopoly of associative power. The institutions too, therefore, were forced to become Potemkin replicas, to serve as masks for decisions that were not their own, and that frequently answered in no way to their interests. Even those institutions whose reality derived from contract were deprived of the moral personality that would otherwise accrue to them, and made part of the great machine. Thus was the government of men replaced by the administration of things, as all persons, corporate and natural, were reduced to things.

Power was henceforth exercised in a spirit of calculation: a purely instrumental view of association (as a means to the transmission of power – a 'transmission belt', in Lenin's phrase) accompanied a purely instrumental view of the individual (as a means to his own replacement, by the New Socialist Man). Neither men nor groups were to be treated as ends in themselves, but all were subject to a single imperative, which recognized no limit to its actions, since it was without the principle of answerability from which the sanctity of limits derives.

The 'socialist legality' of Stalin granted legal personality to Potemkin institutions. But it was a Potemkin personality, and no individual could be sure of binding a corporate person either by law or by contract. The agent that dictated institutional choices – the party – possessed only defective personality, and could not be sued. The greatest criminal, who was also the greatest tortfeasor, could be brought before neither the criminal nor the civil law.

The process that I have described was not everywhere successful. And even when most successful, it leaves one corporate person standing triumphant amid the ruins of social life: the party itself. But it is a monstrous person, no longer capable of moral conduct; a person that cannot take responsibility for its actions, and one that can confess to its faults only as 'errors' imposed on it by misguided members, and never as its own actions, for which repentance and atonement are due. The moral personality of this all-encompassing Leviathan is impaired: unable to view others as ends in themselves, it lacks such a view of itself. It is set outside the moral realm, in a place of pure calculation, blameless only because it denies the possibility of blame. Like its short-lived disciple, the Nazi Party, it is a corporate psychopath, respected by none and feared by all.

When Sir Ernest Barker voiced the fears of the decent liberal Englishman and criticized the incipient 'collectivism' of Gierke's idea of the corporation, he failed to understand that personality requires mutuality. The autonomous rational agent exists in reciprocal relation to his kind, and is a person only to the extent that he acknowledges and defers to the personality of others. The true corporate person is as much bound to respect the autonomy of individuals as it is bound to respect the autonomy of groups. A world of corporate persons is a world of free association: it is the antithesis of collectivism, which imposes a world of conscription, where all association is centrally controlled and all institutions are things. Collectivism involves a sustained war, not on the individual as such, but on the person, whether individual or corporate. The trouble with Hitler was not that he listened to the voice that speaks through Fichte, Hegel, and Gierke, but that he listened to that other voice, which sounds through Robespierre, Marx, and Lenin, and that promises to reduce the intricate moral fact of personality to the single seizable commodity of power.

My reflections have been inspired by Gierke rather than dictated by his argument. He left to others to draw the philosophical implications from his conception of the personal *Genossenschaft*, and merely indicated the many ways in which Enlightenment ideas – by promising a freedom that is detached from every historical experience of membership – were at war with the deeper freedoms upon which society depends. The conception of a universal natural law, whose authority owes nothing to history and which transcends the bonds that unite and divide us, leads to a new and all-embracing conception of sovereignty. The law of the modern state abolishes every customary jurisdiction, makes and unmakes the associations that have been so patiently instituted over time, and recreates by edict, and as a form of servitude, the corporation, which would otherwise arise slowly and naturally as the realization of our liberty.

Gierke died in 1921, before the terrible truth of totalitarian government had been widely recognized. Yet he bequeathed to us the conception through which the impersonal order of totalitarianism can be understood and condemned. It is because institutions tend intrinsically toward personality that they enrich our lives and give value to our enterprises. It is because they are autonomous that they inspire our loyalty; and it is because they are answerable for their actions that our own personality can grow within their tutelage. It is to such facts as these that Burke was obscurely referring in invoking the 'little platoons', and to which de Tocqueville also paid tribute when he enumerated the saving graces of American democracy.

To understand the strength of Gierke's conception, we should return in thought to the world of thing institutions and ask ourselves what the individual lacks in that world. The primary lack, I believe, is the long-term view. No obligation endures there – not even the obligations of love and friendship – beyond the lifetime of the individuals who undertake them; nor does

any obligation exist toward those who are not present to recipro-
cate it. The unborn and the dead are not only disenfranchised:
they have lost all claim on the living. Their claims can be acknowledged only if there are persons who endure long enough to
enter into personal relation, both with us, the living, and with
them.

The true public spirit – the spirit from which civil society and
all its benefits derive – requires just such a projection of our
duties beyond the grave. The care for future generations must be
entrusted to persons who will exist when they exist; and if there
are no such persons surrounding me, how can I have that care,
except as a helpless anxiety? I can enter into no personal obligation that will bind me to past and future souls, nor can you. Only
a corporate person can enter such an obligation, and only
through corporate persons, therefore, can the relation to the
unborn and the dead be made articulate and binding. (Thus
when, as in aristocracies, this relation is made articulate through
the family, the family ceases to be the bond of present love, and
becomes an institution, with a personality distinct from those of
its members.)

That this relation to the unborn and the dead is necessary for
the fulfilment of the rational agent is something that we should
not doubt. For it forms the premiss of self-justification. The
individual is justified by the knowledge that he did right by
those who survive him, whom he never knew and who promised
him nothing; and equally by those who preceded him and
bequeathed to him, unknowingly, their store of trust. In the
broadest sense, then, the corporate person is necessary to the
ecology of rational agency, and without such constructs our
aims will be as truncated as our lives. One might say of corporate persons generally what Joubert said of the old civil and
religious institutions of France: *ce sont les crampons qui unissent
une génération à une autre.*

From: *The World & I,* March 1989.

6

MASARYK, PATOČKA
AND THE CARE
OF THE SOUL

In conversation with Karel Čapek, Masaryk, with the confidence of a man who has fulfilled his mission, summarizes his outlook in a single word: 'concretism'. The reader might imagine that Masaryk is referring back to the arguments of the *Versuch einer concreten logik*, which was published at the outset of Masaryk's academic career.[1] However, this latter work is not really a defence of 'concrete' thinking, in the sense in which Masaryk was later to oppose concrete thinking to the systems of German philosophy. It is an exercise – profoundly influenced by Comte – in intellectual taxonomy. Concrete logic, Masaryk argues, has the task of uniting the rules governing the various sciences in a single system.[2] He compares this logic favourably with the 'abstract' logic of the philosophers,[3] but gives so unsatisfactory an account of it, and shows himself so little aware of the importance of the true science of logic that was (at the very moment when he wrote) being teased into reality by Gottlob Frege, that we can hardly consider his work to constitute either a genuine assault on the pretensions of German philosophy, or a real contribution to a philosophy of Masaryk's own.

Nevertheless, the emphasis on the 'concrete individual' was to remain dominant in all Masaryk's philosophical writings, and to form the refrain of his political rhetoric. In the *Versuch*, Masaryk associated the idea of individuality with the priority which he accorded to the Cartesian *cogito*. It was Masaryk's belief that the Cartesian argument provided the definitive refutation of philosophical materialism, and the premiss of all genuine knowledge. The *cogito* must be taken as 'the starting point of our scientific thinking',[4] since it alone can be established

74

with the complete, foundational certainty that is necessary for knowledge.

Like his teacher Brentano, Masaryk combines the Cartesian theory of consciousness with a repudiation of 'subjectivism' and 'idealism': and in particular of the German idealism which, arising out of Kant's *Critique of Pure Reason*, had found such overwhelming expression in the philosophy of Hegel. Although consciousness is self-guaranteeing, and although this guarantee is offered to each of us *subjectively*, this does not authorize the idealist's division of the world into subject and object (a division which, once admitted, can never be overcome). I too am an object, both for myself and for another,[5] and the fact of consciousness is a fact about a real and objective world.

At the same time, we must not become so objectivist as to deny the existence of the conscious self, or to represent the world as containing nothing but 'material' processes, upon the stream of which the individual rides helplessly like a cork on the tide. In *Otázka sociální* (*The Social Question*) Masaryk tried to show that the 'ultra-objectivism' of Marx is as destructive of true science as is the pure subjectivism of the idealists. Indeed, Masaryk argued, in their attempts to read the whole social world as nothing but a material process, Marx and Engels had been driven to describe the world as though it were really mental. Dialectical materialism understands nature through laws that have their true application only in the world of concepts.[6] Marxism, like every form of extreme objectivism, is really an illusionism: its attempt to displace consciousness from the centre of our knowledge, leads, by an inevitable paradox, to a description of the material world as itself a kind of conscious process.[7]

Masaryk's hostility to idealist philosophy is partly explained by his horror of collectivism – whether in its Hegelian or in its Marxian form.[8] A student of Marxism is brought face to face with the destructive results that follow, when pseudo-profundities take hold of half-educated minds. In his study of suicide, Masaryk had identified this 'half-education' (*Halbbildung*) as a major cause of modern man's disorientation. And the diagnosis was only confirmed by his subsequent analysis of Marxism – a philosophy which entered the world already fitted to the emotional needs of the auto-didact, and already armed with an impenetrable shield against criticism. Observing the effect of Marxism, first on the German critical tradition, and then on that Russian soul whose peculiar mixture of primitive mysticism and moral audacity he was to analyse in *The Spirit of Russia*,[9] Masaryk could not fail to recognize Marxism as a most dangerous intellectual contagion. If one wishes to find the roots of Masaryk's opposition to German idealism, they are to be sought partly here, in his justified apprehension of what ensues when collectivist theories are poured into half-instructed minds.

However, Masaryk's hostility to Kant, the founding father of German Idealism, dates from the earliest days of his university career, long before his interest in Marxism. It is a hostility which goes to the root of Masaryk's intellectual personality. Kant was condemned for his defence of a morality whose form and whose terms were exclusively philosophical, the property of elaborately self-conscious beings. Even so, in the last analysis, Masaryk's moral, political and religious ideas are profoundly Kantian, and dependent on Kant's arguments for their ultimate justification.

This deep intellectual need for Kantian philosophy will be more clearly understood if we return for a moment to the thinker who was to become, directly or indirectly, one of the greatest influences on modern Czech philosophy – Franz Brentano. Masaryk's particular understanding of the Cartesian *cogito* was derived from Brentano. The *cogito* attributes self-evidence neither to a mathematical proof, nor to a law of logic, nor to any other kind of 'eternal truth', but to a concrete, empirical and contingent fact – the fact of consciousness. It therefore provides the key, whereby philosophy can move out of the realm of necessities, into the world of concretely existing things. Starting from this premiss, we can hardly avoid the conclusion that consciousness and its intentionality are the basic objects of knowledge, and that nothing about the world can be more certain to us than the truths that are presented in our own mental life. Such was the starting point of Brentano's *Psychology from an Empirical Standpoint*, and of the later philosophy of Brentano's other famous pupil, the Moravian-born Edmund Husserl.

Brentano and the phenomenologists took as their primary study the 'intentional' character of mental processes: the fact that our states of mind represent the world, and endow it with 'sense' or 'meaning' (*Sinn, smysl*). Through the writings and seminars of Husserl's pupil Patočka, this idea was later to play an important role in the evolution of Czech thought. And in Husserl's treatment of it we find important connections with the themes of Masaryk's philosophy. Like Masaryk, Husserl believed that the 'sense' of the world is to be found in its moral aspect; in a letter of 1935, he even describes Masaryk, the friend of his youth, and his 'first teacher', as the one who had awakened in him 'the ethical conception of the world and of life.'[10] Husserl's philosophy culminated in a study of the European 'crisis' which recalls, in its anxieties if not in its style, the central concerns of Masaryk's social philosophy – in particular, the disorientation and fragmentation of man, under the impact of a knowledge that delivers no account of his place in the world. Phenomenology was nevertheless too contemplative, and too 'subjectivist' an exercise for Masaryk, who saw the meaning of life not as something to be received, like the Eucharist, through private experience, but as something to be won and tested through deeds. Husserl looked for forms of knowledge and understanding which would return the human subject to a central place in the scheme of things. Only then, in a final victory over the false objectivism of science, would the sense of the world be restored to us. For Masaryk, this pursuit of a 'knowledge in subjectivity' was too obscure and too theoretical an enterprise, and too remote from that real engagement with the moral life which was, for him, the only cure for man's anxiety. The conscious subject was certainly, for Masaryk as for Husserl, the centre and foundation of the human world. But to believe in a 'subjective essence', a 'first-person substantiality', is to mistake the true significance of the 'I', which resides not in reflection but in activity.

How then should we interpret Masaryk's frequent emphasis on truth in human conduct, and his adoption of the Hussite motto, that 'truth will prevail'? There cannot be a conflict, Masaryk argued, between truth and morality.[11] Indeed, ethics asks us to serve the truth diligently and wholly.[12] This 'living in truth' (as recent Czech writers have described it[13]) demands much of us. But, Masaryk implies, it is the only course of action that is compatible with our conscious nature. If that is so, however, it is surely because of the reason made clear to us by Kant – namely, that a self-conscious being is a rational being, and as such compelled to respect reason in his actions, and in the actions of others. 'To live in truth' is to demand and to acknowledge the absolute right to live by reason. It is to obey a law which is binding on all, to bow before reason in all its forms, and to leave around every rational creature the moral space which his reason needs for its embodiment. It is to live without special pleading, and to treat each rational being as an end in himself. In short, it is to obey the categorical imperative of Kant.

If we look for the true justification of Masaryk's hostility to collectivist thinking, therefore, and of his defence of liberal egalitarian values, it must be found not in Brentano, but in the great and resounding argument given by Kant. From this argument many things (a wary philosopher would say, too many things) follow. Not only is the sanctity of the individual provided with a philosophical guarantee – a guarantee more real, and more imbued with meaning, than any that Brentano and Husserl were able to derive from the Cartesian *cogito*. The place of the individual in society, and the legitimate sphere of his activity, are determined unambiguously for every rational being. Those vast collective schemes for the remaking of the human condition are instantly condemned: to instigate them we must do what we are categorically forbidden to do by Kant (and categorically enjoined to do by Lenin): we must treat the individual person not as an end, but as a means to his own replacement, a 'stage on the way' to a future and more perfect being. In place of the great totalitarian schemes we have only small-scale work – *drobna práce* – which permits us to strive for the improvement of our situation, while remaining obedient to the moral law. Each individual is endowed with an equal store of rights, and a sphere in which he alone is sovereign. Others may intrude into his sphere only by invitation, or else to their disgrace. The body politic becomes legitimate not when it is established by a collective or a general will, but when it is formed by the individual wills of individual people, to each of whom it leaves that sacred sphere of right without which obedience is unfree. At the heart of every legitimate order, therefore, is the precious core of self-reflecting, self-validating existence, the sacred hearth at which the self is warmed by its own self-emanation: the sphere of *svébytnost.*

Of course, Masaryk would not have presented those ideas as I – borrowing from Kant – have presented them. His defence of Palacký's *práce drobná* was conditioned by his belief that, in the liberal conditions of the Habsburg empire, the Czech question, however deeply it inquired into the depths of political order, could be gradually and peacefully resolved. Nevertheless, we should leave aside – in searching for the philosophical foundations of Masaryk's political thinking – the historical context of its utterance. To look for a philosophy is to search for what justifies, and not for what explains. Suffice it to say, then, that the main contours of Masaryk's world-view follow so naturally from Kant's theory of the individual that we ought to experience some surprise at Masaryk's hostility to Kantian philosophy. Despite his rejection of the extreme form of individualism espoused by Max Stirner[14] – the form of individualism which sets every man at variance with his fellows, in the pursuit of a power and a gratification that is uniquely his – Masaryk believed in the rights and freedoms of the individual. And it is a lamentable fact that, in looking for a basis for his individualism, he turned not to Kant but to that most slippery of all foundations – the Cartesian *cogito*, with its attendant idea of consciousness as an 'immaterial' process. The existence of the soul was, for Masaryk, the indisputable truth upon which rested the entire structure of religion and morality, and which, properly understood, would provide the sole and sufficient justification of an egalitarian and democratic politics:

> The existence of the soul is the true foundation of democracy – the everlasting cannot be indifferent to the everlasting, and immortal is equal to immortal. It is from this that love of one's neighbour acquires its peculiar – one might say metaphysical – significance.[15]

That was the furthest that the ageing Masaryk was prepared to go by way of a metaphysical commitment – and of course it was no further than those instinctive apprehensions of the world which had informed his first prayers as a child. How does the fact of consciousness establish the immortality of the soul? And why should one soul be equal to another, simply because they are both immortal? Those are questions which Masaryk does not ask.

Generally speaking a belief in the immortality of the soul has made the acceptance of human inequality easier, rather than harder. It is one result of religious decline, and of man's loss of hope for an eternal salvation, that human equality (equality *here and now*) has become the unquestioned basis of moral sentiment, and the principal object of political aspiration. We can see, therefore, what a slippery basis Masaryk has chosen for his democratic individualism, and how much safer his outlook would have been, had he entrusted it to the arguments of Kant. For whether or not the *Critique of Practical Reason* justifies democracy, it at least establishes that all rational beings are, as moral subjects, equal citizens of a 'kingdom of ends'. Their equality before the moral law justifies their equality before the law of man. This, in my view, is the only political equality that a philosopher should value, and the only concession that he should make to the egalitarian fashions of our time.

The moral egalitarianism of Kant may not justify democracy. What it *does* justify, however, is a theory of human rights, and the political practice which follows from it. The categorical imperative provides the 'natural law' of the medieval jurists with a secular grounding – and it is to this natural law that Masaryk looked in explaining what he meant by the *ideály humanitní*.[16] Since every rational being is to be treated as an end in himself, it follows that no one can be rightly enslaved, killed, injured or violated. Moreover, each rational being must be addressed as such: he must be given reasons for doing what we wish him to do, and cannot be coerced in defiance of his conscience. The individual therefore has inviolable rights, and above all the right to 'live in truth', in obedience to a moral law which is valid only so long as it is freely obeyed and consciously adopted.

The Kantian path to the defence of human rights has had an influence, direct and indirect, over Czech thinking – over Jungmann, Palacký and Havlíček, and more recently over Emmanuel Rádl and Ladislav Klíma. So far as I know, however, it has not been properly set out by a Czech philosopher in our century, even though there is nothing more vivid in the Czech experience, than the sense of what a man loses when he loses his rights – when he can no longer 'live in truth' except at an unacceptable cost to himself and his family. Masaryk's own reconstruction of the moral law barely advances beyond a Wordsworthian 'intimation of immortality'. Such has been the influence, on Central European thought, of Brentano's attempt to identify the constants of morality through axiology and the study of moral consciousness,[17] that the source and ground of morality has been repeatedly referred to something 'inner' – to a subjective awareness which is also the focus of an infinite 'care'. Thus when Husserl, in his influential work *Die Krisis der europäischen Wissenschaften und die transzendentale Phäno-menologie*,[18] addressed himself to the problem of modern disorientation, he saw it as a problem of consciousness. Man, Husserl argued, has renounced the immediate forms of know-ledge, in which meaning and certainty are contained, and embarked on an uprooted science, whose pretence at objectivity is little better than a denial of the thinking subject. Science threatens to undermine the *Lebenswelt*, which is the first object of our apprehension. It threatens, therefore, to rid the world of meaning. Husserl made much use, in this work and elsewhere, of the idea of a 'transcendental self'. But he seems to have had little knowledge of Kant's earlier exposition of the idea, and no recognition of the powerful arguments for the conclusion that the transcendental self has reality only in the practical reasoning which subjects it to a mortal law.

Husserl's pupil, Jan Patočka, takes these ideas further, though with a consciousness now, of the conflict between Kant and phenomenological thinking, and of the need – in the context of Central European philosophy – to reconcile those conflicting currents, and to channel them both into political theory. It is a fruitful exercise in the history of ideas, to study the transforma-tion of Masaryk's morality in the works of Patočka, and to observe the extent to which phenomenological method and Masarykian culture, filtered through the Heideggerian idiom of Patočka, engage immediately with the post-war experience of Central Europe.

In his later writing, Husserl – drawing on the hermeneutical tradition established by Dilthey – presented philosophy with a novel task. It is for philosophy to describe the world as it is *understood* – the world revealed to us in experience and in practice, the world in its innocence, prior to the fall into scientific explanation, free from the unnatural regimentation that is imposed on it by the concepts of scientific theory. Husserl described this revealed world as the 'concrete a priori', and gave to it the title of *Lebenswelt*, *Naturwelt*, and sometimes *Umwelt*. In his early work Patočka took over the term *Naturwelt* – natural world (*přírození svět*) – and described it, in Masarykian terms, as a 'concretely lived world' (*konkretně prožívaný svět*).[19] The world which we confront, bears the imprint of the perception, understanding and activity through which we encounter it, and our knowledge of it – whether theoretical or practical – is essentially 'concrete', tied down to the circumstances of its acquisition.

It is difficult to doubt that this *Lebenswelt* exists, as a publicly given and publicly recognized object of knowledge. And, while it may be, in a sense, an 'aspect' of the objective world, it is, in its fundamental contours, neither isomorphic with, nor reducible to, the world of science. If the *Lebenswelt* is an object of knowledge, however, it is only because it satisfies the following requirements, all of which are implied in Patočka's early study:

1) It is single and unified, in the manner of a Kantian 'a priori intuition'. That is, whatever relations structure the *Lebenswelt*, these hold between any two items within it. (If it is spatial, then any two items within it are spatially related; if it is temporal, then any two items within it are temporally related, and so on.)

2) It is common and public. Not only is my *Lebenswelt* a single world, so too is it identical in outline with yours. Without this supposition – the supposition that we 'live in the same world' – communication is impossible, language unintelligible, and reference to the *Lebenswelt* meaningless. (Such, at least, is the conclusion of Wittgenstein's 'private language' argument.)[20]

3) It is essentially *for* us, to be understood not 'as it is in itself', but as an object of epistemological and practical possibilities.

It is by virtue of those assumptions that 'cultural criticism' of Patočka's kind can include and, in a sense, gain support from, philosophical analysis. Cultural criticism involves the public expression of features of the world which we confront in our practical thinking and emotional life. And Patočka shared the Hegelian assumption common to many phenomenologists, that man's experience is essentially historical, and is not at one time what it was at a preceding time. Thus, while the outline of the

Lebenswelt remains the same from generation to generation (as it must if the voices of the past are still to speak to us) its topology changes. What is 'given' to a twentieth-century European is subtly different from what was 'given' to an Athenian Greek. Cultural criticism therefore impinges upon philosophy, precisely in the philosopher's recognition of the historical nature of his subject matter. And among the items that are 'given' to twentieth-century Europe, is the concept of history itself. Our world is presented to us already burdened by a past, and by the meanings and interpretations of those who have gone before. Hence, argues Patočka, the great spiritual problem of our time – the problem of *dějinnost*, or 'historicity'. He puts the problem succinctly thus: *Otázka je, zda dějinný člověk se chce ještě příznávat k dějinám*[21] – 'The question is whether historical man wishes still to *confess to history*.' It is our failure to make this 'confession', according to Patočka, which has deposited us in the dead world of *každodennost* – the 'everyday' world of our modern sorrows.

In order to understand Patočka's argument, we must acknowledge the primacy of 'meaning' (*Sinn* or *smysl*) in the world which is 'given' to us. Meaning, argues Patočka, belongs only in the world as lived – that is, as grasped and acted upon in the concrete situations of human experience. Precisely what is included within 'meaning' is unclear. But it is certain, from Patočka's studies of Masaryk,[22] that he wished to argue that *value* is a part of meaning, and along with value, obligation and all that might be subsumed under the idea of 'the sacred'. Meaning is embedded in the given, since it is inseparable from the conceptions whereby the world is grasped. At the same time, Patočka seems to say, meaning can be lost: there is an important sense in which the *Lebenswelt* then ceases to exist. Or rather, it persists in fragmented form, with no intrinsic order which enables us to find our position within it. We are then threatened by an unmediated confrontation with a 'merely objective' world – the world of science. This merely objective world makes no room for us, for it repudiates the subject of experience, and hence the subject of action and response.

This theme is not novel to Patočka – indeed he takes it from Husserl's *Krisis*, in which it is argued, in effect, that only phenomenology can enable us to repair the *Lebenswelt* that was rent by science. However, the theme is really far older than Husserl, and indeed goes back, as Patočka recognized in his second study of Masaryk, to Kant's *Critique of Practical Reason*. The theme is the incommensurability between our vision of ourselves as free beings, in a world which is 'open to our agency', and our vision of ourselves as a part of nature, subservient to the laws of causality of which science alone provides knowledge.

In treating this theme, the philosopher exposes himself to enormous intellectual dangers, and not all of these dangers were avoided by Patočka. For example, there is the constant danger of denying one of the three axioms of phenomenology that I proposed above – of arguing, for example, that the Lebenswelt of one man is unrelated to the Lebenswelt of his neighbour. There is also the danger of thinking that the Lebenswelt is not, after all, given by the internal structure of experience, but by some theoretical idea – some idea of human nature which may be, not the common property of all, but the specialized concern of a few self-conscious academics. Nevertheless, without venturing to assess how far Patočka's treatment of the theme may stand up to the most searching philosophical scrutiny, I shall try to isolate what seem to me to be some of the most interesting, and potentially defensible, theses presented in his later work.

In his lectures on the philosophy of history, delivered privately in Prague shortly before his death,[23] Patočka draws a contrast between two modes of reflective knowledge: myth and philosophy. The myth knows all in advance; it concerns an archetype, an event that is over, and which can only be repeated. Philosophy, however, knows nothing, except the essential formlessness of the world. It begins from wonder (Greek: thaumazein), and at first sees only what is boundless and uncontained: apeiron. The world, for philosophy, as yet awaits its interpretation.

Hence philosophy must take as its premiss the structure of appearances, while recognizing that we are not the creators of this structure, even though, without us, it would be nothing. Boldly, and characteristically, Patočka then argues that, in this philosophical exercise – the interpretation of experience – lies the true meaning of Europe. The philosophical task is undertaken afresh by each generation, and is present, not only in the sophisticated exercises of academic discussion, but in the very structure of common experience.

Patočka borrows a phrase from Plato: tēs psuchēs epimeleisthai – the care of the soul (starost o duši). That, he argues, sums up the effort and the achievement of European civilization, which has created the concrete reality of the philosophical enterprise – the polis, in which a more than worldly truth and justice achieve embodiment.[24] This civilizing effort, Patočka suggests, has been repeatedly destroyed, first in Greece and then in Rome. No doubt he would also recognize other epochs of destruction, but the one that particularly interests him is the twentieth century. The sign of this destruction is the disappearance of the polis, which is the concrete reality of our care for the soul, and its replacement by a world of mere objectivity, a world faced with which man is compelled to retrieve meaning *inwardly*. That, precisely, is the task of philosophy at these moments of crisis, namely, to provide the 'care' of the human soul, without which the meanings of our world will be dispersed forever into nothingness.[25]

Patočka displays an intellectual vice which seems generic to the Central European brand of cultural criticism: the need to advance through dichotomies, dividing the world *a priori* into oppositions which are understood in terms of their spiritual meaning. Thus, throughout the *Two Studies of Masaryk* and the *Heretical Essays*, the reader confronts a world divided between light and dark, day and night, overground and underground, historicity and everyday, the *heimlich* and the *unheimlich*. I do not know whether these are one dichotomy variously described, or a bundle of dichotomies, united around a single theme – the theme of man's spiritual desolation. However, it is important to recognize their main origin in the work of Dostoevsky (and in particular in *Brothers Karamazov* and *Notes from Underground*) if we are to understand the meaning which they conceal from Patočka's reader. Patočka wishes to refer, not to any abstractly conceived intellectual divide in the world of modern man, but to a 'lived reality', a fracture which is there in the ordinary experience of the twentieth century, and which is perhaps more apparent to a novelist than to a philosopher. If the philosopher has a place, it is through his ability to relate this fracture to a theory of the totality from which it derives. This totality is the restored *Lebenswelt*, in which the central experience of European civilization is a discoverable part of the 'natural world'.

This new philosophical task (which is, in fact, the perennial philosophical task, re-written to the idiom of our times) consists in the identification of man's historicity, and the description of that 'care of the soul' which once again enables us to 'confess to' history in our lives. Patočka's concept of historicity has seemed to many – and in particular to many Czechs – to express, much more concretely than Masaryk's *ideály humanitní*, the promise of philosophy in the modern world, and to provide the language with which to describe the fracture in the *Lebenswelt* of Central Europe. Only historical man can attain historicity; and I think that Patočka wished to describe the world of the Old Testament (and presumably the world of the Hindu and the Buddhist, and any other world that has yet to be absorbed into the precipitous movement of European civilization) as in some sense 'prehistorical'. (Certainly that seems to be the implication of the Prague lectures.) True historical man, who alone needs historicity, is beset, at times of crisis, by the disappearance of the concrete reality of his historical attachments. He does not find the public world in which the care of the soul is a recognized state of being: his *polis* can exist, if at all, only inwardly. The public world contains only the routine technicalities of 'everyday life', a life from which meaning has been expunged, and in which the only important value is life itself – the intricate task of daily survival. In response to this, he may take refuge in exultation. That is, he may excite himself into a kind of dionysiac frenzy, in which all consciousness of his situation is destroyed. For it is easier to close one's mind to the *Lebenswelt* than to confront its fractured reality, and to see through that fracture to the meaninglessness of the everyday. Exultation may take many forms; however, as Masaryk saw, its characteristically modern form is revolutionary politics: the extinguishing of all scruples, all *care*, in the tumult of an uncomprehended purpose. This is the final, insensate, substitution of a 'morality of goals' for the 'morality of sense (*smysl*)'.[26] Historicity involves acquiring what the exulting person also acquires, a separation between myself and everyday life. But it is a separation achieved, not at the cost of consciousness, but *through* consciousness. Hence it returns us to the 'care of the soul'.

How do we interpret that theory? As I have remarked, its *philosophical* status is to some extent questionable. It belongs to the same stable as Hannah Arendt's description of the 'instrumentalized' condition of the world of modern experience, and the resulting 'banality' of its evils. (And the writings of Arendt have been as influential in post-war Czech philosophy as those of Patočka.) Like Arendt, Patočka was looking for another, localized, more concretely understood, language, with which to express Heidegger's analysis of the world of *techne*, which surrounds us and which challenges us to 'care' (*sorgen*). The resulting theory must acquire a *universal* character. It must be something more than a 'handle' given to this or that local disaffection. It must describe a distinct intentionality which lies open to any self-conscious creature, and into which he might 'fall', whether or not through some fault of his own. It is in his attempt to display this 'universality' that Patočka produces the most interesting part of his analysis: the theory of the twentieth century as war.

According to Patočka, the wars of the twentieth century have been of a kind previously unknown, and can be understood only when we see in them the fractured intentionality of modern European experience. The modern war expresses the triumph of 'everyday life', and the absence from human intercourse of the meaning (*smysl*) which shows the inner relation between the world and the subject who apprehends it. In this everyday world, life is everything, and death is non-existent. The thought of death has been banished, and there is no value beyond the value of life itself. All has been concentrated into the routine of survival, and no one looks over his shoulder at the shadow which dogs his steps.[27]

But this 'day-time' world of the everyday is purchased at a price. It depends upon the night from which we flee and which is its unillumined side. Others must be sacrificed, in order that night should be overcome. The war is a kind of permanent sacrifice of life for the sake of life: a propitiatory offering to the night. Those who go to it go without cause, and with no apprehension of the meaning of what they do. They go only because the war is there, a constant destruction, into which they disappear without trace. The everyday man, who has renounced the care of his soul, and who therefore takes no responsibility for his existence, secretly needs that world of utter destruction. In that world the price of life is paid, and 'senselessness' is all-triumphant. The war is the consequence of a life voided of sense, in which the void itself rises up to extinguish life.

And yet, in that night, into which the soldier goes without purpose, lies the reality of sacrifice, and in sacrifice, an awareness of freedom. For a moment I am not merely swept along by the banalities of the everyday. My own reality as a soul, whose nature is to care, is brought home to me. In the moment of sacrifice, therefore, there comes an intimation of the meaning which everyday life has swept away.

War, according to Patočka, has become the normal condition of modern man, who lives in a state of total mobilization, confronting now battle, and now 'peace', in the same frame of mind. He takes responsibility for neither, and in neither is he confronted by a meaning that shows him how he might continue to care. Only at that one point – the point of sacrifice – does he for a moment break out of the prison of everyday life, and there, in that 'life at the apex', he experiences the only form of *polis* to which he may attain: the 'solidarity of the shattered'.

There is undeniably something drastic about Patočka's language, and this drastic quality can be discerned in much of his later writing. He frequently dwells upon the thought of death, upon the 'heat death of the universe', upon Spenglerian visions of '*Untergang*', and upon the morality of ultimate gestures, as explored by Dostoevsky. There is, indeed, a streak of Slavonic melancholy in Patočka, as in his hero Masaryk, and in both men this gave rise to a fascination with the Russian soul, and an attempt to describe the mysterious cavern at the heart of existence where the Russian soul seems to have pitched its dwelling. Since this drastic quality expresses precisely what is *local* in Patočka's experience, it must, I believe, be subtracted from his writings by any critic concerned to discover their universal meaning. I say that it expresses what is local, since I believe it to be a record of the peculiar experience of Central Europe, where it is indeed true that war continues to dominate the structure of life, and haunts the shadowy underside of a world which is both senseless and everyday.

It is particularly regrettable to an English reader of Patočka to find the extent to which the Czech philosopher was detached from English influence – the influence which so many of his predecessors had preferred to the intoxicating surge of Teutonic idealism, and to the melancholy extremism of the Slavs. But it is a testimony to what has happened to Bohemia that Patočka's conception of the 'everyday' should now be so much more vivid to his countrymen than the pre-war fashion for a very English form of ordinariness, as this was described and upheld by Čapek. The 'ordinariness' and trust of the English Tory is a record of the inner life of an undestroyed *polis*. It is the intimate self-familiarity of a society that is fundamentally at peace with itself, and in which the soul is cared for by the natural justice of a common law. Patočka's everyday is in fact the inner life of a destroyed social order, an order sown with the seeds of distrust, in which the conditions for spontaneous agreement no longer exist. The 'fully mobilized' mentality of the modern Central European is, however, precisely what is least European about him. It is precisely what has been imposed upon him by the triumph of a system which is at war with Europe, and at war, also, with itself.

If we understand Patočka, not as a philosopher of the modern consciousness, but as a critic of the communist order, we can, I believe, discover by means of his writings a new and important 'crisis' in the experience of Eastern Europe. There it is indeed true that the everyday is void of sense, that it is phenomenologically impermeable, with every passage through which the soul might have passed – every place where the 'I' might still exist in consciousness of its ultimate responsibility – permanently sealed up. Of this world it is indeed true that the 'morality of goals' has replaced the 'morality of sense', that all value is located 'elsewhere', in a promised state for the sake of which man must expend himself in senseless labour. Of this world it is true that the man who refuses the everyday is *'podzemní'*, and that such an 'underground man' is 'without qualities', a pure subject, the mere form of freedom without content. And of this world it is also true that its normal condition is precisely what is most abnormal about it: the condition which describes itself in the language of 'peace', 'liberation', 'brotherhood', and every other secular abstraction, and which thereby reveals its senselessness, its closure to the 'sacred', and its reality as war.

Such ideas are a long way from the Masarykian thoughts that first inspired them, and a long way too from Husserl. Yet they bear the imprint of both philosophies, and continue the enterprise begun by Masaryk, which was to show that the individual soul is the foundation of social order and that the care of the soul, and the care of the *polis*, are two aspects of a single concern.

Reprinted from: Josef Novák (ed.), *On Masaryk*, Amsterdam: Rodopi, 1988.

7

ANALYTICAL
PHILOSOPHY
AND EMOTION

It is probably as difficult for continental philosophers to envisage an 'analytical philosophy of the passions' as it was for Spinoza's contemporaries to understand how he might treat the same subject *more geometrico*.[1] Yet, while we may regret the narrowness, the fruitless technicality, and the philistinism of analytical philosophy, there is no reason to suppose either that the analytical school is less able to study the human soul than its rivals, or that it is more disposed to technicality and philistinism than they. Indeed, so far as those particular defects go, I believe that phenomenology is just as likely to display them. The fault lies, not so much with the particular school to which the writer happens to belong, as with the contemporary pressure which causes those without literary gifts to write and publish. Only the closing down of universities on a massive scale could remedy this situation; and that is as much as to say that it will not be remedied.

Two ideas have had a decisive impact on the philosophy of mind, as practised by those working in the analytical tradition. The first is the argument given by Wittgenstein, against the possibility of a private language.[2] The second is the resurrection, due largely to Hilary Putnam[3] and Saul Kripke[4], of the idea of real essence, and the consequent theory that there is a distinction between necessary and *a priori* truth. Wittgenstein's argument, if valid, seems to put paid completely to the idea that we can learn about our states of mind by 'looking inwards' – by seeing them from the 'first person' point of view. The enterprise of 'Cartesian meditation', which invites me to lay hold of the 'inner essence' of a feeling, by separating it in thought from all objective circumstance, is an illusion. There is no 'inner essence', and no method, but only madness, involved in the pursuit of it. If I wish to understand my emotions, I should study not how I feel, but how you feel. I should ask myself how I identify this state of mind in you, what role the concept of emotion plays in the description of your life and behaviour. This is not to deny the reality of the self, or of the viewpoint which constitutes it. But the self too is a publicly recognizable phenomenon. You too are a self, and you too view the world as I do, from the elusive 'point of view' of the subject who is neither out of the world nor wholly in it. The errors of the Cartesian theory, and of the many theories which have stemmed from it, are the direct result of the attempt to describe the first person viewpoint from the point of view of the first person.

Wittgenstein's argument presents an important – and so far unanswered – challenge to Husserlian phenomenology. But it leaves a residual problem which is perhaps the greatest that analytical philosophers confront: the problem of the self, and of the 'first person' viewpoint. Just what could be meant by those ideas, and how are we to reconcile them with the science to which our public language seems inexorably to draw us? At least one recent philosopher – Thomas Nagel[5] – has suggested that there *can* be no reconciliation between subjectivity and the world of science, and argues, in Kantian fashion, that our world encloses a metaphysical mystery, and that this mystery is *us* (or at least *me*). I feel some sympathy for Nagel's arguments.

The resurrection of the idea of 'real essence' has yet to make a full impact on the analytical philosophy of mind. Some recent philosophers have argued that real essences are a matter for science to determine, but that science makes no use of mental categories. Mental concepts, they argue, are inherently 'superficial', involving a classification of objects in relation to human interests, rather than with a view to scientific explanation. Mental kinds are therefore not natural kinds, and have no essence – or at least, only a 'nominal' essence, derived from our habits of classification. Such nominal essences are to be discovered through conceptual analysis. In this area, therefore, philosophy, as the analytical tradition has conceived it, is uniquely qualified to cast light on what concerns us.

We should not lose sight, however, of the important place in our mental concepts of the idea of explanation. Almost everything that we say in describing the mind of another has an explanatory intention, and involves commitment to some causal hypothesis. Our mental descriptions, like all our descriptions, are the first steps in science. And as the science of behaviour develops, it will bring order and discipline to the descriptions which first inspired and guided it.

It could be, nevertheless, that ordinary psychological descriptions, while they involve causal hypotheses, are impermeable to theoretical elaboration. That is, it could be that the various mental states that we classify together as beliefs, or as desires, or as sensations, have no common scientific essence: their distinctive features have to be explained case by case, and in a variety of ways. If that were so, then 'folk psychology', as it has been called, would not be directly derivable from the science of behaviour, and its laws would retain an irremediably *ad hoc* character. Nevertheless, we should still be able to say something about the real essence of a state of mind – something over and above the analysis of the concepts used to classify it. But what, exactly, could *philosophy* say about this essence, and how? In which direction does the analysis of concepts lead us, and where precisely does it leave us in the lurch? Or is there no lurch?

I mention those vast methodological questions partly so as to explain the state of flux in which the analytical philosophy of the emotions now finds itself. In what follows I address myself more directly to the question of *what* emotions are, illustrating, as I do so, some of the more important lines of enquiry that recent philosophers have pursued, and adding one or two thoughts of my own. I have no final answer to the question of method: I do not know whether emotions, for instance, have real essences, nor do I know how best we could discover what those real essences are. I suspect, however, that the concept of the self – which enters so forcefully into our feelings – is so inherently resistant to scientific analysis, that the real essence of the mental states that involve it will never be easily discovered, or easily described.

The ancient division of mental states into actions and passions recurs throughout the history of Western philosophy, and it might seem that it is now so questionable and threadbare as to be of no heuristic significance. I think, however, that the division still needs to be taken seriously. If we were to seek a prephilosophical classification of states of mind, then we should identify, as the fundamental feature of emotions, the fact that they are motives to action. Emotions are the states of mind *out of* which an agent does what he does. You act *out of* jealousy, anger, love or remorse, and it is this 'out of' which, in the first instance, needs explaining. Now it seems clear that the motives of actions cannot themselves *be* actions. For if they *were* actions, then they in turn would require a motive; else everything should be motiveless – a chain of actions, each springing from its predecessor, but with no other reason than itself. Hence, if we are to capture the common idea of a mental motive, we must distinguish those states of mind that are actions, from those that are not, and among which motives are included. Therein lies a proof of the ancient view that emotions (motives) are all passions – things suffered, rather than things done.

Passions cannot be commanded. But nor can judgments or beliefs (beliefs being the mental states that find expression in sincere judgments). I can ask you to believe that p: but you will do so only if I give you sufficient evidence that p. In which case you will believe p in any case, whether or not I command it. There is no such thing, therefore, as obeying the command to believe something. Are beliefs then passions? And should they provide our model for the emotional life?

There is certainly a tendency to argue that *some* beliefs are passions – namely, those beliefs which lie at the heart of our emotions, and without which our motives would be divorced from the process of rational assent and criticism. Some philosophers, however, have shown a disconcerting tendency to write of emotions as though they were *nothing but* beliefs or judgments. A case in point is Sartre, who, in his *Sketch for a Theory of the Emotions*, seems to make little or no distinction between terror and the recognition of 'the terrifying', anxiety and the recognition of 'the *angoissant*', and so on.[6] The emotion emerges from his analysis as a kind of charm or ritual, whereby I try to overcome the world, by directly changing my cognitive stance towards it.

It is clear, however, that belief or judgment is at best a *component* in an emotion, and insufficient in itself to capture the motivating force. Sartre was misled by the deceptive simplicity of mental descriptions, which seem constantly to imply that all mental states are of a single kind. (This is the simplicity which trapped Descartes and Spinoza into describing all mental states as 'ideas', and which exerted a similar influence on Locke, Berkeley and Hume.) It may be that emotions, like beliefs and desires, have 'intentionality'. But intentionality is not necessarily a unified phenomenon, nor must it always be explained in the same way. We might accept Brentano's idea, that intentionality is distinctive (even if not definitive) of mental phenomena[7], but reject those monolithic theories of 'the intentional' which have been so important in continental phenomenology. Our beliefs may be true or false; our concepts may refer or not refer; our desires may or may not come to pass – in every case our mental state contains, as it were, a gap or recess into which reality might fit. It is this 'relation of fit' that is captured in the idea of intentionality. But why should all 'fitting' be construed on the model of belief – in terms of the true and the false?

Consider desires, for instance. My desire for x is mutually entwined with, and existentially dependent upon, certain beliefs about x. But is the relation between the desire and x, the same as the relation between the beliefs and x? They have this in common, that the object is in each case intentional; which is to say that there may or may not be some entity corresponding to it outside the mind (a material object which 'fits' into the mental recess). But they are also crucially different. For one thing, a desire seeks to *change* its object – to take it into possession, to eat it, destroy it or make love to it. For another thing, desires are not made *true* or *false* by their object, and when they remain unfulfilled this may not be a question of cognitive deficiency.

There has been a tradition in British philosophy – going back at least to Hobbes – which explains motives in terms of the confluence of beliefs and desires. Hobbes defined fear, for example, as 'aversion with opinion of hurt from the object'. A modern analytical philosopher might wish to add only one thing to such an analysis – namely, the element of causality. It is not so much the *addition* of a belief that bestows on a desire its character as a motive (as jealousy, say, rather than envy, hatred or resentment); rather it is the *causal relation* between that belief and the desire which springs from it. What makes my present passion one of envy, say, rather than jealousy, is that the desire to harm the object springs, not from the belief that he has what *I* could have had did he not possess it, but from the belief that he has something that I may not ever have obtained.

The belief-desire analysis of motives is extremely popular among analytical philosophers for two reasons. First, it seems to reduce emotion to more manageable and more general components: belief, desire and the mental causality that binds them. Secondly, it seems to account for the complex intentionality of emotions – an intentionality which, on this analysis, springs from two independent sources, a belief and a desire, each focusing in its own special way on a single object. This enables us to explain, in particular, the following otherwise puzzling features of emotions – features which have been apparent at least since Aquinas's lengthy discussion in the *Summa*:

1) An emotion is a cognitive state, which might be refuted by the world. The explanation of this feature is that emotions are founded on beliefs, which can in turn be true or false. When I believe falsely that my son has died, my grief is a kind of *error*.

2) Emotions reflect the cognitive capacities of the creatures who possess them. This is an obvious consequence of (1). Thus animals, which can be sensibly said to fear things, cannot sensibly be said, for example, to resent, disapprove or grudgingly condone them.

3) Emotions have 'formal objects': that is, there is some description that an object must satisfy, or be thought to satisfy, if it is to be the object of a given emotion. This description is determined by the 'defining belief' upon which the emotion is founded. Thus the object of fear is 'something harmful', the object of remorse, 'something evil done by me'; and so on.

4) Emotions have motivating force. This is explained simply, by the assumption that emotions include desires.

5) There is such a thing as the justification of emotions. For emotions can be criticized and defended in two separate ways: first, through theoretical reason, in that they involve beliefs which may be true of false; secondly, through practical reason, in that they involve the commitment to action that is essential to desire. (This shows how we might conclude that it is wrong of Jack to love, resent or be angry with Jill.)

All those are positive results of the analysis. Nevertheless, it cannot be accepted in the straightforward form that an analytical philosopher might desire. Two difficulties in particular deserve consideration, difficulties which derive from areas of thought and experience that do not have the prominence in analytical philosophy that they have elsewhere. The first difficulty is familiar to all students of aesthetics. Many of our emotions have imaginary objects – that is, objects believed by the subject to be unreal. Such objects are defined not by a belief but by an act of the imagination, in which judgment is denied or suspended. My emotion on observing the death of Desdemona has *the death of Desdemona* as its object; yet I do not believe that there is any such event. Nor do I have a desire to interfere, nor to do anything else that would otherwise be appropriate to the circumstance of murder. So how are we to explain this particular 'direction upon an object', in which both belief and desire are, so to speak, suspended, and yet in which the full strength of an emotion is none the less felt? It seems that we must develop a definition of 'thought' that is wider than either judgment or belief – a definition more nearly approximate to what Frege had in mind, when he argued that 'assertion' is no part of the content of a sentence[8]. And we must do something similar for desire. We must show how we can be moved, without being moved to action, and how this experience can nevertheless be important to us, in just the way that motives are.

The second difficulty is rather more subtle. Emotions do not involve thoughts and desires directed upon the *object* only, but also other thoughts and desires concerning the *subject*. An emotion is a kind of bridge between subject and object, and its direction onto the world is also a 'situating' of the subject. It is indeed doubtful that we can separate, in thought, our conception of the object of desire, hatred, remorse or vengeance, from our conception of ourselves in desiring, hating, remorseful or vengeful circumstances. Emotions involve an element or dramatization, in which the self looms large, as the bearer of sacred burdens. They are liable, therefore, to the kind of corruption known as sentimentality, in which the subject veils the object completely, and becomes the sole and exclusive object of attention. (Sentimentality can be seen, from the Kantian point of view, as a way of treating the object as a means – a means, in this case, to my own self-glorification.) Our emotions are also susceptible to important transformations, as we shift attention from the first to the second person, and again to the third-person point of view. The self engaged is not the same as the self observed, and the person who sees himself from outside in the act of love or vengeance feels differently from the person whose act is through and through saturated by the first-person point of view.

In fact, however, many of our emotions exist only *because* we can switch between the two perspectives – between the 'inner' and the 'outer'. Thus sexual emotion involves a constant shifting of attention, of a kind that is possible only in a fully moral being. (Hence sexual emotion lies outside the emotional repertoire of children and lunatics.) The moral emotions themselves – remorse, guilt, shame, approval, pride and self-complaisancy – involve a definite attempt to place the self in direct relation to the world, and to experience the encounter with the self's inner freedom. The thought-process here is immensely complicated, but certainly not something that could be captured simply in terms of a belief, a desire and a causal relation. The emotion is not merely an affirmation, it is also a transformation of the subject: a shaping of the self against the background of a moral order.

Phenomenologists are used to those difficulties, which are discussed in various contexts by such thinkers as Scheler[9] and Schutz.[10] They are also able to deal more cogently than analytical philosophers with the important concept which Husserl introduced into philosophy, and which proves indispensable in explaining the higher emotions – the concept of the *Lebenswelt*.[11] The *Lebenswelt* is not a world separate from the world of science, but a world differently described – described with the concepts that designate the intentional objects of human experience. Such concepts may not, and in all probability cannot, feature in the best scientific theory of the universe. For all that, they are indispensable to us, since they describe the focus of our attention, and signal the occasion for action. It is through *these* concepts that the world is seen as meaningful, and it is the comparative neglect of them by analytical philosophy that has led to its impoverished account of the human emotions.

In a recent book I have tried to overcome the inherited deficiencies of the analytical school, and to give an analysis of the most exasperating of all human passions – sexual desire – in terms that are responsive to the truths conveyed by phenomenology.[12] Sexual desire, I argue, has an 'epistemic' intentionality: it involves a process of discovery, and takes its direction from what it finds. It therefore has no precise initial goal, but only a 'course': what you desire emerges during the process of a co-operative act, in which another is the principal object of attraction. My desire is for another person, seen as a person, but at the same time identified in thought with his body. In seeing the other as an incarnate self, so too do I see myself: and this experience of mutual incarnation determines the conceptual structure that lies at the heart of desire. (It is from this experience that the relevant fragment of the *Lebenswelt* is constructed.)

The goal of desire, as it emerges from the process of desire, is that of bodily union. But union is wanted only as and in so far as the body of the other is perceived as identical with his self: a centre of action, feeling, observation, judgment and responsibility. I argue that – while we do indeed see each other's bodies in such a way – we are also constantly tempted to transgress through this perception, and to locate the centre of another's being not in the body but elsewhere or nowhere. The urgent need to hold you *in* your body, and to find your perspective and your responsibility there, in the contaminated flesh, is what gives rise, I argue, to the many paradoxes of desire.

The analysis I give is 'third personal': that is, it involves the study of the publicly recognizable expression of desire, rather than its 'phenomenological character'. Nevertheless, it places the first person perspective at the heart of our sexual experiences. Hence the analysis is forced into areas which analytical philosophy normally avoids, and is couched in terms which are perhaps surprising for a British philosopher. Rather than expand further on what I have written elsewhere, I shall merely mention three of my conclusions.

1) Animals do not experience sexual desire, since they have no concept of the self.

2) The goal of sexual desire cannot be described without making a distinction between the normal and the perverted; moreover, rational beings really do have a reason to avoid sexual perversion.

3) Traditional sexual morality, with its emphasis on abstinence, chastity, modesty and love, was probably right, even though it may be too late, now, to return to it.

Analytical philosophers are apt to say that no philosophical argument *could* lead to such conclusions; therefore your argument must be invalid. On the other hand, if the business of philosophy is to explain and to sustain the deliverances of common sense, it may be time that we ceased to be intimidated by this fruitless call for an *a priori* proof.

From: *Topoi* 6 (1987).

8
MODERN PHILOSOPHY AND THE NEGLECT OF AESTHETICS

The Greeks were deeply interested in the question of aesthetics, and their philosophers discussed them in a variety of contexts – moral, political and metaphysical. Nevertheless aesthetics, conceived as a systematic branch of philosophy, is an invention of the eighteenth century. It owes its life to Shaftesbury, its name to Baumgarten, its subject-matter to Burke and Batteux, and its intellectual eminence to Kant. Its irruption into the terrain of philosophy is one of the most remarkable episodes in the history of ideas. In Schiller's *Letters on Aesthetic Education*, the newly discovered faculty of aesthetic judgment is given the sacred task that was once laid on the shoulders of religion: the task of preparing man for his life as a moral being. In Hegel's *Lectures on Aesthetics*, art is presented as the successor to religion, an all-embracing form of consciousness in which the truth of the world, at a certain point of spiritual development, is most perfectly distilled. Art and the study of art form the highest point to which man's self-understanding may attain, before emancipating itself from the sensuous, and passing over into the sphere of abstract concepts, philosophical reflection, and natural science – the world of *Wissenschaft*.

What Hegel said was a kind of nonsense. But what he meant was true. Or at least, true enough to serve as the starting-point for discussion. Art, culture and the aesthetic experience have been removed from the central place in philosophical speculation which they briefly occupied. In their place we find science, logical theory, and the rigour – or *rigor mortis* – of semantic analysis. This transformation in philosophy has accompanied another and larger change. The triumph of scientific thought has caused such self-doubt, such a loss of faith and simplicity, in those subjects which have had the articulation of man's self-image as their purpose, as to raise the question whether a humane education is any longer possible. At the same time, philosophy's retreat from the study of art and culture has left a vacuum. In its absence, any kind of nonsense can take root and stifle the natural growth of meaning. Here is an instance of what happens to literary criticism, when philosophy abandons it:

> Even before it 'concerns' a text in narrative form, double invagination constitutes the story of stories, the narrative of narrative, *the narrative of deconstruction in deconstruction*: the apparently outer edge of an enclosure, far from being simple, simply external and circular, in accordance with the philosophical representation of philosophy, makes no sign beyond itself, towards what is utterly *other*, without becoming double or dual, without making itself be 'represented', refolded, superposed, *re-marked* within the enclosure, at least in what the structure produces as an effect of interiority.

Those words occur in a book put together by a collection of staid and bewildered American critics who, having looked in vain for a philosophy that would give sense and direction to their enterprise, at last hit on Jacques Derrida (the author of the passage) as the answer to their problems.[1] Their purpose was to display to the academic world that criticism is alive and well and living in Yale, where, thanks to Derrida, it has discovered a new method and outlook. The name of this method (or anti-method) is deconstruction.

I do not pretend to know what deconstruction is, although apparently it tells us that texts have neither author nor subject-matter, and that reading is impossible. But I should like to reflect on what is implied, when those who are the trustees of a literary tradition as deeply interwoven with life and feeling as ours has been, should consider themselves to be studying nothing more warm or more compromising than a 'text', and should be able to draw no more useful conclusion from their studies than that reading is impossible. Surely something has been lost, when those artefacts in which every possible meaning had been deliberately concentrated, should be offered to the world as 'unreadable'? Surely philosophy has been neglectful of its duties, if it has allowed matters to proceed to such a pass?

There are some lines of George Seferis, in which he seems to reflect on the burden placed on the modern Greek by the classical culture which surrounds him:

I woke with this marble head in my hands
which exhausts my elbows, and I do not know where
                                    I shall put it down:
it fell into the dream, as I was emerging. . . .

Just such an image occurs to me, when I hear words like 'text'
and 'deconstruction' on the lips of a modern critic. The work of
art lies in his hands, as encumbering and uncanny as an ancient
marble whose meaning he cannot fathom. Such a critic seems to
be no longer immersed in a civilization, but rather awakening
from it, into a flat and desert landscape – a 'post-cultural' world.
The 'text' is a piece of dream-débris, a burden of which he can
rid himself only by analysis, or 'deconstruction'. And in none of
this does life play any part.

The collapse of English studies into deconstruction is not, in
my view, the cause but the consequence of philosophy's inertia.
If literary critics now seem so unable to appreciate the difference
between genuine reasoning and empty sophistry, it is partly
because philosophy, which is the true guardian of critical thinking, has long ago withdrawn itself from their concerns. When
the agenda of philosophy is so narrow and specialized that only
a trained philosopher can understand it, is it then surprising
that those disciplines which – whether they know it or not –
depend upon philosophy for their anchor, should have slipped
away helplessly into the night?

But is the cultural isolation of philosophy really so recent a
phenomenon? Some would argue that, in jettisoning its links
with art and literature, philosophy has returned – after a period
of Romantic and post-Romantic aberration – to its traditional
role in the modern world, as the handmaiden of the sciences. If
we look at the first century of modern philosophy – the century
of Bacon, Descartes, Locke, Spinoza and Leibniz – we see
philosophical speculation arising in the wake of scientific experiment. Then as now, it was science which set the agenda for
philosophy; and if modern philosophers have been so deeply
concerned with logic, probability theory, linguistic analysis and
the behavioural sciences, this is because those branches touch
upon the frontiers of science, and address themselves to difficulties which, if they are not solved, will hamper the process of
discovery. If modern philosophers have been so exercised by the
'mind-body' problem, for instance, it is largely because, until it
is solved, scientists will not know what they are observing,
when they study human behaviour and its causes.

On such an account, the rise of aesthetics was more of a
temporary disturbance: an indentation in the smooth project of

philosophical enquiry, caused by the neighbouring explosion of the Romantic movement. And Romanticism was itself the product of man's sudden and urgent need to find meaning elsewhere than in church, and in some other posture than on his knees. All revolutions in philosophy either serve to launch some new science, or else exhaust themselves in futile enquiries of which we soon grow tired. Aesthetics came into the world simultaneously with social philosophy: and the comparison between them is significant. Out of social philosophy, economics and sociology were born. But out of aesthetics – what has come out of aesthetics, if not futile enquiries of which we have now grown tired?

There is some truth in the retort. But it needs careful examination. Two features distinguish the philosophers of the seventeenth century from their modern descendants. First, they were fully integrated into the cultural life of their times; second, if they did not look to aesthetics for the source of meaning and value, it was because they were, with a few exceptions, sincere believers in a benevolent God, whose redemptive purpose they read more directly in the laws of the created world.

Thus Bacon, Descartes, Locke, Leibniz and Spinoza were, despite their scientific leanings, practising participants in a literary culture. They wrote well – in the case of Bacon and Descartes, surpassingly well. Leibniz composed poetry, and Bacon essays which are as great as any in the language. Even Locke, clumsy though he sometimes was, expressed himself in a manner so succinct and vivid as to enrich intellectual discourse forever after. Consider the following passage, from the *Second Treatise of Civil Government*:

> Though the earth and all inferior creatures be common to all men, yet every man has a 'property' in his own 'person'. This nobody has any right to but himself. The 'labour' of his body and the 'work' of his hands, we may say, are properly his. Whatsoever, then, he removes out of the state that Nature hath provided and left it in, he hath mixed his labour with it, and joined to it something that is his own, and thereby makes it his property.

The simplicity of language in such a passage is one with the complexity of thought. Each word is used with a full sense of its value, not only as a vehicle for abstract reasoning, but as a purveyor of images. And of course the principal image – that of the workman as mixing his labour, and therefore himself, with the thing that he produces – has lived in the educated conscience ever since, resurging in countless ways in the writings of Smith, Ricardo, Hegel, Marx and their modern followers.

The second distinguishing feature of our forebears is equally important. Each of the philosophers to whom I have referred was a believer, for whom the meaning of the world is neither created by philosophy nor dependent upon philosophy for its construction. Spinoza, it is true, concluded that God is identical with the world, and therefore that many of the claims of theology are erroneous. But he at once set out to show how a person may find peace and happiness in the very recognition of that disturbing truth. And Spinoza's language, as he bent to this task, became so fully alive as to convey a message well beyond the reach of abstract argument. Even Spinoza, therefore, the most forbiddingly technical of the seventeenth-century philosophers, was able to speak directly to the heart. Goethe records, in a moving passage of *Dichtung und Wahrheit*, the effect that this solemn, mathematical prose was to exert over him:

> That wonderful utterance: 'Whosoever loves God, cannot strive that God should love him in return', with all the preceding sentences upon which it rests, with all the following sentences which spring from it, filled my entire meditations. To be in everything unselfish, to the highest unselfishness in love and friendship, was my greatest desire, my maxim, my rule, and so that insolent remark which follows – 'if I love you, what is that to you?' – was spoken directly into my heart.*

The fact that the meaning intended by Spinoza was not the meaning understood by Goethe is of small account, beside the evident force, whereby one man has impinged through the written word upon the life and feeling of another.

In both the respects to which I have referred – cultural participation and religious belief – contemporary philosophy differs completely from the philosophy of the seventeenth century. With rare exceptions, the contemporary philosopher is isolated from the surrounding literary culture, with no grasp of style or rhetoric, and with little instinct for linguistic nuances. Of course, there are philosophers with genuine literary gifts – Quine, for instance. And the stylistic insufficiencies of the remainder resemble those of the average practitioner of literary 'deconstruction'. Nevertheless, there is, in the idiom of modern philosophy, such a poverty of emotion, such a distance from the felt experience of words and things, as to cast doubt on its

---

* The insolent remark to which Goethe refers is a line from his verse novel, *Hermann und Dorothea*.

competence as a vehicle for moral and aesthetic reflection. Here is an example of what I have in mind, taken from a recent work of aesthetics:

> I start with some action A that some person P wants at time t_1 to do at time t_2. One possibility is that P believed at t_1 that he cannot perform A at t_2. Then P at t_1 has no action-plan for performing A at t_2. Alternatively, P may believe at t_1 that there is a chance that he can perform A at t_2; but there may be no action A' distinct from A such that P believes at t_1 that he might be able to perform A_1 at t_2 and that if he did so he might thereby generate A. In such a case, let us call the unit set, (A), P's *action-plan* at t_1 for performing A at t_2. But thirdly, there may be at least one ordered set of actions $(A_1 \ldots, A_n)$, such that P believes at t_1 that he might be able to perform A_1 at t_2 and that if he did so he might thereby generate $A, \ldots$, and believes that he might be able to perform A_n at t_2 and that if he did so he might thereby generate A_{n-1}. In such a case, let us call the n + 1-tuple of actions, $(A, \ldots, A_n)$ P's *action-plan* at t_1 for performing A at t_2. Let us call A the *goal* of that action-plan. And let us call A_n, the *terminus* of the plan.[2]

To understand what is so objectionable in that style, is to understand the spiritual temptation which leads people away from true philosophy into pseudo-science. The whole paragraph is a kind of fraud, an introduction of redundant terminology from set theory, in order to capture one simple fact, namely, that a plan of action involves a goal, together with the steps chosen to achieve it. Nothing is subsequently done with the technicalities, which serve merely to give a quaint appearance of rigour to banality.

The stylistic catastrophe of analytic philosophy is a subject for another occasion. I shall merely record my opinion that the alienating prose of our philosophers is due not to expertise but to idleness – to a failure to pursue a thought to the point where it *speaks itself*, in words of its own. (It is precisely this self-utterance of thought that we find in the passage quoted from Locke.) Style is the search for simplicity and naturalness, for the phrase which not only says what you mean, but also embodies within itself all the nuances and hesitations that would enliven the reader's judgment. Philosophy severed from literary criticism is as monstrous a thing as literary criticism severed from philosophy. In each case the result is a kind of intellectual masquerade, a phantom world of discourse, whose principal subject-matter is itself. In philosophy, as in literary criticism, the written word has largely ceased to address itself to living creatures. Only if it contains a theoretical truth, therefore – a truth to be measured by the exacting requirement of the sciences – can philosophy be justified. This partly explains the peculiar affectation of scientific language on the part of many modern philosophers – even though the real hard work of science lies beyond their competence.

It is the second difference between the seventeenth-century philosopher and his contemporary descendant that interests me. If we examine, from the standpoint of the historian of ideas, the episode in philosophical history to which I referred at the outset, then we cannot fail to notice that the rise of aesthetics was simultaneous with the Romantic movement, and with the loss of confidence in revealed religion. In Kant's *Critique of Judgment* the point is already explicitly made, that the sense of God's immanence – the sense of the world as created, and of personality as shining forth from all its aspects – is to be derived from the very same faculty which has beauty as its object and judgment as its goal. It is through aesthetic contemplation that we confront that aspect of the world which was the traditional concern of theology. We cannot prove, by theoretical reasoning, that there is a God; nor can we grasp the *idea* of God, except by the *via negativa* which forbids us to apply it. Nevertheless, we have intimations of the transcendental. In the sentiment of beauty we feel the purposiveness and intelligibility of everything that surrounds us, while in the sentiment of the sublime we seem to see beyond the world, to something overwhelming and inexpressible in which it is somehow grounded. Neither sentiment can be translated into a reasoned argument – for such an argument would be natural theology, and theology is dead. All we know is that we can know nothing of the transcendental. But that is not what we *feel* – and it is in our feeling for beauty that the content, and even the truth, of religious doctrine is strangely and untranslatably intimated to us.

In Kant's third Critique we see, in remarkably explicit form, the historical meaning of that shift in emphasis which was to place ethics and aesthetics at the centre of philosophy. The *Critique of Judgment* situates the aesthetic experience and the religious experience side by side, and tells us that it is the first, and not the second, which is the archetype of revelation. It is aesthetic experience which reveals the *sense* of the world. Of course, the 'sense' turns out to be, for Kant, precisely what religion had assumed it to be. But suppose we do not accept that conclusion? Suppose we look for the meaning of the world in aesthetic experience, while reserving judgment in matters of faith? This would be to give to aesthetic interest an importance comparable to that which once had attached to religious worship. It would hardly be surprising, in that case, if aesthetics were to move from the periphery of philosophy to the centre, so as to occupy the place which, in the centuries before Bacon and Descartes, had been occupied by theology.

In the nineteenth century we do indeed find philosophers for whom aesthetics provides a central subject-matter and a central task. I think of Schiller and Hegel, of Kierkegaard, and above all of Nietzsche, whose flight towards the aesthetic followed an act of deicide unparalleled in the history of thought. And if proof is needed of the ease with which the aesthetic may replace the religious as an object of philosophical interest, it is to be found in the thought and the personality of Nietzsche. Nietzsche's philosophy arose out of art and the thought of art: it involved an effort to perceive the world through aesthetic value, to find a way of life that would raise nobility, glory and tragic beauty to the place that had been occupied by moral goodness and by faith. And of course, Nietzsche is one of the great stylists, rivalled among those philosophers who came after him only by Wittgenstein.

No such philosopher could exist in the Anglophone tradition, for the simple reason that, if he did exist, he would not be called a philosopher, either by others or by himself. He would be identified as a critic or a social theorist, as an essayist or a reformer. Nevertheless, the transformation heralded in Kant's *Critique of Judgment* also took place in Britain. The search for the meaning of the world shifted from speculative theology to aesthetics, just as it had done in Germany. It is thanks to Coleridge, Arnold and Ruskin that students at a British university are now in a position to learn that there are more serious problems on earth than are dreamed of in analytical philosophy.

Nor did literary criticism lose, in our century, its place in the vanguard of the English-speaker's quest for meaning. The debates that were begun in the last century by Arnold and Newman were carried over into our times by Eliot, Chesterton, C. S. Lewis and finally – last representative of a 'great tradition' – F. R. Leavis. And it was perhaps only in the famous 'Two Cultures' debate, in which Leavis made mincemeat of C. P. Snow's suggestion that there could be a 'culture' of science, that the question which had bothered Central European writers for upwards of half a century was at last articulated in Britain.[3] The question is a philosophical one, and of the first importance. Nevertheless, it is a singular fact that it was left to a literary critic to articulate it, and a singular fact, too, that no major analytical philosopher has subsequently shown the slightest interest in what he said. It is hardly surprising, in view of this, that Leavis dismissed philosophy in general (and Cambridge philosophy in particular) as a subject which had lost contact with the human world.

I shall express Leavis's position in his controversy with Snow in my own terms. To possess a culture is not only to possess a body of knowledge or expertise; it is not simply to have accumulated facts, references and theories. It is to possess a sensibility, a response, a way of seeing things, which is in some special way redemptive. Culture is not a matter of academic knowledge but of participation. And participation changes not merely your thoughts and beliefs but your perceptions and emotions. The question therefore unavoidably arises whether scientific knowledge, and the habits of curiosity and experiment which engender it, are really the friends or the foes of culture? Could it be that the habit of scientific explanation may take over from the habit of emotional response, or in some way undermine the picture of the world upon which our moral life is founded? Could it be that scientific knowledge leads precisely in the opposite direction from a culture – not to the education of feeling, but to its destruction, not to the acceptance and affirmation of the human world, but to a kind of sickness and alienation from it, an overbearing sense of its contingency?

The question returns me to my theme. For Leavis the task of culture was a sacred task. Culture had in some way both to express and to justify our participation in the human world. And the greatest products of a culture – those works of art that Arnold had called 'touchstones' – were to be studied as the supreme distillations of this justifying force. In them we find neither theoretical knowledge, nor practical advice, but life – life restored to its meaning, vindicated and made whole. Through our encounter with these works our moral sense is liberated, and the fine division between good and evil, positive and negative, affirmative and destructive, made once more apparent, written everywhere across the surface of the world.

To take such a view is to raise the aesthetic to the pinnacle of authority upon which Kant and Schiller had placed it. And, given his sceptical premises – his Lawrentian belief that value is not transcendent but immanent, contained in life itself – Leavis can hardly stop short of the conclusion that, whatever consolation and significance men have sought in worship, they may find it more securely in the modern world through culture. The touchstones of our culture convey to us the meanings which others have found in liturgy, ritual and prayer. It is unsurprising to find Leavis pointing to Bunyan and Blake as his authorities, or to find him extolling, as landmarks of our literary tradition, the Bible of King James, and the now vandalized liturgy of the Church of England. For it is precisely in sacred works and liturgies that the emotional memory of a civilization is recorded, and it is in the works of prophets that a language strives to its utmost towards the perception of a justifying sense.

Leavis's attack on the idea of a scientific culture has all the character of a holy war – it is a defence of the faith against the infidel, of the Israelites against the Philistines. It is interesting that the word 'philistine', used so as to denote the enemy of civilization, entered the English language from Germany, through the writings of Carlyle. The expression was coined by the German students of Schiller's day, and immortalized on their behalf by Robert Schumann. In borrowing it, Carlyle, Arnold, Ruskin and their followers entered the battle on Schiller's side. The confrontation between science and culture that we find in Leavis is foreshadowed in the conflicts between Coleridge and Bentham, between Arnold and the Philistines, between Ruskin and the immovable apparatus of Podsnappery by which he saw himself surrounded. All of them are heirs to that conception of the aesthetic which we find in Kant and Schiller, according to which aesthetic experience stands in the place of worship, our key to the moral health of humanity and to the meaning of the world.

In my view, the question discussed by Leavis and his forebears is not only philosophical; it is one of the most *important* of all philosophical questions. Nor has it been entirely ignored by philosophers. For one in particular – Edmund Husserl – it was central to what he called, in the apocalyptic idiom of Central Europe, 'The Crisis of the European Sciences'. To put in a nutshell a thought which may or may not be contained in the tens of thousands of Husserlian pages, it is this: science has offered us a paradigm of objective knowledge. According to this paradigm, all reference to the subject of experience is to be eliminated from the description of the world. In seeking to emulate science, the various studies, even those which have man as their primary subject-matter, have tried to abstract from what is given in human experience, to purge the human subject, so to speak, from the archive of knowledge, and to achieve a kind of Stalinist history of the world, in which all persons are unpersons. The attempt, however, is fraught with paradox. For the human subject is the starting point of enquiry, and to refine him out of our science is to lose sight of the very thing that science endeavours to explain.[4]

I agree with one part of Husserl's claim. It seems to me that there are forms of understanding (*Wissenschaften*) which do not possess the objectivity of natural science, being derived from man's self-conception, rather than from the impersonal observation of natural processes. Nevertheless, they possess another kind of objectivity, a convergence upon a common fund of superficial truth, which entitles them to their own claims to knowledge. If philosophy has a central task, it is to protect these forms of knowledge, to anchor them once again in human consciousness, and to strike down the pretensions of science to give us the whole truth of what we are.

I draw a contrast between two modes of understanding: scientific understanding, which aims to explain the world as it is: and 'intentional understanding', which aims to describe, criticize and justify the world as it appears. The second is an attempt to understand the world in terms of the concepts through which we experience and act on it: these concepts identify the 'intentional objects' of our states of mind. An intentional understanding therefore fills the world with the meanings implicit in our aims and emotions. It tries not so much to explain the world as to be 'at home' in it, recognizing the occasions for action, the objects of sympathy, and the places of rest. The object of such an understanding is not the scientific universe described by scientific theory, but the *Lebenswelt*, the world as it is revealed, in and through the life-process which attaches us to it.

This distinction explains what I have called the 'priority of appearance'. Scientific penetration into the depth of things may render the surface unintelligible – or at least intelligible only slowly and painfully, and with a hesitancy that undermines the immediate needs of human action. (Such is the case, I argue, with the critical phenomenon of sexual desire.[5]) As agents we belong to the surface of the world, and enter into immediate relation with it. The concepts through which we represent it form a vital link with reality, and without this link appropriate action and appropriate response could not emerge with the rapidity and competence that alone can ensure our happiness and survival. We cannot replace our most basic everyday concepts with anything more useful than themselves – even if we find concepts with greater explanatory power. Our everyday concepts have evolved under the pressure of human circumstance, and in answer to the needs of generations. Any 'rational reconstruction' – however obedient it may be to the underlying truth of things and to the requirements of scientific objectivity – runs the risk of severing the vital connection which links our response to the world, and the world to our response, in a chain of spontaneous human competence.

The concepts which inform our emotions bear the stamp of a shared human interest, and of a constantly developing form of life. Whence do they come? The answer is implicit in Leavis's attack on Snow: these concepts are the gift of culture, being neither consciously made nor deliberately chosen but evolved over generations. It is by the use of such concepts that the moral reality of our world is described: concepts of good and evil, sacred and profane, tragic and comic, just and unjust – all of them rooted in that one vital idea which, I would contend, denotes no natural kind, and conveys a classification that could feature in no true scientific theory of man: the concept of the person. The concepts of a culture classify the world in terms of the appropriate action and the appropriate response. A rational being has need of such concepts, which bring his emotions together in the object, so enabling him – as the Hegelians would say – to find his identity *in* the world and not in opposition to it. A culture, moreover, is essentially shared; its concepts and images bear the mark of participation, and are intrinsically consoling, in the manner of a religious communion, or an act of worship. They close again the gap between subject and object which yawns so frighteningly in the world of science.

Estrangement from the world is the poisoned gift of science. For Coleridge and his followers the same estrangement attaches to utilitarianism – that morality of the Philistine which was launched into the world by the smiling idiot Jeremy Bentham, and which has marched onwards ever since. The hostility to 'Benthamism' was inherited by Leavis, and became fundamental to his moral vision. And one can see why. Utilitarianism represents the attempt by science to take charge of our moral lives: the attempt by the objective perspective to displace the subject from his throne. The utilitarian sees the world not as it appears to the agent, but as it is in the eyes of the omniscient observer. The utilitarian moralist rises above the individual's predicament, and sees the meaning of his actions in their long-term success or disaster, freely availing himself of concepts which form no part of the individual's reasoning.

Suppose a tribesman is dancing in honour of the god of war. To the observing anthropologist, steeped in functionalist and utilitarian thinking, the dance is a means to raise the spirits, and to increase the cohesion of the tribe, at a time of danger. This description both explains and justifies. Nevertheless, it does not tell us what the dance means to the dancer. If the tribesman thinks of his dance in that way, then he is alienated from it: he loses his motive to dance, once he borrows the language of the anthropologist. His first-person reason for dancing (because the god demands it) is precisely opaque to the third-person perspective: by shutting the dancer within his dance, it abolishes the distance between agent and action. Of course, in this case, the first-person reason is founded in error: there *is* no god of war. But a culture need not be rooted in error: it may remain 'on the surface', in the way necessary to engage with our acts and emotions, and at the same time free itself from superstition. It then ceases to be a culture only, and becomes a *civilization*, sending its branches into theology, philosophy, art and law.

Even when it has launched itself, however, on the path of critical thinking, a culture cannot forswear 'the priority of appearance'. If it is to offer us the precious gift of participation it must resist the pursuit of an unobtainable objectivity. Utilitarianism fails as a moral theory because, aspiring to objectivity, it begins to justify actions in terms which remove the motive to engage in them. Utilitarianism purges our actions of their sense, by displacing the concepts under which we intend them. (Consider, for example, how the utilitarian justification of punishment erodes the will to punish, by abolishing the concept of retribution through which punishment obtains its 'sense'.)

In our post-Enlightenment world, it is natural that we should look elsewhere than towards religion for the 'sense' of our actions. And Kant was in a way right to single out the aesthetic as, so to speak, next in line to the Eucharist, as the source of meaning. The object of aesthetic understanding is given to us in and through experience, and has no life outside the 'intuition' in which it is embodied. In aesthetic judgment, therefore, we aim to achieve the finest possible understanding of *how things seem*. All art is semblance, and (Plato notwithstanding) this is the source of its value. Art brings us to the very same point that we are brought to by religion – to an experience saturated by meaning, whose value overwhelms us with the force of law. In aesthetic experience we perceive the fittingness of the world, and of our place within it. For a moment we set aside the relentless curiosity of science, and the habit of instrumental thinking. We see the world as it really seems: in Wallace Stevens's words, we 'let be be finale of seem' (although there are other emperors besides the emperor of icecream). In the aesthetic moment we encounter a unity of form and content, of experience and thought. This fact, which places the meaning of aesthetic experience outside the reach of science, explains its peculiar value. In the moment of beauty we encounter directly the sense of the world; and in tragedy the most terrible things may cease to be strange to us, and cease to be so metaphysically threatening. Even the nothingness of death may be overcome. In tragedy, death is not a nothing, but a something, a part of that very order which it seems to deny. Death exists in tragedy as a pattern in the world of appearance, and is lifted free from its absurdity. (In tragedy, a man's death becomes part of his life, as the edge is part of a painting.)

When meaning and experience are welded so firmly together, the first is secured against scepticism. The habit of uniting them in contemplation is the aim and reward of aesthetic education – of that induction into a culture which Leavis recommends. The aesthetic understanding locks our modern dancer within his dance, just as an unquestioned culture locked our warrior tribesman within his:

> O Chestnut-tree, great-rooted blossomer,
> Are you the leaf, the blossom, or the bole?
> O body swayed to music, o brightening glance,
> How can we know the dancer from the dance?

Aesthetic experience, which stands outside instrumental calculations and outside science, is therefore of the greatest practical import to beings like us, who move on the surface of things. To engage now with those distant parts of my life which are not of immediate concern, to absorb into the present choice the full reality of a life which stretches into distant moral space, I must lift that experience out of the immediate preoccupation and endow it with a meaning, in which my humanity is embodied and accepted. Hence I have a need, as a rational creature, for aesthetic experience, and for the habits and customs which engender it. No utilitarian calculation can substitute for this experience, which consists in a projection forwards of the acting self. The ability to participate imaginatively in future experiences is one of the aims of aesthetic education: without that ability, a man may have as coherent a purpose as he likes; but he will not know what it is like to achieve it, and his pursuit of it will to that measure be irrational. Failure to appreciate this point, I have argued, underlies the disaster of utilitarian and modernist architecture – an architecture which denies the priority of appearance, and denies the tradition which has formed and educated the human eye.[6]

Philosophy, to the extent that it takes the study of the *Lebenswelt* as its primary concern, must return aesthetics to the place that Kant and Hegel made for it: a place at the centre of the subject, the paradigm of philosophy, and the true test of all its claims. Philosophy, I have suggested, ought not to be the hand-maiden of the sciences; it should be, rather, the seamstress of the *Lebenswelt*. Philosophy must repair the rents made by science in the veil of Maya, through which the wind of nihilism now blows coldly over us. And, even with the needle and thread of concep-tual analysis, this labour of piety can begin.

And there is, as I remarked at the outset, a great need for it. Unless philosophy resumes its place as the foundation of the humanities, those disciplines which have the human world as their subject-matter will be exposed to intellectual corruption. Tempted now by the *fata Morgana* of deconstruction, now by sociological pseudo-science, they will wander from their pur-pose, in a desert of unmeaning, and dwindle into parched unwholesome remnants of themselves. The defence of humane education therefore requires the defence of philosophy. But philosophy can be defended only if it has aesthetics at its heart.

From: *The Times Literary Supplement*, 5 June 1987.

9

AESTHETIC
EXPERIENCE
AND CULTURE

Aesthetics has two fields of study – art and aesthetic interest – and the question which comes first, in the hierarchy of philosophical argument, should be given more attention than is commonly accorded to it. My own belief is that a philosophical understanding of art must wait upon a theory of our interest in it. If such theories tend to be arid and unappealing, it is not because they have been detached from the study of art, but because they make no reference to the wider phenomenon of which art is an instance: the phenomenon of culture. Like art, aesthetic interest and experience are cultural phenomena. They share in the health and sickness of a culture, and partake of its history, its morality, its fund of belief, and the sense of community from which those things derive. If we wish to understand the role of innovation and tradition in art, I believe, we must first understand their role in culture.

Kant's 'antinomy of taste' has received no canonical statement, either from its author, or from the many who have fallen under his influence. Nevertheless, the opinion is widespread that Kant was right in divining a tension, if not a contradiction, within aesthetic interest. Aesthetic pleasure is immediate. Its meaning is contained indissolubly within it, and cannot be detached from the experience which presents it to us. At the same time we feel a need to justify our aesthetic pleasures, to subject them to criticism and analysis, and to give arguments for the *value*, and not just explanations of the pleasingness, of the objects from which they arise. But how is this possible? If it is the experience that matters, and if its meaning lives undetachably within it, how can we say why it matters? How can we make aesthetic meaning into an object of rational judgment?

To express the paradox, we must give a clear exposition of its two components. And this has never, to my knowledge, been done.[1] We can give examples of aesthetic meaning – the aspect in a painting, the expression in a melody, the emotion in a line of verse – but what is the theory which explains and unites them? How is it, exactly, that meaning and experience *belong together* in aesthetic interest, and in what way is the first undetachable from the second? The answer given is usually vaguer than the question – 'freedom from concepts', 'the inseparability of form and content', 'the heresy of paraphrase', 'concept *versus* intuition', 'telling *versus* showing' – and tends to carry such a weight of contentious philosophizing as to be ill-fitted for survival in a competitive world, falling rapidly prey to the beasts of linguistic analysis.

Similarly with the second component of the paradox. Kant spoke of the 'universality' of aesthetic judgment, of the 'demand for universal agreement', and so on. But those phrases are vague, and also misleading in their suggestion of a *legislative* frame of mind, of the kind so brilliantly explained and defended in the Kantian ethics. Certainly, we are disposed to judge in terms of right and wrong; we see the aesthetic not just as a realm of pleasure, but also as a realm of value; it matters to us that others should agree with our judgments, and with the reasons that we give for them.

On the other hand, many people, not seeing how there can be justification which has neither the truth of a belief nor the rightness of an action as its object, have become so sceptical of the critical enterprise as to renounce altogether the right to aesthetic judgment. For such people, the core of aesthetic experience lies in the first component – the experience of meaning – and the second is cast to one side. Such scepticism notwithstanding, the practice of criticism still needs an explanation. Faced with what has been said in recent years about modern architecture, are we really to believe that aesthetic experience can be detached from judgment and still be what it is? Moreover, a person who claimed to enjoy works of art, and to be seriously interested in their meaning, and yet who assured us that he made no judgment of their value, would puzzle us. And the greater the work, the deeper the puzzle. Is he merely refusing to *utter* his judgment? Is he deceiving himself? Is his interest truly aesthetic, truly that interest which motivates the creation of art and unites us in enjoying it? If he makes no judgment, then this implies that his experience does not matter to him, as ours does to us – it has a different place in his life. But then it must be a different experience. (If what John calls 'love' does not matter to him as love matters to the rest of us, then what he feels is not what *we* mean by 'love': its mattering is part of what love, in our sense, *is*.) This returns us to Kant's original idea: the aesthetic experience steps into our lives at precisely the place where evaluation is demanded; to reject the ideas of right and wrong is to remain insensible to beauty.

Some light is cast on the Kantian paradox by returning aesthetic experience to its context, and studying the general phenomenon of which it is an instance. There are other states of mind besides the aesthetic, in which meaning and experience are intimately conjoined, and where questions of right and wrong seem forced upon us. In particular, there are acts of worship, religious rites and ceremonies, and all the varied 'graces' and 'epiphanies' which fill the literature of religious ecstasy. These experiences may involve an aesthetic component. But they are not purely aesthetic, for a reason familiar to Kantian philosophy – namely, that they have an ultimate purpose, which is to involve, to save, and to convey the sacred truth of things. We do not participate in religious rites merely so as to contemplate their meaning, and to enjoy them as we would a symphony. We participate for the sake of our salvation and with a view to the truth.

Nevertheless, there are interesting similarities with the aesthetic experience. Although the purpose of an act of worship lies beyond the moment – in the form of a promised salvation, a revelation, or a restoration of the soul – it is not entirely separable from the act whereby we approach it. God is *defined* in the act of worship, far more precisely than he is defined by any theology, and this is why the forms and details of the ceremony are so overwhelmingly important. The meaning of the rite refers to the transcendental; but it inhabits the empirical moment with all the tenacity that we recognize in art. Changes in the liturgy take on a momentous significance for the believer, for they are changes in his experience of God – changes, if you wish to be Feuerbachian, in God himself. The question whether to make the sign of the cross with two fingers or with three can split a church, as it split the Orthodox Church of Russia. So can the question whether to use or not to use the Book of Common Prayer or the Tridentine Mass. Enlightened people often mock at these controversies, and profess not to understand why we should retain, say, the Tridentine Mass, save 'for aesthetic reasons'. Such people see the resemblance to aesthetic interest in the act of worship, but they do not see the difference – namely, that what is at stake is salvation. In participating, through word, thought and gesture, the believer is effecting a change in his spiritual standing. The ceremony is not so much a means to this end, as a prefiguration of it. In the Mass the believer comes face to face with God; and the urgency of the ceremony lies there.

In societies of the kind that are sometimes called 'traditional', such episodes form a large part of the experience of membership. Indeed, if we reflect on the role of initiations, marriages, baptisms, funerals and 'rites of passage', we might think that these experiences, properly received, are what membership *consists* in. But of course they must *be* properly received. The visiting anthropologist, standing behind the screen of his scientific interest, is excluded from the sense of membership. He does not *have* the experience, precisely because, unlike the people whom he studies, the meaning which he seeks (the meaning of a scientific truth) lies beyond the data which point to it, and can be understood apart from them.

Consider also the aesthetically-minded tourist, who stands in the wings of the ceremony in a state of contemplative pleasure. He too is no participant: he too is excluded by his attitude from a sense of membership. But his case is importantly different from the anthropologist's. To understand the ceremony aesthetically you must be aware of its meaning: the ceremony *embodies* a meaning, which is inextricable from its beauty. No doubt you could have a partial aesthetic understanding, which focused on the outline alone. You could see the rite as a dramatic ballet, just as someone might appreciate a painting as a harmony of colours, without seeing that it contains a face. In both cases, however, there is more to be seen; and until you see the more, your understanding is deficient. In aesthetic understanding you see the religious meaning embodied *in* the ceremony: you have the same sense of unity that is offered to the worshipper, but without the cost or the benefit of worship. Just as you could not understand *Parsifal* if you did not hear, in the music of the Eucharist, the upward reaching of man's soul to God, and the downward tending of God's grace and majesty, so you could not understand the Mass, if you did not respond to precisely *this* in it – even if you do not respond to it with the eye and ear of belief, which are reserved for the worshipper alone.

The example points to an interesting observation. Assuming that the tourist *understands* the beauty of the Mass, then its content is, for him, precisely what it is for the worshipper, even though his attitude and experience are different. In neither case is this content detachable from the ceremony that embodies it: the ceremony *shows* God's presence, and even for the worshipper no other 'mode of presentation' will 'do just as well'. The

Mass is not, for the worshipper, a means of access to some independent truth: it is the very substance of the truth it offers.

How then does the experience of the worshipper *differ* from that of the aesthetic tourist? The answer lies in the theory of imagination. The worshipper *believes* himself to be in God's presence; the tourist merely imagines this, in one of the many modes under which imagination operates. (He might imagine that *he* is in God's presence; or imagine the worshipper he observes being in God's presence; or imagine himself *being* the worshipper he observes and also being in God's presence, etc.[2]) In all cases the content of imagination and the content of the corresponding belief are (and, as I argue elsewhere, must be[3]) precisely the same. Likewise the content of the believing experience is indistinguishable from the content of the corresponding experience in imagination.

The practical consequences of believing are different from those of imagining (you don't flee from imagined disasters as you do from those believed, or else who would go to see a tragedy?) The one experience is charged with purpose, while the other is a matter of contemplative pleasure and 'the free play of responsible thought', as I am inclined to put it. But there are further points of similarity, and it is these which principally concern me. To identify those points I shall take a clearer and simpler example than the Roman Catholic Mass.

Consider, then, a ceremony of initiation, as practised in some isolated tribe. At a certain stage of life, the boy stands ready to become a man. To do this he must undergo initiation. Thereafter, and for the first time, he obtains the full privileges of membership, and becomes a man, who erstwhile was a boy. But what exactly does being a man consist in? It is not a biological but a spiritual transition that is effected. The initiate experiences his new condition, and knows what it is, in and through the act of initiation. From *his* point of view – rather than the point of view of the observing anthropologist – the meaning of manhood is first revealed there.

But the meaning survives the experience. Having entered manhood, a new form of life is available to the initiate: he sees things in a new way, by relating to them as an adult – his experience is no longer *preparatory*. His initiation confers a changed sense of belonging and a changed intentionality. Circumstances provide occasions for action which previously wore only a neutral aspect; others speak of duties and freedoms which were before only guessed at; while others still, which were once saturated with the call to obedience, are now subdued to his will, and shorn of their old authority.

There are other ceremonies which await him. He attends each year the initiation of those who grow behind him, and re-enacts as a man what he first underwent as a boy. The ceremonies are an important source of renewal, and year after year, although he knows them inside out and can speak their every word, he returns to them with gratitude. The meaning that he first obtained from them has not been wholly separated from the experience. He comes back to it, as a person returns to his favourite works of art, for something important which he can describe only in halting and imperfect terms, and which he can identify best by a gesture – which points to the ceremony itself.

I have briefly described a small fragment of 'common culture', as I call it.[4] As we know from the work of the great anthropologists (who arrived on the scene of history just in time to capture the last examples of a disappearing innocence), the pattern I have described was once universal, and survives in secret in many of our 'sophisticated' ways. It suggests the following evident, but by no means trivial observations:

1) A common culture is a form of participation. We can study it, learn about it, and contemplate it aesthetically – but all those attitudes fall short of *having* it. One *belongs to* a culture, and no amount of study can suffice to take us from outside to inside the privileged relation.

2) To enter a culture it is therefore not sufficient to be instructed in it. Something like *initiation* is required, even if instruction is a necessary preparation. (This does not mean that initiation must occur all at once and ceremonially, as in my example; it may be a slow process, beginning at birth, and marked by no line of transition into the state of adult membership.)

3) Through a common culture, a person is joined to something greater than himself, and the world as he perceives it (his *Lebenswelt*) is transformed accordingly. Each culture defines a distinct intentionality – a 'way things seem' – which is offered to the participant, but not to those who stand outside.

4) Membership gives meaning to the world, by offering occasions for action, a right and wrong procedure, and those ready concepts which close the gap between thought and action – concepts of virtue and vice, of sacred and sacrilege, of seemly and unseemly. A common culture impresses the matter of experience with a moral form.

There is only limited scope, in a true common culture, for change and innovation. Indeed, innovation is never a value in itself, but at best a necessary accommodation to changes arising from outside. Too much innovation – especially in those customs and ceremonies which provide the core experience of membership – is inherently threatening to the culture. Tradition, on the other hand, is of the essence. One way – maybe the principal way – in which this kind of membership is understood, is as a form of union with the unborn and the dead. Through membership I see the world as it was seen by those who went before me, and as it will be seen by those who are yet to be. Hence I rise to an exalted perspective, a perspective above my own perishable being. Through the ceremonies of membership, 'my eyes are opened', and I see the world no longer as an object of my own paltry needs and appetites, but as it really and eternally is. Through the ceremony of membership, therefore, God enters the world, and makes himself known.

The attitude of a common culture to innovation is necessarily one of suspicion and hostility. Much more is at stake than the scoffing rationalist can conceivably imagine (if he *could* imagine it, he would cease to scoff). Innovation can take place, if at all, only in the spirit advocated by Burke: the spirit of a reform which aims to conserve. Innovation must therefore be construed as a renewal of something more fundamental than the detail changed: a casting away of accidents and perversions. The innovation must *prove* itself, by showing that it already *belongs* to the tradition which it seems to challenge. It must adapt itself to the tradition, and in doing so it will adapt the tradition to itself.

Earlier I compared the aesthetic experience of a religious ceremony with the act of worship itself, and argued that the *content* may be, and ideally ought to be, the same. However, where in the one case stands belief, filling the soul of the participant, in the other case there stands imagination, urging the spectator to step momentarily into a frame of mind that he may not endorse. Where in the one case there is a lifetime's commitment, closing the gap between thought and desire, in the other case there is a moment of meaning, which lingers afterwards only in attenuated form. Nevertheless, the aesthetic experience tells us what the act of communion is like. Not only does it preserve the content of the ceremony: it also shares its form. Both are examples of the interpenetration of experience and content; and both are the vehicles of a 'repeatable' meaning, one to which we return again and again in search of refreshment. The ceremonies of membership, the Mass, the Friday prayers, the service of the Synagogue – all have the inexhaustible character of art. A man who repeated Newton's laws to himself, again and again, would strike us as strange: for it is enough simply to know them. But the man who repeats the Hail Mary five hundred times, or who recites the Sura of the Cow from morn to night, is far from strange. That is what religion is. In just the same way, to be musical it is not enough to know the classics: you must come back to them, again and again – sometimes you may wish to play through the same sonata ten times in succession even though you know it by heart.

Armed with those comparisons, let us now return to the problems of aesthetics. Aesthetic experience is the core of 'high' culture. It is extremely hard to describe the relation between a high culture and the common culture from which it grows.[5] High culture involves new levels of understanding, not all of which are available to every member of society. It has its roots in religious experience, and it may sometimes have (as in my example) religious experience as its object. But it also has a life of its own, and can grow away from its origins, as the art of our civilization has grown away from the Christian Church which first inspired it. At the same time, when a high culture detaches itself in this way, it preserves the memory of a religious sentiment: a core experience of membership in which God was once revealed. High culture is a meditation on its own 'angel infancy', and that is why, I shall suggest, we value it so highly.

Like common culture, therefore, high culture exhibits the topology of membership:

1) It is a form of participation. You can study it, learn about it, 'deconstruct' it. But no amount of scientific or pseudo-scientific knowledge will ever suffice to join you to it. To belong is to gain access to the *experiences* that it contains, and to receive those experiences properly is to understand them as acts of communication which enfold the unborn and the dead.

2) Entering a high culture therefore requires some process of *induction*. Of course, there is no rite of passage, no foreseeable transition. For each person the crucial awakening comes in his own time and in response to his own particular object. The experience nevertheless has something in common with initiation. It is a kind of grace, and once it has come, there is neither going back nor the desire for it.

That is why criticism is distinct from structural (or post-structural) analysis. Criticism aims to awaken, to open another to an experience and the meaning contained in it. Humane education has criticism as its primary purpose, and the question whether criticism is possible, when a common culture is lost, is the real question underlying the current 'crisis in the humanities'.

3) High culture acts on both the individual and his *Lebenswelt*. I shall illustrate this point through an example. Shakespeare's plays present an imaginative picture of man and his fulfilment, of moral motives and their consequences, of situations and meanings defined by a real common culture. By means of them

we confront the noble, the innocent, the majestic, the pious and the just; and also the vicious, the unseemly, the hellish, the sentimental and the base. Although these experiences are offered in imagination, the concepts contained in them are precisely those once received in belief. Such art captures the meanings of a common culture, and preserves them for an unbelieving age. Someone who knows and understands *Othello*, therefore, no longer sees evil as easy-going people see it.

4) Participation in a high culture therefore brings meaning to experience. It is a meaning imagined, rather than a meaning believed. But it may edge us towards belief, and sometimes stops – as in Eliot's *Four Quartets* – only on the threshold of commitment.

The world of imagination is one of freedom and experiment. A high culture may therefore rejoice, as ours has done, in innovation, and constantly amend itself as expectations change. This might lead us to think that high culture is in one respect the opposite of common culture: that innovation is here always acceptable, and that no limits can be set to its success. It is remarkable to observe, however, that only second-rate artists and critics have ever thought in that way. True artistic innovators justify themselves in the terms used by religious reformers. They describe themselves as 'renewing' the tradition which they seem to violate, and as integrating their work into pre-existing patterns. This is especially true of the great modernists: of Eliot and Pound in literature, of Schoenberg and Stravinsky in music; and even of many of the founding fathers of modern painting – witness Renoir, Degas, Kandinsky and Matisse.[6]

I shall venture a brief explanation of this curious phenomenon. Every high culture is rooted in a common culture, and in a core experience of community. It returns to this core experience with undiminished longing, as we also do by means of it. Innovation begins in earnest when the core experience is vanishing: and the goal of innovation is precisely to testify to what is lost, in the new circumstances of forgetting. For only by maintaining the chain of memory can art engage our aesthetic interest.

The original experience of community provides the 'sense' of a high culture. When the experience dwindles, high culture replaces it, and stands sentinel at the common grave. Such is the great modernist art – the art of Joyce, Eliot, Mann and Rilke. There is also the little modernist art, the art of lamentation which, finding the world bereft of membership, dwells on the experience of loss, and invokes the idea of meaning only to laugh at its insubstantiality. Such is the art of Beckett, Camus, and

Walser. Both kinds of art are important. One, however, continues to unite us in imagination to the unborn and the dead; the other merely reminds us that we are sundered from them irremediably, and have lost the exalted perspective which is theirs. This second kind of art should never be taken as seriously as it takes itself; for if the world is *really* meaningless, then so is the art that tells us so.

We must distinguish innovation from strangeness. A work from another tradition – a Noh play, for instance – can engage our sympathies, despite its strangeness. For it enshrines an experience which we imaginatively share. If art is strange in the manner of a Noh play, this is because it is the sincere testimony to a real but distant culture. But there is art which is strange because it detaches itself entirely from every common culture. The core experience, the 'sense', is missing. Such art can have no lasting interest for us. Its meaning is neither 'ours' nor 'theirs'. An example may help: the manifestly *unstrange* church parable, *Curlew River*, by Britten. Here the forms of the Noh play are reinterpreted, integrated into the harmonic and liturgical tradition that is ours, and used to convey a religious meaning all the more moving for being both 'ours' and 'theirs'. There is here not only an imaginative reaffirmation of the core experience, but also an *extension* of it, an act of cultural generosity which is also an act of loyalty to the tradition within which Britten composed.

If it is not too presumptuous, I should here like to offer a picture of modern culture – one that it would take volumes to establish, and the establishing of which is worth no one's while, since by the time the work is completed, the capacity to understand it will have disappeared. Our high culture grew out of an experience of faith founded in a divine revelation. All the forms of Christian community have shared in that original experience, and nurtured cultures that perpetuate its memory. With the decline of faith, our historical forms of membership have lost their appeal, being everywhere replaced by arrangements in which contract and law substitute for the gift of a common identity. (I say 'everywhere', though of course, some of the heirs to our culture also live in totalitarian states, where neither contract nor law have much authority: for such people the imaginative preservation of the core experience is even more important than it is for us.)

It is part of the genius of Christianity to have made way for this transition.[7] Christianity *separated* its God from the original experience of membership, dividing the intimation of the sacred in two, and reserving for the transcendental the pious emotions which were not to be dissolved in the tribe. The Church, with its law and its corporate personality, comes between God and society, mediating the sacraments to man, and therefore opening his heart to the idea of a universal order. This universal order – the heavenly Jerusalem – is envisaged first through obedience, then through law, and finally through contract (by which time the Kingdom of God has become the Kingdom of Ends). This is why the Mass – the mediated sacrament, with its moment of 'transubstantiation' – is such a decisive experience, and why it provides us with so persuasive an example of embodied meaning.

The high culture of Europe acquired the universality of the Church which had engendered it. At the same time the core experience of membership survived, to be constantly represented in the Mass – the 'communion' with God which is also an enactment of community. It is in this experience that our common culture renewed itself, and the art of our culture bears witness to it, either by honouring or by defiling the thought of God's incarnation. The high culture of Europe has therefore begun to assume a vast importance. It is our last glimpse of the sacred, the last memorial to an experience without which our free and easy manners will bring us face to face with Nothing. It stands as a bulwark between us and the uninterpreted world. Should we ever cease to renew our experience of the sacred, the contractual order will certainly give way. But the result will not be some new and vital community, some new 'core experience'; it will be the regimented *disorder* of the totalitarian state.

I do not ask you to believe any of that, and Marxists of course will be appalled by it. But it enables me to return from this highly speculative survey of culture, to the Kantian paradox from which I began. The difficulty was to see how one and the same mental act could involve both an immediate pleasure in embodied meaning, and an affirmation of 'right' and 'wrong'. The matter becomes less puzzling if we return the aesthetic experience to its context. Aesthetic experience belongs to high culture: its 'sense' lies in a common culture upon which it is a sustained reflection. The content of such a high culture is valuable to men in every period: but it becomes irreplaceable once the core experience of membership is lost. We strive always to recuperate that experience, since it provides the *original* of meaning, the clue to the interpretation of our world. The experience of meaning is *to be defended*: it comes to us hedged round with interdictions, and with invocations of holy dread. It therefore exists only for those who recognize a right and wrong in having it: who distinguish the right gestures, and the appropriate details in the sacramental moment. 'Right' and 'wrong' denote the same considerations that motivate the conservation and reform of liturgies. What is at stake in the world of belief – the survival of a core experience of membership – is at stake also in the world of imagination. The critical faculty is therefore not an addition to the aesthetic experience: it is its priestly part. Criticism is the work of vigilance, whereby the tradition is safeguarded, and the interpretation of the world made available to those who are yet to be.

PART II
CRITICAL ASIDES

10

PLAYWRIGHTS IN PERFORMANCE: PINTER, STOPPARD AND BECKETT

I PINTER'S PROGRESS

Important playwrights do not just interpret the world; they also change it. Since their invention, the Shakespearean types have dominated both life and literature, and there is scarcely a suburban residence in modern England that could not be adapted to the dramatic requirements of a Falstaff, a Lear, or a Hamlet. Jonson, Sheridan, and Congreve added their quota of charlatans and fops, while Beaumarchais and Goldoni taught the lower orders to share the limelight with their masters. The theatrical moulding of human personality continued until the novel – that secret weapon of the bourgeoisie – captured the market in manners. Under the impact of Smollett and Dickens the theatre dwindled into melodrama. The swan-songs of Oscar Wilde and Noël Coward provided splendid caricatures, but it was soon perceived that they are of limited utility. Lady Bracknell may hack her way through social undergrowth; but what does she do at the breakfast table, and what does she do in bed? You can be Hamlet anywhere, and at any time, but Lady Bracknell only in company, and at most once a day. Roles which have such circumscribed application are of little service to the modern person, whose life is mainly conducted in private, and who seeks guidance in the most intimate predicaments.

Ibsen's characters announced this new state of being to the world. They came on to the stage clad in roles which hampered them and which they were visibly impatient to discard. They sought for a tone of voice adapted to the solitude to which fate had consigned them. Out of desire to be deeper than appearances, they harboured private, even anti-social, intentions. By a miracle, Ibsen transformed their lives into drama. He forced communication from creatures too stark and self-preoccupied to measure their words by any public standard of decorum. As a result, they were destroyed by the enormity of their own language, driven to tragic finality by the rash exaggeration of their speech. In Ibsen's drama it is the very failure of the characters to become characteristic that constitutes the success and meaning of the play. Hence there is no theatre less theatrical, no theatre less able to renew our wardrobe of worn-out social roles.

The twentieth-century has shown a remarkable reversion to type. Habituated to the monstrosities of Ibsen, critics did not at first understand the language of Samuel Beckett's tramps, or Pinter's proles. What is in fact pure, distilled, social utterance, was passed off as 'Theatre of the Absurd', whose merits were no different from those of Eugène Ionesco. It seemed impossible that people, real people, should speak like this, that they should walk about the stage without once mentioning some weight of moral isolation, some individual suffering or tragic destiny. Slowly, however, the public began to accept the new tones of voice.

Of course, it was a long chalk from Shakespeare. Nevertheless, here were styles, manners, qualities of experience, that could be taken from the sparse situations on the stage and applied repeatedly, from day to day. The idioms of Beckett and Pinter were as adaptable as Falstaff's bluster or Hamlet's grief. You could use them at parties, at meals, in the factory, on the bus. You could pick up girls with them, nor did they let you down in bed. To be a Beckett tramp or a Pinter prole gave you a handle on experience. It filled the voice with meaning, endowed hesitations with a kind of integrity, and lent authority equally to words and to silences. Although Beckett and Pinter have less in common than meets the eye, nevertheless they share a fundamental premiss: their characters are raw, vulnerable, dangerously exposed to one another. They speak words carefully, with painful consideration, as though every excess of communication puts their existence at risk. Words are swords to them, but also shields. The characters are ill at ease in company, but alert to language. Hence their utility for the modern theatre-goer, who lives, eats, drinks and breathes embarrassment, and who is never more embarrassed than by his recognition that he has no great message, and no private destiny, to convey.

*

Since his majestic attempt to 'eff the ineffable' in the trilogy of novels, Beckett's literary career has involved a paring away, a steady elimination of all embellishments to his central theme. Although Beckett defines social sentiments, in social language, he has, in the end, only one character, and that character is a living ('if you call that living') contradiction: the self who struggles vainly to be the object of its own regard, the ghost which flits before every aspiration. To present this theme, Beckett originally required hallucinatory details, aborted stories, quarrelsome observations, narrated by subjects who fade first into each other, and then into the page. Beckett's subsequent minimalism is a stylistic achievement, an emancipation from redundancies.

Pinter's career has been in a way comparable. The triptych of short tableaux, *Other Places*, when seen in relation to *The Birthday Party*, or *The Caretaker*, represents a considerable economy and condensation. But Pinter's minimalism, while influenced by Beckett, is quite unrelated to the style or meaning of Beckett's recent playlets and pamphlets. It proceeds, not from the attempt to whittle down a single experience to its metaphysical pith, but rather from a constant venturing into new realms of experience, so that hesitation and silence take on increasingly masterful forms. Beckett's tone of voice is tetchy, disappointed, a kind of *gran rifiuto*, in the face of the perpetual elusiveness both of the 'thou' and the 'I'. Pinter's voice has no such universal meaning. While it grows always from the impossible confrontation of human beings and their arbitrary desires, it varies minutely with the situation to which it is applied. Pinter's scenarios are carefully observed and ultra-realistic representations of English society. There has been a marked 'upward mobility' over time: but even the most recent pieces remain wedded to actual situations, studied by an author whose ear for ordinary speech is preternaturally fine.

Family Voices (the first of the three tableaux) tells of a house in which characters from all periods of Pinter's career are assembled: a sluttish, good-for-nothing Mrs Withers; an old proletarian Mr Withers; another Mr Withers whose insane theatricality allows Pinter to recapture the set-piece style of the early plays; even a Lady Withers, whose title, however, proves baffling to the adolescent narrator. In this play, as in *Landscape*, there is no dialogue, only interlocking speech, as one character's voice flows into the silence vacated by the other's. A mother and a son write to each other letters which are never sent, or which, if sent, never arrive at their destination. To their lonely, reaching voices, a third is added, that of the man, husband of the one, father of the other, who has died since contact was lost. The situation de-

prives Pinter of the device with which he established his tone of
voice, the familiar English repartee. The tense atmosphere of *The
Caretaker* depends upon the to-ing and fro-ing of question and
answer, from which the set speeches emerge as declarations of a
longing comic in its ordinariness, and pathetic in its inability to
elicit a response. *Family Voices* consists of questions which cannot be answered, and answers that wing off into the void in
hopeless search for questions that would explain them. Were the
mother and son actually to make contact, one feels, the intensity
of their communication would be unbearable. But their non-
communication is the source of a new comedy and pathos, as
each slowly adjusts to the absence of the other.

The connection which is feared and longed for in *Family Voices*
is granted in the sequel, *Victoria Station*. A cab-driver is con-
tacted by his controller, who speaks from an office upstage,
while the driver answers from the illuminated car below. Brilliant acting from Paul Rogers and Martin Jarvis turns this little
jeu d'esprit into high comedy, although again with a note of
pathos. The controller, who obtains only bizarre, vacant-seem-
ing responses, is at first exasperated, then angry, and then filled
with loathing for this 274 who lies like a barrier across the stream
of ordinary experience. But the loathing turns to need, and finally
to a kind of tenderness; the driver likewise develops a need for
the controller, imploring him not to seek the services of any rival.
'Don't have anything to do with *135*', he cries. 'He's not your
man. He'll lead you into blind alleys by the dozen. They all will.
Don't leave me. I'm your man. I'm the only one you can trust . . .'
And strangely, despite 274's inability to understand the simplest
order, his words ring true.

The two characters are in the original Pinter mould: ordinary
people suddenly thrown out of orbit by an arbitrary act of communication. But words, cast across the distance between the
office and the cab, acquire unpredictable meanings. The characters become increasingly vulnerable with every verbal impact.
By the time the scene fades it is clear that their lives have been
irreversibly transformed. The controller leaves his office in
search of the driver, like a man who turns his back on home and
family for the sake of some catastrophic love.

A Kind of Alaska the final tableau, continues the theme of
distance. However, the distance is not of space but of time.

A victim of sleeping sickness (such as described by Oliver
Sacks in *Awakenings*) is brought to life by an injection of *L-Dopa*,
after twenty-nine years of comatose inertia. The play describes
her bewildered reaction, a child's soul in a middle-aged body,
the fallen face of a ruined aunt, who listens to a voice, her own

voice, describing birthdays, boy-friends, and parties. Judi Dench's stunning performance conveys both the fear of the woman, and the forthright, virtuous cheekiness of the child, as they contend for possession of a body which has lain vacant for a generation. The woman, Deborah, is attended by a doctor, and by the doctor's wife, Deborah's younger sister. The effect of Deborah's illness is captured by the doctor's words: 'Your sister was twelve when you were left for dead. When she was twenty I married her. She is a widow. I have lived with you . . .' The words of the bystanders are succinct, hesitant, overcome, while the sufferer herself rushes into speech, stumbles, retreats, and then impetuously rushes again.

The scene is realistic, and uncompromisingly painful. It perfectly illustrates Pinter's boldness, and his appetite for new material, in which he shows a scrupulous attention to an actual, but uncanny, predicament. Beckett's Cartesian observer could never sustain such concentrated interest. The Beckettian subject lives only in the dark, the limedark of his ruminations. While filled with compassion, it is a compassion inspired by failure, itself born of metaphysical impossibility, to relate to the world or to himself. It is, in Malone's words, the

> foul feeling of pity that I have often felt in the presence of things, especially little portable things in wood or stone, and which made me wish to have them about me and keep them always, so that I stooped and picked them up and put them in my pocket, often with tears, for I wept up to a great age, never having really evolved in the fields of affection and passion in spite of everything.

This is nothing like the fellow-feeling which Pinter carries into all predicaments, and which underlies his repeated disclosure that communication, far from being impossible, is in fact too much with us, a constant threat to our half-established natures. Words assail us with the inescapable fact of other people, and we try in vain to escape their accusations. 'What do you mean by that?' asks Emma, in *Betrayal*. 'I don't *mean* anything by it', replies Jerry. 'But what are you trying to say by that?' she persists. 'Jesus. I'm not *trying* to say anything. I've said precisely what I wanted to say.' But the implication is firmly established that, merely by speaking, Jerry has said too much, or at least far more than he intended.

One feature of Deborah's situation might have appealed to Beckett: she is beyond the world, lodged in her body like a pilot in a sinking ship. Unlike Beckett, however, Pinter cannot accept the situation as anything other than abnormal. For him, as for Deborah herself, it is a terrible falling away from the life that is to be desired. Hence the situation becomes urgent; Deborah disconcerts us, like someone in an epileptic fit. The threat that lurks in language concentrates in her; we can pierce her in a thousand ways with knowledge; we can make her squirm. But because she is not in control of her experience, it is we who squirm, fearing our own aggression. Alone among Pinter's characters she is utterly alone. Her voice cries from an unreachable ultimacy of human experience, across an unbridgeable gulf of time. While we pity her, we do not know whether it is she, the child, or she, the woman, who evokes our sorrow.

The critics have been lavish in praise of *A Kind of Alaska*. But surely, whatever its merits, it cannot really be described as theatre. Deborah's unmanageable experience obliterates the drama. In the face of it, the subsidiary characters become gauche and frozen. None of the three can obtain a consistent tone of voice; in the nature of the case, every voice is suspect.

When Davies, the caretaker, describes his shoes, saying, 'You see, they're gone, they're no good, the good's gone out of them', the idiom leaps out at us, joining us to the cheerful spirit of survival. In *Victoria Station*, the controller veneers his sentiments with idiom, saving us again from sharing his perplexity. In *A Kind of Alaska*, however, everything is stark, raw, absolute. The spectator, sensing the impossibility of response, suffers a growing discomfort. The Pinter voice no longer operates. There is no consolation, no idiom, no normality. The spectator, outraged by sufferings which are without resolution, withdraws his futile sympathy.

Oliver Sacks was deeply disturbed by the effects of the drug *L-Dopa*. His description of the new miseries that were to confront his patients as they struggled, often in vain, to come to terms with the imperfect consciousness which their illness had left them, is heart-rending. It is hard to imagine a clearer refutation of the myth upon which Beckett has relied in all his writings – the myth of the transcendental spectator who lurks, untouched and untouchable, within the arbitrary folds of human flesh. Pinter has never given twopence for that myth. He rightly perceives that a nothing would do as well as this transcendental something about which nothing can be said. It is the writer's responsibility to study words; human beings exist, not behind, but within their utterance. Deborah is neither more nor less than the words which come from her. The theatre of embarrassment perpetually forces us to discard the illusion that there is an ego hiding behind our discourse. But this refutation of the ego creates a need for its opposite, for community, for idiom, for the consoling tone of voice which turns the individual into a type, and disaster into comedy.

Once, on the road to Notting Hill, Pinter came across a tramp, a familiar of those parts, who sometimes wheels his pram-load of rags and newspapers beneath my window, muttering through a beard clotted with drying slobber.

On this occasion the tramp had set up his newspapers in a pile before him. The bundle was detached, immobile, outside the sphere of his possessions. He berated it in an angry voice; under the impact of his insults, the bundle acquired an ego, or at least, as much of an ego as the rest of us. Crime upon crime was laid at its feet. As the frenzy of denunciation increased, the passers-by began to steer further and further away from him, until stepping precariously in line, along the edge of the curb. The tramp was bathed in sweat, his face red and swollen, as though from the discomfort that he caused.

Pinter had joined the line, and then duly swerved away. But as he did so the ranting stopped, and the voice cried 'Hello, *Harold Pinter!'*

The playwright froze, the cursing was resumed at once, more loudly than before, and the eyes of the blushing tramp remained fixed on the pile of offending newspapers. Pinter hurried on, away from the street theatre in which he had been typecast.

The tramp had recognized his author, but then turned from him towards the comfort of abusive words, refusing further contact. It was as though a choice had been made: Beckett or Pinter. The first gives you peace of a kind, but also immobility and isolation. The second gives you audience, meaning, social identity, but also a terrible consciousness of others. The tramp had chosen Pinter as his author, and then, in the very choice, regretted it, throwing himself with a renewed fervour into curses and insults. Deborah had made the same mistake, for she too could not survive the perception that she does not belong. She too was made untouchable by her rash and sudden contact; and she too, having no idiom to save her, blushingly suffered in the centre of the stage.

II   THE REAL STOPPARD

One of the worst things that ever happened to civilization was the invention of art. It is not certain when the disaster occurred. Some date it as far back as the eighteenth century, when the infinitely tedious idea of the sublime stirred in the minds of ordinary decent folk the suspicion that they were missing something. Others argue that Schiller and Hegel were the culprits, the first for arguing that aesthetic education is a necessary preparation for civil life, the second for describing art as though it were almost as important as Hegel.

But these are speculations. What is certain is that, throughout the nineteenth century, German intellectuals snapped at us with the idea of art. Although we English put up a stout resistance, we Podsnapped back in vain. By the end of the nineteenth century Art definitely existed, as a single, all-engrossing, European ambition, an exclusive club to which everyone, from prince to peasant, from priest to politician, aspired. When King Ludwig II of Bavaria abased himself before Richard Wagner, he was giving public expression to the prevailing social order, by propitiating its sovereign deity. And when Hanslick, horrified by Wagner's influence, defended the ideal of the 'absolute art' of music, he was simply reiterating the mystic's outrage, upon seeing his god made finite and believable in the graven images of the multitude. But all art corrupts, and absolute art corrupts absolutely. Absolute art rotted the people's conscience. Within a few decades it had virtually abolished life. It became the received idea that art should have no subject besides itself; nothing else was pure or significant enough to merit its attention. Nothing else could bear the infinite burden of meaning which is the right and the duty of divinities. Like Aristotle's God, art must remain above and beyond the world, timelessly thinking itself.

For a while the fraud worked miracles. Art poured its scornful brightness on the world, creating shadows in all the places where civilization had placed its light. Under the glare of art, the ramshackle endeavours of ordinary humanity seemed obscure and unintelligible. Traditions and moralities, constitutions and laws – all were eclipsed by it. In the shadows, however, the *schwarz-Alberich* of revolution gradually came into being. Places of power fell one by one to its control, and when the people began to perceive at last the emptiness of Art's promise, it was too late to return to the life which they had abandoned. Modern people live as they can, and wander where they may, in a world where the two great illusions of Art and Revolution compete for every meaning. The gods are no longer trusted, but they have effectively cleared the world of rival myths. This is why true humanitarians are accused of being revolutionaries, and true conservatives of being aesthetes. Nobody can quite believe, any more, that there could be a principled pursuit of a civil order which defers to neither ruling illusion.

That self-referential art and self-indulgent revolution grow from the same soil is a proposition with which Tom Stoppard is familiar, and there are few modern playwrights who could bring a more formidable intelligence to bear on it. Stoppard's own plays – which are, almost all of them, plays within plays – grow from the demand that Art should be its own subject. At the same time politics provides their occasion, and no politics fascinates Stoppard more than that which has issued from the revolutionary consciousness.

In *Travesties* (1975), he exploited the accidental, or not-so-accidental, coincidence in Zurich of Tristan Tzara (the arch proponent of the Absolute in Art) and Lenin (the arch political absolutist). With them also is James Joyce, and much of the play – a clever collage made from Oscar Wilde's *Earnest*, the Ithaca chapter in *Ulysses*, Lenin's letters and speeches, and Tzara's boyish nonsense – is devoted to the contrast between Dada and *Ulysses*. There is no doubt whose side Stoppard is on. Joyce's novel, like Tzara's badinage, is supremely conscious of its artistry; but it also justifies every word by a vision of reality, whereas Dada is nothing more than self-advertisement. 'If there is any meaning in any of it, it is in what survives as art', says Joyce, who demolishes the talentless self-reference of Dada, but will not deny that it is art, and not life, which is the purveyor of value. But Joyce poses a question: does art have reality because life is its raw material, or does life gain reality from the meanings contained in art? What, in short, is the real thing? Lenin, who stands apart from the other characters, sifting his benighted pedantries, shows the relentlessness of the shadow world. Yet it is not a real world, Lenin's words are dead, unfeeling, a patter of urgencies which occasionally rattles across the stage. Revolution can be translated into slogans, but not into art. Hence, if all meanings must be borrowed from art, revolution remains unmeaning, a seething pool of darkness, always advancing, always betraying, but never real.

But when revolution has cleared the world of its old significance, something still remains. In the artless desert of the totalitarian state a germ of reality struggles to exist, and to be born again. This struggle for existence provides the theme of Stoppard's most unconventional creation, a play for orchestra (*Every Good Boy Deserves Favour*, 1978), and also that of his most conventional, the effective television drama called *Professional Foul* (1977). In this second play Stoppard shows just what is at stake in the call for 'human rights' that was epitomized in the Czech *Charter 77*. In a cleverly contrived 'lecture within a play', he argues that it does not matter if there are no natural rights.

The point is rather that all social relations, and all morality, are founded in individual encounters. There cannot be society without the experience of self; and from that experience grows the inescapable sense of a sphere of inviolability. To deny rights is to deny the individual's sense of himself as a member of society, and so to deny society. The totalitarian denial of the self is therefore also a self-denial. In being everywhere, the totalitarian state ceases to be anywhere. Its massive power is, as the Czechs like to point out, also a banalization of power, an invasion of all experience, all society, and all power, by a sense of pointlessness. The vast machinery of the revolutionary state proves itself unreal.

So there is something, after all, which provides the criterion against which meanings may be measured – a criterion outside art, and outside, or inside, politics. But how can we summon up this 'individual existence', or *svébytnost*, which can be understood only as a remainder? Before the invention of Art, novelists, playwrights and poets were able to provide the social context and moral security with which to describe and to justify the individual self. Outside society, however, the self is nothing, a substance without attributes, matter without form. When society renews itself, then the individual also is renewed. But when society decays, the individual retreats into inscrutable subjectivity. How, then, can we guarantee his reality, and how obtain from him the significance which we desire?

Here we see the great puzzle that confronts modern art. Art can be the fount of reality only if it can also guarantee the reality of the individual, whose experience contains the clue to what is real. But the individual lies outside art, and outside the laws of art, hiding behind every mask, every persona, that art provides for him. The individual can be crushed, but not commanded.

To return to the allegory – his is the free spirit for which the *licht*-Alberich craves. In one sense he is made by his god; in another sense he makes him, since without him no god can endure. Hence the Wotan-like mastery of Joyce – who created in Bloom the free individual outside art, who would also be art's guarantee. *Ulysses* presents the type of modern creativity. Art must derive its subject from itself, but art must also conceal art, so that we can take its subject for real. The *schwarz*-Alberich of revolution also needs the individual, because revolution needs the meaning which the individual alone controls. However it cannot create the individual, but must appropriate, enslave, and abolish him. The *licht*-Alberich of art creates the individual, but gives us no guarantee of his reality. Art scorns society, and so denies the conditions from which the individual grows. The magic of Joyce lies in his massive, all-embracing tolerance towards our social nature, and in the illusionism which convinces us that he has resurrected the common man.

In what is perhaps his most brilliant play, Stoppard expresses his intense dissatisfaction with the self-involvement of modern art. *Artist Descending a Staircase* (1972), written for radio, shows two ageing painters, Martello and Beauchamp, who were young in the era of Duchamp (from whom the title is adapted). They are quarrelling over the death of their companion, Donner, also an artist, who fell (or was pushed) to his death, containing within himself the unsolved riddle of their existence. It transpires the dead man alone had felt true love, towards Sophie, the blind mistress of Beauchamp. At his death Donner was working on a realistic portrait of Sophie, who herself had died, perhaps by suicide, and in any event by defenestration, on being rejected by Beauchamp. Donner's return to artistic realism comes at the end of a life of aesthetic experiment. As Donner says, 'I very much enjoyed my years in that child's garden of easy victories known as the avant-garde, but I am now engaged in the infinitely more difficult task of painting what the eye sees . . .' But of course, the eye no longer sees it: so where lies the reality of the portrait? Only in Donner's love for Sophie, who rejected him, and who therefore refuted his love. Or did she? She loved only the artist whom she saw, before her eyes failed, beside an abstract painting at the trio's first exuberant exhibition. But had she perhaps confused Beauchamp's abstract with Donner's? With failing sight, how is it possible to distinguish between paintings, each of which abstracts towards the same point of insignificance? So had she in fact loved Donner thinking him to be Beauchamp, or rather, Beauchamp, thinking him to be Donner? What would it be, in any case, to love the individual, rather than his qualities, and what can art show that is more than quality? In a dizzying concentration of philosophical jokes, Stoppard points both to the comedy, and to the seriousness, of dead Donner's predicament. Donner's art is nothing without the individual experience which is its reality, but this experience is founded in an art which provides no definition or guarantee. What, in all this, is the real thing?

The title of the new play, *The Real Thing*, is shared with a famous story by Henry James, in which two pathetic old-fashioned individuals (confident at least of their reality, since it is the product of a social order which they have yet to question) are forced by penury to pose for a painter. A fatal mistake. In the glare of art their social guarantee, and hence their reality, evaporates. Only anxiety remains. Stoppard's artist is Henry, a playwright – brilliantly performed by Roger Rees – who lives in the dilemma posed by his art, not knowing whether his experience is the creature or the creator of his plays. Stoppard, whose plays are not so much drama as audio-visual metaphysics, is of course a gift to the talented producer. Nevertheless, both director, Peter Wood, and designer, Carl Toms, deserve the highest praise for their seemingly effortless production. By virtue of their work everything is presented so clearly as to be totally obscure, in just the way that the 'real thing' is obscure whenever it gets up on stage. All the principals are actors, engaged in speaking lines which Henry might have written, and sometimes has written, so rehearsing before him the enigma of his existence.

Once again the revolutionary consciousness appears, in the person of an ignorant Scottish soldier, Brodie. Brodie has become a fashionable radical cause, having taken part in a Peace March, burning a wreath as he passed the Cenotaph, and so ending up in jail on a charge of arson. Much of the plot turns on this character, who appears only at the end, but who is the recipient of concern from Henry's second wife Annie, finely acted by Felicity Kendal. While in prison Brodie writes a play about his experience, including his meeting with Annie on a train. Annie seeks to have this play performed. Through Henry, Stoppard is able to strike some well-aimed blows at the posturing of the radical chic, and at the emotional fantasies which find release in facile indignations. But what Henry objects to is the terrible abuse of language which the revolutionary consciousness entails. Brodie, says Henry's friend Max, 'got hammered by an emotional backlash', and Henry protests, 'No, no, you *can't* . . .', so precipitating a quarrel for the sake of words. Or is it for the sake of words? Max complains that 'that's what life's about – messy bits of good and bad luck, and people caring and not necessarily having all the answers. . . .' Henry's obsession with language, he implies, is no more than a snobbish isolation from the ordinary conscience.

Max's words are intended to support Annie, but it turns out that she cares neither for Brodie nor his cause, but only for the theatrical gesture with which she had originally enticed him into it, while Brodie himself, we discover, so far from being the real thing, is a jumped-up creation of the theatre, the quality of whose sentiments is revealed by the appalling language of his play. Henry cunningly compares Brodie's play to a cudgel used in place of a cricket bat: 'What we're trying to do is to write cricket bats, so that when we throw up an idea and give it a little knock, it might *travel*. . . .' – and the image is developed in a masterly and devastating criticism of the radical butchery of language:

I can't help somebody who thinks, or thinks he thinks, that editing a newspaper is censorship, or that throwing bricks is a demonstration while building tower blocks is social violence, or that unpalatable statement is provocation while disrupting the speaker is the exercise of free speech. . . . Words don't deserve that kind of malarkey. They're innocent, neutral, precise, standing for this, describing that, meaning the other, so if you look after them you can build bridges across incomprehension and chaos. But when they get their corners knocked off, they're no good any more, and Brodie knocks corners off without knowing he's doing it. So everything he builds is jerry-built. It's rubbish. An intelligent child could push it over. I don't think writers are sacred, but words are . . .

In the end, we are to understand, the fault of Brodie's language is not that it is crude, heavy, gratuitous – although it is all of those – but that it is *unreal*. Nothing speaks from it, nothing comes out of it, besides itself. By posturing as the *real* thing, the thing outside art, it loses the aid which art can bring. It too becomes self-referential. But unlike art, which strives always to make room in its centre for the individual experience, the jargon-ridden language of revolution makes room only for itself. Its self-reference is of a more deadly kind; it is like a blind drawn down over our only window on the world, where we stand hopelessly looking for that elusive thing, the self.

In the second act the tone of the play becomes increasingly serious, as Stoppard tries to provide the reality which he has promised, the reality, as it transpires, of love between Henry and Annie. But the writing becomes looser, and at times disjointed. Too much cleverness has been stored in the first part of the play, and there is little room for more. Only the theatricalization of Brodie has yet to be accomplished, in a little vignette of slapstick; when it is over Henry and Annie are left wordless and incomplete. In one way this is inevitable, but it prompts one to reflect on the imperfection of Stoppard's art.

Stoppard is not a dramatist – he does not portray characters who develop in relation to each other, and generate dialogue from their mutual constraints. He strings characters like puppets on a line of repartee: his masters are Wilde and Shaw, and his ideal of dialogue is an exchange not of feelings, but of epigrams. The real thing is never in his words, which contain only the idea of it, in the form of brilliantly staged metaphysical conundrums. The result is of course good theatre, and, when acted with the verve of Felicity Kendal and Roger Rees, utterly compelling. But it is the *effect* of theatre – a kind of theatresque – and an effect without a cause cannot be described as quite the real thing.

III   MINIMAL BECKETT

I cannot think without thinking about something, or feel without feeling towards something. And I exist as a subject only to the extent that I think and feel. The subject seems crucially to depend upon the object which is the focus of its attention. But what is this object? It exists in my thoughts; but my thoughts give me no reason to believe that anything exists outside them. The object exists, therefore, because the subject thinks it. Subject and object exist in precarious interdependence, joined by the mysterious relation of 'about'. But what then is the subject? Nothing can be said about it, and every attempt to imprison it in words leads to exhaustion. You can catalogue the objects observed, but you never get to the subject who observes them. So what *are* you cataloguing? Not, in fact, the objects, but only the impression of them. Impressions belong to a subject; the object remains un-described, and indescribable. Subject and object constantly elude each other's grasp, and this 'aboutness' which seems to denote the most intimate of possible relations, and also the complete absence of every possible relation, is nothing more than a contradiction.

That conundrum has been the spur to a great philosophical ambition. It provided the unifying motive behind all German idealism, dictating now the 'transcendental subject' of Kant, now the 'universal ego' of Fichte, now the 'will and representa-tion' into which Schopenhauer partitioned the world. Subject and object stalk each other through the works of nineteenth-cen-tury philosophers. They have close encounters: in Hegel's *Phenomenology* the one is briefly master, and the other slave. For the most part, however, they keep their distance, and are still to be found circling each other unreconciled in the works of Husserl and Heidegger. In Sartre they make another attempt to live together, and end up like some ill-matched old couple, cheer-lessly and tediously denouncing the self-contradictory nature of their relations.

Nietzsche dismissed the old conundrum as a tissue of lies and illusions, woven by the 'catastrophic spider' Kant. But Nietzsche also said that human fulfilment lies in discovering the illusion which fortifies the will to power. An illusion upon which so many generations have built their ordinary, decent, inauthentic existence ought not to be dismissed so disdainfully. And besides, who is doing the disdaining, if not a subject? and what if not the object, is disdained? Even Nietzsche is condemned to think 'about' what he condemns.

When a writer turns away from the social world, almost invariably it is in order to climb the rainbow of 'about' and creep towards its unknowable extremities. If he turns towards the object, then, like Kafka, he becomes lost in the obsessive investigations of a dog or a land-surveyor, overcome by the infinite inaccessibility and inscrutable concreteness of 'other' things. This way lies anxiety and eventual madness. If, on the other hand, the writer turns his gaze towards the subject, then he becomes lost in nothing, or rather (to do it metaphysical justice) in Nothing. He is in the position of one attempting to observe his own gaze. That way lies silence, but also, as Samuel Beckett shows us – and it is Beckett's major achievement – a kind of pathos.

To reach the end of this path is not just hard, it is strictly impossible. But the pure subject can be approached by degrees, by the artistic equivalent of Hegel's 'labour of the negative'. It is necessary to pare away all relationships, and indeed the very language of relations, so as to leave the 'I' alone at the centre, or periphery, of the stage. Or rather, not the 'I', but (to borrow one of Beckett's titles) Not I. The theme is already broached in the trilogy of novels (*Molloy, Malone Dies,* and *The Unnamable,* 1951–53):

'Do they believe I believe it is I who am speaking? That's theirs too. To make me believe I have an ego all my own, and can speak of it, as they of theirs. Another trap to snap me up among the living. It's how to fall into it that they can't have explained to me sufficiently. . . .'

And:

'Enough of this first person, it is really too red a herring. I'll get out of my depth if I'm not careful. . . .'

But into whose depth, then, is the Unnamable trying to sink? He remarks that 'any old pronoun will do, provided one sees through it', but who is this 'one' who is doing the seeing, and what does he see? In *All Strange Away* (1976) Beckett invents a new grammatical case to contrast with the first person as its final opposite: 'Light off and let him be, on the stool, talking to

himself, in the last person, murmuring, no sound, Now where is
he, no, Now he is here. . . .' And the mouth in *Not I* (1973)
reaches moments of hysterical climax at which it forces itself,
with the true chastity that overcomes desire, to resist the first
person case. At these moments the observing figure makes a
movement. This movement, Beckett says, in his notes to the play:

> consists in simple sideways raising of arms from sides, and
> their falling back, in a gesture of helpless compassion. It les-
> sens with each recurrence till scarcely perceptible at third.
> There is just enough pause to contain it as MOUTH recovers
> from vehement refusal to relinquish third person.

In the novels, this refusal of the first person is effected also by
the constant renaming of the characters, and the narrator's positing of himself as identical with the characters he creates, or not,
according to whim. The fiction thereby becomes intertwined
with the self of the narrator, and the self becomes a fictional
artefact, the 'narrator narrated' in Beckett's words.

On one reading, the trilogy might be taken as a kind of
extended satire on the human disposition to believe in the existence of the 'I', to assume that it is the true repository of value,
the fount of life. With a charming pun, the Unnamable sums up
centuries of human frailty: 'But can that be called a life which
vanishes when the subject is changed? I don't see why not.'
Naturally, 'I' can never see why not, since while the 'I' persists
the subject has not changed – or if it has, this is a fact which
cannot be perceived from 'my' point of view. At the same time,
in the early works, the emotional pressure of the prose pushes in
another direction, towards the view which persists beneath
Sartre's cynicism, of the self as the true individual existent, the
infinitely valuable thing which we can know as subject, but
never as object, and which is the only thing which ultimately
matters, or minds.

But even in the early work, Beckett has been avid for the
poignancy which lies, he believes, not in the self, but behind it,
in the pure, pared-away perspective from which the transcendental subject surveys the inexistent world. In recent work he
has attempted to approach this poignancy more directly, balanc-
ing on the illusory arc of 'aboutness', so as to divine the strange
substance from which it is composed. Already in the trilogy he
hints at an answer: the 'foul feeling of pity', says Malone, 'that I
have often felt in the presence of things, especially little portable
things in wood or stone. . . .' And it becomes steadily clearer in
the plays and playlets that Beckett's subject is the 'helpless com-

passion' referred to in *Not I*. In order to approach this sentiment more nearly, Beckett has composed theatrical pieces in which the subject, by providing his own object, contrives to vanish from the scene. Thus Krapp, who listens to himself on tape, strategically prevents his voice from exposing it(him)self:

> TAPE: . . . What I suddenly saw then was this, that the belief I had been going on all my life, namely – (KRAPP *switches off impatiently, winds tape forward, switches on again*) – great granite rocks the foam flying up in the light of the lighthouse and the wind-gauge spinning like a propeller, clear to me at last that the dark I have always struggled to keep under is in reality my most – (KRAPP *curses, switches off, winds tape forward, switches on again*) – unshatterable association until my dissolution of storm and night with the light of the understanding and the fire – (KRAPP *curses louder, switches off, winds tape forward, switches on again*) – my face in her breasts my hand. . . .

Thus, by editing himself, Krapp removes himself from the stage. At the same time, his relation to the world is reduced to a suffering absence of relation, in which he himself, or rather, he unselfed, is the single term. A voice of pure lyrical suffering speaks from the tape, carefully choosing words in which the idea of 'about' is tenderly cradled, even though there is neither subject nor object to which it can be attached.

Krapp's Last Tape (1959) is a step away from the tragicomedy of *Endgame* (1957). But it does not achieve the lyricism of the new playlet, *Rockaby*, presented this winter at the Cottesloe Theatre, in an accomplished performance by Billie Whitelaw.

An old lady rocks quietly in her rocking-chair, while her own, perhaps younger, voice speaks into the auditorium, longing for another human soul, another individual, a creature like me. The voice remembers a room with an only window, from which the woman looked out on to 'other only windows', where the blinds were drawn. The image is developed with considerable subtlety, exploiting every verbal nuance (as in that 'only'). The impression is created of an ineffable gentleness of semi-contact. The window, which frames all experience, also lets through the 'helpless compassion' of 'about'. Billie Whitelaw, as she overhears, or underhears, the words, conveys suffering, and also calm. Her face remains unmoving, like a perfect Noh mask, borrowing its expression from the words which pass over it like mobile shadows. Every now and then the voice refers to another. It pauses on two unexplained words – 'Whom else?' The grammatical weight of the phrase is enormous. The other is inaccessible ('else'); at the same time he cannot exist as a subject. He is never more than object for me; always only 'whom'.

The few words uttered by the protagonist, in chorus with the voice, predict her eventual cessation – although, whenever the voice fades, the woman calls plangently for 'more'. At last, however, she acquiesces, ceases her rocking, and allows her head to fall slowly forwards. The simple image is extraordinarily effective. Although there is, in a sense, no person to whom the feeling of release is attached, that too is part of Beckett's meaning. The woman's voice, her *principium individuationis*, evaporates; with it evaporates the futile contrast between subject and object. The thought is Schopenhauer's, but it has been clear since Beckett's early monograph on Proust that Schopenhauer is, for him, the preferred interpreter of the metaphysical conundrum of the self.

The theme of self and other is, in fact, the master theme of modern literature. We are told that we must treat others not as means but as ends. Only thus, argued the catastrophic spider Kant, can we see them as subjects. Hegel attempted to show the catastrophe involved in the attempt to treat another as object alone: the catastrophe experienced one way by the master, and another way by the slave, in the cruel contradiction that binds them. Beckett displays Hegel's master and slave in *Waiting for Godot*, in the characters of Pozzo and Lucky; and here, we see, is a kind of drama. By contrast, the pure Kantian understanding between the tramps negates all drama. In its lyrical pathos, its infinite hesitation and vulnerability, it already anticipates Beckett's later attempts to 'eff the ineffable'. To observe the subject is also to negate him. The subject retreats before every gesture. Since he can never be object, he must exclude every compassion that is not purely 'helpless.' *Rockaby* is the final point of this pilgrimage towards the ineffable. What can Beckett now do, but repeat himself, discovering new ways of avoiding the self who repeats?

It seems, however, that he has more to show us about the 'catastrophe' of Lucky and Pozzo. A remarkable festival was held last summer in Avignon, under the title *Une Nuit pour Václav Havel*, organized by the *Association Internationale de Défense des Artistes* (AIDA). Several writers contributed pieces dedicated to their imprisoned Czech colleague, who is presently serving six years hard labour for having felt too strongly the compassion for humanity which finds a voice, of sorts, in *Rockaby*. Beckett's contribution to the festival was called *Catastrophe*. The central character, the protagonist in an unspecified play, remains completely silent, while a producer, his assistant, and a lighting

engineer prepare him for display. The others circle the protagonist, barking out orders, taking notes, occasionally adjusting
his posture. The protagonist merely trembles slightly, his head
bowed; gradually the petulant instructions of the producer confer on him the pathos which they seem designed to negate.

At one point the assistant lifts the protagonist's hat. *'Le sinciput
te plaît?'* she asks. *'Faudra blanchir'*, is the laconic reply. The
assistant drops the hat, and, taking her notepad, records *'Blanchir crâne.'* In business-like tones the protagonist is returned to
the 'catastrophe' of Lucky and Pozzo. However, beside the brusque tyranny of the producer, one senses also the helpless compassion of the assistant, who can do nothing but obey. In her
eyes, we feel, the protagonist remains a feeling subject, a
perspective on the world which contains her. Hence, for her, he
retains his intolerable value, as that inaccessible something
about which nothing can ever be said. Eventually silence
triumphs, as in every Beckett play. One senses, then, the truth in
the producer's closing words: *'Il va faire un malheur. J'entends ça
d'ici.'*

It is just such a *malheur* that the Czech state has prepared for
itself. Havel made the mistake of refusing to think of his countrymen as objects, of calling to them in their 'other only windows'
over which the blinds are drawn. This obviously was the act of a
reckless criminal, and he deserved to be enslaved. But, as Beckett
shows, nothing can compensate for the loss of the subjective
perspective, the loss of compassion. To lose compassion is to
lose 'aboutness', and so to lose the world. Slavery is the greatest
defeat for the enslaver, since he thereby puts himself beyond
dominion. That is the *malheur* which Beckett's producer foretells,
and which Beckett condemns so eloquently in all his recent
plays.

From: *Encounter*, January, February and March 1983.

11
PETER FULLER
AS CRITIC

With this declaration of faith, which is also a confession to his lack of it, Peter Fuller summarizes the critical standpoint which he adopts in *Images of God*:

> I believe a debate about the spiritual in art is long overdue. Indeed, in all that clutter about the political and social dimensions of art which went on during the last 15 years, very little attention was paid to what, after all, must be seen as among the most central of all questions affecting art and craft in our century: the severance of the arts from religious tradition and their existence within an increasingly secular culture. Modernist art historians tend to regard this as unproblematic. But incorrigible aetheist (*sic*) and aesthete that I am, I believe it to be a moot point whether art can ever thrive outside that sort of living, symbolic order, with deep tendrils in communal life, which, it seems, a flourishing religion alone can provide.

Fuller's attitude is nicely captured in the felicitous misprint: an 'aetheist' is presumably one who believes in the god-like function of aesthetic endeavour, while being militantly certain that nothing in the world or out of it is really god-like. Peter Fuller is a proselytising aetheist, impatient alike with those who deny man's need for religion and with those who yield to it. If art speaks to us of a consolation which life withholds, it is also, he believes, because it speaks to us of God. The aetheist does not believe in God. Nevertheless, he believes in treading the path to which art beckons him, and which leads to an empty grave, and a faint, barely discernible odour of divine putrefaction.

Fuller is a talented critic, with a lively eye, a lively intelligence and a lively pen. He is also led by his aetheism to be unremittingly serious. He knows the heights to which real art aspires

146

and to which it occasionally raises us. He knows the difference between the work which shows us truth and value, and the work which merely tinkers. And – rare among contemporary art critics – he knows the extent to which the rhetoric of modernism has provided an opportunity to fools and charlatans, and the extent to which the harsh discipline of art has yielded to the brash impatience of the salesman.

It is this sense of the disparity between the great art of the Western tradition and the paltry nonsense of the art market that provokes Fuller's frequent outbursts – against Georg Baselitz, for example, dismissed in a flow of invective which, like many of Fuller's negative appraisals, fails to justify the passion that compels it. Fuller's failure to describe the image of Baselitz's painting leads one to suspect that his passion has a religious, rather than a critical, meaning. Baselitz is rejected, one feels, not for his pretensions, his cheap originality or his offensive subject-matter, but for his profoundly nihilistic vision of the world, and his desire to paint human, animal and vegetable forms untouched by light or gladness. Fuller's praise for Henry Moore – nicely expressed and seriously felt – stems from the same emotional root. In Moore, as in the sculptures of Glynn Williams, Fuller finds an affirmation of the human form which is also a recognition of the spiritual need which speaks through it. The plastic values of these sculptors are not separable from their moral sense: they touch the human form as something sacred, whose meaning transcends the matter that conveys it. Against the model provided by Moore and Williams, Fuller is surely right to dismiss so much of the art-school junk that clutters the path of the practising critic. Nevertheless, he is perhaps insufficiently careful to discharge his primary critical obligation, which is to describe what he sees in such a way that we are tempted to agree with him.

Fuller is hostile to fashions and trends, and is in many ways one of the most reactionary art critics now writing. Nevertheless he has been able to carry his message home to readers who would otherwise be reluctant to accept it – readers immersed in the modernist and post-modernist aesthetic, in the morality of self-expression, and in the rootless nihilism which calls itself 'authenticity'. The trick, as Fuller abundantly displays, is to repeat at the top of your voice that you are a radical and a socialist, that all the criticisms of modern fashion are directed at capitalism, consumerism or even 'Thatcherism' (Fuller is nothing if not up-to-date in his description of the Enemy); to impress on the trendy reader that he is mistaken not in his radical posture, but only in his failure to perceive that the party tricks which catch his fancy are merely the latest and most cunning disguises of the 'bourgeois' illusionist. Fuller goes further, and declares himself to be a 'historical materialist'. But either he doesn't mean it, or he doesn't know what it means. For he is passionately convinced of the value of art, not as an economic force, but as a 'live tradition' whose power resides entirely in its spiritual meaning. Art, for Fuller, is no illusory epiphenomenon, generated like a will o' the wisp from the churning bog of material production, but the stuff of human existence, a motive as powerful and as precious as life itself.

In fact Fuller is no more a socialist than I am. He recognizes that aesthetic experience is meaningless without evaluation, that evaluation means discrimination, and that discrimination breeds order, hierarchy and a respect for the past. He looks on the modern world with a profoundly Victorian sensibility. His masters are Ruskin and Morris, the first of whom he admits to be a conservative, and the second of whom was indeed a radical, but radical about nothing so much as conservation. Fuller's repeated and effective invocations of landscape and the 'organic community' lying dormant within it show the place where his aesthetics and his politics are joined, in a seam that is as fragile as it is carefully woven. His principal concern is for the destiny of scarce resources and precious achievement, in a world made harsh by materialist obsessions. If the aesthetic experience has such importance for him, it is partly because it reminds him of the fragility of our achievements and the overwhelming debt of gratitude that man owes for a world which, whether or not it had a creator, certainly was not created by himself. If that is what it is to be an aetheist, then perhaps we should all be aetheists too.

Peter Fuller's admiration for Ruskin finds more careful and telling expression in *Theoria* (London, 1988), subtitled 'art and the absence of grace' – a work in which socialism is no longer either a dominant theme, or an obvious item of commitment, a work, therefore, which (unlike *Images of God*) has called down upon its author all the vindictive fury of those who write in the 'good old cause'. Ruskin argued that we understand the moral significance of beauty only by contemplation (*theoria*), and not by the pursuit of sensual pleasure (*aesthesis*). Lacking faith, however, man can no longer contemplate the beauties of nature; instead he loses himself in sensuality, preferring works which are 'ministers to morbid sensibilities, ticklers and fanners of the soul's sleep'.

Faith is necessary if we are to love the world. Conversely, Ruskin thought, by studying to know and love reality, we regain (in altered form) the safety of faith. This was the task he set himself, recording every lovely form, every colour, light and texture in exquisite drawing, and also in words: always in the hope that God would be revealed to him. His sentences were sometimes laboured and pedantic; but they wrapped themselves around their subject-matter like strands of ivy, clinging tightly but delicately to every part.

Ruskin was one of Proust's masters. If the prose of his French disciple has proved more lasting, it is partly because Proust retained the relish for detail, while jettisoning the search for God, and with it the high moral tone. In the annals of English literature Ruskin now appears as a finger-wagging preacher, speaking from a lectern richly carved by himself, to a hall that is ever emptier as the years wear on.

Such is emphatically not the hero of Peter Fuller's study. Fuller's Ruskin is a contemporary, walking agitated beside him through the modern world, speaking in nervous tones of a predicament that is not only Ruskin's but Fuller's, and not only Fuller's but also yours and mine. The two men are alike in many respects: living through their intellects, and yet remote from and contemptuous of the academic world. Fuller sees in Ruskin the first anti-modernist, the first major thinker to recognize that the task of modern art is not to lose itself in free experiment but on the contrary to hold self-consciously to tradition, as the guardian of truth. Modernism, Fuller believes, is an assault on art which is also an assault on morality, and therefore on life itself. While promising 'liberation', it merely drives us from art's enchanted castle into a barren desert, where neither faith nor hope nor charity can grow.

Modernism's success, Fuller suggests, is due in part to the triumph of science, which imprinted on the nineteenth-century mind the image of universal progress – progress even in those spheres, such as art and morality, where progress generally means decay. Modernist art has taken over from science as the vehicle of disenchantment. It is the busy broom which sweeps away the last cobwebs of faith, the last vestiges in the here and now of an eternal and transcendental meaning.

Ruskin provides Fuller with the vicarious experience of a faith barely vanquished, and so enables him to experience the poignancy of his own condition as an aetheist, acutely aware of what he has lost in losing God, who knows that a world without grace is a world which makes no room for art, for morality, or even for man. It is the religious experience, in its many forms, which stands between man and mechanism, which draws a line through the utilitarian balance-sheets, and tells us that the pursuit of profit profits nothing. And that is why true art – the last reserve of religious feeling – matters to modern man. In a series of eloquent chapters devoted to Nash, Moore, Bomberg and their like, Fuller once again argues that the true art of our century attempts to recuperate the experience of sanctity: the sanctity of the human form, and of landscape. It involves an attempt, in the teeth of Darwinian disenchantment, to see the world as created. The false art of our time celebrates a realm of instant pleasure, and asks to be assessed as part of it. The gallery of guilty ones grows larger every day: not only Baselitz, but also Gilbert and George and Julian Schnabel are now entombed there, drawing Fuller's condemnation in proportion to the accolades that are heaped on them by the corrupt machinery of the art world.

Fuller is too subtle a critic to be taken in by the redemptive claims of socialism. Even in *Theoria*, however, he focuses his attention on the single commodity – power – which enthrals the socialist mind. His profound spiritual analysis of modern society accompanies, in consequence, a shallow conception of its politics. Mrs Thatcher is not unlike Fuller: another decent soul attempting to stem the tide of self-indulgence. To ascribe the collapse of British culture to something called 'Thatcherism' is, at best, to confuse cause and effect, at worst to write for effect, and to affect a cause.

From: *The Listener*, 20 June 1985; *The Sunday Telegraph*, 1 January 1989.

12

PICASSO AND THE WOMEN

As the demand for biographies increases, so does their quality decline. For reasons that have little to do with the love of literature, and still less with the love of life, biographies are now comprehensive, packed with trivial detail, and burdened by a scholarship which, through its obsession with fact-finding, raises up an insuperable obstacle to truth. Modern biographies are generally opposed to any conception (other than a sentimental one) of the heroic, and are therefore unable to justify the interest that they arouse. All are very long, and all explore – with the impertinence of an age for which no human greatness must be allowed to obscure the fact of our equal littleness, and for which no human character must stray beyond the bounds of the cosy and the frail – the most intimate features of their victims' earthly journey. Most are written in an easy-going, middle-brow patter, reminding their readership that the lives of the great can be described in terms of the very same conceptions as rule the feelings of the gullible. In short, the modern biography is an exercise in vicarious living: and vicarious living is the enemy of life.

Mrs Arianna Stassinopoulos Huffington's book about Picasso (*Picasso: Creator and Destroyer*, 1988) is no exception. However, unlike most instances of its genre – which tend, on the whole, to be well received by critics engaged in the same lucrative pastime – it has met with almost universal condemnation. Many reviewers have warned against reading it; others have advised us to wait for John Richardson's four-volume alternative, due to start appearing next year. (According to Richardson, Mrs Huffington's work is 'as dim-witted as it is mean-spirited' – fortunate qualities in a book published a year before one's own.) The principal cause of this hostility lies in the fact that Mrs

151

Huffington has broken one of the unwritten rules of modern biography. She has written without that ghastly commodity called 'empathy': the capacity to present one's victim as feeble and forgivable, a genius perhaps, but at bottom just like you or me. She has invited her readers to live for five hundred pages in the manner of Picasso, and at the same time reminded them that in doing so they commit a terrible wrong. In every other way, however, her book is a competent instance of a genre that no person of taste would have the slightest inclination to read were he not, like the present reviewer, paid for doing so. Mrs Huffington chatters fluently; she has collected a mass of interesting information; her subject too is interesting, and she has woven her material together in a racy narrative packed with sexual episodes. What is primarily wrong with her book is what is wrong with the whole genre to which it belongs: namely, the failure to perceive that biography is an art, whose greatest exponents – Plutarch, Johnson, Aubrey, Evelyn – offer us the drama and the meaning of a life through the rectifying prism of aesthetic form, reducing each person to the episodes, and the number of pages, that his inner truth requires. Serious biography is therefore suspicious of facts, and at war with scholarship. If Picasso emerges from Mrs Huffington's chatter as demeaned and diminished, this is not because she emphasizes the demeaning side (though she certainly does), but because she does so unremittingly, and at enormous length, until Picasso is entirely buried beneath the case against him.

It is the mature and ageing Picasso who principally interests her. Gone is the charming, antic Bohemian, with his clown nose, his dancing eyes, and the children clinging to his shins. Instead we find a raging Minotaur, fired by an egotism that turns from lust to despair as the years wear on and the human wrecks accumulate. Picasso's sexual obsession, Mrs Huffington implies, reveals a need to dominate the other sex, to reduce and subjugate the source of love, so that love could be obtained at will and without payment. But whether those feelings – which permeate the book – stem from Picasso rather than Mrs Huffington is a matter of some doubt. It occurs to me that someone who can sustain for five hundred pages an unflagging interest in an unruly penis, while finding little to justify its antics, does not have a strong claim to the moral superiority that is assumed by Mrs Huffington.

Not that she fails to make her case: for it was already all but made by Françoise Gilot, who has favoured Mrs Huffington with some new revelations. Even if her use of such hearsay evidence is, to put it mildly, less than fully critical, the reader is persuaded by the sheer weight of it. Clearly Picasso exerted an enormous sexual fascination over women. He also used that fascination in a most unscrupulous way, not only to gratify his desires, regardless of the dependence that he thereby created, but also so as to maintain a permanent balance of moral power in his own favour. It may be, too, that he was as disposed to betray his friends as his mistresses, and that he was as cruel to his children as to the women who flocked to receive his punishments. For, as John Richardson expressed it in a recent interview:

> Picasso . . . was a cannibal. You'd be in a room with him and he'd take on each person in turn, look into your eyes as if you were the only one who interested him. He'd remember a particular painting that you had liked on a previous visit, and tears would come to your eyes . . . And nothing would please him more than your tears . . . It was an amazing performance, and he'd do it all around the room until, at the end, the group suffered from nervous exhaustion.

But, as Mr Richardson goes on to show, there is another side to this, one that only dimly engages Mrs Huffington's attention: 'He had taken the energy from everybody, their love, their thoughts. When he stood, he was full of energy and then he'd walk into the studio and work all night on it.' The love and life that he drained from his victims was (in their eyes) transformed into art and sanctified. For Picasso flourished at a time when art had become redemption, and the artist stood in for God. To love him, and to offer up one's soul to him (not to speak of one's body), were almost obligatory passions among those who sought Picasso out.

This peculiar cultural circumstance – the emergence of the artist as god, priest, and sanctifier – helps to explain the hostility directed toward Mrs Huffington. As I have suggested, her book is a fairly conventional specimen of its kind: relentlessly prurient and sexually unassuageable, distinguished only by the implied criticism of its subject. Mrs Huffington is not convinced that anyone, even a genius, has the right to live as Picasso lived. For her, the pretence that artistic creativity is a sign of godhead, and that the moral law can be freely broken for the sake of art, is only a pretence. To say as much, in a book devoted to the major artist-hero of our century, is to provoke as lively a feeling of moral indignation as the art establishment is capable of experiencing. For this establishment lives by the myth of artistic licence, which it invokes in justification of all its antics: of its endless moral transgression, and its relentless assault on human dignity. Among the reviewers of Mrs Huffington, only Paul Johnson in *The Spectator* – who sees this matter (as he sees every matter) from the perspective of Roman Catholic morality – could find the grounds for whole-hearted praise. The others have resented the suggestion that the man who breaks all aesthetic conventions, so as to achieve a new and glorious form of beauty, is not entitled to break all moral conventions too. As John Golding put it (in *The New York Review of Books*), Picasso 'was somewhat like a force of nature, and in the morality stakes he saw himself as *hors concours.*'

Picasso was not the first artist to use the modern attitude toward art to such stunning sexual advantage. Many others (not the least of them Richard Wagner) had made a go of it. But Picasso was perhaps the first to leave no place in his art for the self-criticism that such conduct demands. In all its forms, his images tell us, the erotic experience is wholesome and life-affirming. Its griefs and jealousies are but the sauce to its inexhaustible nourishment, and his one message to his many admirers was 'go – or rather come – and do thou likewise.'

And they did, seduced by the promise of an ecstasy beyond the reach of law. For the fact remains that the women whom Picasso exploited surrendered willingly to him. For the most part they were adults (just), presumptively responsible for their actions, with a knowledge of good and evil. Having surrendered, they invariably returned for more. Some, like Marie-Thérèse Walter (who played Echo to his Narcissus until her self-inflicted death), accepted the outrageous terms he imposed on them with a kind of gratitude that their lives were so radically and brutally simplified by his dictatorial power. Picasso's love for his women invariably dwindled: but while it lasted it was real – real enough to awaken the most ardent reciprocal passion, and no more deceptive in its brevity than the love of man for woman tends to be, when freed from the sacrament of marriage.

Running through Mrs Huffington's narrative are certain peculiar assumptions: namely, that if women are exploited by men, it is always the *men* and not the women who are to blame; that women are not accomplices in their own destruction; and that they do not, in permitting it, make their own contribution to the destruction of men. A man who made similar assumptions about women, and who wrote accordingly, would be dismissed by the modern American critic as sexist. It is perhaps a testimony to the power of feminism that no American reviewer of this biography has yet used that word to describe it – but if the word means anything, here is a clear instance of it. As Lord Gowrie expressed it in a review in the *Daily Telegraph*: 'The people who loved and were exploited by Picasso were loved and immortalized in return; there is no evidence that any of them, including Gilot, would have wished it otherwise.'

Picasso was a sinner – but so were his accomplices; and if he is to be singled out for special blame, we need to be told why it is that his women should be exonerated, when they were as willing as he was, and when the terms were (as a rule) quite clear. It seems to me that Mrs Huffington's ultimate complaint against Picasso is that he was sexually attractive, and used his attractiveness to get what he wanted. But there are attractive women too – Mrs Huffington is one of them – and they also make use of this advantage in the pursuit of their desires. This 'using' is not necessarily a calculating thing: the aspiring painter Francoise Gilot was not calculating when she first offered her young body to the genius whom she adored. But it was a pretty good way to begin a career as a painter.

Picasso was a witty man, and his quips and aphorisms are scattered through Mrs Huffington's pages. At the same time, his wit, like the wit of Cocteau and Guitry, arose from, and played with, a peculiar and never-to-be-repeated social context. Mrs Huffington does not succeed in evoking that context: indeed, she scarcely tries. It is partly for this reason that the charm of Picasso is reduced to his sexual prowess: nothing else remains of his magnetic social presence, once the surrounding society has been erased from its description.

A more important cause of the diminishing of Picasso, however, lies in the fact that Mrs Huffington is not much interested in Picasso's art. She accepts uncritically the dubious thesis of John Berger: that late Picasso evinces a decline into sterility and emptiness. Berger explained this by arguing that Picasso (through his success) became too much a part of the consumer civilization that he had begun by challenging. Unlike Berger, Mrs Huffington is taken in neither by Marxism nor by Picasso's own attempt to appropriate its justifying banner by becoming a member of the Communist Party. It is worth remarking, however, that membership of the Communist Party is, for the Parisian intellectual, usually a way to *épater les bourgeois*, and rarely signifies (as Mrs Huffington would have us believe) love of totalitarian power, or indeed of any power other than the power of the self.

Late Picasso was 'sterile', Mrs Huffington argues, because the artist himself was sterile: the burnt-out remainder of his own work of dissolution. Commenting on Roland Penrose's introduction to the 1960 retrospective at the Tate, in which the critic described Picasso's work as 'born of an understanding and a love for humanity,' she remarks that this is as true as Orwell's slogan 'War is Peace'. Her evidence for this judgment makes no reference whatsoever to Picasso's art, but dwells instead on the post-coital quarrelling with Françoise Gilot. By such means we should be able to discount not only the love and understanding expressed by Picasso, but also that conveyed in the art of Stendhal, Balzac, Wagner, and Dickens. The fact is that an artist may, in his life, yield cheerfully to temptation, and nevertheless recuperate, through his art, the values and the vision that are betrayed in his behaviour. To say this is not to justify him; it is rather to emphasize that the story of a man's soul can be told in many ways and the story told in his art may contradict the testimony of his life. To write a biography of Picasso in which his art is silenced by the avalanche of his misdemeanours is to miss the meaning of Picasso.

But what should we say of Picasso's art? That he was a genius I do not doubt: though less of one than his protean powers suggest. Picasso opened more avenues to empty and nihilistic image-making than almost any painter in history. But he left it to the mediocre talents who came after him to explore those avenues: he himself stood always outside them, with his face turned to the sun. To say, as Mrs Huffington does, that Picasso 'brought to painting the vision of disintegration that Schoenberg and Bartók brought to music', and to insist that in this he 'took to its ultimate conclusion the negative vision of the modernist world', is to misunderstand the entire effort of European culture in our century. Picasso's art should not be seen as disintegration, but rather as an attempt to re-order and re-integrate what had *already* disintegrated, under the impact of forces outside the artist's control. Faced with the unseeable fragments of the modern world, Picasso sought to reassemble them, so as to make them visible and to reveal their truth. The modern world may be ghastly; but the modern artist has no other world to play with. And, as Picasso showed, he can still discover in this world an order and a purity that justify his work.

From: *National Review*, 9 December, 1988.

13
BEASTLY BAD TASTE

The astonishing thing about Gilbert and George – and the only thing that is likely to be memorable – is that they freely admit to being without taste or the desire for taste. Their work (it could hardly be called art) is easy to understand for the simple reason that it contains nothing to understand. At the same time, it has the form of defiance: it successfully ritualizes the game of originality, as this has been played up and down the country over the past four decades.

The work of Gilbert and George should be seen as the final production-line version of a romantic archetype. At the beginning of the Romantic era, Blake had declared that 'Jesus was an artist' and, Nietzsche was to add, a corrupt and corrupting one. By the end of the century, the crucified artist had become a popular salon figure, condemning through his art the pompous nothingness by which he was surrounded, while at the same time exemplifying it in another form.

In the popular imagination the task of the artistic revolution was thus glamorized: untalented and trivial people began to posture as artists in order to enjoy the easy-won glory of the bohemian form of life. What had begun as an attack on the banalities of l'art pompier became another mode of tasteless banality, and on the whole a less agreeable one.

The new cult of the artist-prophet – which was to bestow on dadaism, surrealism and the later lunacies of Duchamp, the crown so hard-won by Courbet, Manet, and Cézanne – ceased in time to be the property of the educated few and became instead a universal cliché and also a weapon in the hands of the philistines. Salon art was again triumphant: not in the form of cloying nudes and grotesque anecdotes of saints and heroes, but in the form of a mechanical spontaneity, a trashy novelty-mongering whose one intention was to 'challenge' whatever style had last commanded the market.

Ugliness, morbidity, emptiness, and obscenity – all were posi-
tively encouraged, and, by the late 1960s, when the products of
the baby-boom began to roam the streets in arty costumes, the
nadir had been reached. Non-conformism had become an iron
conformity, novelty a platitude, and emptiness the only form of
signification. This was the time of Pop Art and Andy Warhol, of
a commercialism of the 'liberated' gesture, when the prophet-
artist had been assimilated entirely into an anarchic middle-class
and become a normal citizen in a lawless world. *L'art pompier*
had been replaced by *l'art Pompidou* and the claims of taste were
as much set aside by the new establishment as they had been
scorned by the nineteenth-century salons. The doors of the
nation's public and private art galleries were thrown open to
Gilbert and George.

The works shown at the 1987 Hayward Gallery exhibition and
at the Anthony d'Offay Gallery are vast, flat, lurid squares and
oblongs, too large to sit comfortably in any but the grandest
private houses and sure to destroy the grandeur of any place that
houses them. Their titles are lifted from the gutter – 'two cocks',
'tongue fuck cocks', 'friendship pissing', 'shit faith' and the like
– while the images fail to be disgusting only because Gilbert and
George are so devoid of artistic talent as to be capable of producing no emotion whatsoever. They have little understanding of
surface or light; their colours are those of the playground and the
supermarket, and their lines are executed either photographi-
cally or in the hard-edged manner of the comic strip.

None the less, they are masters of hype, and can find for any
painting, however boring, some suitable paragraph of art-school
lingo with which to market it:

> with fine-brained ghastliness of good intentions each fitting
> part fits in and tunes to the rising whole. Sweet delicate mas-
> siveness of purpose and desire. Twinkling compartment/cells
> of energy inspire us with blood-thoughts. A thousand people
> whizzing with their blood from cell to cell, and another
> thousand heavy fixed hard to desk with work for pleasure
> ambition. Some for their first day and some for their last. Rot
> on for us dear lighted sign of life, prove good and get loved as
> a form.

With brazen effrontery they lay claim to every possible moral
and artistic virtue:

> We believe in the Art, the Beauty, and the Life of the Artist
> who is an eccentric Person with something to say for Himself.

We uphold Traditional Values with our love of Victory, Kindness and Honesty. We are fascinated by the richness of the fabric of Our World and we honour the High-Mindedness of Man as the ultimate Form and Meaning of Art. Beauty is Our Art.

It is curious to turn from those bathetic words to such triumphs as 'Buggery Faith', four cartoon penises prodding with their fly agaric noses one of those explosions which (in the Beano world which nurtured Gilbert and George) would be marked Zap! Wham! or Powee! One can see how words like 'beauty' have undergone, in their jargon, a peculiar transformation, like that suffered by 'democracy' in 'people's democracy', or 'violence' in 'structural violence'. The word is being used to mean its opposite. Where there is an absence of beauty, impossibility of beauty, the overthrow of beauty's empire, there Gilbert and George stand drivelling their ritual paean of the beautiful, uttering the word in the same tone of voice as they utter 'shit', 'fuck', 'cock', and 'buggery'.

Gilbert and George ceaselessly remind their admirers that they are clever people. And, in a sense, they are. But their cleverness amounts to nothing that could be called imagination or intelligence. For the real test of their value lies in the works themselves rather than the words which package them. And in the works one finds only ritual gestures: empty rhetoric without a theme. The aim of being 'of their time' has been deliberately divorced from judgment: there is no attempt to assess their time with a critical understanding or with an eye for what is real.

Gilbert and George describe their paintings, or rather photo-daubs, as 'visual sermons'. But there is no lesson to be derived from them, no understanding, guidance or discrimination. Their works are as remorselessly undiscriminating as the world from which they spring and which they pretend to celebrate. Their idiom is that of the advertisement and their subject-matter – well, their subject-matter is Gilbert and George, whose figures appear in almost all of them, and whose half-digested obsessions are transcribed onto their surfaces with the same painful urgency as guides the hand of the graffiti 'artist' in a public lavatory. Their sole skill is in having made self-advertisement profitable, in having sold as creative masterpieces works which have no aesthetic quality at all.

In a sense, theirs is the culmination of the advertiser's art and the realization of every advertising agent's dream: to devise an advert which *sells itself*, for which no product is even necessary, and which, rejoicing in the assumed dignity of art, is wrongly imagined to be a bargain at whatever price. Gilbert and George are certainly gifted; and if their gifts appeal to such as Charles Saatchi then it is because they are practising the same trade as their patron.

It would be wrong to say that what they are doing is original: Andy Warhol showed the way. But by operating as a pair, they have gone one further than Warhol. They have produced works which cannot even be read as individual expressions, and which therefore have closed off the one remaining avenue in which significance could be sought. It is plain for all to see that their works mean nothing: and therefore that anyone, whatever his state of learning or cultivation, can understand them. Their commercial success depends on this demotic quality. The new species of patron – the state cultural apparatus, represented by the Arts Council and its officials, and the fast-thinking, restless yuppies of the Saatchi school – is anxious to justify its financial power in terms which make no reference to élitist ideas of taste and discrimination. Patronage in the modern world, even when administered by a private person, tries to free itself from aristocratic overtones; it must pretend to follow popular judgment, not to lead it. The result is that those like Gilbert and George, who are least worthy of public patronage, are most likely to receive it – whether in the form of the Turner Prize, or, as now, in the form of a state-subsidized, international touring exhibition, displayed at choice venues all over the civilized world.

As an economic phenomenon, one might sensibly praise their work. From the point of view of political economy, the artist has a vital role to play in a market: by charming the rich (including the new impersonal rich of the state bureaucracy), he ensures the constant redistribution of accumulated resources. He maintains in a state of flux that which would otherwise become moribund and ossified. At this level he is indeed the highest form of advertiser, the one who induces those who have more money than they need to release it again into the general cycle of production. Thanks to the artist, all kinds of otherwise useless people – auctioneers, gallery attendants, art teachers, students, photographers, critics and journalists – find gainful employment, and the well- or ill-gotten gains of the patron are cast once more into the economic air, to accumulate in new and surprising places.

This function is displayed by Gilbert and George in its purest form, since the realm of taste and aesthetic value is by-passed by their work altogether. As the Marxists would put it, their 'art' has ceased to be part of the superstructure and has attached itself to the economic base. And if the rubbish displayed on the walls of the Hayward Gallery has any spiritual significance it resides in this: that spiritual significance, as a category, no longer has any role to play in the sale and purchase of 'art'.

A work can now perform its economic function without being loved or admired; nobody need be enchanted by it or moved by its deeper meaning. The money pours through it unresisted, like sewerage through a drain, and the civilizing function of art – the function which justified all this extravagance and caused the patron to benefit from his purchase as much as the artist from the sale of it – has been finally set aside.

From: *Modern Painters*, March 1988.

14
WHO OWNS ART?

It is more and more a received idea that art is a public asset, which should be owned by the people as a whole. But when the people are mentioned, guilt and doubt inevitably rush in behind them. Which people? Do we mean all of them or only some? Do we have to mix with them, or is it enough to keep them at arm's length while diligently advocating their right of admission to municipal museums?

The questions are familiar to all sceptical observers of the volatile New York conscience. The idea of the people – one of the most singular legacies of the French Revolution – remains a shibboleth in educated circles. It is for the sake of the people that all noble enterprises are undertaken, and, as the ultimate beneficiaries of art and culture, they, it seems, are the true owners of the treasures of mankind. If rumour has it that this or that private house contains interesting art, the educated conscience at once cries for its doors to be prised open so that the people may rush in.

I have often stood before some minor masterpiece in a crowded museum and reflected on how much deeper and more lasting pleasure it would bring were it to be hanging above the mantelpiece in a private house, receiving from its domestic circumstances some of the warmth and sympathy that are art's due. I have often had cause to compare the unfeeling connoisseurship of our museum culture with that passionate love of the rare and the miraculous which is to be found in the pages of Goethe and Reynolds, Hugo and Fromentin, and which arose when people of taste were forced to nourish their sensibilities on a hard-won diet of examples and on experience gained at the end of taxing journeys.

But the days of the passionate amateur are over. Art is a public concern, and ripe for public ownership. We are asked to believe that the works of art that are housed within a nation's borders belong, or ought to belong, to the people who reside there. Can we really believe such a thing?

Take the recently publicized case of the Elgin marbles. Do they really belong to the people of England, to the people of Greece or to the people of Turkey? The marbles were taken from the Parthenon by the seventh earl of Elgin during the course of a work of restoration that he himself had initiated, at great personal expense, and with intentions that were, by the standards of art collectors, largely public-spirited. The marbles were taken to England; Lord Elgin was certain that their Ottoman custodians would otherwise consign them to the lime kilns. After a parliamentary inquiry into the legitimacy of Elgin's transaction, the marbles were acquired by the nation, for a sum that only partly covered the enormous cost of their transportation. The Greek government now claims these treasures as an immovable part of its 'national heritage' and is trying to bring diplomatic pressure to bear to persuade the United Kingdom to relinquish its claims.

The case could be generalized. One may think of the plundered portions of Europe that have ended up in the United States – not merely paintings but whole monuments and even buildings. One may think of the massive spoliation of the temples of Laos and Vietnam by the likes of André Malraux, who, making deft use of his Western connoisseurship, was able to enrich himself in unprecedented ways. One may think too of the sculpture and decorative art of tribal Africa, so readily surrendered to the admirers of Picasso by those for whom art was neither a coherent concept nor a recognized object of exchange. A whole continent was thereby swept clean of its artistic heritage, and remains blind to the fact. A peculiar kind of civilized curiosity, which sees value in the 'primitive', has made the primitive into an article of mass production, a degraded form of airport souvenir.

The result has been devastating. Native African art was vulgarized to satisfy an appetite for the 'primitive' that is profoundly alien to African culture. For what primitive person sees himself as such, until his culture has been shattered forever? You could say that the Africans have been victims of a most terrible fraud. Not only has their taste been perverted, but the artworks have been removed that might have provided them with the standard against which to judge their present labours. Surely, then, we owe them a great debt of restitution? And what better way to pay it than by securing the return of the many transported objects to the territories whence they came, there to take their rightful place in museums accessible to the people who created them?

The question is not one of legal ownership. No doubt, insofar as law governed any of these transactions, they were frequently validly accomplished. The question is, rather, one of moral ownership. To whom does a work of art *really* belong; who has the underlying spiritual claim to it? The most straightforward answer – the artist – is no better than straightforward. For the artist has died, without heirs apparent and without expressing a desire for the restitution of his work.

Hence the modern answer, the answer of the guilty liberal conscience: the true owners of the work are the people from whom the artist sprang. Is this answer more plausible? I believe not. For who are these people? Those related by race or blood to the artist? If we say so, then we allow a dangerous fiction – the idea of race – to dominate our otherwise impeccably liberal guilt feelings. Should we refer, then, to the people who now occupy the territory where the artist lived and worked? But by what right do they occupy it, and as a result of what conquest or what *coup d'état*? Should we then say that it is not the people but the state that has the most serious claim to the national assets? But the state too may have changed beyond recognition. In what way is modern Italy the same state as the assemblage of Renaissance princedoms or the Soviet state the same as the Tsarist empire? Besides, how many artists would wish their patrimony to belong to the great instruments of coercion that rule the lives of their unhappy descendants? It was certainly not for this that they laboured, but for some more honourable thing, such as money, a woman or the glory of God.

The only plausible idea is this: the people in question are constituted by a culture. They consist of all those individuals who share the culture of the artist. If we say this, however, then the case for restitution collapses. Either these people have retained sufficient hold on their culture to safeguard its monuments, in which case we need no longer feel guilty that some of them have been scattered abroad; or else they have not, in which case they have ceased to exist as a cultural entity and have no greater right to the works of some previous epoch than has anyone else. To return the products of their ancestors' labour is to return unspeaking relics to people for whom they have no inner meaning.

Let us forget all this guilt. Let us recognize that, among those who claim ownership of art, the greatest entitlement rests with the private purchaser, with the person who has sufficiently loved an object to make a sacrifice in acquiring it. It is he who is the true guardian of culture, and without his enterprise and observation it is certain that little would remain of the art of the past – as little as would remain of the Parthenon sculptures had Lord Elgin not had the sense to bring them to England.

From: *ARTnews*, September 1983.

15
RADICAL CRITICS

I HAROLD ROSENBERG

Harold Rosenberg's neat, self-confident judgments of contemporary art were widely respected. He had the gift, not only for spotting talents, but also for finding words that would sustain a public interest in them. At the same time he stood aloof from the world of dealers and impresarios, whose fraudulent protégés he would happily ridicule whenever they threatened to displace his own chosen favourites – Gorky, de Kooning, Barnett Newman – from the centre of the stage. Rosenberg therefore provided the art-world of the 1960s with its touchstones, and also with a necessary core of seriousness and relevance. Without Rosenberg this market might have blown up at any moment: a whole section of the economy, as vital to America as was the building of pyramids to Egypt, would then have collapsed ignominiously.

The Case of the Baffled Radical (Chicago, 1986) consists of articles and interviews from every period of an active career. It does not have the verve of those celebrated collections – The Tradition of the New, and The Anxious Object – whose titles herald the wealth of illuminating paradox contained in them. Nevertheless, it includes one first-rate essay – an introduction to a book of Avedon's photographic portraits, in which Rosenberg discusses the aesthetic potential of photography, and the differences between photography and painting. 'The art of painting', he argues, 'is a generator of distance, both between the painting and the spectator and between the painting and its subject. In contrast, the photograph leads the mind into the actual world – if it is of a nude, it will make one think of women, not art.' Thus, with clipped, sudden phrases, Rosenberg alights on a profound critical perception. The transparency of a photograph, which seems at first sight to make portraiture so easy, in fact makes it hard. In photography almost everything that matters lies outside the artist's control: to assert control over the final image he must daub it like a painter, and so destroy the photograph. Rosenberg does not quite draw that conclusion, which would lead him to show less respect towards Avedon than is compatible with the task of introducing him. But he makes an impressive attempt to remind us of the labour, the discipline and the detachment of the true art of portraiture.

Many of the essays have a political content, and in an extended discussion of F. R. Leavis, Rosenberg makes it clear that criticism, or at least Leavis's criticism, is as much a political as an aesthetic enterprise. *Scrutiny*, the journal which Leavis edited, is castigated because 'it had set itself against Progress, democracy, and political liberalism, and . . . had occupied a sector in the battle line of anti-modernism established by *L'Action Française*, the New Humanism, the classicism-royalism-Catholicism formula of T. S. Eliot, the literary agrarianism of the Old South, and the cultural Fascism of Ezra Pound'. The diatribe is uncharacteristic, which is just as well, since it contains some pretty gross fabrications. Pound, for example, may have been hoodwinked by the Duce, but is 'cultural Fascism' the correct description of the invocations of courtly love, the melancholy testimonies to the grief of exile, and the jeremiads against 'usurocracy' which form so much of the poet's work?

Rosenberg is adamant that he is not reactionary like Leavis, but impeccably (or at least only slightly peccably) liberal. And in a sense he is right. He does indeed reprimand American liberals of the 1930s for so fervently excusing the Soviet Union – 'as extreme a case of misapplied generosity as any recorded in human history'. But he has nothing to say about the 'misapplied generosity' that later exonerated the Viet-Cong and the Khmer Rouge, and which now finds its object in SWAPO, the ANC and the Sandinistas. For Rosenberg was, on the whole, fairly tolerant towards movements which paid lip-service to democratic values, and which were prepared to prove their sincerity by allying themselves with the Soviet Union. If that's what makes a liberal, then Rosenberg was certainly a liberal.

However, he gives his own definition. Liberalism, he writes, is 'an expression of generous feelings, particularly towards the poor, the badly treated and dependent people'. American conservatism, in contrast, is 'merely a series of rationalizations for holding onto what one has'. And 'since its kernel is personal hoarding, as a point of view it is a joke'. Such remarks betray an extraordinary ignorance of the common people of America, who are motivated in their conservative sentiments as much by charity and religion as by desire for wealth. By 'generous feelings' Rosenberg means the disposition to spend other people's money on schemes for which one assumes no liability, and by 'hoarding' he means prudence – the necessary virtue without which charitable intentions are neither generous nor sincere.

Elsewhere Rosenberg draws the political agenda more broadly, so as to cover law, liberty and constitution as well as wealth. In writing about Watergate he half recognizes that justice could not, in the circumstances, be done to President Nixon, who had already been tried and convicted by the press. Reading people like Rosenberg one realizes that Mr Nixon's crime was not so much his offence against the constitutional delicacy which liberals had so suddenly and miraculously discovered in themselves, as his desire to hold on to office at a time when all decent journalists recognized America's need for a liberal President.

Discussing the Nuremberg trials, Rosenberg again shows his sense that justice is hard to come by when the victim has been publicly vilified before being legally condemned. In this case Rosenberg is motivated by real and justifiable passion. It is interesting, therefore, that the resulting view of crime and punishment has a strongly conservative flavour. Punishment, he reminds us, is an objective recognition of the individual's responsibility for his evil actions, and its purpose is not reform or deterrence but retribution. Punishment gives form to the natural desire for revenge, and at the same time assuages and replaces it. Forgiveness is the prerogative of the victim; the judge who usurps this privilege adds to the victim's humiliation and compounds the moral burden of the crime. Such a view of punishment – applied, not to Nuremberg but to the normal course of justice – would evoke a storm of protest from the liberal establishment, and if Rosenberg gets away with it in this case, it is because he is writing of Nazis, and writing as a Jew.

Nor is this the only place at which Rosenberg is trapped by his conservative instincts, even if it is the place where he is most evidently 'mugged by reality'. In a series of interviews, he repeatedly expresses his doubts about the modern world, about the media, about technological progress, and about the anti-élitism of Washington politics. At times he sounds like a polite and good-natured Leavis (if that were possible). It would not be right to say that Rosenberg is *consistent* in this reactionary posture. But he is a good enough democrat in the matter of his own emotions to let each of them raise its voice: and the majority turn out to be profoundly sceptical of human progress.

Nor does Rosenberg take much comfort from modern art, which he describes as a 'form of anxiety', and whose effect on politics, he argues, can never be direct. (If you aim for a direct impact, what you produce is not art but propaganda.) He believes that artistic values are as vulnerable as all other values to 'the crushing power of cash', and he is suspicious of government subsidies as a means for the maintenance of artistic creation. To have seen the pure gold of art forged into monetary value awoke him, in the end, to an old Wagnerian perception. The man at the forge was the modernist critic, who showed that whatever is painted can also be sold. And as Rosenberg acknowledges, that critic was Rosenberg.

II   T. J. CLARK

If we take social history seriously, then art seems to be too small a part of it to justify independent study. On the other hand, if we take art seriously, then social history seems to have no clear application to it. Great art transcends its circumstances, while minor art is too easily discredited by them, too easily made to seem, when brought into relation with its origins, like a social climber come home to the slum.

The easiest way to make the social history of art look interesting is to re-write history according to some aesthetic paradigm. If history becomes art, then art has a place in history. For instance, if you divide history into periods, associate each period with a spiritual condition, and then invent some tragic, comic, or at any rate aesthetic 'law of motion' which takes you from one period to the next, then you have a social history that lends itself to the analysis of art. One such historical system is that of Hegel. Another is that of Marx. For the contemporary art historian Marxism has the greater appeal. To bring together in a single gesture the factitious moral intensity of the radical with an aesthetically pleasing historical 'science' is to provide a powerful critical method. Not only can you now fit the work of art into its social context with almost mechanical exactitude; you can also cast judgment on the work and its context together.

T. J. Clark is a kind of Marxist, who adopts, as does Michel Foucault (the thinker who seems to have most powerfully influenced him) the schoolboy's guide to history provided by the *Communist Manifesto*. The nineteenth century is the period of 'bourgeois' civilization, and the 'bourgeois' period begins in 1789. It is also the period of 'capital' and, increasingly, of the consumer society created by capital, in which human wants, needs and satisfactions are successively dismembered and 'commodified'. Like Foucault, Clark is deeply suspicious of the 'bourgeois', and of 'capital', both of whom stalk through *The*

Painting of Modern Life (London, 1985) in personified form, malignant and pervasive powers against which art raises its voice in fine but feeble protest. It is 'capital' which creates and re-creates the city, as the forum of its vile transactions. 'Capital', Clark tells us, 'devises a set of orders and classifications which makes the *city* unintelligible,' and its interest in doing this is to neutralize the possibility of 'collective action and understanding.' 'Capital' doesn't want people to get together; it doesn't want them to be united and happy; it doesn't want them to be interested in anything save the commodity which it provides, and into whose strait-jacket it ruthlessly constrains them.

'Capital' acts, however, through the medium of human beings. One such was Baron Haussmann, whose plan for the new Paris is, for Clark, a triumph of policemanship. The city of Haussmann is the new city of 'capital', the city of marketable images, of commodities, of objects and people in flux, of solitude, class division, and prostitution. 'Haussmannization' is 'the essential form of capitalism in the mid-nineteenth century.' And so on.

Such easily manufactured insights are far from persuasive: or persuasive only to someone who does not question the Marxian morphology, and who sees 'capital', rather than the free market and free association, as the distinctive mark of the 'bourgeois' city. If 'Haussmannization' is the *essential* form of capitalism in the mid-nineteenth century, then why was London not also 'Haussmannized'? (Besides, what does the word 'essential' mean in such a context?) Clark argues roughly as follows: the mid-nineteenth century was the apex of the period of 'capital'. The important cultural events of the time are therefore to be assigned to 'capital' as their cause and meaning. Social history is a matter of spelling out the meaning, for all to see. This, of course, is to assume the truth of Marxist historical analysis and not to prove it. Moreover, the game of 'meanings' can be played by other rules. Why not see Haussmann's plan as part of the French rationalist tradition in architecture, which began with Boullé and Ledoux, and which culminated in the *ville radieuse* of the socialist Le Corbusier? Why see in Haussmann the logic of 'capital' (i.e. of the free market), and not the steady march of a force that revealed itself, at last, in the planning mentality of the modern state, with its egalitarian ideology, and profoundly interventionist outlook? Clark's persistent marxising provides neither inspiration nor insight; moreover, it blinds him to the aesthetic merits of the boulevard style. If Haussmann hadn't done it, think who might have tried his hand later, when the bleak and equalizing ideals of modernism had destroyed the last vestiges of architectural taste.

The central chapter sets Manet's great *Olympia* within the social context of Haussmann's Paris. Here is the *boulevardienne* in all her naked insolence, usurping the satin couch of Titian's Venus. The figure, Clarke argues, challenges not only the category of 'prostitute' and the myth of the *courtisane*, but also the bourgeois order, whose identity and sexuality are somehow tied up with such categories and myths. Manet's *Olympia* testifies not only to the sexual transaction in its new 'commodified' form, but also to the reality of social class, as it is both reproduced and transgressed by the bourgeois client who pays for the flesh of the proletarian. The image shocked the world of 'capital' by presenting the social reality of its sexual hunger.

Clark's analysis is serious, sensitive and suggestive. It is also obscure. Prostitution is an ancient and persistent feature of the human condition; so too is social class. If a painting can challenge the first of these categories by bringing it into relation with the second, there is no reason to think that this achievement is either distinctive of the 'bourgeois' period, or particularly expressive of its spiritual peculiarities. Once again, Clark's thought is quickly overrun by Marxist incantation, and the reader has little opportunity to consider what he is being asked to believe.

There follows a more general analysis of Haussmann's Paris. This takes as its focal point Manet's *Bar aux Folies-Bergère* (again sensitively analysed), and covers – with many fascinating and ably documented references – the life of the cafés and boulevards. Clark argues that the idea of the 'popular' expressed in the songs, lyrics and antics of the *café-concert*, is really a bourgeois invention, a mythologizing and confining of the lower orders; a kind of barrier to 'collective' action and even a covert 'policing' of the working class. The paranoia again owes much to Foucault, and generates some remarkable conclusions, among which the following is by no means untypical:

> The middle class in the later nineteenth century . . . had not yet invented an *imagery* of its own fate, though in due course it would do so with deadly effectiveness; the world would be filled with soap operas, situation comedies, and other small dramas involving the magic power of commodities.

This class obsession would be more tolerable if Clark told us what he means by 'class'; but he doesn't. By any normal understanding, the 'middle class' constantly provided, throughout the nineteenth century (and any other century for that matter) artistic imagery of its fate. To take but one example: what is Wagner's

Ring if not an account of the fate of the middle class (and indeed of every class), when subjected to the 'magic power of commodities'? And if Wagner was not middle-class, who was?

Clark seems to think that only *bad* art can be bourgeois, and that anything of value must therefore stem from some other source. (This displays the snobbery that lies at the heart of Marxism.) It is of course true that any work of value breaks free from its 'class origins' and is misrepresented by the attempt to re-attach it. But if that is Clark's meaning, then he ought to see how little Marxist social history has to tell us about the meaning of art.

From: *The Salisbury Review*, April 1986 and *Artscribe*, September 1985.

16
THE PHOTOGRAPHIC SURROGATE

Painting was shocked into self-consciousness by the invention of the camera, though not, perhaps, into true self-knowledge. If the purpose of painting is to copy appearances, and to place a frame around the world, then photography can do this just as well or better. So why trouble to paint, and where does the *art* of painting reside?

Over the century and a half of their irritating persistence, those questions have attracted two broad answers. One says that the purpose of painting is *not* to copy the world, but to do some other thing: it is in this other thing that the art resides. The other says that photography is as much an art, and for the same reasons, as painting is. The first leads inexorably towards abstract expressionism and the death of painting; the second leads to 'photo-realism' and the montages of Gilbert and George. Such is the terrible price that we have paid for taking the camera seriously.

Croce and Collingwood made what was perhaps the boldest attempt to defend the first answer, and to uphold the dignity of art against the vulgar world of image-mongering. They argued thus: art involves two separate tasks: representation and expression. Only expression, however, is proper to art, and integral to the experience of beauty. The delight in representation is not, as such, aesthetic: it looks beyond and through the work of art, to the thing depicted, which is the real object of attention. Photography is the most developed form of representation, and, as such, ministers to curiosity, nostalgia and idle fantasy. A photograph is never interesting for its own sake, as art must be, but only as a substitute for something else.

Painting may use representation – but only as a means. The *end* of painting is expression. All art gives objective form to experience, which lives inseparably within it. Impressionist paintings provided the Crocean ideal of art: they do not show us the world, but express an *experience* – an 'intuition'. And this experience is inseparable from the shapes, colours, harmonies and patterns that are set upon the canvas.

By that argument, Croce and Collingwood hoped to safeguard the realm of art from its modern enemies. Photography is confined by its nature to the task of representation: it shows the world, but expresses nothing. It is the visual equivalent of journalism, pampering the appetite for knowledge, while destroying, through its expressive incompetence, the act of communication – the resonance of each to each – which is achieved through art.

The argument is wrong: not because photography is an art on a par with painting, but because photography does not represent anything at all. It may be an art, but if so, it is not an art of depiction.

Representation occurs in painting; it also occurs in literature, where there is no question of copying the way things appear. Literature and painting represent things, not by copying them, but by expressing *thoughts* about them. The word 'about' is one of the most difficult in the language. It seems to denote a relation – between thought and its subject matter. But we can think and speak about non-existent things, and what could be meant by a relation between objects, one of which does not exist? Painting is exactly analogous to thought and speech. If you paint a subject, it does not follow that the subject exists, nor, if it does exist, that it *is* as you paint it to be. And your painting can be of a man, even when there is no particular man of which it is a painting. In the jargon of philosophy: the relation between a painting and its subject is an intentional, not a material, relation.

A photograph is caused by its subject, and causality is a material relation. Hence the subject of the photograph must exist, and if a photograph is of a man, there is *some particular man* of whom it is a photograph. Furthermore, the photograph will always show the subject, within limits, as it really appeared from a certain angle: and this, indeed is the root of our interest in photography. Of course, the appearance may be deceptive, but the deception lies in the thing photographed, and not in the process of recording it.

Hence photographs are incapable of displaying things which are unreal. I may take a photograph of a nude and call it *Venus*. The result, however, is not a photograph of Venus; still less a photographic representation of her. It is a photograph of a representation of Venus: the representational act, the act which establishes the 'intentional relation' with Venus, was completed before the photograph was taken. Photographic fictions are really photographs of fictions; the camera itself is without imagination. Interest in a photograph – even in the arty photographs of a Robinson or a Lartigue – is always interest in the thing photographed, whose existence can never be in doubt. Interest in a painting is in the presentation of a subject, which exists, as a rule, only in the act of presentation. That is why there is no room, in the art of painting, for vulgar curiosity, or for those vicarious emotions which hunger for what is distant, disengaged, but real.

By its very nature photography can 'depict' things only by resembling them. It is only because photographs look like their subjects that we were ever tempted to compare them with paintings in the first place. In looking at a photograph, therefore, we know that we see something which actually occurred, *as* it occurred. This fact dominates our response to the picture, which becomes in consequence transparent to its subject. If the picture holds our interest, it is because we are interested in the thing 'shown within'. The beauty of a photograph is seen as a beauty in its subject, and if the photograph is sad, it is because the subject is sad. Consider, for example, Roman Vishniac's superb records of the Central European ghettoes between the wars. The emotional density here belongs not to the picture but to the thing displayed, and is entirely dependent upon our knowledge that *this is how things were.* Hence there cannot be a photograph of a martyrdom which is other than horrifying. To take an aesthetic interest in a photograph of martyrdom is to sink into moral corruption: the corruption involved in looking aesthetically upon the sufferings of men. By contrast, a painting of a martyrdom may be serene, as is Mantegna's great crucifixion in the Louvre. The painting, because it tells a story, can create the distance between itself and its subject matter which is necessary for aesthetic judgment. The photograph is unable to do this, since it lacks the technique whereby the subject and its mode of presentation could be held apart.

Well, you might say, why not *invent* that technique? Suppose that we do so. Suppose that we try to make our photographs so that it no longer matters whether their subjects exist, or whether they look like the things depicted. In such a circumstance, we begin to separate our interest in the picture from our interest in the thing displayed: perhaps we can now take an aesthetic attitude to the one which is not also an aesthetic attitude to the other; perhaps medium and content have at last been pulled apart.

Unfortunately, there is no way of determining in advance

which detail is relevant to an aesthetic interest: every detail can and ought to play its part. At the same time, the causal process of which the photographer is victim puts almost every detail outside his control. Even if he does intentionally arrange the folds of his subject's dress and meticulously construct, as studio photographers once used to do, the appropriate scenario, that would still hardly be relevant. For there seem to be few ways in which such intentions can be revealed in the photograph. For we lack all but the grossest features of style in photography; and yet it is style that opens the way to the question, Why this and not that?

Let us assume nevertheless that the photographer can exert over his image the kind of control that is exercised in painting. The question is, How far can this control be extended? Certainly, there will be an infinite number of things that are accidental. Dust on a sleeve, freckles on a face, wrinkles on a hand: such minutiae will depend initially upon the prior situation of the subject. When the cameraman sees the plate, he may still wish to assert his control, however, choosing just this colour here, just that number of wrinkles or that texture of skin. He can proceed to paint things out or in, to touch up, alter or *pasticher* as he pleases. But he has now *become* a painter, precisely through taking representation seriously. The photograph persists only as a kind of frame around which he paints.

The culmination of this process can be found in the techniques of photo-montage, as used by such artists as László Moholy-Nagy and Hannah Höch. Here our interest in the subject has been genuinely separated from our interest in the image, to such an extent that, as in painting, we can be entirely indifferent to the existence and nature of the originating cause. But that is precisely because the photographic figures have been so cut up and rearranged in the final product that it could not be said in any normal sense to be a *photograph* of its subject. Suppose that I were to take figures from a photograph of Jane, Philip and John and, having cut them out, I were to arrange them in a montage, touching them up and adjusting them until I have a telling representation of a lovers' quarrel; it represents a lovers' quarrel because it stands in an intentional, rather than a causal, relation to a quarrel. Indeed, it is to all intents and purposes a painting.

The history of the art of photography is, I believe, the history of successive attempts to break the causal chain by which the photographer is imprisoned, and to impose a human thought between subject and image. It is the history of an attempt to turn a mere simulacrum into a mode of discourse, an attempt to discover through technique (from the combination print to the soft-focus lens) what was in fact already known as art. Occasionally photographers have tried to create fictions, by arranging their models and props according to the requirements of some imaginary scenario. But a photograph of a representation is no more a representation than a picture of a man is a man.

The true talent of the camera is not to produce representations, but to provide us with surrogates and reminders. Hence, like the waxworks, it provides us with the means to realize the situations which fascinate us. It can address itself to our fantasy directly, by showing what is absent, untouchable, but *real*. This is surely what distinguishes the scenes of violence which are so popular in the cinema from the conventional death-throes of the stage. And it is this too which makes photography incapable of being erotic. For it presents us with the object of lust, instead of the imaginative symbol of it. The photograph is a realization of the thing desired, and therefore gratifies the fantasy of desire long before it has succeeded in imagining and reflecting on the fact of it. The medium of photography, when bent towards the sexual and the violent, is inherently pornographic.

Of course, there are other, and better, uses for the camera. We wish for portraits of our friends, hoping to be reminded of their appearance and to renew our affections towards them. But why is the result so disappointing? In order to understand aesthetic appreciation, Wittgenstein once said, 'I would have to explain what our photographers do today – and why it is impossible to get a decent picture of your friend even if you pay £1000' (*Lectures and Conversations on Aesthetics*, ed. Barrett, p. 7). Because photography is understood through a causal relation to its subject, it is always, for us, the record of a moment: that sudden smile, that vanishing embrace, that flicker of a long since dead emotion. Painting aims to *capture* the sense of time, and to present its subject as extended in time. Portraiture is not an art of the momentary, and the true portraitist paints into the features of his sitter a whole narrative history. The causal relation which fixes the photographic image is a relation between events, and it is only by deserting his craft and taking up a pen, a brush or a pencil, that the cameraman can adjust his image so as to break free of the moment. (This is surely what Brady manages in his portrait of Queen Emma.)

A photographer can aim to capture the fleeting moment which gives the most reliable *indication* of his subject's character. He may look in the moment for the sign of what endures. But a sign is not an expression. A man may give a sign of his guilt by blushing; but he does not thereby express his guilt. Similarly, a photograph may give signs of what is permanent, despite the fact that it cannot express it. Expression, however, is what we need in a worthwhile portrait. We can never rest content with a photo of our friend. We seek the visual narrative of his character, through which to recreate the object of our love. Even in the realm of portraits and reminders, therefore, it is impossible that photography should displace the art of painting or even begin to compete with it.

Photography is here to stay, and will always call forth the mostly vigorous protests on behalf of its aesthetic pretensions. And it is not difficult to see why. Photography is democratic: it puts into the hand of everyman the means to be his own recorder. To defend its artistic pretensions is to make everyman an artist. To attack them is to imply that the ability to create, to appreciate, to resonate – the ability to stand back from the world and record its meaning in an aesthetic judgment – is the property of the few. Such a thought will always be greeted as deepest heresy, in an age which builds its institutions and its monuments on the myth of human equality.

From: *Modern Painters*, March 1989.

17
IN SEARCH OF AN AUDIENCE

The recent London performance of the completed parts of Stock-hausen's operatic cycle *Licht*, served to remind British music lovers of the distance which their own music has travelled since this impertinent German last asserted his absolute right to their attention. Of course, not everyone who sat through those long hours of attitudinizing was equally regretful. At each perfor-mance there would appear a small band of ageing trendies – bald now, more neatly dressed, and with fashionable earrings in their prominent ears – who rose in paroxysms of applause. But for the majority of the audience Stockhausen's combination of por-tentous symbolism and musical vapidity marked the end of an era. If this composer, the darling of the 1960s, had failed so signally to advance beyond the manner and the *Weltanschauung* of those years, why should we continue to subject ourselves to the hours of quasi-religious devotion that he demands? And why should we strain to fathom the meaning of scores which, despite their factitious complexity, conceal so small and uncer-tain a core of musical good sense?

Such scepticism is by no means new. What is new is that we can openly express it. We can now say, of this spectacular suit of clothes, that it has no emperor. During the 1960s and 1970s the British musical public succumbed, like the rest of Europe, to the tyranny of the avant-garde, and it became necessary to accept without question everything that defied the 'bourgeois' ear. Boulez and Stockhausen were appointed honorary guardians of our musical conscience, and for a decade or so the native tradi-tions were downgraded, scorned, or ignored entirely. During those years Benjamin Britten – a musical genius comparable in range and imagination to Stravinsky, and in everything as British as his name – continued to write scores of an ever-

increasing refinement and luminosity, each one achieving new
melodic insight and new harmonic radiance. They were greeted
by the ordinary music-lover with sincere but quiet gratitude,
and for that very reason were disdained by the avant-garde. For
the trendy critics, the true originality of *Death in Venice, Curlew
River,* and *A Midsummer Night's Dream* – an originality born of
taste, discipline and a profound respect for natural harmony –
was as nothing beside the false originality of Stockhausen,
whose extravaganzas were presaged by such careful marketing,
such a barrage of interviews, announcements, debates and
glossy programme notes, and such a formidable outlay of public
expenditure, that the entire musical profession acquired a commitment to praising them, long before their emptiness could be
heard. For several years, the feigning of musical ecstasy became
a national pastime, and people without the faintest record of
musical culture found themselves prompted into fierce, but
unopposed, partisanship, on behalf of works which had little
significance besides the fact that they were furiously and
defiantly new.

The avant-garde came before us as the final repudiation of the
nineteenth century, and the scientific cure to every romantic
excess. In truth, however, *avant-gardisme* is no more than the
latest, and most feeble, manifestation of a central Romantic idea:
the idea of the artist as separated from society, possessed of new
and astonishing truths which raise him above the lives of ordinary mortals, a scourge and redeemer to whom all is secretly
permitted. As the Romantic movement lost its initial confidence,
it strove to perpetuate itself in both art and politics, by contrasting its ambitions with the dullness and subjection of the ordinary 'bourgeois' world. *Épater les bourgeois* became the signature
of the disaffected artist, the guarantee of his social credentials,
whereby he demonstrated his aristocratic entitlement and his
contempt for the usurpatory dominion of the rising middle class.
Under the dual influence of Marx and Flaubert, the bourgeois
emerged from the nineteenth century transformed out of all
recognition from his humble origins. He was the 'class enemy' of
Leninist dogma, the creature whom we are commanded by history to destroy; he was also the repository of all morality, all
convention, all codes of conduct that might hamper the freedom
and crush the ebullience of *la vie bohème.* Much of the efforts of
the French intelligentsia in our times have been devoted to
completing the portrait. The aim has been to create the perfect
enemy: the object against which to define and sharpen one's
authenticity, an authenticity guaranteed by its transformation
into art.

This negative self-identity explains what is perhaps the strangest feature of the musical avant-garde: its use of technicalities – both theoretical and practical – in the justification and presentation of its novel sounds. Serialism should not be understood – for all Schoenberg's protestations – as the 'emancipation of the dissonance', or as the discovery of a new dimension of expressive sound. It should be seen as an elaborate pretence of musical discipline, a congeries of rules, canons and theories, and a mock exactitude (manifest at its most comic in the scores of Stockhausen) which strives in vain to overcome the listener's sense of the arbitrariness and senselessness of what he hears. The affectation of artistic order is a mask for inner disorder. True musical constraint depends not on intellectual systems, but on custom, habit and tradition – on the forms of a common musical culture. It depends precisely on that 'bourgeois' audience which the avant-garde set out to kill with insults.

In *Die Meistersinger* Wagner portrays, in schematic form, the components of a musical culture – although it is a culture that stands in need of renewal. In this idealized bourgeois community, music serves as a *lingua franca*, uniting and harmonizing the many occupations upon which the life of the town depends. David provides to the aristocratic interloper Walther a touching description of the current musical conventions: the weird, frozen ornaments of a local style, in which variety is also a monstrous uniformity. Each style, each detail, each constraint, participates in a common musical substance – the substance of tonality, whereby these diverse musical entities are brought together into a harmonious whole. Tonality is the symbol of the broader harmony of the town, the harmony of co-operation which disaffected radicals denounce so childishly as 'bourgeois'.

Walther looks on the musical diversity of Nüremberg with contempt, seeing in it no more than its shabby provinciality, its arbitrariness, and its monotonous sameness of flavour. The rules which David teaches to him are no more to him than the ossified remainder of practices which impede the artistic impulse, and place a barrier between him and the prize: the muse Eva (who is also, however, daughter of the principal citizen of Nüremberg). His own musical idiom separates him from the hide-bound burghers. His is a free-flowing, constantly modulating, unstructured melody, in which the principal ingredient is feeling – or so it seems to him. When at last he contemptuously rejects the title of 'Master', and with it, the civic pride of the Nürembergers, it is in order to show his freedom from the pettifogging constraints of a dead musical tradition.

But what had brought him to this point? Only the persuasive

power of his song, which had carried the people with it, establishing its reality as music by creating the audience which could hear it as such. Walther's success lay in his creation of an intelligible musical idiom. In being understood, however, his song became part of the culture that he had spurned. When Hans Sachs rebukes the Junker for his fine contempt, he gestures to the meaninglessness of an art that has no audience, an art that defies the community of listeners, and the local attachments which unite them. Such an art, he implies, is nothing in itself, and also, in its nothingness, a kind of cancer in society. By scorning the common culture of the town, it scorns also the social existence which makes culture possible. This aristocratic contempt for the life of the market place is a two-edged weapon, which, in wounding the community, wounds also itself. For it damages the common life upon which all individual gestures, however original, however sublime, depend for their meaning.

Walther acquiesces, and receives his reward. And in truth he has deserved it. For throughout the opera, fragments of his *endlose Melodei*, turns of phrase, chromatic questions and answers, a free restlessness of ornament and rhythm, have been slowly seeping into the surrounding music, and rescuing it from the exhaustion of which it stood accused. The chorus begins again, and reaffirms the mutual dependence of the old and the new, the original and the conventional, reminding us that the pompous C-major theme of the Mastersingers is, in fact, the natural bassline to Walther's song. Tonality triumphs, and, in its triumph, is also transformed.

The avant-garde, like the vanguard party, set out to 'liquidate' the bourgeoisie. Under its baneful influence the musical culture of Europe was rapidly dying. The spontaneous order of music depends upon amateur performance, concert-going, a healthy mixture of old and new, a broad familiarity with the sounds and the rhythms of the moment. It is inimical to the avant-garde, which brings with it the new and artificial order of the Welfare State. 'Music Festivals' now provide the public alternative to the gramophone, and the means whereby the State dispenses its nameless patronage, securing for an arbitrary handful of composers the occasional luxury of a first performance. However, it is *second* performances that every composer longs for – since these are the sign that he has a following, that someone other than the impersonal bureaucrat is prepared to pay for his music. He wishes his works to be part of the *repertoire*. And since there can be a repertoire only where there is an audience that will ask for it, the composer must cultivate the normal bourgeois ear.

The recognition of this truth has dawned on the British musical world in recent years with such vividness, that it is possible now not only to reject the avant-garde and its wilful snobbery, but also openly to profess an allegiance to the principles of tonality. (There has even been a printed T-shirt, bearing the slogan 'Tonality rules – O.K.?'.) Among younger composers there has emerged a remarkable movement for 'the emancipation of the consonance', in which five names stand out as particularly important: Nicholas Maw, Robin Holloway, Oliver Knussen, and the brothers Colin and David Matthews who, having fallen first under the influence of Maw (himself deeply inspired by both Britten and Walton) became, as Britten's resident scribes and helpers during his last years, the receptacles for the master's final and maturest cogitations.

Neither Oliver Knussen nor Colin Matthews would think of himself as fighting a battle against the avant-garde, still less a battle on behalf of tonality. Each is eclectic, anxious more to build on achievements than to establish a habit of repudiation. Knussen is perhaps London's most striking musical personality, and his expertise as a conductor of modern music has made his vast, slow, shabby figure a familiar sight in the concert hall. Knussen's music is bright, clear and meticulous, quite unclassifiable by any system other than its own, while Colin Matthews expresses himself in vital, often percussive sounds which, for all their tenacity of purpose, defy the logic of tonality, moving off constantly into new regions, and employing harmonies which support the melodic line without inviting it in any particular direction. Nevertheless, to listen to Knussen's remarkable opera *Where the Wild Things Are*, or to Colin Matthews's lyrical Cello Concerto, in which the solo part seems to speak out with a human intonation, over finely orchestrated clusters of sound reminiscent more of Szymanowski and his Polish followers than of previous English concerto writing – to listen to these works is to return from the sterile wilderness of the avant-garde to a place of warmth and energy, in which musical sounds grow from each other with a natural and organic impulse.

An air of the early twentieth century also pervades the music of David Matthews, who, in a remarkable series of string quartets, combines the experimental method of modernism with the contours and cadences of tonality. The Fourth Quartet, a work of considerable beauty and unaffected directness, ends in a movement that might have been composed by Britten, with a soaring melody in the idiom of *Peter Grimes*, and a firm tonal logic that finally resolves itself into the triad of D major. This quartet, like the Second Symphony and the Violin Concerto, expresses a conscious resolve on the composer's part to re-establish contact with his audience – and in particular with the cultivated amateur, from whose life and enthusiasm the possibility of a public music ultimately derives. As young British composers recognize, the problem is to resuscitate the immediacy and appeal of tonality without lapsing into the mesmerizing vulgarity of the American minimalists, for whom tonality has been, on the whole, merely a novel form of self-advertising grossness.

Few living composers are more adept in the language of tonality than Robin Holloway, whose exuberant Serenade in C, played often and with evident relish by the Nash Ensemble, has scandalized forward-looking critics by its historical impossibility. Like many impossible things, one can believe in it only after a certain mental exercise. But you do not need the stamina of the White Queen to be persuaded by this delightful music. As we all know, the pure language of tonality is so redolent of discarded meanings that it can now be used only with a certain ironical detachment. Holloway's irony in this piece is the irony of Flaubert – *l'ironie qui n'enlève rien au pathétique.* In more recent tonal compositions – the *Serenades* in E and in G – he leaves irony entirely behind him, making fluent and affectionate use of the lighter commonplaces of classical chamber music. His manner in these pieces, while somewhat 'cubist' in outline, seems entirely to regain the innocence of the originals.

Holloway first came to public attention in 1970, with *Scenes from Schumann*, a strangely compelling and utterly novel work, in which Schumann songs are re-cast in a resistant harmonic medium, appearing not distant and inaccessible but on the contrary disconcertingly close in this modern perspective, as though we were for the first time looking them straight in the face. This lyrical masterpiece was followed by more grandiose and cumbersome works. In recent years, however, Holloway has returned to his earlier idiom, with a much surer and maturer grasp both of tonality and of the many ways of discreetly re-affirming its fundamental values. Most impressive, perhaps, have been the *Romanza* for violin and orchestra, and the magical Viola Concerto – a piece of sustained song comparable to the Cello Concerto of Elgar (from which it quotes obsessively, one of those rocking phrases which, as Berlioz and Brahms had already discovered, bring the virtues of the solo viola into startling prominence).

In such works, as in the Szymanowskian Cello Concerto of Colin Matthews, and the quiet, consoling Violin Concerto of David Matthews, we can perceive the full extent of our return to the idea of music as an art of communication between composer and audience. For these composers of the younger generation, the lesson of *Die Meistersinger* has been learned, and their thought has returned to that crucial dividing line of twentieth century music – the period of Schoenberg's first experiments in serialism, of Stravinsky's coloristic harmonies, and of the last flowering of British romanticism in the late works of Elgar.

Not every composer of the new generation has learned the lesson of history, however. There exists a rival school, led by Brian Ferneyhough, the composer still selected by anti-bourgeois critics as uniquely deserving of unqualified praise. His scores, patterned with subsidiary notes, dense with unhearable cross-rhythms and mounted on the most acerbic harmonic progressions, have been fervently imitated by such younger composers as Chris Dench and James Dillon, whose products are designed, like Ferneyhough's, for export to avant-garde festivals in France and Germany. Indeed, Ferneyhough himself was clearly designed for export; for he now lives and works in Germany, and addresses his countrymen only in the occasional programme note, written in the pretentious language of the Frankfurt School, and reminding us that, across the water, the obsessions of the 1960s are unfortunately not yet dead.

From: *The Salisbury Review*, January 1987.

PART III
THE POLITICAL
DIMENSION

18

THE IDEA
OF PROGRESS

The idea that the human race, as it moves through history, is always advancing towards some ideal state is an old one. In his *History of the Idea of Progress* (London, 1980), Professor Robert Nisbet argues that it is as old as Western civilization, if not as old as mankind. Nisbet discerns the idea in the myth of Prometheus, in the pastoral vision of Hesiod, in Roman and Christian antiquity, even in the chronicles of the Middle Ages and the Renaissance encomiums of classical learning. He consciously opposes the orthodox theory that the idea of progress is distinctively modern, a product of the rise of science and of the secularization of Western culture. It is, he believes, one of the perennial values of mankind, a source of hope in all ages, which is expressed sometimes in secular, and sometimes in religious terms.

Nisbet is an impressive scholar, armed with an effective card-index. He produces carefully chosen quotations to show that men as diverse as St Augustine and Adam Smith, Thucydides and Hegel, Fontenelle and Cotton Mather, all shared a common faith in the progress of mankind. Even Vico, the first great advocate of the cyclical view of history, is said to have had a progressive streak. The evidence for this is that he called his principle work the *New Science,* and how could he have used those two words, Nisbet asks, if he did not have a lingering attachment to modernity?

The thesis sounds suspicious to say the least. Augustine believed in the Fall and in the perpetual need for redemption. Thucydides thought that the Peloponnesian war presaged the end of civilization. While Hegel prophesied that the owl of Minerva will fly only with the gathering of dusk. Adam Smith held that human nature is a permanent datum, capable of reaching an equilibrium from which it is neither natural nor desirable to depart. Surely an idea that can be fitted to all those philosophies, even though they seem mostly designed to resist it, must be a rather empty one. Either it is a truth so trivial that any thinker is bound to recognize it. Or else it has some ritualistic quality which requires that even the most sceptical pretend to accept it, on pain of being reviled and cast out. Or perhaps Nisbet is just wrong in thinking that so many people at so many periods of history have believed in inevitable progress. To settle the question we must look at the idea more closely; and Nisbet's book is timely, since there is no doubt that, despite overwhelming evidence, the belief in the necessary progress of humanity still has a fair measure of support.

In 1920 J. B. Bury wrote an influential work, *The Idea of Progress*, in which he argued that the concept of progress is a modern one. He emphasized the particular brand of optimism that was associated in the seventeenth century with the rise of science, and which had begun with Descartes' attempt to base knowledge in reason alone. The idea of progress, he claimed, went with a taste for modern as opposed to classical literature. It went with a rejection of ancient and dogmatic authority. It went with admiration for scientific achievement and with a belief in the superiority of reason over revelation. It was rooted in Copernican cosmology, in the growth of urban capitalism and an educated middle-class, in the Protestant ethic and the spirit of self-help and self-enlightenment. In short, the idea was one harmonious part of the familiar transition from the Renaissance to the modern world, to be explained as the offshoot of social, scientific and economic changes which displayed themselves in this and countless other ways.

Such a theory is fairly significant, whether or not it be true. The idea of progress gains content from the social context and political expectations with which Bury combines it. Remove that context, as Nisbet does, and it is impossible to see what the idea amounts to. In what respect are men supposed to progress, towards what, and how? Are we speaking of scientific knowledge, of technology, of social harmony, of moral and political perfection? At the end of Nisbet's résumé of Western thought, it seems as though every age has made empty noises about 'not putting the clock back' and 'moving with the times'. I find it hard to believe that these undignified phrases would have touched the heart of a Thucydides or a Cicero. The Fifth Monarchy Men at the interregnum believed that the future would be better because the world would be violently destroyed. Marx believed that it would be better because man would have mastered nature and so freed himself from the tyranny of private property. Liberal thinkers of the Enlightenment believed in the future because darkness and superstition would be swept away. In short, the idea of progress, divorced from its historical context, is so wide as to include every form of human aspiration. Someone who so hated the world that he set out to destroy it in a nuclear holocaust would count as a believer in progress, in Nisbet's terms. For he would certainly regard the future as an improvement. I find it hard to believe that our greatest thinkers have entrusted their values to an idea that is so vague as to bear the distinctive marks of none of them.

Nevertheless, it is true that some people see history as a process of linear development, while others see it as cyclical, or random, or as a permanent struggle without resolution, or as a slow and inevitable decline. These pictures are more or less arbitrary, in that the evidence is compatible with all of them. But the one that is chosen will reflect the attitude of the man who adopts it, and will form and transform his thinking in countless significant ways. When I consider the particular picture that is associated with the idea of progress I find myself overcome by scepticism. The idea of mankind moving ineluctably from bad to good, so that whatever belongs to some previous age should never be repeated, is so absurd that it is hard to understand how reasonable people could subscribe to it. For one thing, it involves a contradiction. If mankind necessarily moves towards the good, then the injunction not to 'put the clock back' becomes senseless. Many quite sophisticated believers in progress have been caught in this contradiction. They have wanted to say that the progress from bad to good is as inevitable as the change from past to future, and at the same time to warn us not to thwart it. Either the process is necessary, in which case warnings and exhortations are absurd. Or it is not, in which case it might be just as reasonable to go back as to go on.

Two thoughts lie at the heart of the belief in progress, a truth and a falsehood. The truth is that we can plan only for the future, and not for the past. And it is irrational to plan except for the better outcome. So man, being a rational animal, must always act with a picture of how things can be improved by his action. Sometimes, in order to give himself confidence, he will project this picture into reality, feigning to believe that things are already as he would wish them, or that impersonal forces will ensure the realization of his hopes. So people are always willing to follow the man of faith who assures them, whether on the authority of divine revelation, or on that of infallible science, that the world is inevitably moving in the direction they desire. History presents many examples of these men of faith; the fact that half the globe is now ruled on the strength of myths forged by one of them is some testimony to their power.

The falsehood behind the belief in progress is that time alone makes a difference. The moral and human attributes of an event are supposed to be explained in part by the time when it occurs. If one event occurs later than another, then it must be guided by the more beneficent influence of that later time. The inevitability of time's movement from past to future – which only philosophers and madmen would dispute – is thereby transferred to the moral sphere. The absurdity of this belief was pointed out by one of Nisbet's leading progressives, Immanuel Kant. The position of an event in time, Kant argued, confers no special power on it, since time itself is without causality. Time is not a process, but a dimension in which processes occur. And power belongs to processes alone. These can as well be circular, reactionary, destructive or chaotic, as linear, progressive and in the interests of all. A belief in progress, which tells me nothing about processes that are supposed to bring progress about, is merely a 'pernicious superstition', in the words of Dean Inge. Of course, many people have been victims of it, just as many people have believed in magic, metempsychosis, and in every variety of mysterious thing.

The chiliastic mentality has entered a period of quiescence. I doubt, however, that it will allow us much respite. It will return, when it returns, with just the same destructive intentions that have guided it in the past, finding nothing but evil in the perceivable, and nothing but good in the unknown. Nisbet introduces us to the post-medieval disciples of Joachim, who had tried to hasten through sword and torch the time of terror that must precede the millennium. He describes the zealots of the Puritan Revolution, the Jacobins, the modern demagogues such as Lenin, Stalin, Hitler and Mao, well aware that these agents of persecution and crime have had for their justification a sense of necessary historical development, and were every bit as galvanized by it as the Crusader by his sense of God's need for vengeance against the infidel. All those facts are familiar. Yet the idea of inevitable progress still retains its appeal. Why should that be so? I shall suggest three reasons.

The first is that the idea of progress is a myth, and all myths require belief in a supersensible reality. The future is supersensible, since, no sooner have we perceived it, than it is past. Hence, if you wish to believe something that flies in the face of all the known facts of human nature, you are best advised to believe it of the future, which is forever unobservable. In that way the implausible is made irrefutable.

The second reason is more interesting. It seems to me that the belief in progress has almost always involved some kind of confusion between the realm of science and the realm of values. In the normal course of events, and failing catastrophe, the stock of scientific knowledge must inevitably grow. Once made, a discovery is more often adopted than lost, and, once adopted, new discoveries are built on it. With the advance of science comes the advance of skill. In the last century this skill was dignified by the name of 'man's mastery over nature'; now it is called 'technology', out of a nervous recognition that it might not be all that it was cracked up to be. Technology must advance from year to year, a fact which is transformed by Marxist theory into the vital proposition that productive forces always develop. But what do we make of this fact? Clearly technological advance affects our means, not our ends, so it can never be said to be good in itself. It will produce as much evil when put to evil ends as it will produce good when put to good ends. As Adorno once put it: 'No universal history leads from savagery to humanitarianism, but there is one leading from the slingshot to the megaton bomb.' But there is, I think, a further consideration that is often overlooked, and which leads to the confusion that I mentioned. Consider the body-builder, who, having swelled and tightened every useful part of himself, ends by forgetting the advantages of doing so. He takes refuge in a familiar fantasy. He becomes obsessed with his body, and begins to regard as ends in themselves the muscles which he originally acquired as means. His body becomes paralysed by inaction, or else devoted to the single-minded cause of its own improvement, without any sense of what it is being improved to do. So too in technology. Habits of thought are engendered which lead people to consider as an end in itself what is at best a means. And they then begin to worship it, endowing it with magical qualities which distract their attention from serious values. As their means become their ends, so do they lose both end and means together.

This process is nowhere more vividly illustrated than in the art of architecture. Nobody disputes the immense sophistication of means introduced into modern building by new materials, new manufacturing processes, and new engineering skills. But, apart from architects, almost everyone disputes that the transformation has been worthwhile. A sense of the ends of human conduct is more easily lost than gained, and this loss is visible in the cheerless sophistication of modern architectural styles. If you admit that there is something of the utmost value which is hard to acquire and easy to lose, then the myth of progress will never again be persuasive for you. The less so, as you come to realize that one of the things that threatens what you value, is the desire endlessly to improve on it.

The third reason for the continuing belief in progress is fear. The belief in providence, destiny and divine retribution absolves men from the trouble of controlling things. Having done the utmost that lies within human power, it seems permissible to leave the rest to God. As men lost the belief in providence, they began to feel responsible for events, even for the large events which had previously been left to divine wisdom to regulate. At one period it was possible to believe that scientific knowledge, advancing within the framework of an accepted moral order, would enable men to deal with the task that devolved on them in God's absence. This was the age that Bury described. During the last century, however, despondency set in. It became apparent that men do not have the capacity to control the world. While there were determined optimists, like Marx and Spencer, for whom the miracle of providence could be recreated under the guise of scientific law, the tone of the century is one of melancholy. Nisbet regards the nineteenth century as the century of progress, confirming his vision by quoting from such recognized sources as the infantile Comte and the profound but unpersuasive Marx. In fact such thinkers were exceptions to their time. If we turn from social science to the more perceptive and troubled thoughts that find expression in art, we discover something very different. We encounter the spleen of Baudelaire, the grief of Tennyson, the nihilism of Flaubert, the didactic admonishing of Ruskin, the death-worship of Wagner and his disciples. We find, too, the architecture of the Gothic revival, with its sombre nostalgia for a vanishing social order, and its categorical denial of the god of technology. The so-called century of progress produced every variety of gloom, pessimism and revulsion, and its greatest aesthetic achievement, Wagner's *Ring*, contains the most conscious and thoroughgoing rejection of the myth of progress that has ever been embodied in art.

This loss of faith stems from a combined sense that man alone is answerable for his destiny, and that man *alone* is unable to control it. It is fear of the vast and directionless forces that govern us which leads to the Comtian and Marxian forms of optimism. But it seems to me that their systems have the quality more of incantation than prediction. The stronger a force, the more we fear it, and therefore the more we are disposed to appease it through an act of worship. As men find themselves faced with the problem of making the world, and begin to recognize, what had been apparent long before, that the task is impossible, they feel their increasing littleness beside the forces of history. Out of fear they attach themselves to any belief that will represent these forces as beneficent. Hence there is a 'willing suspension of disbelief' concerning the tragedies of recent history, or any other matter that will bring sobriety into our moral and political attachments.

This fear explains, I think, the almost incredible adherence of intelligent beings to the Marxist theory of history. It also explains the belief in the 'market' as an impersonal force that will regulate self-interest and ensure that all is right with the world. It explains almost every secular fetishism of our more than usually fetishistic age. Whether the belief in progress is a more rational response to this fear than Pascal's wager is not for me to decide. But one thing at least seems certain. There is no greater proof of the unreality of human progress than man's continuing disposition to believe in it.

From: *PN Review*, no. 24, October 1981.

19

MAN'S SECOND DISOBEDIENCE: REFLECTIONS ON THE FRENCH REVOLUTION

> They who had fed their childhood upon dreams,
> The play-fellows of fancy, who had made
> All powers of swiftness, subtilty, and strength
> Their ministers . . .
> Did . . . find, helpers to their hearts' desire,
> And stuff at hand, plastic as they could wish, –
> Were called upon to exercise their skill,
> Not in Utopia, – subterranean fields, –
> Or some secreted island, Heaven knows where!
> But in the very world, which is the world
> Of all of us, – the place where, in the end,
> We find our happiness, or not at all!
>
> (*The Prelude*, Book XI, lines 124–44)

Of all the great events in modern history, few have been so assiduously moralized as the French Revolution. It was a revolution conducted, so to speak, in the mirror of its own approval, obsessively recording its daily progress, and bequeathing to posterity not only its new concept of virtue and its new species of crime, but also a new language through which both crime and virtue could be meditated. Even now the Revolution is often considered in its own self-image: as a single vast occurrence, a transformation in the order of things, whose effects were felt throughout society, and whose causality lies deeper than the will of individual men. There are historians who protest against that monolithic conception – Richard Cobb, for example, who unceasingly reminds us of the waywardness, indifference and mute *attentisme* of the provinces during the Revolutionary years.[1] Not the least among the Revolution's legacies, however, is the rooted belief – which no patient Cobbery has yet managed to eradicate – that 1789 marked the entry on to the stage of history of new forces, new political conceptions, and new forms of deed.

I am not a historian. Nevertheless, it seems to me that the French Revolution – however it was caused, however it ended, and whatever it produced – enshrines a process which does have precisely the unity which the Revolutionists proclaimed. I have in mind the events which we describe, in retrospect, as Jacobinism, and which marked the birth of the 'revolutionary consciousness'. Whatever the causes of the Jacobin power – catastrophe, conspiracy or cock-up (to mention the three most plausible theories of history) – its meaning, for conservatives at least, is of a total and perhaps unprecedented change, not merely in the conduct of politics, but also in the aims and aspirations of mankind. Nor is this reaction peculiarly English. Even if nothing else in Taine deserves our credulity, he should be given credit at least for this: that he identified in the Revolution a force that was new to the world of politics, and which also demands our moral judgment.[2] In what follows, however, I shall draw little from Taine, and much more from two earlier conservatives: Burke, from whose astonishingly prescient essay[3] the theory of modern conservatism derives: and Tocqueville, recognized on all sides as the wisest, if not the truest, commentator on those great events.[4] I also owe a debt to François Furet, whose *Penser la Révolution Française* takes a step in the direction that I too shall travel.[5]

Reaction to the Revolution has had two connected aspects: an attitude to the events themselves, and a further attitude to their representation. It is part of the genius of Burke and Tocqueville to have recognized (as neither Michelet, nor Taine, nor even Carlyle seemed to recognize) the extent to which events in the Revolution became responsive to their own interpretation – the extent to which the *self-consciousness* of Revolution became the principal agent of social and political change. The meaning of revolutions is, I believe, to be found exactly here: in the consciousness which guides and inspires them and which, arising out of unbelief, fills the vacuum of man's longing with a belief in collective man. The Revolution involved a war against religion: an attempt to re-create the world as a world uncreated. The modern conservative cannot fail to see in it, therefore, a fatal anticipation of that other and more terrible revolution which modelled itself, not on the events of 1789, but on a canonical representation of those events, and on a general theory of history in which revolution is described as the primary – indeed the only – form of real social change.

As with that later revolution, the French Revolution has found constant sympathy in the hearts of liberal and progressive thinkers. However wedded to the ancient politics of compromise, however appalled by what they deem to be 'temporary excesses' and fanatical *jusq'auboutisme*, the believers in progress and enlightenment have on the whole seen the Revolution as a positive contribution to their cause. To the good Buckle it seemed as though only mental decay could explain Burke's revulsion towards the events of 1789.[6] While acknowledging the vileness of much that was done thereafter, Buckle, like Michelet, Tawney and many a like-minded spirit, counted the ultimate cost as less than the vast initial benefit. In vain did Tocqueville argue that the progress, such as it was, had already occurred (a point made powerfully also by Burke); in vain did he point out that the anger unleashed against the aristocrats did not cause, but on the contrary, was caused by the steady erosion of their power;[7] in vain did he show that the ancient habits of oppression had all but vanished, and that the Revolution arose less from a struggle against absolute power than from the *absence* of power in that very central place which had been so foolishly prepared for it. All those wise observations, along with the profound psychological analysis of the new forces which had been swept into the central vacuum, made little impact on the progressive historians of the nineteenth century, just as similar truths about Tsarist Russia have been overlooked by the countless well-meaning commentators for whom the October Revolution was a step in the right direction, a leap forward into the modern world that had been for too long, and too cruelly, delayed.

It is fair to say, however, that the tide has now turned against progressivism. In a striking work, René Sedillot summarizes the results of recent scholarship, and argues that *le bilan final* – two million dead and the almost complete cancellation of every civil liberty being only parts of it – is offset by no discernible long-term advantage, either to France or to mankind.[8] How accurate is Sedillot's assessment I do not know; in what follows, it is not so much the measurable destruction as the spiritual condition of revolution which will engage my attention. More important in assessing that condition is the theory of the Revolution which has done the most to inspire it: the theory of Marx, or at least, of the Marxists. According to this theory, 1789 was a 'bourgeois' revolution, a transition from 'feudal' to 'capitalist' relations of production, which toppled the 'superstructure' of politics and law, and also the ideology which had inhabited it. Many versions have been assumed or justified – by Jaurès, Mathiez, Lefebvre, and their followers. Its traces survive even in the sophisticated *jeux d'esprit* of Michel Foucault, and in what Alfred Cobban calls the 'myth' of the French Revolution.[9] The relative paucity of Marx's own references to the events of 1789 suggests that he may have glimpsed the glaring truth about them – namely, that they provide a paradigm refutation, rather than a confirming instance, of his theory of historical change. The withering away of the feudal order had occurred long before the Revolution, and had involved the overthrow neither of the prevailing system of politics nor of the law which sustained it. By the time of the Revolution the remaining vestiges of feudalism were irksome ties and privileges which bore little relation to the real economic life of the nation and which were an object of resentment for that very reason. Whatever the ultimate causes of the Revolution, it is absurd to suppose that intellectual changes were not first among them: changes in what Marxists call 'the 'ruling ideology'. I do not mean only the writings of the *philosophes*, or the literary activity that surrounded them and which the authorities tried feebly to suppress. (Feebly by modern standards, at any rate, and feebly too by the standards of the Revolutionaries.) I mean also the incredible burgeoning of intellectual curiosity in eighteenth-century France: the local academies and literary societies;[10] the journals, libraries and museums; the *cabinets de lecture*; the movement for a secular education which had already led, in 1762, to the fatal (if to some extent understandable) suppression of the Jesuits; the pamphleteering, the atheistical diatribes; and the admiration for America and the American revolution, fuelled by a Benjamin Franklin who was to become, in Daniel Mornet's words, *l'homme le plus à la mode de Paris* during the years 1777–84.[11] And from the *political* changes initiated by this intellectual transformation there emerged a profound *economic* change: a change not towards capitalism but away from it, not in the direction of market relations and the wage contract but in the direction of price-control, rationing, and the re-infoedation of the worker. (The very same causality – from ideological frenzy to economic stasis – can be witnessed in all the revolutions inspired by Marx.) If the Marxist theory means anything, then this is exactly the sequence of events that must conclusively refute it, and no Ptolemaic system of epicycles, no 'relative autonomy', 'uneven development' or 'determination in the last instance', could possibly recommend the theory to anyone who looked impartially at the facts of eighteenth-century France.

Why, then, has the French Revolution been so often seized upon by Marxists as providing their paradigm of historical change? The question goes to the heart of my subject-matter. The French Revolution – or at least, that central episode upon which revolutionaries focus their attention – was the work of intellectuals, a manifestation of what Tocqueville called *la politique littéraire*.[12] The revolutionary consciousness lives by abstract ideas, and regards people as the material upon which to conduct its intellectual experiments. The charm of the Marxist theory is in describing revolutionary transformation as *inevitable*, and as originating wholly outside the realm of ideas: the experiment therefore is certain to succeed, and the human cost is down to history itself. Hence Marxism both sanctions the politics of ideas and at the same time excuses everything done in the name of it. It washes clean the guilty conscience in the same flood of ideas that first instilled its guilt. And, by excusing the Jacobins, Marxism covertly proposes them as an example. (Thus for Lenin, the revolutionary is 'the Jacobin indissolubly tied to the organization of the proletariat, which has become conscious of its interests as a class'.[13])

Tocqueville justly remarks, and with some amazement, that *parmi les passions qui sont nées de cette révolution, la première allumée et la dernière éteinte a été la passion irréligieuse.*[14] He goes so far as to suggest that the Revolution was animated by a *génie antichrétien*: although it was a *génie* which expressed itself with a monkish zeal, being less the child of Voltaire's tolerant deism than the re-creation, in modern dress, of the attitudes pilloried in *Mahomet*. It is this anti-religious zealotry which provides the first important clue to the revolutionary mentality.

The revolutionists had been schooled in the sceptical attitudes of Burke's 'literary cabal'.[15] Many of them also saw in religion a bastion of ancient privileges, and an unwelcome instrument of conciliation between the estates. However, the hatred unleashed against the Church at the very outset of the Revolution transcended anything that might be inferred from those two currents of opinion. Like the hatred towards the nobility, it was fed less on present injustices and corruption than on myths and stories: it was, in Burke's words, a 'work of art', like the 'anti-bourgeois' propaganda of subsequent revolutions. The hatred of the Church should be seen, I believe, as the hatred of a new priesthood for the old. The Church was less an obstacle to the work of Revolution, than a rival in its quest for the possession of men's souls. It was Sieyès, himself an unbelieving clergyman, who first announced the Revolution's astonishing claims over the human subject: 'The nation is prior to everything. It is the source of everything. Its will is always legal . . . The manner in which a nation exercises its will does not matter; the point is that it does exercise it; any procedure is adequate, and its will is always the supreme law.'[16]

As Cobban rightly says, such ideas do not belong to the Enlightenment (which had, at least in its intellectual aspect, stood for limited government and individual rights), but to a new order of political thinking.[17] Claims previously made only in God's name (and certainly never in the name of a king) have been transferred to, and imposed upon, the human world.

The first act of the Revolutionary Assembly was therefore to expropriate from the Church its lands, liens and revenues. This property had not always been wisely used. Nevertheless there can be no question that it was a greater public benefit in the Church's hands than in the hands of the Assembly, which used it merely as security for its own escalating debt, and ruined in a few years the savings of centuries. Furthermore, the church property contained much that had been given in perpetuity. The Assembly saw no obstacle in this fact, counting the will of the dead as nothing beside the pressure of its own self-made emergency.

The transfer of church property was no more than a first step: but it is a sure indication that the spirit of Jacobinism was triumphant long before the Jacobins took power. The Republic was now firmly set on the path which led towards its new religion. The ecclesiastical orders were to be dissolved and the loyalty of Catholic priests demanded: the 'non-juring' priest was to go in fear of his life, precisely because he recognized that the oath demanded of him was incompatible with his greater oath to God. Before the practice of the Christian religion had been entirely forbidden in the name of Reason, the Revolution began to introduce its own religious ceremonies: the Federations, described in ridiculous and glowing terms by Michelet, as occasions where 'man fraternized in the presence of God'.[18] And as the new Republic began to make itself, in this way, into the principal object of piety and the master of religious ceremonies, it conceived the ambition to transfer to itself all the functions of the Church. These functions – marriage, baptism, moral instruction, the provision of societies and ceremonies – were removed from the priesthood, not so as to return them to society, where they arose and whence the Church itself had captured them, but so as to bestow them on the State, as episodes in its own mystical legitimacy. It is to the French Revolution that we owe the new kind of 'civil marriage',[19] the civil holidays, the civil ceremonies, and, in due course, the partial expropriation from the family of its children. The motive was twofold: sacrilege, and re-consecration. The Revolution sought first to rid the bonds between people of their ancient sanctity, and therefore installed in the place of the Canon Law of marriage its 'Laws of Marriage and Divorce', calculated to undo as many marriages as were solemnized. (The Soviet code on 'family and marriage', introduced on 18 September, 1918, had precisely the same intention.) At the same time the Revolution sought to involve the State, as a mystical presence, in all the deepest human ties and aspirations, and so to attach their fund of pious feeling to itself.[20] Robespierre's Festival of the Supreme Being – in which, when all was revealed, the Supreme Being was seen to be mystically identical with the Revolution itself – was no eccentricity of an isolated fanatic. It was the culmination of a movement which expressed itself throughout the war against the Church. The advance of the Revolution saw not the abolition of the feudal order (which had long since disappeared), but a re-infoedation of the people, with the State as universal lord. Christianity had to be replaced with a creed more suited to this new obedience, a creed which did not insist so embarrassingly on the fact that the individual is answerable for his soul to God alone, and is the property of no earthly master – not even of the State.

What was this new creed which jostled aside the ancient claims of Christianity? Here we find one of the most interesting features of the revolutionary mentality, a feature to be observed as clearly in modern Leninism, in Maoism, and in the campus credos of the 1960s. The system of belief, while it has the same ability to absorb refutations and demonize opponents as traditional religion, is almost entirely devoid of content. Its goals and ideals are specified in terms so vague and sloganizing as to possess no real authority beyond that which must inevitably accrue to them in the course of battle. All that is certain – though this alone is sufficient – is that the world is full of obstacles to their realization, and that these obstacles must be destroyed by every means to hand. Of course, there was a philosophy – or, if you like, a theology – which the likes of Robespierre would summon to their aid when posing as men of principle. (In using the word 'posing' I do not mean to imply that they were not themselves taken in by their posture: on the contrary, the revolutionary mentality involves a constant process of 'self-captivation'.) The important fact, however, is the total lack of curiosity shown by the Jacobins as to what the People or the Nation might actually consist in, or as to how Liberty, Equality and Fraternity might actually be achieved. This absence of curiosity, which was in no way shared by the American Founding Fathers, is a permanent characteristic of the revolutionary consciousness. It can be seen in Marx, in his impoverished and impatient descriptions of the 'full communism' towards which history is tending. And it is even more evident in the writings of Lenin, in which the blocks of wooden language are constantly shifted so as to conceal the goal of communism from view.

In his attacks[21] on the 'prissy' Robespierre, the humourless Saint-Just, and the cranky puritanism of the Terrorists, therefore, Richard Cobb seems to me to miss precisely what is most interesting about these people, and most decisive in determining the character of their government: namely, that they in fact have *no* principles, *no* absolute restraints, and recognize no moral obstacles. Their doctrine proposes the goal of popular sovereignty. But it is a goal so vaguely described, so inherently made in the image of its own perpetual postponement, as to argue that doctrine had, for them, some other purpose than to guide, limit and cast judgment on their actions. Its purpose was not to forbid but to permit, not to judge but to exonerate, not to limit conduct but to enlarge it to the full extent of their moral exorbitance. Like the doctrine of 'full communism', it had no other meaning than to license destruction of existing things: it was not so much a system of belief as a system of unbelief, a means to the de-legitimization of rival powers, and to the undoing of true commitments.

The decisive feature of the revolutionary credo, therefore, is its provision of a criterion of legitimacy that no actual institution can ever pass. Rousseau recognized that he had provided such a criterion in the *Social Contract*, and at one point begged his reader's patience, saying that the apparent contradiction in his argument was no more than apparent.[22] He never troubled, however, to correct the appearance – nor could he have done so, for here, uniquely in Rousseau, appearance is reality, and the flow of slick deception is interrupted by the truth. All revolutionary ideologies are alike in this respect: 'direct democracy', 'social contract', 'the classless society', 'full communism' – all are names for the illegitimacy of actual things, rather than descriptions of a real alternative. The same is true, I would suggest, of the 'Rights of Man', at least as understood by the French Revolutionaries. Having made its Declaration, the Assembly at once went on to reject a proposal that the Duties of Man and of the Citizen should also be included. The Assembly did not wish to hear of duty and obedience; it sought for an instrument of rebellion, a doctrine that would undermine authority, not one that would restrain and discipline its own powers. Those who sever the demand for rights in so brusque a fashion from the burden of duties have, it seems to me, no desire to establish the institutions that will translate this metaphysical abstraction into a real social truth. The patient work of politics has already been set aside, and the word 'right' occurs on their lips not as a clearly defined goal but as a slogan, whose purpose is to carry forward the work of war.

The same is also true of the words 'the People', which Hannah Arendt has described as 'the key words for every understanding of the French revolution'.[23] For Arendt the term 'people' is saturated by the downward-directed compassion of the semi-privileged, towards *le peuple toujours malheureux*, as Robespierre described (and made) them. In fact, however, that connotation was no more than the necessary sentimentality of power. 'The People', like 'The Rights of Man' functioned as an instrument of de-legitimization. It is easy to show of any institution that it is *not* identical with 'the people': impossible to demonstrate that it *is*. One after the other the old instruments of law and compromise must fall before the hatchet of this potent word. It was to obtain no use more precise than in the phrase 'the enemy of the people', which licensed the elimination of whomsoever stood in the Revolution's way.

Of course, there is a positive *image* attached to such words as 'people' (and the more recent 'proletariat'), and this image is immensely important to the self-consciousness of revolution. The revolutionary lays claim to a *constituency*: but this constituency is removed from the real world by his very assumption of the right to speak for it. Thus any member of the working class who speaks out against the revolutionary communist becomes a class 'traitor'. As Lukács put it, one must never mistake 'the actual, psychological state of consciousness of proletarians for the class consciousness of the proletariat'.[24] Only the Party (the priesthood of revolutionaries) can tell you what the proletariat is thinking. Similarly only the Jacobins had access to the mind of the 'people', whose protesting members thereby merely 'betrayed' their collectivized identity, and ceased effectively to exist. The critics of the Jacobins therefore conveyed themselves to the guillotine as surely as the kulaks offered themselves to the firing squad. Something similar can be witnessed, too, in modern feminism, which pretends to speak for all women, and which turns in fury on the actual woman who, by failing to be a feminist, 'betrays' her sex. In all such cases the alleged constituency has been removed entirely from the real world: it has become something discarnate, a spirit force whose reality exists only in the moment of its conjuration. In Furet's words, *le peuple n'est pas une donnée, ou un concept, qui renvoie à la société empirique. C'est la légitimité de la Révolution, et comme sa définition même: tout pouvoir, toute politique tourne desormais autour de ce principe constituant et pourtant impossible à incarner.*[25]

Nothing positive, then, is offered in these sloganizing words by way of a belief or commitment. Indeed, the Revolution ensures that there *can* be no independent truth of the matter, as to what the rights of man, or the will of the people consist in. All procedures which might be used to determine those things are no sooner instituted than destroyed. Decree follows decree in such profusion as to cancel the certainty of law; the constitution is so vague and abstract, and so detached from any procedure for its invocation, as to serve as the flag on the masthead of the ship of state, rather than the hand at the wheel. Soon the citizen comes to recognize that he has no means of knowing, in advance of the drift of power, what the crucial terms refer to. They gain application only after the event, and if he then discovers that the enemy of the people was not Jacques, Marie or Hubert but himself, this too has no justification, and is further proof of the innocence, the other-worldly blamelessness, of power. The terms of the doctrine become warnings, which fill up the place of moral duty with the more pliable material of fear. The parallel with modern revolutionary ideology is remarkable. The function of ideology in the Marxist state is not that people should believe it.[26] On the contrary, the function is to make belief irrelevant, to rid the world of rational discussion in all areas where the Party has staked a claim, and where it is rash for the ordinary citizen to venture. These are the areas in which opposition takes root, and by issuing its ideology, the Party provides a guide to conduct – but a guide so vague that only by doing nothing can you improve your chances of survival.

The effect of revolutionary ideology is to introduce a kind of incurable nihilism into the social order, to infect all public processes with the sense that they are without justification, and to be understood merely as the passing drift of power. It therefore acts so as to negate the process of politics – the process which has the conciliation of rival interests as its meaning and its goal. By proclaiming a purely abstract 'Liberty', the Revolution facilitated the destruction of the qualified and partial liberties which come through the work of compromise. By offering abstract Right, it legitimized the destruction of law, and so made the concrete rights of citizenship impossible to claim. By proclaiming the sovereignty of the abstract People, it was able to remove power, privilege and property from every association of actual human beings.

With the ideological destruction of politics comes also a new form of language, in which power is decked out in glowing euphemisms, while its enemies are demonized in readiness for their 'liquidation'. Here too there is an interesting parallel between the French and the Russian Revolutions. Within a very short time the Assembly is talking to itself in a kind of Newspeak: those opposed to its measures are conspirators and heretics, or else the personal apex of obscure impersonal forces which surround the innocent fount of power: the clergy, the emigration, the counter-revolution. In place of individuals and their decisions we find a strenuous contest of energies: 'progress' against 'reaction', 'liberty' against 'despotism', the Revolution against the Old Regime; to which we can now add socialism against capitalism, bourgeoisie against proletariat, fraternal relations against imperialism. This *pan-dynamisme*, as Françoise Thom has called it[27], is a quasi-syntactical feature of revolutionary language, by which it drives the idea of personality from the description of power. In the debates of the Jacobin club the members of the Gironde appear not as persons, but as manifestations of a force – *le girondisme* – just as the opponents of our modern revolutionaries are but the visible sign of 'opportunism', 'deviationism', 'bourgeois revisionism', 'infantile leftism' and the rest. (Interestingly, Lenin explicitly compares 'opportunism' to the 'girondisme' which had so exasperated his Jacobin predecessors.[28]) The individual critic becomes 'an enemy of the people', whose rights are automatically cancelled by the 'people' from which they were originally derived – in just the same way as the privileges of the 'anti-socialist' are inevitably cancelled by his opposition to the 'socialism' which is the source of all available goods.

This is not the place to attempt a survey of the *langue de bois* of the French Revolution. A few examples may, however, help to show the workings of a mental process remarkably similar to that so chillingly satirized by Orwell, and so familiar to anyone who enters either a communist country or a British sociology department. In Aulard's collection of documents from the Jacobin Club[29] we find opponents described as *scélérats ligués avec l'étranger*; as *un ramas de factieux et d'intrigants*; as *un peuple de fripons d'étrangers, de contre-révolutionnaires hypocrites qui se placent entre le peuple français et ses représentants*, or simply as *ceux qui se groupent pour arrêter la marche de la révolution*. By contrast the *comité de surveillance* is a *sentinelle de la liberté*; the scaffold *l'autel de la patrie*; interrogation a *scrutin épuratoire*; and of course soldiers have long since ceased to be soldiers and attained the dignity of *défenseurs de la Patrie*. The language recognizes only *patriotes* and *suspects*, and proceeds with the same dichotomizing logic that has been persuasively analysed by Petr Fidelius, in his study of the editorials of *Rudé Právo*[30]. While the Jacobin club was perfecting the new mode of discourse, the public was being conscripted into the use of it. People were no longer to address each other as Monsieur or Madame, but only as *citoyen* or *citoyenne*: a word which was, in time, to acquire the same inverted-comma use that now attaches to 'comrade' in every communist country. (See Flaubert's *L'Éducation sentimentale*.) The ancient names of streets and communes were discarded, as were the names of the calendar. It is as though the revolutionists sought to destroy not opposition only, but the language through which opposition could be focused.[31] Here is an example of the process, contained in a submission on 12 November 1793, to the National Convention, from a zealous representative in Cahors:

> *J'ai trouvé ce département fanatisé, royalisé, girondisé, l'esprit pub-*
> *lique tué, un petit noyau de patriotes molestés, n'osant qu'à peine*
> *s'avouer montagnards; j'ai tout défanatisé, tout republicanisé, tout*
> *montagnardisé, tout ranimé, tout regenéré. Sociétés populaires*
> *épurées, administrations, tribunaux, municipalités purifiées,*
> *comités de surveillance crées; aristocrates, royalistes, fanatiques,*
> *girondins reclus; muscadins mis en réquisition, monopoleurs,*
> *egoïstes, richards, indifférents, sangsues du peuple pressurés . . .*[32].

As with its Marxist successor, such Newspeak also permits a novel kind of duplicity, in which words are used to mean both of two opposing things, and so emptied of all sense besides that conferred on them by power. Robespierre and Marat's discovery of the 'despotism of liberty' is but the extreme example of a process of semantic dissolution, prefigured in Rousseau's notorious 'forced to be free', which can be seen in all the revolutionary terms: liberty, equality, fraternity, people, republic – all are robbed of their sense, melted down, and reforged in a single weapon.

The destruction of language is part of a larger and more interesting destruction, of discourse as such. By 'discourse' I mean all those spontaneous exchanges through which people meet each other on terms, and reconcile their varied interests. The world of the revolutionary is one in which the other is either wholly *with* you, or wholly *against* you. Since he is Other, and therefore not transparently known, you can never assume the total identity of interests which would place him securely on your side. It follows that opposition cannot be *met*: it is not the object of negotiation, and can be the beneficiary of no agreement. Opposition is to be destroyed, *épuré*, 'liquidated'. As Saint-Just said in 1794, 'a Republic is constituted by the total destruction of that which is opposed to it'.[33] But this 'total destruction' (like all the 'total' ambitions of revolution) cannot be guaranteed. The result is, therefore, a universal suspicion of others and of the world. The revolutionary enters a world which has already secretly betrayed him, and from the very beginning he must expend his energies in rooting out the source of this betrayal – the 'enemy forces' which, in his pan-dynamic vision, are everywhere pulsing behind the illusory social calm. It is no accident that the Revolutionary Assembly established its 'Committee of Inquiry' into conspiracies (which was eventually to become the Committee of General Security) within months of obtaining power. The reign of suspicion was already installed, just as soon as the Tiers État – spurred on by the *trente voix*, but by no means controlled by them – forsook the path of compromise. The idea of betrayal was thereafter uppermost in its thoughts, growing until it had absorbed the whole of the Revolutionists' attentions. By 25 January 1792 Robespierre was speaking in the following terms: *Ils vous trahiront avec art, avec modération, avec patriotisme; ils vous trahiront lentement, constitutionellement, comme ils ont fait jusqu'ici; ils vous vaincront même, s'il le faut, pour vous trahir avec plus de succès.*[34] *Ils vous trahiront constitutionellement*: there speaks the authentic voice of revolution. For the revolutionary, all forms of constitutional government, all forms of parliament in which the outcome cannot be determined in advance by himself, are really forms of betrayal, for the very reason that they grant a voice and an influence to opposition.

We should not be surprised, therefore, at the extraordinary structure of central and peripheral committees which evolved during the course of the Revolution. Cochin has shown how a network of extra-governmental institutions was established in Brittany, in the years prior to 1789, and how a kind of 'dictatorship from above' was already exercised over 'patriots', long before the formation of the National Assembly.[35] Cochin pictures the *comités de correspondance particulière* as establishing a power 'machine' which was already geared for the subversion of the political process, and we should not ignore the resemblance of this 'machine' to the 'parallel structures' of modern revolutionary societies. The resemblance becomes yet more striking after the Revolution. More and more power is taken from the constitutional bodies and vested in committees, whose answerability to the Convention becomes increasingly a matter of form. The 'Central Committee of General Defence' was already in existence by 1792 (before the Terror), and the Committee of Public Safety emerged as the central, *secret* offshoot of this body. This latter committee was empowered to appoint its own *commissaires*, so enforcing its will throughout the country, and instituting a system of control remarkably similar to Lenin's democratic centralism, with the clubs making decisions which were then imposed upon the municipalities. By this time power was exercised wholly *outside* the Constitution, as it is in the Leninist state. The process culminated in the famous law of 14 Frimaire an II (4 December 1793): officially a measure for the reform of local government, but in fact ensuring the abolition of local government and the destruction of all institutions through which some degree of representation might be granted or achieved. All authorities and officials were placed by this law under the immediate control of the Committee of Public Safety (except for the police, which remained with the Committee of General Security). Henceforth government would be conducted in secret, and imposed by a network of 'transmission belts' (to use Lenin's idiom) on local activists obedient to the central command.

Those facts are well-enough known. What is not always admitted, however, is that, far from being aberrations, they are the correct expression of the revolutionary mentality. Suspicion, betrayal, a sense of universal enmity; measures which 'have not yet gone far enough'; contempt for compromise, and a demonization of opponents – all these are implicit in the revolutionary ideology, and require just the kind of government by conspiracy that has everywhere been the consequence of revolution. The power which acts 'in the name of the people' moves in a mysterious way. Those who exercise it do so in secret, without impeachment or compromise, and with nothing but a doctrine to establish their claim. Someone, they suspect, somewhere, disagrees with them and is therefore betraying them – for disagreement has treachery as its only outlet. The revolutionaries resort to ever more drastic measures in order to destroy this 'traitor'. Nevertheless, despite their efforts, despite their virtue, the enemy (who is, in truth, a projection of their own incurable fear of him) returns constantly to haunt them. At last they confront him: their very measures give reality to the monster of their dreams. But, by a wondrous alchemy, he comes before them in the guise of their own ideal. It is the people who must bear the revolutionary's insolence, and it is the people who finally rise against him in despair. (Hence Robespierre's need to distinguish the 'true' (imagined) from the 'false' (real) people; and hence Lukács's distinction between the mere proletarians themselves and the 'class consciousness' which is their 'truth', and to which only the party priesthood has access.) The only question, therefore, is whether the revolutionary can organize his network quickly enough, and efficiently enough, to prevent the people from combining against him. La Vendée was a near thing: later revolutionaries, while approving the method of genocide initiated by their French predecessors, have taken more precautions.[36] Not wishing to resort to terror in a moment of crisis, they have resorted to terror at the outset, and made it the normal condition of their liberated State.

When we come to consider the Terror, therefore, we should bear in mind that this event has recurred in later and more perfect instances. As with later terrors, that of the Jacobins has its ranks of 'progressive' apologists, arguing with Mathiez that the violence came from below, out of the just grievances of the *sans-culottes*[37], or with Greer that it was a reaction to people who genuinely wished to destroy the Revolution and who must therefore expect what they got.[38] Others have referred (in terms later used to excuse the Soviet terror, and still used to justify the poor Sandinistas in Nicaragua) to the 'emergency' caused by enemy 'encirclement'. None of those excuses should mislead us: the real question is, who created the revolution's enemies, and how? If I pillage your house, murder your wife, rape your daughter and torture your son, then of course I have to resort to 'emergency measures' if I am still to enjoy your co-operation in these domestic reforms.

Burke wrote his great essay in 1790: everything that I have described he had already noticed. As yet the King had not been executed, the Jacobins had not staged their *coup d'état*, the public rejoicings were still believable. But the spirit of the terror existed already; it remained only to transcribe it in legal form. Consider the law of 4 December 1792, a law which was frequently to be cited in the Revolutionary Tribunals. 'Whoever proposes to establish', it decrees, 'any power detrimental to the sovereignty of the people shall be punished by death.' Not 'tries', but 'proposes'; not 'illegal', 'unconstitutional' or 'seditious', but 'detrimental to the sovereignty of the people'; not 'fine' or 'imprisonment', but 'death'. And the whole thing is worded in such a way that no *mens rea* is required. It is no excuse that I did not *intend* my proposal to be 'detrimental to the sovereignty of the people'. Indeed, I could hardly know how to intend or to avoid such a thing, since only my accusers have the authority to define it. And on their definition hangs my life. There is embodied in the very form of such a law the abrogation of natural justice which was to conclude in the Terror. Moreover, the law is the perfect expression of the revolutionary doctrine, as I have described it. It permits everything to power, and allows nothing to its victim. Those interested should compare its wording with the sections of communist codes dealing with subversion, sedition, and 'damaging the interests of the State at home and abroad'. They will see that we are not dealing here with some judicial accident, but with the revolutionary mentality itself.

Of course, one must not overlook the relative mildness of the French Terror. Even at its height it never managed more than three or four thousand executions a month, and the total – including the *noyades* and similar atrocities – scarcely amounts to a day's work for a modern revolutionary. All the same, it is a sobering thought that the French prisons contained 400,000 people between 1793 and 1794: in appalling conditions which ensured the death of vast numbers of them. (The Bastille had disgorged precisely seven inmates when it was stormed four years before.) It is also a sobering fact that most of those held or executed were either political offenders, captured by the same vague language as that used in the law of 4 December 1792, or else ordinary people accused of the equally arbitrary 'economic' crimes. Nor were the victims united by any 'class interest' or 'emigré attachment': 84% of those executed belonged to the Third Estate, and by far the largest group among the sufferers was that of the working class.[39]

Rather than dwell on the actual cost of the Terror, however, it is more instructive to examine the new form of 'justice' which it inaugurated. We have already seen one instance of it. But it is by no means the most astonishing. Like other revolutions, that of France had recourse to retroactive legislation – even when the decree involved a penalty of death.[40] For it regarded law neither as a means for the resolution of social conflict, nor as an instrument of justice, but solely as a way of legitimizing its own insolent dealings. Like the doctrine of 'the People', the 'law' of the French Republic was a self-conferred title of approval, which the patriots pinned to their breasts with all the illusory dignity of a Brezhnev awarding one more medal to himself. Absurd crimes were invented, and given their Newspeak titles: *incivisme*, 'fraternizing with the emigration', 'making proposals detrimental to the sovereignty of the people', etc. A new class of offenders was discovered: the emigrés, strictly comparable in their liturgical function and ultimate fate to the kulaks of Stalin. The laws dealing with these monsters filled two huge volumes, and were so worded as to place on the accused the obligation to prove that he was *not* an emigré, and also so tortuously elaborated as to make this burden impossible to discharge.[41] Trials were frequently conducted by military commissions, and without right of appeal; eventually, after the Law of 22 Prairial (10 June 1794) there ceased to be any real distinction between crime and the suspicion of it, and the gap between accusation and guilt was finally closed.

The destruction of law in the name of legality is also, I suggest, a natural consequence of the revolutionary mentality. Lacking the spirit of compromise, the revolutionary also lacks the sense of law which springs from it. Law, for him, is a command, an edict, a pursuit of 'war by other means', to parody Clausewitz. It is not what it is for the man with *Rechtsgefühl*: a *procedure*, whose truth and justice lie hidden elusively within it, beyond the reach of any peremptory command.[42] Certain features of legal procedure are necessary for justice: the judge must be independent, the accused must have a right to defend himself, the law must be certain, knowable and not retroactive; and the record must be kept. No such matters have the slightest significance for the revolutionary, and all were abolished by the Revolutionary Tribunals. Indeed the modern revolutionary goes one stage further, dismissing the law and the judiciary altogether, as parts of the 'ideological state apparatus' whose function is to maintain the dominion of the ruling class.[43] Foucault (who, for all his protests, remained a naïve revolutionary to the end) repeats the worn-out Marxian cliché in stunning form: 'The revolution . . . can only take place via the radical elimination of the judicial apparatus, and anything which could introduce the penal apparatus, anything which could reintroduce its ideology and enable this ideology surreptitiously to creep back into popular practices, must be banished'.[44] (And how typical of the revolutionary, to see the heart of the law, not in its procedure, but in its *ideology*!) The French Revolution, Foucault adds, was a 'rebellion against the judiciary', and such, he implies, is the character of honest revolution everywhere.

Tocqueville remarked that there is the greatest difference between a 'revolution' (such as that of 1688, or that which founded the United States of America) through which law and adjudication continue undisturbed and which has the maintenance of law as one of its objects, and a revolution, such as the French, in which legal continuity is cast aside as an obstacle and an irrelevance.[45] As the example of Foucault shows, the distinction will never be significant to the revolutionary. Armed with his Rousseauist doctrines of popular sovereignty, or his Marxist ideas of power and ideology, the revolutionary can de-legitimize any existing institution, and find quite imperceivable the distinction between a law aimed at justice, and a law aimed at power. His own power is sustained by the promise to abolish it; he is therefore impatient with all institutions which use existing powers, in order not to abolish but to limit them.

That is the thought process which leads to the revolutionary courts. Lenin announced, as one of the ultimate benefits of communism, the 'withering away of law' which was to follow when class conflict had ceased. As a step in this direction he established a new form of procedure, based on the court-martial, but with the added refinement that the rules were not fully knowable in advance of the verdict. The judge can give the verdict only when he is sure that the Party will accept it. In the Soviet court the prosecutor, himself a servant of the Party, can effectively dictate the outcome of a trial (and will do so if the Party has an interest). The model for this Potemkin justice was provided by the Revolutionary Tribunal. And it is now the dominant system of legal procedure in all political trials, not only in the Soviet Empire, in China, Vietnam, Laos and Cambodia, in Cuba and Nicaragua, but also in Syria, Iran and Iraq, and in much of modern Africa.

The decisive features of the Revolutionary Tribunal were these: first the vagueness of the crimes that it was appointed to try. This pattern has been followed in modern revolutionary systems, where all crimes against the State are couched in terms so wide as to permit the entrapment of anyone required, and where there is no authoritative record that enables the citizen to improve his understanding. Under revolutionary justice you are tried, in the end, not for what you do but for what you are: emigré or kulak, Jew or anti-socialist, enemy of the people or running dog of capitalism – in each case crime is not an action, but a state of being.

Secondly, the procurator had effective charge of the proceedings and was under no discipline (in relation to evidence, precedent or procedure) that would compel him to deviate from his predetermined course. Thirdly, the accused was (after the law of 22 Prairial) denied the right to counsel, and could therefore put up no defence. Finally judges and juries were both chosen for their political reliability – a reliability which could in any case be assumed, once the penalties of rebellion were known.

The Paris Tribunal was a crude first attempt, and the Potemkin façade is now far better constructed. Those accused by the revolutionary State today have the right to employ a counsel, provided that he acts as a loyal servant of the Party and does not obstruct the smooth working of the trial. In recent political trials in Czechoslovakia certain lawyers have made the mistake of actually *defending* their clients: Josef Daniš, in the VONS trial, and Ján Čarnogurský in a related trial of Charter signatories. Both found themselves in the dock beside their clients, and condemned to the same penalty as they. The permission to employ a defence counsel is, in other words, a Potemkin permission, just as the procedure imposed on the prosecutor is a Potemkin procedure, which can be set aside whenever the Party requires. Of course, terror has dwindled to the state of 'graveyard stillness' which is the Potemkin equivalent of peace. Nevertheless, the structure of revolutionary justice remains, causing a universal caution, a habit of avoidance, whose main effect is to make the law irrelevant to daily life: a puppet-show whose squeaks and growls have long since lost their audience. If Poles, for example, are the least litigious of people, it is not because they have no quarrels with their neighbours: on the contrary. It is rather that you have to be a fool or a party member to take your quarrel to law. The effect of revolutionary justice is therefore to marginalize the law, to rid civil life of the law's moderating influence, and to force all conflicts underground, where they usefully contribute to the fragmentation of society upon which the totalitarian order depends.

The marginalizing of law is one aspect of the new style of revolutionary politics. There is an immense difference between Parliamentary government on the old model, in which the nobility always occupied the important offices, and the modern forms of constitutional democracy, in which government, like every other profession, has become a *carrière ouverte aux talents*. But there is a far greater difference between both those political systems and the government installed by revolution. Revolutionary government does not exist in order to balance interests and reconcile powers; its office is not that of counsel, nor does it construe its authority in judicial terms, as a final court of appeal in civil conflict. It exists for a purpose, and its legitimacy depends upon hurrying ever onwards towards a vague but imperative goal. Politics ceases to be a part of life, and becomes the whole of it. The philosophy which promises the end of politics, makes politics into the sole human end. Government can be limited neither in its sphere of application nor in its powers, while legitimacy is henceforth self-bestowed by doctrine, rather than acquired by habitual usage. Revolutionary government inevitably moves in a totalitarian direction, absorbing subsidiary social powers, and conscripting the population to its ill-considered purposes. Moreover, because the goal is always receding, the regime must manufacture a conspiracy of enemies, at home and abroad, who are acting so as to thwart its designs. To maintain the state of emergency, a spectacle must be provided: show-trials, executions, dawn arrests and denunciations; propaganda, ceremonies, military parades; and of course the threat, constantly made and often executed, of internal and external war.

A philosophical observation will perhaps clarify those remarks. The task of the French Revolution was to remake the social order in conformity with a 'social contract', to forge a society which was explicitly consented to by all its citizens. All individuals would henceforth be dissolved in a 'general will' whose movements would express their unqualified and unmediated participation: thus would 'the People' be born. In order to produce this 'society consented to', the revolution set about destroying the very process of consent. Traditional society, while not the *object* of consent, is nevertheless the *product* of consent, arising 'by an invisible hand' from the countless negotiations, agreements, votes and compromises that compose the unforced life of association. Philosophers of the 'social contract' attempt to translate this consensual order into an order consented to: to make the results of our contracts into the first object of them. But this is precisely to suppose that we could understand the outcome of social interaction before we had engaged in it: that we could agree *now* on a social order that arises from choices that we cannot *now* envisage.

Because of its goal-directed nature, revolutionary politics declares itself to be uniquely rational, even the rule of Reason itself. But collective rationality arises as a solution to what the game-theorist calls a 'co-ordination problem'. It comes about not because people have a common goal and work out a policy for achieving it, but because they are able to *adjust* their goals, and so create the flexible system of negotiation without which no man is able to respond reasonably or kindly to his fellows. The point has been expressed in many ways: in the Austrian theory of the market, in Burke's defence of prejudice and tradition, in Oakeshott's attack on 'Rationalism in politics'. Only its deep emotional need to ignore all criticism has enabled the revolutionary mentality to remain unaffected by this, the core argument of modern conservatism.

The new goal-directed politics licensed three moves in a totalitarian direction, moves which constituted a triumph for abstract Reason over concrete reasonableness. First came the attempt to absorb civil society into the state. I have already touched on this in the matter of the civil ceremonies. Equally important was the attempt to regulate relations between people, by replacing the consensual process of manners with a species of 'social decree', imposing forms of address and customs on the people in the interests of ideological conformity. In proceeding against the Church, the Assembly also made it quite clear that it recognized the rights of *no* autonomous institutions, and subsequently (18 August 1792) decreed accordingly: 'a state that is truly free ought not to suffer within its bosom any corporation, not even such as, being dedicated to public instruction, have merited well of the *Patrie*.' (Note the Newspeak.) The Republic thereafter permitted partnerships – associations for gain – but dreaded those unselfish people who sought to unite for some religious, charitable, literary or scientific purpose. In fairness to the Revolutionists, it should be said that private charities had suffered considerably in the last days of the Ancien Régime.[46] But they had suffered from that very same disrespect for free association and corporate personality which reached its culmination in the decree of 18 August 1792.

Revolutionary governments have since gone through the same cycle of 'moral expropriations' as the French Revolutionists, nationalizing all institutions, from universities and churches, down to chess clubs, orchestras and discussion groups. (The special case of Poland is the exception which proves the rule.) Everywhere you observe the collapse of institutional life, especially in the countryside of central Europe, once so rich in autonomous associations and local loyalties. Not only have charities been expropriated, and their funds diverted in defiance of trust; charities themselves have been outlawed. The process began after the Russian Revolution, with the confiscation of all church property, the imprisonment, torture or murder of the more active members of the clergy, and the forbidding of any kind of social work on the part of those in Holy Orders.[47] When the first of the great famines arrived in 1921, the Church established a relief committee; but it was at once decreed illegal and dissolved. A civilian committee to provide homes for the millions of orphans created by famine and civil war was also dissolved, and replaced by another organization, under direct command of the Cheka, which had its own uses for homeless children. It is true that the Bolsheviks did, at one point, permit a group of private citizens to form an 'All Russian Famine Relief Committee'. But the function of this Committee was to attract funds from the West (and from the United States in particular). Once the donations had arrived, the Committee was arrested, its organization dissolved, and its funds appropriated for the use of the Party.

Since that time, and until recent changes in Poland and Hungary, there have been few legal charities in communist countries, other than those organized (under great difficulties and in constant risk of expropriation) by the Catholic Church in Poland,

and by the Protestant Churches in East Germany. Of course, there are *illegal* charities – mutual support groups, 'flying universities', and so on. In 1985, for example, certain good citizens of Hungary combined in order to relieve the sufferings of the poor (of whom there are increasingly many) but they were compelled to meet, to raise funds, and to distribute relief in secret, and in constant fear of reprisals. Moreover, the holdings of such charities, lacking the protection of the law, are at the mercy of those who control them. The whole concept of 'beneficial ownership' has been expelled from public life.

That the French Revolution did not proceed so far is less important than the fact that it moved in this direction at all, that it began to use the machinery of the State in order to destroy the institution-building impulse which is the foundation of society. Perhaps it did not need Hegel to demonstrate to us that State and Civil Society are distinct 'moments' in the life of a body politic; perhaps it did not need Solidarity to remind us of the catastrophe that ensues, when the distinction between them (between *władza* and *społeczeństwo*) is abolished. But defenders of the French Revolution often fail to see that the suspicion of civil society lies in the very spirit of revolution and in the 'politics of goals' which it imposes.

The second totalitarian consequence of the new politics was the tendency towards ownership of the individual by the state. As Tocqueville astutely points out, this tendency is present in those statist conceptions of reform that preceded the Revolution and which did so much to make it possible.[48] But it took on a new character and a new impetus with the events of 1789. Besides all that we have already touched on, concerning the administration of justice; besides the system of internal passports, price controls, compulsory loans, and laws against association; besides the interdiction exerted over the publication, expression and even possession of opinions 'detrimental' to the 'People'; besides the attempt to extinguish the national religion of France, and to expropriate its moral functions – besides all this there arose two new and momentous changes in the relation between the individual and the state: the system of compulsory education, and the *levée en masse*. The first of these was brought to fruition only by Napoleon; the second of them made Napoleon possible.

It proved impossible, in the event, to carry through the educational programmes: private schools were permitted to re-open, when it was discovered that no other means existed to ensure the goal of universal instruction. Neutrally described, such a goal can hardly be disapproved of. And from Lenin to the Sandinistas it has been a vital part of revolutionary propaganda to devote itself to campaigns of education (which increasingly turn, however, into campaigns of 're-education' of the kind which can last for a lifetime). Nevertheless, the value that we attach to education should not blind us to the startling fact that the educational level of the French declined during the Revolutionary period.[49] Nor should it cause us to excuse the extraordinary presumption of a sovereign power that obliges us to educate our children, and obliges them to attend schools of its own devising. The new role of the state in our lives is given a further, and chilling twist by Saint-Just, in educational proposals which he did not live to carry through:

> The child, the citizen, belong to the *Patrie*.
> Communal instruction is necessary.
> Children belong to their mother until the age of five, if she clothes and feeds them. After that, to the Republic, until they die.[50]

What Saint-Just here makes explicit in his words is elsewhere implicit in the acts and projects of the Revolutionists. The revolutionary's advocacy of education conceals another and vaster design: to lay hold of the infant soul, and mould it according to his own requirements.

Universal military conscription is at one level merely an extrapolation to the maximum of a practice already familiar in the post-Renaissance monarchies. However, the *levée en masse* expresses a whole new attitude to the condition of citizenship. The entire nation was now to be flung at its 'enemies' (whose enmity was caused, not by the French nation, but, at least in part, by the belligerent policies of its leaders). Any able-bodied man could be called up, at any time and for any cause. It was not only to war that the French population was conscripted: the Revolutionary Armies were given extensive policing functions and maintained as a permanently mobilized vehicle for the execution of revolutionary commands. The Revolutionary Armies, the *commissaires* and *sociétés populaires* together provided a foretaste of the system which was to reach perfection in the *komsomol*. For the first time in history we encounter a society *conscripted for peace*, in which the conditions of peace and war have become effectively indistinguishable. The whole of France lived under a kind of martial law, in which the citizens subjected also served in the army which subjected them. It is true, as the Revolutionaries declared, that each stage in their reform introduced new liberties: but they were liberties for the government, to exert over the citizen rights of ownership that had seldom been known in Christian Europe, and which had never been asserted so extensively. Once again, we have a remarkable foretaste of the pattern to come.

This brings us to the third totalitarian tendency in the politics of goals: the destruction of the economy, and the elimination from public life of the habit of responsible accounting. The expropriation of the church lands sets the pattern for what was to follow. These resources, husbanded over centuries, were squandered almost at once, used first as security for increasingly inflated *assignats*, and finally sold off in the attempt to finance the projects, the bureaucracies and the wars of revolution. The *assignat* provided a foretaste of the 'soft currencies' of modern revolutionary states: pieces of paper whose meaning is a dishonoured promise, and whose ultimate purpose is not to facilitate economic transactions, but to exploit them to the limit of their taxable surplus. The rouble and the zloty, like the chits issued under the 'trucking system', are not only ways of paying the labourer for his hours of work, but also ways of extracting more labour from him through a tax on his subsequent transactions. The same was true of the *assignats*, which were an open mortgage of the entire public capital, including the human capital which was the principal part of it.

By the winter of 1793–4 the economic cost of the Revolution was apparent to everyone: price controls and rationing, queues and black markets, and that slow rotting away of honesty which is the inevitable consequence of an arrangement in which private property is only spasmodically respected, and in which too much is owned by the State. Of course things did not go so far in this direction as they were taken by Lenin and his successors. The idea of an economy *entirely* owned and run by the State had yet to seize the imagination of the power-hungry intellectual. Nevertheless, the decree against *accaparement* (26 July 1793), which dealt out terrible punishments for hoarding, provides an interesting anticipation of the famine-inducing measures of more recent revolutions[51]; while the forced loan of September 1793, combined with the 'General Maximum', were as near as the Revolutionaries – with the means at their disposal – could come to exerting their will over the entire national economy. The result was a destruction of free trade, a re-infoedation of the citizen, and a subversion of the habits of accounting.

This public *gaspillage* is a striking instance of what follows when the dead and the unborn are disenfranchised, as they are by every revolution. Far from being a sentimental indulgence, an irrational brake on the use of present funds, the respect for the dead, and for the will of the dead, is part of prudent husbandry. The recognition that goods are held in trust from past to future generations and that rights of ownership are conditional on responsible accounting, is the true source of social saving. The habit of saving is a form of piety, and the destruction of this habit by revolutionary governments lies at the heart of their economic failure, and of their need to live by spoliation.

This brings me to a final interesting parallel between the French and the Russian Revolutions. The Revolution was founded on a principle of 'de-legitimization': no government was to be legitimate unless it conformed to the principle of popular sovereignty. That this was an implied declaration of war on France's neighbours was made clear in a Decree of November 1792, offering assistance to all peoples who 'rise against their governments'. The threat was carried into reality in February 1793, with the declaration of war against England. Peace and stability were re-established in Europe only after Wellington's victory at Waterloo: by that time the international order had been entirely discomposed, and untold suffering inflicted on the peoples of Europe.

Leninism, being founded, like the French Revolution, in a universalist ideology, regards no national boundary as legitimate, and declares itself on the side of 'liberation' everywhere. Both states illustrate the need felt by revolutionary governments to impose on their neighbours, and to fill the world with protests of Potemkin friendship. (For the Revolutionary, Potemkin friendship is far more valuable than real friendship, since real friendship is freely given, whereas Potemkin friendship is controlled.) The dictated friendship which bound the states of Eastern and Central Europe derived, like the friendship dictated by the Revolutionists to the people of Holland, from the ideology of revolution: from the thinking which removes legitimacy from all actual institutions in the name of an unattainable ideal. The ideology which excuses the monopoly of power, therefore, also justifies, and indeed requires, its unlimited expansion.

Given those similarities, we may well ask why the French Revolution failed to achieve the stagnant durability which was so striking a feature of its successor. The explanation, I venture to suggest, lies not in the ends of the Revolutionaries, but in the deficient means available for their realization. Power came too quickly to the Jacobins, and its seizure was not preceded by that patient work of organization to which Lenin devoted so much of his energy. Their 'party-mindedness' was a fragile and fissiparous thing, which did not survive their own personal downfall. The Communist Party was built slowly, first on a foundation of loyalty and discipline, and then on a clear principle of rational self-interest. Once the Bolsheviks took power the party member was to obey the one above him, and to control the one below, for the reason that only through the Party could there be privilege or power. The first work of the Party was therefore to destroy all forms of advantage that were not provided by itself. This is the secret of communist longevity. Once in power, the entire ruling élite can be destroyed without damage to the structure, and without the rank-and-file acting upon any principle besides that of 'endarkened self-interest'. The Party is sustained not by plans (which are merely liturgical fictions), but by the very invisible hand which Adam Smith had discerned in the market economy.

Furthermore, the Revolutionaries did not fully grasp the value of front organizations, or of the network of Potemkin institutions which play such an important part in dispelling truth from its central place in social discourse, and putting power and ideology there instead. The success of revolutionary government, and its transition to the stable point of 'graveyard stillness', depend upon the ability to produce a public habit of mendacity. False-hood must become a way of life; as Havel puts it, people must learn 'to live within the lie'.[52] The Revolutionists went some way in this direction. But they did not surround themselves with the necessary mask (the *manto*, as the Sandinistas call it), and worked always in the knowledge – fatal to their project – that the truth was still perceivable. In the communist State, with its Potemkin courts, Potemkin churches, Potemkin schools, universities and academies, with its Potemkin patriots like Jaruzelski and its true patriots like Wałesa, Havel and Sakharov presented to the people as Potemkin traitors, we find the ideal of revolutionary order: a State in which the question of legitimacy cannot be answered in the negative, for the reason that, lacking a forum, a voice and a language, it cannot be raised.

But the Revolutionists' comparative failure was not entirely their fault. They lacked the technological resources available to their successors: in particular they lacked the complete control over the means of communication, and the technology of surveil-lance, which have enabled their successors to act rapidly at a distance and to impose their will without delay wherever force is needed. Human progress has overcome the Revolutionists' disa-bility, and there is no longer any reason why a revolution, once successfully established, should thereafter lose power.

I have tried to defend Burke's conservative reaction to the French Revolution; but I am conscious that I have done no more than

identify one spiritual current within that great event. I am conscious too, that I have said nothing to describe its meaning, and
that until I do so, all talk of a conservative 'reaction' must be
premature. In conclusion, therefore, I shall offer an interpretation of the revolutionary consciousness, which will, I hope, explain precisely why Burke and his successors have found it so
abhorrent.

The actions which have occupied my attention involved a
formidable concentration of religious energy. But this energy
was not turned towards the transcendental. On the contrary, the
Revolution placed its gods on earth, and described them in 'the
language of man': liberty, equality, fraternity. Yet what do those
idols amount to? The pursuit of them was to destroy every
imperfect human value – freedom, justice, and fellowship –
which they might otherwise have sanctified. Moreover, they
were to threaten, not only the religious and moral, but also the
aesthetic values of our civilization, mobilizing people behind
one of the greatest acts of organized vandalism in the history of
mankind.[55] These abstractions stepped down into the world of
men from the sphere of metaphysics and laid waste the patient
work of centuries, finding nothing in the merely empirical world
that could match their own geometrical perfection. At the same
time, the revolutionaries began to adore their idols, not in spite
of, but because of the fact that they filled the world with terror.
'Liberty', since it denoted no achievable goal, came to refer to the
purely *negative* principle, that all powers on earth are powers of
usurpation, and could therefore be destroyed. Likewise, 'equality' referred to no achievable order: it meant neither justice, nor
law, nor that 'respect for persons' which was set before us by
Kant. It too had a negative application: it was a weapon against
privilege, a denial of distinction, and an inspiration to the eye
and hand of envy.

Worst of the idols, however, was the third: fraternity. This
most potent of abstractions has been the source of socialist
dreams from the Revolution to the present day. The General Will
of Rousseau, the People of Robespierre, the 'phalanstery' of
Fourier, the commune of Marx, the *fascio* of the Italian anarchists,
the *groupe en fusion* of Sartre: all express the same contradictory
idea, of a free society without institutions, in which people
spontaneously group together in life-affirming globules, and
from which the dead shell of law, procedure, custom and authority has fallen away. The aim is for a 'society without obedience', indeed, for a 'unity in disobedience', where conflict,
competition, domination and subservience are all unknown.
Each version of the dream is as unreal as the last, and none more

unreal than that which has dominated radical socialism in our time: the dream of the great alliance, the 'historic bloc', as Gramsci described it, which brings worker and intellectual together in defiance of established power. Contemplating, Pygmalion-like, the worker of his fantasy, our modern revolutionary is stirred by a passionate love: love for himself, as the architect of this noble vision. The heroic worker combines in his protean personality the contradictory attributes of self-affirming liberty and class solidarity; he is at once the proud individual, answerable to himself alone, and the submissive unit, joined to his companions in the universal sympathy of the 'mass'. As with Robespierre's *peuple*, which cannot be *toujours malheureux* and the object of compassion, and at the same time sovereign, and without the need for a condescending love, so too with the industrial worker. The proletarian of the Leninist must mirror the striving individualism of the alienated intellectual; but at the same time he must display the complete social immersion, the 'class solidarity', from which the intellectual feels himself so tragically sundered. The worker of the future, like the 'People' of Robespierre, must be completely free, and at the same time bound by the consoling solidarity of the oppressed. The contradictory nature of the idol is the immediate result of its having stepped from the transcendental into the empirical realm. And yet the idol is worshipped as such, in full consciousness of its impossibility. This transcendental unity of the 'people', this unmediated, un-negotiated bond in which intellectual and worker are mystically united and dissolved, flesh of each other's flesh, is described precisely by Sartre as 'a concrete totalization continually de-totalized, contradictory and problematic, never closed back on itself, never completed, yet nevertheless one single experience'.[54] And in pursuit of this acknowledged contradiction men like Sartre are prepared to pull down all actual institutions, all actual relations between people, all that is merely negotiated, compromised and half-convinced. As with the Revolutionists, the *real* reference to the transcendental, which is there in the humble forms of ordinary love, is cancelled, on behalf of an earthly idol whose sole reality is to destroy human relations, by measuring them against a standard which they cannot attain.

We are confronted by an astonishing fact, one that we should treat with all due solemnity since it touches on the meaning of our lives. Liberty, equality and fraternity become the objects of religious zeal only to destroy freedom, justice and fellowship. Their earthly reality is precisely Nothing, and the spirit of nihilism blows through them with a force that is all the more mysterious in that we the worshippers provide it.

Let us return for a moment to the religion against which the Revolutionists rebelled, and the fundamental doctrine which the deists and humanists had already cast aside as unfit for human Reason. God, says the Christian, has three natures, and we come to him by three separate paths: when we worship him as transcendental law-giver; when we encounter him incarnate; and when the Holy Spirit moves in and around us in its work of peace. To express the thought in other, and more mitigated, terms: our worship is owed to something that is not of this world, and whose law-giving capacity is inseparable from its transcendence. But this does not mean that the world is *bereft* of God, or that we can find him nowhere in our experience. On the contrary, sanctity comes to us in two modalities; and not to respond to its imperative is to live incompletely and meaninglessly.

The first modality lies in the incarnate person: the animal in whom the light of reason shines, and who looks at us from eyes which tell of freedom. Only now and then – in love, hatred and desire – does the reality of this incarnation overwhelm and trouble us.[55] But the underlying sense of it is there in all respect, and all affection. It is this which forbids us to treat another's life and freedom as expendable, or to weigh his survival in the balance of our own individual profit. Our calculations stop short at the threshold of the other, precisely because his flesh is sanctified. The first effect of the revolutionary mentality is to undo this experience of the sacred. Once the idols have been brought to earth, individual freedom, and the flesh which harbours it, become *property*. They can be placed in the balance of calculation, and discarded 'for the public good'. Revolution leads to murder, for the simple reason that it rids the world of the experience upon which the refusal to murder depends.

The second modality of the sacred lies in counsel, association, and institution-building. In countless ways men combine in a spirit of conciliation, willing to renounce even their dearest ambitions for the sake of agreement with their fellows. In the true council, men are prepared to accept a corporate decision which corresponds with nothing that they previously desired, for the reason that the council itself is vested with authority. The spirit of co-operation may issue in decisions which coincide with the will of no participant: and this corporate will in turn implies a corporate liability, and a corporate right and wrong. In such circumstances the law speaks sometimes of a trust, sometimes of a corporate person, sometimes of an 'unincorporated association' – and through each concept endeavours to give reality to a will, and a responsibility, that attaches to no individual man. It thereby glosses a deeper moral concept, known to Quakers as 'the sense of the meeting', and to the rest of us as 'we'.

This 'we' bears a countenance: it has authority, right, responsibility and freedom. We gladly submit to it, and embody its personality in offices, insignia and ceremonies. For modern man, of course, the ceremonial aspect of membership is more muted than it was, certainly more muted than in the guilds immortalized in *Die Meistersinger* (the only great drama which has a corporate person as its central character). Nevertheless, the ceremony of membership exists, and especially in that haven of free association which is the United States of America. People *celebrate* their membership, just as adolescents celebrated once their transition to the adult world. In such ways, the spirit of counsel surrounds and transforms our lives, enriches the individual and offers him not only an experience of community, but a sense of public validity. From our respect for the 'small platoon' far greater emotions rise in us: our sense of duty is spread more widely than the circle which inspired it, to embrace other places and other times. We come at last to respect the dead and the unborn; and this is the experience upon which free and stable government is founded.

The process of politics thrives, I suggest, only where the claims and duties of the corporation are recognized. The most striking fact about the revolutionary is that – bowing to the idol of a 'General Will', or some other abstract 'fraternity' which knows no mediation, no negotiation and no half-heartedness – he finds himself at once suspicious of real associations. With the advent of revolution the true work of institution-building comes to an end; so too does charity; so too does every other form of combination which lies outside the 'People's' or the Party's control. There results a society devoid of counsel, in which (as Cochin recognized[56]), decisions have all the impersonality of a machine. In this respect too, revolution turns against the world: it leads to the destruction of corporate persons, just as it leads to the murder of individuals, since it has abolished the experience of sanctity which conditions our respect for them.

To put the point in a nutshell: the revolutionary transfers his worship to the world, and so destroys the two experiences of God that are actually contained in it. It is part of *le génie du Christianisme* to have summarized these experiences in the doctrines of the incarnate God and the Holy Spirit. And it is a further instance of its *génie* to have recognized the existence of the Spirit as a person, and so to have founded a personal and independent church. But the language of Christianity is not imposed on us. In more secular idiom – the experience of authority (and therefore the impulse to obedience) comes to us in three related forms: the authority of the moral law, whose foundation is transcendental; the authority of incarnate freedom; and the authority of counsel. If I use the Christian language it is because it identifies more accurately the points at which our lives are consecrated, and which call forth the revolutionary sacrilege.

Moreover, in judging the revolutions of Europe, it is to the religion of Europe that we should turn. The Revolution is, I believe, a supreme act of Christian disobedience. Rather than worship a transcendental God, the revolutionary brings him to earth, and reshapes him in the form of an ideal community. At once the two other forms of obedience are cancelled, and God's face in the world is overcast and imperceivable. The worship of the idol becomes a worship of nothing – but it is a potent nothingness, which threatens everything real. It is the very same nothingness which, captured in a handkerchief, caused Othello to destroy the sacred thing which God had given him – and all for Nothing. As to what, or who, this Nothing consists in, the question answers itself.

(The author is grateful to the Social Philosophy and Policy Center of Bowling Green State University, Ohio, for the leisure necessary to work on this paper.)

Reprinted from Ceri Crossley and Ian Small (eds), *The French Revolution and British Culture*, Oxford, OUP, 1989.

20
TWO ENLIGHTENED IRISHMEN

I G. B. SHAW

Most letters to the press, in my experience, are too long to be published. Since the writers must know this fact, their aim in putting pen to paper cannot be the simple one of publication. In fact, unpublishable letters to the press constitute a peculiar kind of speech-act, and one which does not fit easily into recognized categories. Certainly, they are not addressed to any person so low in the hierarchy of listeners as the Reading Public. It is arguable, indeed, that unpublishable protests are addressed not to men but to God; and that the letter to the press is the nearest that a fully modern person may come to prayer. It is therefore hardly surprising that the recent declaration by the Editor of *The Times*, that unpublished letters would no longer be automatically answered, elicited a response that was less like the clamour of an indignant readership than the lament of an abandoned congregation.

Things were different when Bernard Shaw first began writing to the press in 1875. Judging by the contents of *Agitations: Letters to the Press 1875–1950* (eds. Dan H. Laurence and James Rambeau, London, 1986), editors of the *Star*, the *Pall Mall Gazette*, the *Saturday Review*, and even the *Daily Chronicle*, were quite prepared to publish letters of any length – and no doubt saved themselves considerable sums in doing so. Shaw estimated that he had lost at least four years of creative life in writing 'superfluous letters': nevertheless, he intended the result, even when three or four times the length of a modern feature article, to be read and debated, and took evident pleasure in the upset that he caused.

The reader of Shaw's prefaces, and of *The Intelligent Woman's*

Guide to Socialism and Capitalism, will know what to expect from a volume of his letters. Although Shaw was capable (as in his contribution to the first volume of *Fabian Essays*) of presenting a reasoned argument in a way that demands an intricate and uncertain answer, his rhetorical gifts, and monstrous self-opinion, enabled him too easily to sweep aside the obligation to be serious. His indignation is for the most part factitious, and his strange ability to be most emphatic precisely where he is most mistaken is a source of constant irritation and fatigue. Shaw's reputation does not stand as high as once it did: the wit and charm of the plays are no longer widely mistaken for profundity, and his conceited attitudinizing ceases to amuse. At the same time, he was a titanic force in modern British culture, and the origin of all that is best – as well as much that is mediocre – in the Fabian mentality. The reader of these letters is likely to feel nostalgia for the old *New Statesman,* and for the days when socialism was a half-believable pastime of a charmed upper class. The gaiety and garrulousness of Shaw's commitments contrast refreshingly with the drab resentments that have now usurped their heritage, and Shaw's culture and learning add a dimension to the socialist programme which has long since disappeared.

Nevertheless, except for his brilliant music criticism, Shaw's writings seem now to be devoid of the common sense that he so zestfully affected, and more like the derring-do of a precocious schoolboy than the mature reflections of a man. It is of some interest to discover, in these letters from an unbelievable seventy-five years of active literary production, that neither the style, nor the thought, nor the feeling, shows much tendency to develop beyond the point which they had already reached when, at the age of eighteen, Shaw wrote to *Public Opinion,* puncturing the illusion that the poor of Dublin might attend Evangelistic services simply for the good of their souls.

Perhaps the most interesting section of this scrupulously edited volume is that containing G. K. Chesterton's reply to a Shavian review, and the ensuing letters by both men. Shaw and Chesterton endeavour to refute each other over a question that remains of the greatest interest long after the event: the question whether socialism, in the form advocated by Shaw, must inevitably lead to a 'Servile State' (as Belloc described it), without true responsibility, true charity, true ambition or true individual life. Such was Chesterton's claim, and it was put forward in a style which matches the eloquence and robustness of Shaw. Neither correspondent argues at the depth at which so difficult a question could really be decided. But I do not think that it is merely my own inclination to agree with Chesterton that leads to the sense that, beneath a similar gaiety, and a similar love of paradox, there runs through his style a firm stream of common sense that is nowhere to be found in Shaw.

It is to this exchange of letters that one should return, I believe, in estimating Shaw's value as a polemicist. He is, perhaps, unfairly judged by the letter written after a tour of Leningrad and Moscow, in which he praises the 'new dispensation' established by Mr Stalin. He is certainly unfairly judged by his expostulations against theatrical censorship – in which, like all decent people, he showed himself unable to imagine how far indecency might go. He is perhaps more fairly judged by the letters in which he denounces the ignorant respect for family and motherhood that makes us reluctant to surrender our children to the care of a benign and omnicompetent state. But it is only when caught up in dialogue with an equal that Shaw's mind fully opens, as he composes for himself the theatrical utterances appropriate to his combative role.

Concerning no subject would Shaw be deterred by the minor accident of total ignorance from penning a definitive opinion. When it came to music, however, he was far from ignorant; and when it came to the music of Wagner he was, by the standards of the time, something of an expert. For those with an interest in truth, the letter about the *Ring*, written to the *Daily Chronicle* in 1898 (the year of *The Perfect Wagnerite*), is therefore among the most engaging. It is perhaps hard, looking back on it, to imagine the difficulties experienced by contemporary reviewers in understanding Brünnhilde's denunciation of Siegfried's 'lie'. But Shaw's bold commitment to a total vision of the *Ring*, combined with a minute attention both to the dramatic detail and to the Wagnerian sources, enables him to write with an authority which is elsewhere no part of his achievement. If Shaw had stuck to music criticism he would now be read more seriously. But he would also be read less widely, and, as his letters display, it was width and not depth which provided his contemporary appeal.

II   CONOR CRUISE O'BRIEN

The unifying theme of Conor Cruise O'Brien's book of essays, *Passion and Cunning* (London, 1988), is politics: both political reality and political ideas. As one might expect, South Africa and Israel loom large in O'Brien's perspective. Nevertheless, they do not dominate it, and the reader is treated to a great many serious reflections, on themes ranging from terrorism to academic freedom, from Bobby Sands to Norman Podhoretz, and from Robespierre to Pope John Paul II. Despite the variety, however, the essays are all addressed (if perhaps subconsciously) to a single question: what role is there for an enlightened liberal in a world increasingly persuaded of the damage done by enlightened liberals?

In the title essay, O'Brien argues that Yeats's interest in the Irish blueshirts was not the temporary foible depicted by his posthumous apologists, but a serious attempt on the poet's part to identify himself with a political movement, and to find political expression for his own romantic conservatism. It is not surprising that this well-argued essay caused a stir when it was first published. For it remains true that artists and writers who lend support to any kind of fascism, in any country and at any time, are not pardoned by history – 'history' being another name for the intellectual establishment. On the other hand, of course, you can lend as much support to communism as you like – you can apologize, as G. B. Shaw did, for murder, and paint the most terrible atrocity as a necessary sacrifice – and 'history' will neither notice your crime nor tolerate those who allude to it.

O'Brien is too sophisticated a literary critic, and too honest an intellect, to side with 'history' in this contest. He sees that the crime of Yeats did not diminish his stature as a poet: politics entered his later poetry only to be transformed into something deeper. Moreover, Yeats's toying with fascism never led him to apologize for murder, nor even to notice that murder is precisely what you can expect from a political movement whose main aim is not to negotiate with opponents but to exclude them from power. Maybe that was naïve of Yeats; and maybe his scant respect for parliamentary institutions and negotiated policies showed a culpable lack of common sense. But the fault is by no means rare. Here is O'Brien, in another essay:

> to *Sandinistas*, national humiliation is precisely what Reagan insists on, when he refuses to negotiate with them, and tells them to negotiate with the *contras*. It is not in the nature of *Sandinistas* to negotiate with *contras*. *Not* negotiating with *contras* is what their whole intellectual, moral and emotional formation is all about. *Patria Libre o Morir*.

The passage is intended as a compliment – one among many. Since a Contra is, by definition, anyone who is opposed to the Sandinista revolution, it follows that, in one respect at least, the heroes chosen by Yeats agree with those chosen by O'Brien.

Reading the long essay on Nicaragua I was in fact constantly taken back to the 1930s. Not to Yeats and the few scattered writers like him, but to the many more who were on the side of 'history', and whose utterances on its behalf have been so devastatingly analysed by Paul Hollander in *Political Pilgrims* (1981). In Nicaragua, O'Brien finds a society pulsing with inner dynamism, an ubiquitous hope and faith, an unforced unity and loyalty to the leadership – the very same phenomena which made such an impact on the customers of Potemkin Tours. All his critical sense seems to desert him, as he solemnly repeats the sentimentalities of revolution, finding, in the blocks of Sandinista-speak, a revelation of faith and a promise of liberation. The bathos and self-intoxication of revolutionary politics are breathed in by the author, and out at the reader, as though they were some kind of life-giving oxygen, and not the death-dealing ozone which has extinguished so much liberty and life.

Like many previous pilgrims (to Cuba, China, Vietnam, as much as to the pre-war Soviet Union), O'Brien sees the revolutionary process as expressing a new species of nationalism – one in which a nationalized religion unites the people in the cause of their own regeneration. He also believes that this nationalism somehow justifies the Sandinistas, in a way that their revolutionary socialism would not. In these circumstances, he seems to imply, there is no immediate need for opposition, or for the liberties which are fundamental to it, since the people (with the exception of a few middle-class reactionaries who don't count) are united behind the Sandinistas, and the Sandinistas can speak for them with an authentic voice.

It is by striving to replace the negotiated ties of politics by the unmediated unity of a nation on the march, Julien Benda argued, that intellectuals betray their calling. Since O'Brien refers favourably, in another essay, to *La Trahison des clercs*, it must be that I have misunderstood his argument concerning Nicaragua. On the other hand, most liberal intellectuals in the West seem to agree with what I take to be O'Brien's analysis. The Sandinistas, they tell us, are doing a good job, and their claims to be the 'sole representatives' of the Nicaraguan people are genuine. The only thing that could turn them in a dangerous direction is the foolish policy of supporting the Contras. It is armed resistance which tempts these infant revolutions towards oppression. We are also told (by O'Brien among others) that the Contras cannot win; so support for them is pointless in any case. And besides, the Contras are all gangsters and terrorists.

The argument has been offered on behalf of every revolution since Lenin's. And since, in the present instance, so many intelligent people step forward to uphold it, usually in passionate terms, and sometimes even taking the trouble to go, like O'Brien, to Nicaragua, in order to see it confirmed, I can only conclude that it must be true. These regimes which begin by excluding opposition from politics – so as the better to concentrate on the 'work of reconstruction' – would open their ears at last to dialogue, provided we make sure that opposition, in the mean time, isn't armed. It may be that revolutions in our century (whether nationalist, socialist, or national socialist) have led to party dictatorships; to the extinction of individual liberties, freedom of speech and the rule of law; to mass murder, militarization and economic ruin; to a war on religion and a subversion or invasion of neighbouring states. But the main reason for these tragic developments is that others take up arms against them, preventing the revolution from pursuing its 'natural' course.

An argument of such intrinsic plausibility, backed by so many independent authorities, must command respect. My only slight reservation is that O'Brien leaves unanswered, because unasked, certain somewhat academic questions that trouble me. For instance, how are the courts now organized, and what law is applied? How is justice enforced, and what right of appeal exists? What proportion of trials are for political offences, how are the laws defining those offences worded, and what are the safeguards of judicial independence? What attempt is made to ensure a separation of powers in the political process, and what are the rights of the opposition? What remedies are available to the citizen against the abuse of central power, and who is entrusted to enforce them? Certain dead and discredited philosophers imagined that those were the important questions. What mattered, in their view, was not whether terror had visited a land, but whether there was any constitutional obstacle to its doing so, should 'the process of reconstruction' require. Such quibbles may have occupied the idle hours of Hobbes, Spinoza, Locke, Hume, Voltaire, Kant and Hegel; but that hardly proves their contemporary relevance. The overwhelming consensus of our élite is that we must offer to the Sandinistas the blank cheque of credibility which they demand. Those who are so obtuse as to feel reservations, must retire again to the dust-heap of history.

At several places in *Passion and Cunning* O'Brien expresses his disapproval of the Pope, whose authoritarian conception of the Church seems to him to justify the disobedient priests of 'liberation'. The issue is a touchy one, and, as always, O'Brien gives eloquent expression to the Enlightenment humanism which is his guide. O'Brien is a sincere humanist. He does not merely posture, like Marxists, on behalf of an idea, but believes in the power of human reason, and the virtue of human choice. He is also a defender of the market (a fact which does not prevent the obligatory sideswipes at 'Thatcherite materialism'). These Enlightenment attitudes were severely tested by Nkrumah's Ghana, where O'Brien lived and worked for three years (but which no doubt also had its first festive spasms of 'liberation', and its time of joyful pilgrimage). O'Brien tells a sorry tale of this grim dictatorship, and of the socialist principles that ruined its economy. The Enlightenment attitudes that offer him this perception lead him also to acknowledge complexities elsewhere. He belongs with those who really would like to see a just solution to the conflicts in South Africa and the Middle East, and who really do think that widespread bloodshed would be too high a price to pay for it.

O'Brien's reflections are cleverly and briskly expressed. He shows a commendable respect for his own experience, and for the prejudices that are constantly confirmed by it. If he has less respect for the experience of the unenlightened, then that too lies in the nature of Enlightenment. Those who speak for Reason tend to see only darkness and superstition in their opponents. People like the Pope, therefore, who believe that a world without obedience is a world without sense, are scarcely likely to make any impact on the apostles of Enlightenment. On the other hand, O'Brien is a student of the French Revolution. He is aware of the fact that Reason too can become a god, and that the modest guide of Voltaire, when once set upon an altar, demands an obedience far more terrifying than any of the superstitions at which it scoffs. For a while this god filled the prisons and the graveyards of France. Later it demanded a similar proof of obedience from the Russians, calling itself the Truth of History. I wonder why O'Brien is so sure that 'el Dios de los pobres' is not another of its names? One thing appears certain, at least. In the modern world, it is *this* god which stands behind *les gros bataillons*.

From: *The Times Literary Supplement*, 21 February 1986 and 24 March 1988.

21
THE RED AND
THE GREEN

An Eastern European friend recently took me to see one of the devastated regions of his country, a place which appears on the map as forest land, but where only a few blackened tree-stumps now stand amid a lunar landscape.* We passed through towns and villages which had all but crumbled away, their cement and stucco dissolved by acid rain. We walked beside rivers smelling of ammonia and acetone, where oily water in bright industrial colours swirled between lifeless banks. Palls of yellow smoke lay on the horizon, and beneath them the collectivized fields seemed to stretch lifelessly forever, without hedgerows, plants or animals, and glowing, where the soil had eroded, with a strange bald whiteness, as though suffering from eczema.

We came at last to a smouldering cavern, from the depths of which rose little puffs of sulphurous smoke. Drab grey apartment blocks were perched on the abyss, and children played listlessly between them, their faces pale and sickly, their gestures interrupted by constant nagging coughs. Two hundred metres below us tiny figures could be seen, working at seams of coal. Parts of the mine seemed to be burning, other parts were crumbling under the assault of pneumatic drills. A railway line, spiralling up to the perimeter, carried trucks loaded with coal to the surface, and took them empty down again. Once, my friend told me, a town had existed on this spot – a beautiful Central European market, with a baroque church, winding streets, an old Rathaus and a gay civic square. Discovering coal beneath it, the authorities had sold the town to a Hollywood film company, which had blown it to pieces for the sake of some ephemeral drama.

Scenes like this can be witnessed all over Eastern Europe. It would need a Dickens or a Zola to describe their full intensity of

* It is now possible to reveal the fact that the friend described in this article is Pavel Bratinka, the country Czechoslovakia, and the town Most.

degradation, just as it would need a Kafka to describe the utter helplessness of the people, as the anonymous, unanswerable, impersonal machine of communism sweeps them towards the greatest ecological catastrophe the world has ever known. Yet no one in the West seems to be concerned about a disaster whose long-term consequences will affect us all. Not even the Greens have taken much interest in the ecological results of communism. When the Chernobyl accident occurred, distracting them for a moment from their anti-capitalist posturing, their first thought was to blame, not the irresponsible system of communist government, but nuclear power in general, regardless of who attempted to exploit it. Their second thought was once more to forget the Soviet Empire, and return to the attack on the capitalist 'system', campaigning now for a removal of nuclear installations from the only countries where they are likely to be wisely operated and responsibly controlled.

'Why is it,' my Eastern European friend asked me, 'that the Greens who come to tell us of their heroic struggle, fail to understand that the principal enemy of our environment is socialism? Why do they imagine that, in order to exhibit a true concern for future generations, one must be not only an ecologist, but also a feminist, a socialist, a third-worldist, and even a pacifist? Why do they insult us with their self-congratulatory war against Western armaments and Western defence, when they can see how sorely our brotherly neighbour has afflicted us, and how, having ruined half of Europe, he has no option now, but to take charge, should it be possible, of the rest?'

He told me of his attempts to persuade his Green visitors that Western military strength provides the only basis for hope among his countrymen; that feminism – 'that fashion of the pampered' – appears, from his perspective, as simply another weapon in the hands of the enemy, a way of sowing dissension in the only relationship which the communists have yet to control. And as for 'third-worldism', 'anti-racism', and the other fads of his Western visitors, what meaning did they have, to people who were so utterly without power, that they could compare their situation favourably with no one? Yet, he said, he had not made the slightest impact on his kind and peace-loving visitors, who listened patiently to his ravings, and who pitied his moral darkness from the bottom of their copious hearts. For them it was settled that to be Green is to be socialist, to be socialist is to be egalitarian, feminist, pacifist and protesting. It was settled, too, that the cause of all catastrophe is the system of power, regardless of who should control it and how. And it was settled, therefore, that the duty to oppose power arises equally in

East and West. So implacable is the Green's hostility to power –
and especially to power in its 'capitalist' manifestation – that my
friend was driven to conclude, at last, that he was dealing not
with a system of reasoned belief, but with a new religion.

Nothing more clearly illustrates the utopian nature of the
Green movement, and its divorce from any serious appreciation
of the political realities, than its response to the Soviet Empire.
Last summer's report (1986) from the Friedrich Ebert Foundation
showed that the Eastern bloc is on the verge of environmental
catastrophe. The majority of waterways and lakes are now
irreversibly polluted, and land in many places is rapidly becoming unusable for agricultural purposes. In the Soviet Union factories operate in many towns without any control over the out-
flow of poisons. In the GDR only 17% of rivers contain drinkable
water; in Poland 80% (unofficial figures suggest 95%) of all
rivers and lakes are irremedially polluted, while 11% of all children between 8 and 10 suffer from respiratory disease. According to figures published in *New Scientist*, 66 tons of sulphur per
thousand inhabitants are released into the atmosphere of France
and West Germany each year, while in East Germany, despite a
lower industrial output, the figure is 251 tons per thousand: half
a kilogramme per person per day! In Hungary 18 million tons of
industrial waste are produced annually, only 15% of which is
treated. In Czechoslovakia more than 400,000 hectares of forest
have already disappeared, and land in Bohemia and Slovakia is
now in many places unusable for agriculture. A secret memoran-
dum of the Polish Communist Party, recently circulated in War-
saw, estimates that 43.6% of Polish land is seriously polluted,
with 58.6% of the Polish population living in the poisoned territory. In most of the Eastern bloc countries, statistics from which
political conclusions can be drawn are state secrets; nevertheless,
unofficial figures, patiently collected by those good citizens who
are prepared to risk imprisonment for their country's sake, show
a rapid decline everywhere – including in Hungary – in life
expectancy, and an alarming increase in infant mortality. (An
important source is the *Journal of Independent Medical Thought*
[*Zeszyty Niezależnej Myśli Lekarskej*] which is published underground in Poland. The frightening situation in the Soviet Union
has been described in a book written under the pseudonym of B.
Komarov – *The Destruction of Nature in the Soviet Union* – recently
published in the West.)

Furthermore, the people of the Soviet bloc are powerless to
protect themselves. In Poland, the Freedom and Peace movement, which has tried to organize petitions and demonstrations,
has been silenced and its activities curtailed by arrests and

harassment. Attempts by Solidarity to organize peaceful protests (for example, on 19 February 1987 in Konin, where the
inhabitants are being gradually poisoned by a huge aluminium
works) have been similarly thwarted, often violently, and usually with many arrests. In Romania civil initiatives for the
defence of the environment have been made explicitly punisha-
ble by law, while in Czechoslovakia and the Soviet Union no
such initiatives can be taken without immediate attention from
the secret police, followed by punitive reprisals. Even in Hungary, the Danube Circle, the best organized of all the environmental groups in the Eastern bloc, has found its initiatives
blocked, and its members subjected to increasing pressure from
a government that has closed every official channel through
which their feelings might express themselves. Measures
implemented in the West alone will not be sufficient to preserve
the ecological balance of Europe. Is it not rather puzzling, therefore, that the Greens have paid such scant attention to the dangers presented by 'real socialism', and shown themselves so
hostile to the military strength which alone gives us the *locus
standi* from which to bargain with the Soviet Union? And is it not
surprising that the image of a 'socialist' order still dominates the
conscience of those who have but to open their eyes, to see the
devastation which socialism has caused?

The Green will dismiss my friend's complaint with a contemptuous gesture. 'The economies of Eastern Europe', he will say,
'are not genuinely socialist, but only "socialist" in inverted commas.' To which Michel Foucault used to reply: 'Those inverted
commas should not be around the reality of Eastern Europe, but
around the illusion in your head.' For let us consider the question, from the point of view of political science. The ecological
catastrophe of the Soviet bloc is caused by two facts: public
ownership of the means of production, and the absence of a rule
of law. Both are the inevitable consequence of communism. The
remedy to pollution exists; but it exists only where there is
private ownership of the means of production, under a rule of
law – in other words, where the prevailing system is 'capitalist'.
In communist countries, those who control the means of production are empowered both to make the law and arbitrarily to
evade it. In Czechoslovakia, for example, there are 360 laws
dealing with matters of pollution and environmental health. But
any enterprise can obtain exemption from them, if the Party
officials consider it to be of sufficient economic importance. The
result is that *all* the major polluters remain outside the law.
Nothing could be done by a citizen to enforce the law in a
country where one party monopolizes power, and therefore no

force within a communist country can make any lasting difference to the ecological danger. Only outside pressure – our pressure – can do anything to force the communist bloc to comply
with internationally settled norms, and outside pressure
requires just the kind of military back-up that the Greens would
undermine.

The error of the Greens is the error of the nineteenth-century
socialists. They neglect to see that property involves not merely a
right, but also a responsibility. We justify private *rights*, by
justifying private *duties*. The duty of property – the duty of care
towards all those affected by its use – will be honoured only if
there is some individual on whom the responsibility lies. How
this answerability can be obtained without private ownership is
a question to which the socialist utopians have never properly
addressed themselves. No private owner is sovereign, and all
private owners are therefore subject to law. Moreover, legal
opposition (such as exists under 'capitalism') permits the law to
be influenced by, and changed in favour of, the powerless. This
is precisely what is happening, in the matter of the environment,
throughout the Western bloc. It is happening too slowly. But it is
happening: and its success depends precisely on that private
ownership of the means of production which socialists decry.

The Greens will define their socialist ideals in contrast to the
'state capitalism' of the Soviet Union. Socialism, they will say,
means co-operative ownership, in which workers, rather than
capitalists or the state, control the means of production. Thus
they represent as similar two things which differ – morally,
politically and economically – to the greatest possible extent,
namely, free enterprise under a rule of law, and state production
controlled by totalitarian power. At the same time they make a
radical distinction between two things which differ hardly at all.
Co-operative ownership is simply a *form* of private ownership.
And if it is not to be a threat to the environment, there must be
individual accountability for the depredations which it causes. In
other words, the co-operatives must have managers, with all the
responsibilities (and all the rights) that attach to the managers of
private corporations. Co-operatives are as likely to pollute in the
cause of profit as factories owned by one person, and stand in
just the *same* relation to the law as they do. Like the traditional
firm, they are corporate persons, and their staff are functionally
differentiated, and separately rewarded, in the manner of any
modern industry. Only in the utopian imagination is this
'socialism' really different from capitalist enterprise, and it is
precisely the utopian imagination which has created the catastrophe of Eastern Europe.

The Green, my friend said, is anti-capitalist for the same reason that he is feminist, third-worldist and pacifist – not because he has any clear conception of what he seeks to put in the place of Western institutions, but because he more easily sets himself *against* power than alongside of it. To defend the rule of law is to be 'with' the authorities; to defend free enterprise is to be 'with' the successful and the strong. Such alliances are, for the Green, morally impossible. He is motivated by that identification with the underdog which justified the original sin of Lenin, and which set Russia and its empire on the path to ecological and moral catastrophe. In the Green psychology we find a new version of an old disease: the disease of antinomianism. And it is from the effects of this disease that the trees, animals and people of Eastern Europe are dying.

From: *The Salisbury Review*, December 1987.

22

A NOTE ON BLOCH

Das Prinzip Hoffnung, written during the Second World War, when its author was in exile in America, is regarded in Germany as Ernst Bloch's major work. Not that many people have read to the last of its 1400 pages, or even broached the third and most interesting volume, in which Bloch casts his roving eye over the world religions, and measures the hope which they contain. Nevertheless, this massive, rambling and didactic document – which reads like an obsessive commentary on some undiscovered text – has enormous symbolic importance. It is offered as proof that Marxist humanism can fulfil its intellectual promise, and speak richly and profoundly about the entire human world; as proof that capitalist life and institutions are in every particular assailable; and as proof that socialism provides hope where other philosophies provide only servitude and drab despair.

Bloch was a Jew and a romantic. Both facts marked his thought indelibly. Witnessing the most terrible catastrophe that his race had ever suffered, he was able nevertheless, by a supreme, almost religious exaltation, to cling to the hope that first inspired him – though it was a hope without content, a hope of form and style alone. And, while scattering his pages with Marxian outbursts, Bloch expressed his optimism in the language of Novalis and Hölderlin. He wrote of youth, homecoming and harvest, where his political mentors referred to progress, praxis and production. In Bloch the ideas of false consciousness and alienation are referred back to the vivid images of a Day of Atonement and an Original Sin. Theories were less important to him than archetypes, and Marxism was validated, not by its scientific pretensions, but by its projection into the future of the romantic theology from which it grew.

Bloch settled after the war in East Germany, a gesture which lent authenticity to his Marxist principles. However, his pupils were soon imprisoned and persecuted; he himself was dismissed from his university chair and disqualified from teaching.

Eventually, tired of real socialism, he moved to the West, so as again to bear witness to socialism of the unreal kind. Bloch became the darling of the 1960s radicals, who saw in his celebrations of youth and utopia the true meaning of their revolutionary zeal. If Bloch was useful to the New Left, it was because he seemed to be living proof of the fact that Marxism had not been applied, but rather betrayed, in those parts of the world where it was imposed as doctrine.

The first thing to be said about the English version of this work – *The Principle of Hope*, tr. Neville Plaice, Stephen Plaice and Paul Knight (3 vols, Blackwell, 1986) – is that the translators have done a remarkable job. To have read the book is labour enough. To have translated it, now that its time is past, suggests an uncommon lack of worldliness. And to have translated it so well, so that the flush of adolescent feeling is conveyed to the English reader in all its embarrassing plenitude, shows a devotion to the text equal to that of a Luther or a Dryden. The only question is, whether it was at all worthwhile.

Much of the book is severely dated. The callow anti-Americanism, the understandable but debilitating obsession with the Nazis, the naïve attachment to Marx as prophet and saviour of the modern world – all these must prove as exasperating to the literate socialist as to the reader for whom they convey attitudes which are far from innocent. But these are incidental irritations, significant in revealing openly, what is elsewhere displayed more discreetly, that Bloch was less a critic than a preacher. The interesting parts of the book are those in which Bloch's comprehensive vision – of man poised eternally between hope and despair – is brought to bear on minute experiences. In these parts he can achieve a kind of poetry, even a certain finesse; elsewhere he is merely pompous.

The book consists of loosely connected passages, assembled (perhaps as an afterthought) into sections. As their titles reveal, Bloch fancied himself as a poet: 'A Frugal Meal'; 'The Roast Pigeons'; 'Lunacy and Colportage even here'; 'Glance through the Window'; 'Columbus at the Orinoco Delta'; 'Dome of Earth' – such titles might have been attached to paintings by Max Ernst, with just as much meaning as they are given by Bloch.

The worst passages are those (and they are many) in which triviality is dressed up as sublimity, and given the false authority of a high romantic style:

Very little, all too little has been said so far about hunger. Although this goal also looks very primal or primeval. Because a man dies without nourishment, whereas we can live a little

while longer without the pleasures of love-making. It is all the
more possible to live without satisfying our power-drive . . .
But the unemployed person on the verge of collapse, who has
not eaten for days, has really been led to the oldest needy place
of existence and makes it visible.

In such passages a thought so simple that it goes without saying,
is gradually built into a 'poetic utterance'. But it acquires, in the
process, neither authority nor grace, while losing the simplicity
which is its sole literary virtue. The manner is rendered all the
more exasperating by the naïve leftism which substitutes for
moral sense, and the constant reference to a hope that is never
justified. Indeed, it could be argued that the real cause of the evil
against which Bloch fulminated, was the blind pursuit of unjus-
tified hope. (For what was Nazism, if not another cult of Utopia,
dressed in blood and iron?)

The best passages are striking, even beautiful, and the reader
is often surprised by Bloch's ability to lift from the shallow
stream of rhetoric, nuggets of occasional gold. Book 1 contains a
prophetic section on social dancing, in which Bloch penetrat-
ingly describes all that has been lost through the modern habit of
dancing apart, while invisibly and indissolubly joined to a partner. Volume 2 contains a sensitive account of architecture, while
Volume 3 could be read with profit by any student of comparative religion. Bloch's real talent was as a writer of sermons. His
misfortune was that he had no transcendental belief to which he
might attach this gift, and was compelled to ruminate obsessively on an earthly paradise which he knew to be impossible.

I doubt that Bloch will be read by the next generation of
socialists. Like his contemporaries, Horkheimer and Adorno, he
was a derivative writer, a sentimentalist, and a windbag. Like
them, he was temporarily saved from oblivion by the 1960s. I
hope that his books and theirs will henceforth be confined – as
the publishers clearly expect, having priced these volumes well
beyond the reach of Everypseud – to libraries.

From: *The Salisbury Review*, July 1987.

23

THE LITURGY
OF THE LEFT

Jozef Wilczynski's *Encyclopedic Dictionary of Marxism, Socialism and Communism* (Macmillan, 1982) is an extraordinary document. Its relation to Marxism or socialism, as these are understood in the West, is marginal, and its claims to be 'encyclopedic' must be discounted. Virtually no Marxist thinker is mentioned who has not received recognition or criticism from the Chinese or Soviet Communist Parties, and all the theories and events discussed belong to the 'heroic' stage of Marxist revolution in the present century. Gramsci is not mentioned, nor are any of the influential French Marxists (Goldmann, Althusser, Lefebvre, etc.) of the post-war period. Almost every definition is brought back to a tired old slogan from revolutionary rhetoric – the 'class struggle', 'the dictatorship of the proletariat', 'from each according to his ability, to each according to his need'. Neo-marxism is discussed as though it were entirely a product of US campus frolics in the 1960s, and the influential re-discovery of Hegel by Western Marxists might just as well never have occurred, despite the fact that everything suggestive in modern Marxism – the theory of alienated labour, the analysis of class consciousness, the distinction between civil society and state, etc. – derives from Hegel.

The Marxian doctrines which are referred to are the materialist theory of history (interpreted throughout as 'dialectical materialism', despite the fact that Marx did not use that label, and despite the fact that the 'dialectic' is *demonstrably* wrong), the theory of class struggle, and the labour theory of value. Since all these theories have been refuted it is not surprising to find oneself losing patience with the definitions that are built on them, and only the constant reminder that they form part of a liturgy that our fellow intellectuals in one third of the world are forced to repeat in all their public pronouncements enables one to continue reading – although with mounting horror at the extent of human folly.

If Marxism fares badly, socialism fares worse. 'Socialism' is throughout taken as a technical term of the Marxian theory of history – to denote that system of production relations which supposedly follows on capitalism, and which precedes the final withering away of the state and the emergence of 'full communism'. In the West, however, the term is not used in that way, and indeed most people who call themselves socialists do so in order to distance themselves from the Marxian theory, either because they recognize that the state is necessary to their aims, or because they believe that the Marxian theory has been refuted. It is extraordinary to find Wilczynski constantly deferring to the myth of 'full communism' without any hint of irony. 'According to a prediction of N. S. Khrushchev in 1961', he writes, 'the phase of socialism in the USSR (the oldest socialist country) would last up to 1980 at least, (after which the country would start entering the phase of full communism). But owing to the Soviet economic setbacks since that time, the socialist phase will in fact be much longer.' The idea that socialism might exist, both as theory and practice, outside the Marxian rhetoric, does not seem to have occurred to Wilczynski. All the intellectual labour that went into the making of modern English socialism, for example – the historical analyses of Tawney, Cole, and E. P. Thompson, the social criticism of the New Left, the political theories of the Fabians, the Webbs, Russell, Crosland, and many more – none of this gets more than a casual mention. Admittedly much of it, with hindsight, appears intellectually dubious. But that is clearly not Wilczynski's criterion for exclusion, since he treats us to the thoughts (or rather slogans) of half the Chinese revolutionaries, and to the theories of every half-baked schoolboy who put up his hand at some International, then to enter history as revisionist, opportunist, deviationist, or whatever.

The explanation of this bias must lie in the fact that Wilczynski, although now apparently residing in Australia, did much of his research in Poland. His dictionary is, therefore, a dictionary not of Marxism, or of socialism, but of official Communist rhetoric. Read as such, it is a remarkable and in some ways impressive document: impressive for its unscholarly thoroughness, and remarkable for the deadpan tone which it succeeds in maintaining over 660 pages of double columned text. Not that Wilczynski entirely swallows the party line. He allows himself a few criticisms of Soviet tyranny, and even hints that some fairly disreputable things might occasionally have occurred in China. On the whole, however, he represents his dictionary entries as parts of a believable system of thought, applicable in the contemporary world, delivering definite answers to definite questions. It is difficult to know whether the work is one of propaganda and subversion, although the illuminating definition of 'entryism' as 'boring from within' suggests that it might be. We are told that in socialist countries other than the Soviet Union collectivization has been 'more or less voluntary or has at least been carried out more humanely'. (Admittedly it could not have been carried out *less* humanely). Likewise, in socialist countries the provision of social welfare is as of right, and all need has therefore been eliminated; besides, there is more or less permanent full employment, so that the problem of welfare seldom in fact arises. (It is of course difficult to know the facts. We know that you lose your right to welfare in Poland if you do not find a job within six months, and that you will not find a job if the Party wants you to lose your welfare. One *samizdat* publication puts unemployment in the Soviet Union at fifteen per cent, although it is unclear how the figures are calculated. Of my own friends and acquaintances in Eastern Europe, one puts salt on the streets for two hours every snowy morning in winter; two clean lavatories and stairways on one day a week; two are nightwatchmen where there is nothing to watch; most of the rest work as and when they can, in order to acquire a residence permit in a town. Almost all of them receive less than they would get if they were entitled to welfare.) We are repeatedly told that the dictatorship exerted by the Party *is* simply the dictatorship of the proletariat (or at least its 'logical expression'), and informed for example, that 99.9 per cent of Czechs in 1976 voted for the National Front candidates. (One wonders where the remaining 0.1 per cent now are. In fact virtually no Czech ever attends an election, since the Communist Party fills in your ballot form if you do not attend, and, if you do attend and choose to make use of the procedure for voting secretly – the kiosk is ostentatiously there – you are, to put it mildly, a fool.)

Sometimes Wilczynski shows an awareness that the theory of communism has been criticized. His speciality seems to be economics, and he has great respect for the heroic attempts by Eastern European economists, especially Poles, to provide the concepts with which the modern 'socialist' economy can be described. At the same time he seems to admit that the labour theory of value (which he calls one of the four 'cornerstones' of Marxism) is wrong. When it was seen that the labour theory does not explain price and profit (although it aimed to do so), early Marxists adopted what is now a familiar strategy: they argued that it *does* explain something called 'value', that 'value' is the 'essence' of which price and profit are the 'appearance', and that there remains only a 'transformation problem': how to derive the illusions of the market-place from the realities which they conceal. This excruciating piece of intellectual dishonesty (what one might call 'saving the essences') has led to a mass of Marxian economics in the Soviet Union, and garbled versions of it are presented by Wilczynski. A similar attempt has been made to 'save the essences' in the theory of history, although Wilczynski seems to be less aware of its existence. It provides the unifying thread of dishonesty in Lukács, Goldmann and Althusser, and, in its late baroque excesses, invokes vertigo in the minds of those not independently persuaded that the Marxian theory of history *must* be true.

The four cornerstones of Marxism are, apparently, the labour theory, the materialist theory of history, dialectical materialism and the class struggle. The remaining two are equally, if not more, contentious: as a Pole it is surely possible for Wilczynski to have observed how intensely dated and parochial is the concept of the 'class struggle'. For one thing, the notion of class with which it was associated (where class meant, roughly, position in production relations) no longer seems clearly to apply, or if it does apply, it is not so as to support a theory of 'struggle'. While there are indeed 'struggles' in the world, they are not between 'classes': the struggle in Poland involves a whole people, vainly trying to throw off the yoke imposed on it by an external power, in collaboration, it must be added, with the kind of people who speak the language recorded by Wilczynski. Outside the parlours of the student left, this talk of class struggle seems now to be no more than fantasy.

There is a useful moral to be drawn from Wilczynski's book. I assume that it really does record the main items of political thought that have been contributed by Marxism to political practice, if not to political theory. One begins to see just how disastrous that application has been. The dictionary consists almost entirely of shrill slogans, abortive dogmas, absurd 'heresies' and controversies, for example, the 'one divides into two' versus 'two combine into one' controversy, and pity the Chinaman who was on the wrong side. Events are described in mythopoeic language (the Great October Socialist Revolution, the Great Leap Forward, The Great Industrialization Drive, etc) without respect for historical truth, and every half-articulated perception of society takes the form of an 'ism', of which one might be accused and for which (in the 'heroic' stage) one might have been tried and executed. It is notable that there is not a single concept that belongs to law, and there is no reference to any institution (other than the Communist Party), and that the language of politics – the language which permits people to understand and resolve their conflicts – is swamped by hysterical slogan-shouting from the commanding heights.

If this dictionary is anything to go by, 'actually existing socialism' has successfully abolished all the concepts and institutions, legal, political, social and moral, with which men have, over the centuries, attempted to understand their social condition; it has replaced the enterprise of political conciliation with a dogma of 'struggle', and at the same time deprived opposition not only of its legal status, but equally of its right to describe the real complexities of human existence in a language of its own, without risking the charges of 'bourgeois ideology', 'deviationism', 'opportunism' and the rest. It seems to assert that conciliation, adjudication, accommodation – in short, politics as we understand them – are no more than an appearance, beneath which the 'essence' of the class struggle takes its inexorable course. But there is no such essence, and, even if there were, knowledge of it would no more be relevant to politics than knowledge of the skull is relevant to the interpretation of a face. The revolutionary overthrow of all existing institutions, all existing legality, all existing morality – this has indeed taken place. But no institutions, no legality, no morality, no human understanding seem to have come to replace it. The artefact of centuries was overthrown in the name of a myth of 'full communism', and, while we may take comfort in the fact that 'Lenin defended the validity of objective truth' (he would have been hard pressed to attack it), it is undeniable that the inability of Communism to recognize that its theoretical foundations have been refuted shows a contempt for truth, and for human nature, that is without parallel in political history. Wilczynski's dictionary brings home vividly the almost complete intellectual, social, political, and above all moral isolation of communism in the modern world.

From: *The Times Literary Supplement*, 9 July 1982.

24
IDEOLOGICALLY SPEAKING

I cannot prevent myself from feeling a certain inner revulsion whenever the word *person* is self-consciously summoned to take the place once occupied by *man*, or when the flow of a sentence is interrupted by a distracting use of *he or she* where *he* would once have been mandatory. Far from serving to remove the 'irrelevant' reference to gender from the English language, such practices heighten that reference, and transform it from a harmless quirk of grammar to a vigilant ideological presence. I resent this ideological intrusion, and its insolent dealings with our mother (perhaps I should say 'parent') tongue. But like many who share such reactionary sentiments, I find it difficult to justify them except in ways which are too *ad hoc*, or too *ad feminam*, to gain a hearing from those who do not already share them. It seems to me, therefore, that a great service would be done to the dwindling body of linguistic reactionaries if an argument could be found for their position which is something more than a mere reiteration of it. In this article I search for that argument – though with a despairing sense that it lies, in the end, too deep for words, being presupposed in every word that is used to utter it.

I have mentioned two strategies of 'gender elimination': the substitution of *person* for *man*, and of *he or she* for *he*. They are only superficially similar. A moment's reflection tells us that while the second change is stylistic, the first is also semantic. The word *person* comes to us from the Latin *persona* – originally meaning 'a mask', but transformed by Roman law to designate the bearer of rights and duties, who comes before the law in order that his rights and duties should be determined (or rather, in order that *her* rights and duties should be determined, for *persona*, of course, is feminine). As Sir Ernest Barker beautifully put it: 'it is not the natural Ego which enters a court of law. It is a

right-and-duty bearing person, created by the law, which
appears before the law.'[1] The Roman-law conception passed into
jurisprudential and philosophical usage, so that already in
Boethius the word *persona* is used to denote the human individual, in his quality as rational agent. It is now quite normal
among philosophers to assume that 'personality' belongs to our
essence, and that this puzzling fact is independent not only of
law, but of all human institutions. Personality is no longer something bestowed upon himself by man, but something discovered
in him, by all who would treat him as he really is. It was from this
concept of personality that Kant distilled the Enlightenment
morality which has all but replaced the morality of Christendom.
And it is the classless, genderless – indeed sexless – morality of
Kant whose brilliant rays are dimly reflected in the sermons of
the modern feminist.

   Not all persons are human. There are corporate persons, such
as churches and firms; there are (or may be) divine persons,
angels and devils. Moreover, not everything that belongs to our
humanity belongs also to our personality. The embodiment of
the person in the human organism brings with it a 'human
condition': a bond by which the free being and the animal are
inseparably united, so as to confront the world from the same
eyes, and with the same mystifying countenance, and therein to
wrestle with each other till death do them part. The human being
suffers and dies; he is at one with nature and with the animals,
attached to his flesh and to the flesh of others. He rejoices in the
sight, sound, smell, and touch of things: of his child, his dog, his
horse, and his lover. And all those ineffable experiences are
invoked when we refer to him not as *person*, but as *man*. This
term returns us to our incarnation, and places the flesh where it
should be, in the centre of our moral view:

> man, proud man,
> Drest in a little brief authority,
> Most ignorant of what he's most assur'd,
> His glassy essence, like an angry ape,
> Plays such fantastic tricks before high heaven,
> As make the angels weep.

Even if we considered personality to be the most important fact
of our condition, this could not lead us to the conclusion that we
should refer to ourselves always as persons, or that we do not
need a word to designate our incarnation and to locate us not in
the hierarchy of angels, but amid the throngs of life. To use the
word *person*, where our poets and liturgical writers have chosen

man, is to deny the need to capture our destiny in words of our own.

But why the word *man*? For does this not imply some preference for the masculine gender, some lingering attachment to the view that, when the chips are down, it is men, and not women, who count? If not *person*, why not some other word which is semantically equivalent to *man* in its generic use, and yet free from every resonance of gender? Slavonic languages have such a word – *chelovek* in Russian, *člověk* in Czech, *człowiek* in Polish – whose etymology has nothing to do with man or woman. Why do we not follow suit, perhaps inventing a word for the purpose?

We could indeed adopt this strategy. But think of the cost. All at once we cease to use the word reserved by our language for the most important of the world's phenomena. More: we begin to treat the word as somehow polluted and unclean, to be avoided in polite society and reserved for onanistic use. Our past literature becomes tainted for us, something to be read or uttered with secret pangs of guilt and naughty titters – something that is no longer part of us, as antiquated and absurd as the Roman toga or the Morris dance. The result would be a massive 'deculturation', as we cease to hear the language of Shakespeare and the King James Bible as addressed directly to the modern ear. And, in all probability, the experiment would fail. In a few decades the new word for man would be uttered always in inverted commas, like *citoyen* in post-Restoration France, or *comrade* in the modern communist state.

What is at stake becomes clearer when we consider the other example of 'gender elimination': the use of *he* or *she* where *he* was once the norm. That this usage is inelegant will be freely admitted, even by those who advocate it. One philosopher has even suggested (and used) the alternative device of randomization, so that in neighbouring sentences the impersonal pronoun is now masculine, now feminine.[2] The result is a stylistic catastrophe of unprecedented proportions. In such an idiom, neither the well-turned counsel, nor the poignant perception, can find utterance. Others still have advocated the use of *they* as a genderless third-person pronoun – a usage which has a certain popular authority. Dale Spender even argues that this usage was once universal, and that the rule requiring *he* is the invention of 'patriarchal' grammarians in the nineteenth century.[3] If that were so, then we should have to thank the Victorians for a considerable stylistic gain: try to use the generic *they* consistently, and observe the confusion of syntax and number that immediately follows. In fact, however, the truth seems (as so often) to be the opposite of what is confidently affirmed by Dale

Spender. It is true that there are early instances of the generic use of *they*: 'Each of theym sholde make themselfe ready,' writes Caxton in *Sonnes of Aymon* (*c.* 1489), while Shakespeare has 'God send everyone their heart's desire' (*As You Like It*, 1598). Nevertheless, some of the first examples of the systematic use of *they* as a generic pronoun are in the polemical works of John Stuart Mill, where the author's usual eloquence is expressly constrained by his feminist principles. Seventeenth- and eighteenth-century English almost invariably seems to use *he* as a generic pronoun, and this is what we find in the works that did most to create the literary English of modernity: the King James Bible and the Book of Common Prayer. As these works abundantly demonstrate, the generic pronoun owes much of its power to the fact that it places before us an image of the human *individual*, but in the *general* condition which defines him. It reminds us that all counsels go unheard, until the individual life is touched by them: 'He that findeth his life shall lose it: and he that loseth his life for my sake shall find it' (Matt. 7:39). The occurrence of the generic pronoun in the New Testament is of course influenced by the Greek. But the style of that sentence is the style of the surrounding English language: 'He that is too much in any thing, so that he give another occasion of satiety, maketh himself cheap' (Francis Bacon). Consider what would happen to the writings of Addison, Johnson, Arnold, Ruskin, Dickens, or George Eliot, if every generic pronoun were plural, or if it should appear, when singular, always yoked to its feminine partner, struggling against it in a marriage of inconvenience. Even the law, which speaks not of man but of persons, has need of an individualizing generic pronoun, and therefore employs the standard *he*: 'The words of a testator's will necessarily refer to facts and circumstances respecting his property and his family and other persons and things . . .' – which impeccably tautologous utterance comes to us with the authority of Halsbury's *Laws of England*.

Logically speaking, the pronoun is the equivalent of the mathematician's variable: it stands 'in place of' the noun which fixes its referent. That it should bear a gender of its own is a grammatical fact of no semantic consequence. For semantically, its gender is the gender of the noun for which it stands proxy. The impersonal *he* stands proxy as a rule for *man*: for the general noun which describes us as instances of human life rather than as persons. And once again the complaint will be made that the resonance of gender here involves a reaffirmation of the discredited belief in the precedence of the male sex.

How can such a complaint be answered? First, we should not

neglect the fact that linguistic gender distinctions are far from universal. The Finno-Ugric and Turkic languages provide us with the nearest examples, culturally speaking, of genderlessness, and it is instructive to compare them with the Indo-European languages whose grammar has given so much cause for offence. No doubt there is difficulty in conducting the necessary investigations. But at least the genderless languages give us a point of comparison. And if they tell us anything, it is that the masculine pronoun has little power to oppress the female sex. The historical emancipation of the Finnish woman is part of a wider Scandinavian phenomenon, welcomed by Ibsen and bitterly complained of by Strindberg. It was neither advanced by the Finnish language, nor retarded by the Swedish and Norwegian. The historical subjection of the Turkish woman was an *Islamic* phenomenon, and her partial emancipation, when it came, was not the result of a 'genderless' perspective, but the effect of secularization, and of a quaint old-fashioned belief in modernity. As for the position of Hungarian women, how are we to distinguish it, in general, from the position of women in Bohemia, Moravia, and Austria? Even if we accept the feminist view of traditional Europe as a society based on 'patriarchal' oppression, there seems to be little evidence that pronominal gender has done anything either to reinforce or to legitimize the ancestral power of men.

The feminists would, I imagine, be unimpressed by those considerations. The 'emancipation' of European women, they will argue, was a matter of local adjustment, whereby the chains of male domination were made to chafe less severely, precisely so that the victim should cease to struggle against them. The true oppression is 'structural': it runs through all institutions, not showing itself in overt violence, but maintaining, nevertheless, a persistent and tacit preference for all that belongs to the male. To such a 'capillary' oppression language cannot but add its justifying signature, and what better way for women to free themselves than to cancel masculine dominance in this, its longest-standing citadel?

Our language is particularly unfortunate. For gender usually becomes apparent in English only at the pronominal level. In Romance and Slavonic languages, as in Greek, German, Hebrew, and Arabic, gender attaches to every adjective and every noun. The idea that gender has something to do with the sexuality of the thing described is apt to strike the speaker of such a language as faintly ridiculous. Having introduced the moon as *la lune* I must naturally refer to it thereafter as *elle*. But consider some of the vagaries of gender in those languages which are structured by it. In Arabic, for example, all adjectives qualifying plural nouns which refer to nonhuman things must occur in the feminine singular, while the numeral adjectives from three to nine are used in the masculine gender with feminine nouns and in the feminine with masculine nouns. In Czech there are two masculine genders, one for words which describe 'animate' objects, and one for words which describe 'inanimate' objects; in French the generic pronoun can be either *il* (standing for *quelqu'un*) or *elle* (standing for *une personne*); the Germans refer to girls in the neuter (*das Mädchen*), and agree with the Arabs, French, and Italians in seeing towns as feminine. And so on. All such facts, however interesting in themselves, have not the slightest bearing on sexual politics, and serve only to emphasize the semantic arbitrariness of gender.

In English, however, with a few rare exceptions (such as the personifying *she*), *he* and *she* are used exclusively of things with male or female *sex*. Gender in language is therefore seldom attributed to deep-rooted habits of grammar which are perceptibly beyond the reach of conscious change. It really may seem, to someone faced with the choice of using *he* as opposed to *he or she*, that he is confronting a question of sexual morality, rather than one of conventional usage.

There is an intellectual device that runs through all Marxist and feminist criticism and that is probably the mainstay of radical social analysis in our time. This is the theory of ideology, as adumbrated by Marx and Engels, and the 'hermeneutics of suspicion' (to use Paul Ricoeur's apt expression) which derives from it. According to this theory, historical societies have been characterized by distinctive economic structures, by political superstructures which derive therefrom, and by ruling 'ideologies'. These ideologies arise spontaneously from the social process and render natural and authoritative the prevailing disposition of social and economic power. Ideology includes systems of belief, such as religion, but it is always more than that. It is a form of what Marx called 'consciousness', and what current Foucauldian jargon prefers to call 'discourse': a mode of systematic representation of the world. This mode of representation may also be systematically false, in the way that lenses can be systematically false – not so much by authorizing this or that erroneous conclusion, as by employing concepts and categories that distort the whole of reality in a direction useful to the prevailing power. Marx believed that there could be a scientific, or unideological, consciousness, and that such a consciousness would be true to reality, in the manner of lensless spectacles. Recent offsprings of the theory have tended to forgo that interesting claim, using the theory more as an instrument of criticism than as a prescription for any 'correct' understanding of the world. For the Foucauldian, suspicion is all, and power, stark power, lurks behind every discourse, even the discourse which tells us so.

Such a theory has almost unlimited capacity to disestablish existing authorities. Whatever you say, it can penetrate behind your utterance and establish conflagration in your camps. No claim to truth or objectivity can survive its proof that your very *choice of words* is steeped in self-serving falsehood. What matters is not the objective truth-value of a judgment, but the ideological quality of the 'discourse' which is employed in it, the implication being that objectivity and truth either have no independent authority, or else are but another 'mask'. Truth and objectivity are created *within* a given discourse, which are therefore unable to assess it from any point of view that is not its own. 'Truth' is but another name for self-serving error. Nietzsche came close to believing this self-refuting proposition. Feminists frequently embrace it in all its absurdity:

> Piercing through to the essence of this debate, Adrienne Rich (1979) summed it up succinctly when she stated that "objectivity" is nothing other than male "subjectivity". The patriarchal order is the produce of male subjectivity and it has been legitimated and made "unquestionable" by conceptualizing it as "objectivity" . . . The meanings encoded under the rubric of psychology, or history, or even biology, for example, have also been political, although not necessarily frankly so. That these meanings have not been open to question, that they have been justified on grounds of "objectivity", is no longer a defence, for "objectivity" – as it has been defined and appropriated by males – is just as much a political act as any feminists are currently engaged in.[4]

This seductive way of thinking does not stand up to a moment's philosophical analysis: if the patriarchal order has been made 'unquestionable' by our discourse, how is it that Dale Spender and her colleagues are able to question it? If 'objectivity' is another patriarchal mask, what of the theory that tells us so: is it objectively valid, or not? (Neither answer is available; and yet there is no third possibility.) And so on. Nevertheless, ideological criticism seems to offer a method and a goal to the study of literature. In every age critics have recognized that their concern is not with the literal truth or falsehood of a text, but with the values, emotions, and resonances that are conveyed by it. But why are they so concerned? Ideological criticism offers an answer, and one which justifies the critic as no other answer has justified him. Criticism exists, it tells us, precisely to go behind the spurious claims of truth, and to discover the power which is seeking to make use of them. By doing that, we show to be artificial what had been previously perceived as natural, and we expose the reality of choice where choice has been denied. Stripped of ideology, the world becomes a 'field of action': the disinterpreted world is *ready for change*.

Ideological criticism has immense charm. For it too can play its part in that 'brokerage of power' which it denounces. It promises precisely to *transfer* power, from the one who now possesses it to the one who unmasks him, from the speaker of prevailing discourse to the zealous critic who lays bare the realm of choice. This is why ideological criticism has all but conquered the academic world and become the intellectual centre of the humanities. It is the final vindication of the donnish life; the instrument which gives to the teeth-gnashing fantasist his longed-for power over the world of real things. The ideological critic can never stop short at criticism, however. Always he seeks to legislate: to fill the consciousness of men with the ultimate choices that he discerns, and to force open every door against which ordinary humanity has stacked its moral baggage. What is the consequence of this legislative impulse?

When Lenin and his band of Bolsheviks took power, they were in the grip of Marxist theory, and sincerely believed that their task would be impeded not only by the bourgeoisie, but also by the Russian language, which had hitherto been steeped in bourgeois ideology. They therefore began to devise a new 'discourse', one that would be transparent to the truth of history, and from which the lurking ideology of the 'class enemy' would have been expelled. Each thing was to be referred to by its proper (that is, Marxist-Leninist) name. People were divided into 'exploiters' and 'the proletariat'; references to authority, to the sacred, and to law were either put in inverted commas or else qualified with some pejorative adjective like 'bourgeois'. 'Revolutionary legality', when it came, bore only a superficial resemblance to that 'bourgeois legality' which it replaced, just as the newly invented 'masses' had no connection with the 'common man' of bourgeois thinking. The old language of human relations was also to be purified: 'proletarian solidarity' took the place of individual friendship (indeed, friendship between individuals became something like a contradiction in terms); and terms like 'peace' and 'friendship' were to be applied henceforth not to negotiated relations between those with unequal power, but only to relations of *equality*, in a world in which the 'class struggle' had come to an end. (The resulting semantic transformation of the word *peace* – according to which there can be peace only when both parties to it have 'accepted socialism' – has had fatal diplomatic consequences.)

It is of no great consequence that the 'scientific' theories which inspired the new language are false. Human error has been built into language from time immemorial without destroying man's capacity to correct it: the capacity to say of witches, that there are none; of the Emperor, that he has no clothes; and of patriarchy, that its days are numbered. Of more consequence is the emergence of a phenomenon which is perhaps peculiar to the modern world: the phenomenon which the French and Russians call 'wooden language', and which we might call, in honour of Orwell's satire, newspeak. Recent studies by Petr Fidelius and Françoise Thom cast interesting light on the syntax and vocabulary of communist language and both suggest that the revolutionary attempt to *impose* an interpretation on events, by embodying it in discourse, has in fact diverted language from its referential function.[5] It makes no difference that the purpose was to *emancipate*, to reveal the choices that had hitherto been cancelled by ideology. Vocabulary, syntax, logic, and style all take on a new purpose, which is not to describe the world, nor even to interpret it, but to *uphold the interpreting power*. The interpretation is no longer understood in relation to the world (the world is of no relevance to the 'correct' use of language), but in relation to the political power which decreed it. Linguistic deviations are assessed according to whether they accept or question the tacit claims of power. Hence what matters in any criticism is not its truth or falsehood, but whether it accepts or rejects the legitimizing language.

In Czechoslovakia, for example, you could write that the 'fraternal assistance offered by the Soviet Union to the people of Czechoslovakia in 1968 did not lead to effective normalization, and only partially eliminated the counterrevolutionary forces', and the implied criticism would be assigned to some bureaucratic category and ignored. But were you to write 'the Soviet invasion of our country conferred the greatest benefit in reestablishing the Leninist system of party dictatorship', you would be arrested at once: not for praising the invasion, but for using language transparent to the thing described. You would have broken the circle of newspeak, whereby words rise free of reality and return always to their dominating purpose, which is to conceal and render 'natural' the ruling power. Facts are of secondary importance, and can be amended as linguistic propriety requires. While no party ideologist believes the theories of Marx, all recognize that truth and reference have no serious part in the public discourse of communism. Language is used in another way. Actual events are therefore generally described in abstract terms, as peculiar impersonal processes, contending in a nebulous region of pure power; people are seldom mentioned by name, and actions are assigned to no real personality. Reality appears always as a contest of opposites: 'positive' and 'negative', 'progressive' and 'reactionary'. But only one thing remains clear: that the power which speaks these terms is 'correct', and in no need of criticism from those who are not already absorbed by it.

Here is an example, taken from Mikhail Gorbachev's 'new thinking for our country and the world':

> Many competent specialists admit that social and economic development in Soviet society can be accelerated and that success in the current drive for restructuring will have positive international consequences. They justly reason that the world community can only stand to gain from the growing well-being of the Soviet people and further progress of democracy. The scope and scale of the social and economic programs undertaken by the Soviet Union bear evidence of, and offer material guarantees for, its peaceful foreign policy. . . . Leaving aside many evaluations and estimates that we see as disputable, we, on the whole, regard this position as realistic and welcome its predominantly constructive orientation.[6]

This passage, chosen at random from a book which proceeds in that vein for 250 pages, could have been written by a party computer; perhaps it was. No people are identified: only 'competent specialists', 'evaluations', and 'estimates'; no events are described: only a vaguely characterized 'development', 'restructuring', and 'further progress in democracy'. (Further than what?) We are offered a glimpse of 'social and economic programmes', and are invited to admire their scope and scale: but what they are, and who is in charge of them, we cannot tell. Everything is bent to the sole task of emphasizing that the Soviet Union is not a threat (it has a 'peaceful foreign policy'), and that to recognize this fact is 'positive', showing a 'predominantly constructive orientation'. The passage is succeeded by another, following the Manichaean logic of newspeak, in which those who say that *perestroika* is simply a device to enhance and consolidate the power of the Party are denounced as liars and war-mongers, propagators of 'scares concerning dynamism in domestic and foreign policies', who 'hope to cause our people's mistrust towards the leadership'. These enemies of the people, we learn, are 'ready to use anything to achieve their ends'.[7]

The enemy – thus vaguely and abstractly characterized – has no other quality than his determination to speak referentially: he is the one who refuses to enter the charmed circle of newspeak and decides instead to call things by their names. Interestingly enough, Gorbachev concludes his invective by confronting the enemy directly, and in the course of doing so, covertly admits that what the enemy says is true: *perestroika* is indeed another word of newspeak, designed to name and legitimize the Party's monopoly of power:

> today members of the Politburo and the Central Committee are unanimous as they have never been before, and there is nothing that can make that unanimity waver. Both in the army, in the State Security Committee (the KGB), and in every other government department, the Party wields the highest authority and has a decisive voice politically. The drive for perestroika has only consolidated the Party's position, adding a new dimension to its moral and political role in society and the state.[8]

The language here is no different from that used by previous leaders, and is as devoid of referential purpose as theirs. But woe betide the person who refuses to speak it, and who, in defiance of the Party, insists on calling a spade a spade.

A student of communist newspeak will be struck by an extraordinary paradox. The attempt to chase ideology from language, to achieve a discourse transparent to social truth, has in fact produced the opposite: a discourse that is *opaque* to truth, precisely because it is devoted to uprooting 'class ideology'. Such a discourse has *become* an ideology, in the Marxist sense: an instrument for legitimizing power. But it is nothing *else*. As Thom and Fidelius have demonstrated, its referential function has all but 'withered away'; so too have the possibilities of deliberation. It is impossible to use such a language to suggest that things might be *fundamentally* changed. It is, moreover, a language in which honest communication is next to impossible, and in which all agreements are cancelled in the very act of making them, since neither the subject nor the object of agreement can be defined.

The example returns me to the feminist attempt to expropriate the language of dissent. The feminist, like the Marxist, is deeply suspicious of power – at least, of power in the hands of others – and shares the Marxist conviction that power lurks within the structures of our thought and language and must first be expelled from *there*. Modern English is a 'patriarchal' discourse and this, for the feminist, is the most important fact about it. The need arises to expose the underlying patriarchal assumptions, and to offer another language, free from ideology and transparent to social truth. As with Leninism, what is offered is *emancipation*, an opening of the world to previously cancelled choices. And, I suspect, the long-term consequences could well be the same as those of Leninism: a complete *ideologization* of language, and a displacement of its primary referential function, so that it ceases to be a medium of rational decision-making, or a means to conversation with one's kind.

Langue de bois emerges only with the seizure of power, and the subsequent emergence of a public discourse of warning. But the way is already prepared for this event by a theory which sees nothing in language *besides* power, and which represents all decisions of style, syntax, and semantics as ultimately reducible to transactions in an ideological 'struggle'. In this respect, the language of modern feminism can be compared with that of Lenin: a vigilant, depersonalized meditation on a world gripped by hostile powers: 'an acute and impassioned *attentiveness* to the ways in which primarily male structures of power are inscribed (or encoded) within our literary inheritance', as one feminist critic has expressed it.[9] The feminist, like the Marxist, wishes to uproot and destroy the power that hides itself in language.

Marxist suspicion was directed towards what Hayek would call the 'catallactic' aspects of thought: the aspects which arise 'by an invisible hand' and which, while the result of many choices, are themselves never chosen. Like prices in a market, the structures of language are unchosen outcomes of a myriad individual decisions. In this, the follower of Adam Smith might argue, lies their wisdom. They provide solutions to problems that are generated and solved socially. These problems cannot be fully understood by one person, and could never be solved by a plan. Nor can the natural solutions that mankind has hit upon be improved by some steering committee of experts. Such a committee would wish to impose as *law*, and in the teeth of human instinct, a solution which can exist only as a tacit convention. Just as the Leninists ended by displacing the primary functions of discourse and producing a monstrous, all-encompassing version of the very evils that they claimed to fear, so, I suspect, will the feminists produce a new *langue de bois* of their own. The sole study of the user of this language will be to dispose his words and thoughts in accordance with the rules of ideological correctness. Truth, reference, deliberation, and honest feeling: these would take a secondary place, and be recognized, if at all, largely as masks adopted by the patriarchal enemy. When this happens, the writings of English-speaking feminists will be as unreadable as the speeches of Gorbachev.

25
SEXUAL MORALITY AND THE LIBERAL CONSENSUS

The liberal view of the state requires government by consent. The most plausible version of this requirement formulates the test of legitimacy in these terms: the legitimate state is the one that each individual citizen would consent to, in those circumstances where consent derives solely from the principles of rational choice. In our time the most famous exponent of that idea has been Rawls; but it can be recognized, in one form or another, as fundamental to Enlightenment thinking. The state ought therefore to be neutral regarding all those matters over which rational people might reasonably disagree. By a wholly natural movement of thought, the liberal tends to conclude that morality and its enforcement are no business of the state. To make the state into the guardian of morality is to give privileges to a *particular* morality, and therefore to those individuals who subscribe to it. But other individuals, whose values differ from those endorsed by the high command, may be equally reasonable in affirming them, and equally entitled to live as their conscience dictates. They could never rationally consent to an order that forbids this right, and therefore no such order can be countenanced. The only conceivable liberal order is one that remains morally neutral, standing above and beyond those particular 'conceptions of the good' which motivate the various ways of life that are subsumed by it.

Built into that argument is the assumption that rational beings may reasonably differ concerning the requirements of morality. Kant denied this assumption, on the grounds that moral principles emerge directly and necessarily from the autonomous exercise of practical reason, and that every rational being will, in those circumstances where his reason is unclouded, spontaneously affirm a common moral code. Moral neutrality seems to follow from the liberal view of the state, only on the assumption that the ordinary principles of rational choice – principles which every individual can be expected to endorse – do not fully determine the content of morality. That is the assumption made by Rawls, and by many other liberal thinkers. And it is an assumption that is easily made, given the manifest fact that ordinary people, even though rational, must invariably be prompted by something other than reason – a religion, for example – if they are to have a clear idea of right and wrong. A problem then arises for the liberal world-view. These ancillary forces which turn us to the moral life are not as a rule tolerant of rivals. They are not 'experimental' attitudes; on the contrary, they derive their power from an authority that countenances no alternative. God's will cannot be countermanded, and, once revealed, cannot be disobeyed. The very fact that it provides the certainty which reason never offers makes religion immune to argument, and intolerant of those who reject its counsels.

Faced with this dilemma, the liberal conscience tends to turn in one of two directions: either it reverts to the metaphysical morality of Kant, affirming that reason alone determines the content of morality, or it retreats by degrees from the moral view of things, replacing praise and condemnation with an uneasy toleration which, while pregnant with guilt-feelings, denies the reality of guilt. Neither solution is comfortable. The first has the unwelcome consequence that the state is, after all, entitled to enforce a moral code – the code, whatever it might be, that spontaneously emerges from the exercise of reason. The second has the equally unwelcome consequence that no merely human power can be allowed to impede man's corruption, but that almost every 'option', however repugnant, is but another form that liberty may take.

An illustration of the liberal dilemma is provided by homosexuality – a practice which has often been condemned, but which is now permitted wherever the liberal conscience holds sway. It is true that the liberal is not obliged to countenance every human impulse: he will argue that some fragments of traditional morality can be reconstructed on his principles, and endorsed and upheld by the law. For it has always been central to the liberal idea that rational beings will not consent to be harmed by their neighbours, so that practices which threaten harm can be outlawed and the implicit agreement of everyone safely assumed. But aside from forbidding murder, violence and theft, this way of thinking leaves us powerless to determine the path of others' salvation. So vague is the concept of 'harm' that it is never clear what activities can be condemned by it. Do we condemn homosexuality because it might lead to disease? Or do we condemn the disease? In the latter case, our moral obligation is not to refrain from buggery, but to look for a prophylactic against the effects of it. The moral status of the act becomes incalculable: best, therefore, to permit it, for fear of losing that most precious of political commodities, the consent of the one with whom we disagree.

Although the liberal may find homosexuality 'distasteful', therefore, he tends to regard this as a fact about himself, of no intrinsic moral interest. Distaste is not the same as disapproval, and disapproval must always be withheld until the case is proved. The legacy of this world-view (if I may so describe it) has been a certain confusion in the minds of those who do not spontaneously share it. For while many people have little sympathy with homosexuality, they hesitate to describe it in the terms which otherwise would come so naturally to them, as immoral. In an age of liberal consensus, nobody is more severely censured (and censored) than the anti-liberal. With the growth of proselytizing homosexuality, which seeks to enter schools and households with the liberating message that there are rival 'orientations', the situation has arisen in which parents seek desperately to shield their children from an influence which they are forbidden to condemn.

I shall consider the case of homosexuality since I believe not only that it is of the first importance at the present time, but also that it leads us, when properly considered, to an important insight into morality. The terms 'moral' and 'immoral' have traditionally been used more of sexual conduct than of conduct of any other kind. Under the influence of liberal ideas, however, they have been gradually voided of their sexual application, and reserved instead for those areas in which agreement comes easily, and in which the liberal conscience is naturally at home – areas of calculation, where cost and benefit seem clear. (Hence the peculiar examples in books of moral philosophy: ought I to visit Auntie Jane in hospital, or ought I instead to attend the meeting of the Academic Council? Ought I to shoot the intruder now, or ought I to wait until I know that he is armed? In these dilemmas the great question is avoided – the question what sort of man I should *be*? This may be a religious question: but it is also at the root of the two most vivid secular moralities that I know – those of Aristotle and Nietzsche.)

Traditional sexual morality tends to lean on two kinds of teaching – the theological, which advises us that the body is

God's image, and must therefore not be defiled, and the familial, which tells us that the sexual act is not what it appears to be (a project for individual pleasure), but a commitment which includes others who are not party to it, and indeed who may not be born. The Catholic church has emphasized both those ideas, and described the hidden *telos* of the sexual act as the generation of children. On that radical view all actions – including contraception – which sever the act from its God-given purpose are immoral, in that they disavow our primary commitments, and allow us to put our own gratification ahead of the obligation to life.

It is difficult to make the Catholic teaching clear – even as fine a mind as Professor Anscombe's has notoriously failed to do so. Nevertheless, it seems to capture a worry that is already familiar to readers of *Brave New World*, and to all who have followed with alarm the proposals for 'genetic engineering' which have been made in recent years. If children can be made in laboratories, and by methods which bear no relation to the love-making of their parents, what remains of those commitments which tie the generations each to each, and give us a motive, in our most urgent ventures towards the Other, to safeguard the world for those who have not yet entered it?

Attempts have been made to reconstruct the idea of commitment on purely individualistic premises, without reference to the dead and the unborn who have such an interest in our conduct. Chastity, for instance, may be defended as the virtue which prepares us for love, and for the consolations upon which our happiness depends. (I have developed this argument in *Sexual Desire*.) We might all therefore have reason to control our sexual impulses, in order to reap the greater benefit of consolation. But such an argument hardly seems to capture the weight, or the urgency, still less the extent, of our moral interdictions. Moreover it is powerless to rule against homosexuality: it forbids promiscuity only, something that the wiser proponents of 'the love that dares not speak its name' have in any case always condemned.

The issue becomes clearer when we recognize that there is a distinction between the first-person and the third-person view of agency, and that liberalism, for commendable reasons, has always taken the first-person view as fundamental. For the liberal, the question of social order is the question of my choice – whether I would, in real or ideal conditions, consent to it. Hence the only reasons relevant to the legitimacy of a practice are the reasons individual agents might have for permitting or forbidding it. From this first-person point of view, given 'risk and uncertainty', the constraints of traditional morality appear to have an arbitrary – or at any rate a non-rational – character. From the first-person point of view traditional morality consists of sacrifices – or 'uncompensated costs'. One purpose of religion is to convert these costs into notional benefits – rewards stored up in Heaven, or yet heavier costs foregone in Purgatory and Hell. But when we lose religious belief (and liberalism is, historically, a consequence of that loss), it becomes hard to see why the costs of moral sacrifice should be incurred at all.

But there is also the third-person view of moral agency – the view which sees our actions from outside, and which does not limit its perspective to those features of a situation that can provide a reason for me, here, now. This third-person perspective can arise in two ways: first as the perspective that others take of my action; secondly as the perspective that I might take, were I to step outside the limits imposed by my present motivation and see my action in the context of my life as a whole.

From the point of view of others, the sacrifice required by morality may be a social benefit. Consider the Spartans at Thermopylae. They are motivated by honour, which commands them to stand and die. No selfish calculation could conceivably recommend that course of action. Their first-person reasoning, therefore, which starts from the absolute interdiction of dishonourable conduct, may seem arbitrary, even irrational – certainly not something that a liberal could recommend to others. On the other hand the motive of honour, and the disposition to sacrifice one's life for honour's sake, are useful to the social organism that instils them. A society which can count on these motives has – as the historical experience of the Greeks demonstrates – an immense evolutionary advantage over its rivals. And a society which, like that prevailing in the last days of Rome, is devoid of the spirit of sacrifice, will fall to the first competitor. Those obvious (if shocking) truths provide some justification for a moral education which instils the motive of honour in its pupils.

This third-person perspective on action is not the prerogative of the third person. I can adopt such a perspective on my own action. In doing so, I may find reasons for the cultivation of motives which I presently do not have, but which serve my long-term interest. This, I believe, is the leading idea of Aristotle's *Nicomachean Ethics*. For Aristotle, the self-sacrificing motives, which have honour (*to kalon*) as their goal, serve not only society, but also the individual himself. To discern this, however, is not within the power of everyone: it is not given to the ordinary man to understand that happiness lies in the exercise of virtue, and that he therefore has reason to acquire the self-sacrificing motive. Since a person's practical reasoning must begin from motives that he presently has, it will never be possible for the unphilosophical man, lacking the motive of honour, to acquire that motive by his own reasoning powers; nor will he, acting in a spirit of calculation, approximate his conduct to that of the virtuous man. However, suppose Aristotle is right. Suppose that happiness is man's final goal, the obtaining of which justifies every labour expended in the pursuit of it. Suppose that happiness is 'an activity of the soul in accordance with virtue'. And suppose that virtue is the disposition to pursue what is honourable, regardless of countervailing desires. If this is so, then we are right to instil the motive of honour, even in those people who do not presently possess it, and who, from the first-person point of view, can find no reason to act as honour requires. We are justified not only for society's sake, but for the individual's sake as well.

The hostility to the homosexual act derives from a feeling of revulsion. This revulsion is an instance of a more general reaction to what we might call 'unseemly visions of the flesh'. It is a curious fact that certain uses and aspects of our bodies arouse the most violent reactions. Obscenity illustrates what I have in mind: the sense, which we may find extremely hard to justify, that certain things cannot be looked at, cannot even be thought of. Obscene things display someone as threatened, overcome or extinguished in his body. Our fear of obscenity, like our curiosity towards it, parallels our fear and curiosity towards death.

Sexual revulsion is manifest too in the feeling of shame, described by Max Scheler as a *Schutzgefühl* – a protective feeling, whereby the self guards itself against invasion. A woman, whose sexual feeling, once aroused, may attach her immovably to its object, clearly has a reason to hesitate. She therefore has reason to acquire those *Schutzgefühle*, shame being one, that guard her against any hasty indulgence.

The ordinary person's revulsion against homosexuality can be seen as another such *Schutzgefühl*: a feeling which (rightly or wrongly) protects him from activities in which he might otherwise engage. The object of this revulsion is difficult to describe. Like many of our sexual revulsions (those towards incest and paedophilia, for example) it is inspired by arousal. The object of disgust is not this or that sexual performance, this or that use of the generative organs; it is 'man aroused by man', or 'woman aroused by woman'. Arousal is a reciprocal experience, wilfully generated between persons; the *Schutzgefühl* is triggered by the thought of this experience inhabiting 'flesh of a single kind'. If this seems strange, it is because we tend to think of arousal (wrongly) as a merely 'physical' condition – or else as an experience that we share with the animals. However, as I argue in *Sexual Desire*, arousal is not only the core experience of desire; it is also essentially inter-personal, and essentially compromising.

From the liberal point of view, the question of homosexuality takes a straightforward form: are there reasons why I, who wish to engage in homosexual practices, should refrain from doing so? Whichever way the argument goes (and the liberal can be dissuaded from an 'option', if the costs are high), the homosexual act is purged of the aura of sin which previously attached to it. Buggery is at worst inadvisable. For the traditional conscience, the question takes a different form: thinking about homosexuality starts from the premise of revulsion: an absolute interdiction which blocks off the path to indulgence. The question is no longer whether the benefits of transgression outweigh the costs – one of the costs presumably being the guilt-feelings which my *Schutzgefühl* will almost certainly inflict on me. For revulsion is one of those motives that bring calculation to an end, like the motive of honour: it defines its object as forbidden. I may go against my revulsion; but the revulsion is not to be measured on the scale of costs, and is not overridden even when defied. It possesses the categorical character of moral sentiments generally. The question is whether the feeling can be justified. Is there a reason to instil this kind of revulsion against the homosexual act? And can we do so without violating other moral imperatives? I believe that the answer to both these questions may be yes.

First let us consider the interest of society. What are the social benefits of retaining, and the social costs of abolishing, the *Schutzgefühl* that forbids homosexual intercourse? The social arguments for the traditional view are, I believe, of four kinds:
(i) Traditional sexual morality instils and reinforces an idea of the sexually normal. This idea has a social function, reinforcing the desire of one generation to sacrifice itself for the next. The family embodies this spirit of sacrifice, transforming sexual attraction into a commitment to offspring, which is at the same time a commitment to home. Sexual feeling acquires a solemn character: those unborn have an interest in it, and this interest is transformed into a sense of eternity, which inhabits the sexual passion itself. 'Normal' sexual feeling is for ever. To mark this 'eternal' quality, sexual unions are traditionally enshrined in vows, rather than in contracts. 'Normal' sexual feeling comes to enjoy the dignity of a sacrament.

The liberal view, by contrast, typically sees the sexual bond as an agreement between individuals – 'consenting adults' – who write the terms of the contract according to their own desires. Other generations are not intrinsically involved in their transaction, and become involved only if the parties desire. The sexual act loses its solemnity, and the sacrifices which some people (the 'straights') feel mysteriously impelled to undertake for the sake of future generations come to seem optional and arbitrary. Why go to such trouble merely for the sake of sexual pleasure?

The idea that home-building is the normal result, and the justifying goal, of sexual attraction is so widespread and enduring, that we might be tempted to conclude – on grounds of natural selection – that my functional justification of it is empirically confirmed. At any rate, its loss cannot be in the interests of society. On the contrary: society, whose hopes lie with those unborn, has a reason to avoid any developments which tend to sever sexual passion from the commitment to future generations. Surely, then, the easy permission of homosexual union – as an 'orientation', on a par with that which leads to the raising of children – may offer a threat to social continuity?

(2) According to the traditional conception, the sexual act involves the passing of a threshold, a moving outwards from the self, into a realm that is partly unknown. The body of the Other is a mystery, whose secrets are unlocked by the charm of desire. Sexual possession is also a spiritual awakening; a peculiar sense of responsibility comes from knowing that you have awakened feelings that you do not understand. The heterosexual therefore makes himself vulnerable in the sexual act, and is a solicitor for love and understanding. This experience is hard to describe in philosophical idiom, although it is familiar enough from poetry. Once the possibility of homosexual intercourse is freely admitted, however, what remains of it? Again, it seems to become a 'residue', a discardable option. The body of the homosexual's beloved belongs to the same kind as his own, there is no mystery in its arousal, nor in the desire that animates it. It is not truly 'Other', and lacks the inviolable character which attaches (for a man) to the body of woman. To deal with it there is no need for love or understanding; nor is there a mystery to be unlocked. The loss of the revulsion against homosexuality therefore takes us one step further along the road to the de-sanctifying of the human body. It becomes easier to see the sexual act as an animal performance, rather than a spiritual journey. Again, and for reasons implied in (1) above, it seems to me that society may have an interest in preventing such a loss.

(3) Perhaps as a consequence of that loss, there is, in homosexual union – especially that between men – a vector which tends to

promiscuity. Unimpeded by the shame which governs women, the male homosexual hastens to arouse in another those feelings which he knows in himself. The natural predatoriness of the male is shared by both partners, and the body of the one holds no mystery for the other. When the experience of the other is so familiar and predictable, it can easily become the subject of a contract, and if both parties consent, why should the contract not be acted upon? It may be no accident, therefore, that male homosexuals are promiscuous, once they have lost the *Schutzgefühl* which forbids their desire. The result of promiscuity is to void the sexual relation of commitment. No society, therefore, has an interest in permitting it.

(4) It is undeniable that certain people in any generation, especially men, are attracted to their own sex, and especially to children of their own sex. The *Schutzgefühl* prevents them from expressing their desire, and perhaps even from overtly acknowledging it. Indeed, it turns them against their sexuality, and directs them along the path of renunciation. At the same time, in searching for an outlet for their now 'sublimated' feelings, they tend more and more to take an interest in the young. They become priests, teachers, scoutmasters, and so on. They acquire the character of 'father' to everyone's children, and their role is that of *paideia*, in the Greek sense. If you were to wonder why it is that homosexual impulses are reproduced in human societies, then here is a possible functional explanation: societies benefit from the emergence of a priestly class, which in turn benefits from sublimated homosexual feeling, and the vow of chastity that enshrines it. Homosexuality can confer this beneficial effect, however, only if the homosexual act is the object of revulsion.

I have sketched four lines of justification that might be offered for the *Schutzgefühl* forbidding homosexual intercourse. They are by no means conclusive: nor could a conclusive third-person argument be mounted for *any* of our *Schutzgefühle*. For the facts about society are hard to grasp. (Consider, for example, how we might justify our revulsion against paedophilia.) It is also a further question whether the *Schutzgefühl* is in the interests not only of society but of the agent *himself*. Maybe those things which further the well-being of society also further the well-being of its normal member. But that does not give us what Aristotle promised: namely, an argument to show that the individual must have certain motives if he is to be happy (if he is to flourish according to his nature). When people condemn homosexuality as unnatural they are implying that such arguments exist.

It may nevertheless be true that the individual does have an interest in being sexually normal, according to the traditional conception. For he certainly has an interest in all of the following: in tying sexual desire to love, and love to commitment, in viewing sexual union as a vow and a sacrament, in feeling the urge to sacrifice himself for his children, and to make a home for them. He has an interest in living cleanly and chastely, governed by sentiments of responsibility and awe towards the body of his companion. And he has a reason to acquire those feelings – the revulsion against promiscuity, homosexuality, bestiality, paedophilia, and obscenity – which keep him on the path of decency, and which reassure him of the innocence of his pleasures. He has an interest in all this, because he needs that which can easily be acquired in no other way, unless it be the way of renunciation and *paideia*: knowledge of his proximity to, and right conduct towards, the rising generation. All men need the love of children; and all men need to confirm their values and their lives in terms of what they transmit to their successors. This is part of moral certainty; and without moral certainty man is a prey to unassuageable guilt.

That is only a sketch, and it depends upon assumptions (defended elsewhere) about the nature of sexual desire. But suppose it were true. It would follow that we must, if we can, instil in children the feelings of revulsion that guide them to the normal path. But *can* we do this, and can we do it without infringing any other moral imperative? It seems that we can. For sexual revulsion is pliable. Although it is founded in natural facts, such as the mechanism of sexual selection, it is everywhere re-shaped by education. People are taught to feel ashamed of certain acts, by the opprobrium that is heaped upon those who overtly perform them. However, can such a method of education coexist with the 'respect for persons' which lies (and rightly lies) at the heart of the liberal world-view? In one sense, yes: for the condemnation of those who overtly engage in homosexual behaviour is compatible with the view that each has a right to live as he wishes in *private*. It has always been a requirement of sexual morality, that public scandal be avoided, and private practice concealed. The distinction between the private and the public is indeed integral to any sexual morality that could commend itself to the normal conscience. If you say that those things which are done privately should be condoned publicly – as Diogenes did, when asked why he masturbated in full view of passers-by – then you may soon come to the conclusion that there is no such thing as sexual morality, but only irrational feelings of distaste. If, on the other hand, you recognize that certain acts are shameful, and must therefore be concealed if they are to be performed at all, you may still hold that we have no right to cross another's threshold, into that world of 'rights' where he alone is sovereign, so as to prevent him from performing them. That, surely, *was* the traditional position, in its most civilized form. It is a position, however, which liberalism is in danger of renouncing, when it loses its sense of shame. For it then finds no reason against advocating that which it can find no reason to suppress.

But now we must part company with the liberal. For suppose my contentions are right. Suppose the *Schutzgefühl* forbidding homosexual intercourse is in the interests of society, and also of the individuals who compose it. It is nevertheless true that the arguments for this are hard to understand, especially when expressed in the secular and abstract form that I have given to them. No unphilosophical rational being would come naturally to reject the homosexual 'option', if he did not already possess the revulsion which closes it – at least, not by reasoning. Nor would he, if he lacked that feeling, have any sense either of the sinfulness of the homosexual act, or of the desirability of avoiding it. Only if the revulsion is implanted in him, by means which by-pass his reflective powers, could he ever come to see the *point* of the traditional interdiction. In his formative years, therefore, he must be subject to an educative process which could never be justified from liberal premises. His moral education cannot be a purely 'enlightened' and 'enlightening' one – it cannot be simply a matter of teaching him to calculate the long term profit and the loss, while leaving his desires to develop independently. It must involve an 'endarkened' and 'endarkening' component, by which he is taught precisely to cease his calculations, to regard certain paths as forbidden, as places where neither profit nor loss has authority. There is no force like religion, for endarkening the mind in this way.

If we should ever see our way to justifying that idea of moral education, however, we should probably have to abandon the liberal conception of society. For a society which serves the happiness of its members would then contain a component that could not be a part of the social contract. It would involve practices which close options that a liberal must regard as open, and which could not be recommended purely on the basis of the first-person reasoning of any and every agent. Only those who share the favoured revulsions, or who have worked through the arduous reasoning that justifies them, will see that they have a reason to accept such a society and to live within its institutions.

Which way, then, should we turn? In the liberal direction, the direction of enlightenment, or in the direction of partial darkness? Maybe such a question can be raised only after it has been answered for us, by forces which we cannot control.

This essay was presented as a paper at The Professus World Peace Academy Conference, 'Liberal Democratic Societies: their present state and future prospects', held in London, August 1989. It is published in a volume on morals and religion in liberal democracies by Paragon House Publishers. Printed by permission.

26

THE USURPATION
OF AUSTRALIA

THE 1984 LATHAM MEMORIAL LECTURE,
DELIVERED IN MELBOURNE, AUSTRALIA.

Like the British, the Australians live in a highly politicized
world: a world where vociferous people are constantly asking us
to solve a thousand insoluble problems, to adjudicate a thousand
contradictory claims, to rectify a thousand injustices, preferably
now, or if not now, tomorrow. These demands are put over with
a peculiar fervour, calculated to leave us unable to sleep peacefully at night and unable to do our business during the day.
Their statement also involves a considerable distortion of language. For example, it involves persuading us that inequality,
wherever it exists, and however it was generated, is injustice.

The people who purvey such abstractions have a specific
motive. They hope that, while they can deal in these terms, we
cannot; and therefore that they will win any argument which we
are foolish enough to engage in. But I think that there is an
element of bluff in that. In truth nobody understands the meaning of 'social justice'. When people ask us to rectify the injustices
committed on women, on blacks, on minorities generally, they
are really offering us nothing more than slogans.

Behind their slogans, however, more concrete emotions are
concealed. The radical pursuit of 'social justice' stems, I believe,
from a repudiation of our culture, tradition and history; from a
desire to charge our ancestors with the burden of original sin. I
am told repeatedly that I must regret all that has made me, find in
it nothing that binds me with any obligation; for all my inheritance is founded on oppression, violence and lies. For two
decades the left has been looking for victims, who can be held
forth as condemning everything by which we normally live and
everything to which we spontaneously subscribe allegiance. In
Australia the Aborigines are the fashionable excuse for this

sentiment. The crime against the Aborigines, it is implied, frees me from my allegiance since it shows that my own society has no title to my respect.

This disparaging of one's own culture and history is one of the things I discern most vividly in Manning Clark's influential *Short History of Australia*. Clark contrives to write about the history of Australia without seriously considering (other than the Labour Party) a single Australian institution. His first mention of the universities, for example, comes in the biography of a Labour leader – who, one is told, was educated at the University of Melbourne. The author neglects to mention that the University of Melbourne was founded within fifteen years of Melbourne itself; a fact which indicates a civilizing propensity in Clark's ancestors which he is reluctant to attribute to them. He wishes us to see them as a band of self-seeking marauders, the scourge of innocent Aborigines, struggling for possession of a land that was not rightfully theirs. The idea of them as settlers, whose first concern was to establish institutions of religion, learning and law in benighted regions, is one that Clark cannot tolerate.

That is the first sentiment that I identify in the prevailing radical temper. The second, which I think is equally fierce, is more complex. For the radical consciousness the single, all-important aim, is to free myself from obligations and to be totally unanswerable to anything outside myself. To achieve that aim I must abolish all traditional forms of authority. Three such forms in particular stand out as attracting the hostility of the radical: 'the Family, the Church and the State'. These three institutions have to be either destroyed, or else remade so as to be without any intrinsic claim to my allegiance.

Consider the family. It has become commonplace to describe this arrangement as arbitrary, justifiable only as a private agreement, and lasting just as long as the mutual tolerance of the parties. Anything else is 'oppression' or 'patriarchy' or 'sexism'. At the same time a variety of 'alternative' arrangements are introduced and condoned: homosexual partnerships, one-parent families, and any other liaison however temporary, and however divorced from the great cycle of human reproduction, which could be represented as equally valid, and equally authoritative, for those who choose to enter it. The result is that no authority remains in the family itself; the only authority is that of the individual choice. I am my *own* authority, and hence I am freed from every external obligation that the family seems to impose on me. Not to get divorced when my family seems to hamper my fulfilment is to be merely superstitious or irrational.

Secondly, the church: the way of abolishing the authority of this institution is to 'relativize' it. And the people who are most fond of relativizing the church are the clergy themselves, who display this institution as one alternative among many, and the Christian faith as one system of beliefs among many equally valid, equally legitimate alternatives. These alternative religious beliefs and practices are in fact to be respected far more than the practice which is mine, precisely because they are *not* mine. Anything that is mine has to be despised; by despising it I free myself from the authority that it has over me. I am helped to despise what is mine by cultivating an exaggerated respect for what is alien. Hence the emergence in the modern world of the 'multi-culturist' lobby, which tells us to respect with an assiduous deference all beliefs, however absurd, of other cultures, and to despise all beliefs, however noble, of our own. In Australia, for example, Aboriginal beliefs and customs are to be protected by law and constitution, simply because they are alien to those who wish to protect them.

The third institution, which is to be the principal subject of my talk, is the state. The radical has a certain trouble in removing the authority of the state. For he also wishes to keep the state, as the only instrument whereby his dream of social justice could be realized. The radical has therefore invented what could be called the 'effeminate state'; a state which does not take action in any definite way to protect its citizens or to advance its own interests, but which exists purely in order to distribute the goods of the wealthy to those who are supposedly 'exploited' by them. The effeminate state has no right to command me to fight for it, it has no genuine legitimacy, it has no historical claim; it exists merely in order to care for those who cannot (or will not) fend for themselves.

Those three ways of voiding our principal institutions of authority are familiar. There are reasons behind the radical claim that the authority of these institutions is not absolute. But we must face up to the question of what we should really believe if we were to accept their authority as relative. (One thing that we should have to believe, I argue, is that the radical's programme of 'social justice' has neither political legitimacy, nor persuasive power.)

What should be the conservative response to the radical attack on traditional authority? Too often in recent years the response has been one of bewildered acquiescence. Alternatively, recourse has been made to some rival abstraction to pit against the chimera of social justice. The conservative response has tended to focus on an idea of individual freedom (leading to freedom of association, and of the market); as though freedom were the single value of political existence. Undeniably the ideology of freedom has been politically useful. Nevertheless it commits, I believe, just the same error as is committed by the radical. Like the radical, the 'new conservative' holds that the only true value is my freedom, and therefore that all institutions are equally valid, just so long as I choose them and exercise my choice in and through them. No institution has any genuine authority independently of my choice. Hence there is no authority in the world independent of me. All family arrangements are legitimate provided they are freely chosen; all religions are legitimate similarly (although the idea of a freely chosen religion is undeniably absurd). Finally the state is also valid only because it is a sign of my freedom, and to the extent that I freely submit to it. Many of you never freely chose to submit yourself to the sovereign state of Australia, however, even if some people would like you freely to disclaim your allegiance now. So the liberal outlook is, in the end, extremely hard to accept, and in any case incapable of providing guidance now, at a time when the legitimacy of the Australian state has been called in question.

I shall take the state as a test case. The state is the substance of politics and all our political beliefs depend upon our conception of the obligation towards it. What I called the effeminate state of the radical – the state which occupies itself merely in distributing goods to those who are unable to earn them – is also an *impersonal* state. It removes the elements of personal responsibility and personal duty from public life, and sets up in their place a kind of machine for equalizing people. The state's principal concern is to tax those who have a lot of life's goods and to distribute the surplus to those who have less. People will then be equal in as many ways as they can be *made* to be equal. Obviously, there are limits to this process. But the radical is rarely prepared to specify what the limits are. If you could make people equally beautiful by surgery, perhaps that ought to be done too. Who knows? Perhaps people ought to be made equally intelligent by removing parts of the brain from those who are too clever. There are plenty of equalizing stratagems which the state has not yet employed.

The new social order, in which the state is permanently occupied in creating an equal balance of goods among the citizens, is an order which would be quite different from anything that we know. In particular, in this new order there would be nothing in the state to which allegiance could be owed. Nobody could really feel under an obligation towards this new kind of state. People may believe they have rights against it and think they are being unfairly treated by it. Those who are robbed by it, however, would feel no obligation to give what is taken from them. On the contrary they would try to hide it in Switzerland. Nevertheless, this machine state has an appeal to people in a democratic age. Because it is impersonal, it cannot be identified with any particular human force. Hence it cannot be seen as a mask for individual self-interest. There is no interest group which advances itself through this process of redistribution. Hence, in a democratic age, such a state becomes especially appealing. For it neutralizes the question as to who is gaining over whom. It displaces all such questions, just as it removes every other reference to personal existence. It says: 'I relieve you of responsibility for your existence; and in return you must allow yourself to be bound to an impersonal mechanism which governs your life.'

The impersonal state locates politics outside itself: it encourages the politicization of society, while abandoning all true politics. Its decisions become increasingly *administrative*, and attempts to affirm a national identity, to bring people together for purposes of defence or celebration, seem, under its influence, increasingly foolish. Such attempts presuppose just the kind of loyalty and responsibility which the impersonal state evades, and if they are made it is only because people are still in contact with ideas of legitimacy which are other than those which could adhere to the administrative machine. It is these ideas of legitimacy which provide, I believe, the true foundation of conservative politics.

Faced with this triumph of impersonality, however, the conservative in recent years has had a single strategem. He says that we must affirm the individual against the state, that we must 'roll back the frontiers of the state', as Winston Churchill once put it. Now, someone who says that we must affirm the individual against the state, is not going to carry much credence in the modern climate of opinion. For to those who stand to lose (that is to the weaker members of society, who are the majority), this cry for the individual against the state looks like another cry for the powerful against the weak. The weaker individual is protected by the impersonal state (or at least so he has been persuaded to believe), and the only person who will gain by reaffirming the rights of the individual is the one with power. The majority of people, not being powerful, see no reason why the interests of the powerful should be furthered.

So, in the long run, this conservative rallying cry is counterproductive. It is necessary to have a completely new conservative philosophy, which will confront directly the question of what the state is and what it ought to be. I would summarize this new philosophy in a single idea. The state ought to be a personal, not an impersonal, entity. Let me explain. The state is first of all a set of institutions. It consists of laws, parliaments, and offices. It also exists in conjunction with educational establishments, churches, and a thousand smaller institutions, reaching down into the roots of civil society. Not all these institutions are strictly part of the state, but all belong to the political order. One such institution is this discussion group, a gathering of people who freely come together in order to listen to an opinionated person and then to challenge him to defend himself. Institutions such as this do not exist everywhere; but they are an important part of the political order in which *we* exist. This institution is very small, but it is entwined with a thousand other institutions, together with which it constitutes the 'body politic'. It is protected by a system of laws and by the cultural expectations, shared values and social habits upon which the political order is founded.

All such institutions are personal in a quite specific sense. They have duties towards their members and rights against their members, just in the way that individual people have. They are sources of authority; they make claims over people and they answer questions for them in an authoritative way. (This is obvious in the case of legal and religious institutions; but it is equally true of clubs and societies. It is the prevailing ethos of authority that forbids people, now, to jump up and shout abuse at me. There is an atmosphere of authority – however mild, and however welcome – in this room.)

Institutions exert their powers legitimately over their members; they can also exert those powers illegitimately. They are responsible to their members and also have a kind of sway over them. In those respects they are like persons. They are not machines, but agents answerable to other people in the way that individual human beings are answerable. A further important fact about these institutions, and one which is neglected by almost all modern conservative thought, is that they are neither inventions which we choose, nor the outcome of contracts. On the contrary, they exist in a certain way independently of us, and are even partly responsible for creating us. We exist because we were born into these institutions, nurtured by them and given a certain social and political identity through their works and offices. It is through the medium of institutions that human beings meet and respond to one another.

Thus Anglomorphs (to borrow Dr Knopfelmacher's useful term) have an instinct for justice and fair play. This instinct does not exist everywhere. But it does exist in this kind of society, largely because it exists in the institutions which surround us at birth and which watch over us as we grow up: the school, the family, the church, the club, and the rule of law which they eventually imply. Now, we feel a certain sympathy for the radical, who demands 'social justice' for the under-privileged. But this is because the word 'justice' has a resonance for us. It connects with a fundamental motive in our lives. And what made it possible for us to resonate in this way to an abstract idea? What gave us the sense of justice? Surely, the institutions which are characteristic of our society and of our kind of state: institutions which awakened in us a feeling of responsibility for our fellows.

However, it is precisely the authority of those institutions that the radical wishes to destroy. If he succeeds in his purpose, he also abolishes the sentiments to which he is appealing. There, I believe, is the real contradiction in the radical cause. The radical wishes us to remain civilized beings, motivated by an idea of justice, and at the same time, he seeks to destroy the institutions which make it possible for us to have that idea.

The first task for us, in the face of the radical threat to our social order, is the 'care' of institutions. Institutions, like all people, are fragile things. They are more easily destroyed than created, and they demand from us a willing sacrifice. We have to give of ourselves in order that they can be maintained. We must respect them and add to them. To do so is a matter of political will, and the destruction of this political will is the most dangerous feature of our prevailing social order.

Men like Professor Manning Clark have devoted much intellectual labour to destroying in us the sense of obligation toward inherited institutions. But we are under that obligation and we should take it to heart. If these institutions are so closely tied to our identity, our self-respect requires us to respect them. That is the first maxim of conservative politics: self-respect requires respect for institutions. To the extent that we learn a habit of mockery towards our inheritance, to that extent do we mock ourselves.

This brings me back to the state. The state is the highest of the institutions to which we owe our existence; it is the supreme institution, which protects and endorses all the others. Without the state, all institutions of civil society would be threatened by the first person who chose to exert force against them. The authority of the state goes under the name of sovereignty. Sovereignty denotes the authority to answer questions finally; to settle, for each of us, the question of our allegiance. But the state can have this kind of authority over our affairs only if we accord to it the status of a person, as I have suggested. The radical's 'equalizing machine' could never be a sovereign body. It could not be a source of collective action, a way of affirming our political identity towards the world as a whole. It could never command us or inspire us, as a person commands and inspires; it can only coerce us implacably, opposing our will with its iron laws of motion.

What is the peculiar thing that I have called sovereignty? That is a great question of political philosophy to which I can only sketch an answer. Nevertheless the answer I shall sketch is not without importance for Australians in these times.

Let us take an analogy. I love my father and I owe him an obligation. Why is that? Because he is there, because he nurtured me, because he made me what I am and because he responds to me with warmth, guidance, advice and a reciprocal obligation. In loving my father I do not ask myself how he came into existence. Maybe my father took up some precious 'living space' that might have been occupied by another. Maybe his coming into existence was the occasion of great suffering. After all, one being cannot come into existence without removing resources from others, who perhaps have an equal claim to them. But that is irrelevant to me. What makes my love and respect for my father right, and what makes his authority over me legitimate, has nothing to do with his origins. It is his present existence and my relation to him which count.

Similarly, the state which made me came into existence before me and at the cost of others. That is the eternal law of creation. No living thing can be created in a finite world without curtailing the opportunities of others. That fact has no bearing, however, on the question whether my obedience to this state is justified. What makes my obedience right, and what makes this government legitimate, is the relation between us, to which I owe my life and happiness. A state is legitimate for me because of its relation to *me*.

The machine state of the radical does not have legitimacy. It rids the world of all obligation, including the obligation to itself. If you want a concrete illustration of this you need only look behind the Iron Curtain to the lands of 'actually existing socialism'. There every citizen avoids answerability to the state. Taxes are not paid, contracts between people are not enforced, the black market governs economic life, and law is replaced by the lawless dominion of the secret police. The state intrudes everywhere while being honoured nowhere. Nobody gives anything away to it or trusts it with anything. The citizen regards himself as under no obligation whatsoever toward it. The state has become an impersonal, threatening entity which controls the citizens through fear, but without authority.

The personal state that I would advocate creates an obligation towards itself, because it is the real representation of the life that is mine. It is bound up with me: I find my life reflected in it and its life reflected in me. For I see it as the supreme expression and protection of the institutions which nurtured me and to which my existence is owed. I am answerable to it, because it is also answerable to me, and from our mutual recognition my allegiance grows.

How do I fulfil my obligation towards such a state? In the first place by caring for the institutions which have nurtured me. But to do that I must accept the given historical reality. These institutions exist, not because of my doing, but as a result of a history which preceded me. Like every history, this history will be a tale of suffering and injustice, but those who suffered are dead, and their death has relieved me of the need to care for them (although not necessarily of the duty to honour them).

What does this mean for sovereignty in the modern world? The first thing that it means is that I have no inalienable rights against the state except one. The only inalienable right I have against the state is the right to be respected as a person, as I in turn respect it. What that means in concrete terms is a very difficult question. But we have an idea of what it means from our relation with each other. We all claim from each other the right to be respected. But that is the only general right, every other right depends upon the particular history of the particular relations which bind us.

This has interesting consequences. In particular one could not say that the individual has an inalienable right of property against the state. That is a well known principle of English law. Nobody in English law has an inalienable right to property in land, for land belongs to the Crown. A freehold is a form of tenure from the Crown, which is defeated by certain acts of the person who holds it. The Crown can at any moment revoke it according to due process of law. To accord inalienable rights – in particular, inalienable rights in land – is to imply that the person who holds those rights is released from his allegiance. He is not really part of the state; he has been put outside the jurisdiction. Hence, if the State of Australia were to give to the Aborigines inalienable rights in land it would in fact be treating the Aborigines as aliens. It would be saying: 'you are outside my sovereign jurisdiction. It is not I who am sovereign in your territory, but you.' Therefore to give inalienable rights in land to the Aborigines is to *alienate* the Aborigines, to tell them that they do not belong with *us*.

To return to an earlier theme, 'multi-culturalism' is a recipe of civil war. It is an attempt to legitimize war, by giving to the separate cultures separate *political* identities. Its meaning is: you do not belong with us, and make sure you do not belong; here is a bit of land for you, so that you can carry on not belonging with us in a place of your own. The long term consequence would be disastrous. For we know very well who would win in any conflict between the whites and Aborigines in this land. Of course that is none of the intention of the people who are promoting this move; but lacking a coherent conception of sovereignty they do not, in truth, know what they are doing.

This brings me to the second task for the conservative. The first task, I said, was the care of institutions. The second task is to give up this breast-beating, guilt-ridden desire to throw away our inheritance. We must take confidence in it, believe in it, recognize that in the end we have inherited something which we have no alternative but to accept. This inheritance is mine, and I ought to accept it; it is as right for me to accept it as it is right for the Aborigine to accept what is truly his. The difference between us is that my culture and institutions are living, while his are dead.

Now what is it that you are accepting, in accepting your inheritance? In one case one major feature of our inheritance stands out as conditioning not just the matter, but also the manner of our acceptance: the tradition of common law, and in particular the tradition that rights in the public sphere are adjudicated legally. Rights are claimed before a court of law and adjudicated publicly in open court. The process of adjudication can make sense, however, only if both parties acknowledge a single sovereign. Again if the radical solution of the Aboriginal problem involves splitting sovereignty, it also threatens the legal adjudication upon which any acceptable solution (any solution acceptable to you and me) will depend.

This tradition of adjudication is not to be understood as an isolated convention. It is made possible only because of its integral connection with other institutions and social artefacts; with the institution of monarchy, with Christian culture, with the habit of public association and free debate. Those are immovable parts of our heritage; but they are also threatened by modern ways of thinking. We must therefore 'confess to' them, and re-integrate them into our lives. In doing so, we will recognize the all-important truth that for us social reality can never be truly politicized. That is to say, we could never think of the world as the radical thinks of it – as a constant struggle to instantiate an abstract idea of justice. We will recognize, rather, that the world contains diverse claims that cannot be satisfied, and which are, perhaps, unsatisfiable. We will recognize that the world is full of claims which must remain open, and that it is part of politics to keep them open for as long as possible. The political order consists, for us, of a constant parading of rights, and a constant toing and froing of unanswered grievances. But we should not regret this fact. For we are not politicized beings; we do not believe that politics is the only thing that matters, or that we must re-fashion the world in accordance with abstract political ideals. Tolerance remains a virtue for us; and we accept others in their diversity. The institutions that we have inherited make this acceptance possible precisely by confining politics to a narrow and concentrated sphere. Our world contains a political process – and therefore it is not truly politicized.

The idea of sovereignty towards which I have gestured is not an intellectual dream. It is a fundamental component of the ordinary experience of British people. Of course, they rarely show that this is so. But they do show it in times of crisis. For example, they showed it during the Falklands war. An Eastern European friend made an interesting remark about this war. He said: 'we have been looking on the West with despair for years and years until this event. For the first time in my adulthood, for the first time in twenty years, I have seen a Western government act for no reason other than the fact that it had been insulted. Britain acted spontaneously, regardless of the diplomatic cost, of the legal cost, of the financial cost – regardless of the consequences, and simply because its sovereignty had been held in contempt. And,' he said 'this gave heart to us as no other recent event has done. It showed us that you had not succumbed to the left-wing disorder, to the disease of galloping equality, or to the nonsense which seemed to us for so long to have weakened you.'

My friend's observation was, I think, true to the experience of the Falklands war. When the real thing – our national sovereignty – was threatened, all the conflicting claims for social justice evaporated overnight. People responded as they should, with their loyalties intact. If I urge you to take confidence in those loyalties it is because I believe in the testimony of that experience. I believe that the confidence is already there.

There is, finally, a third task for conservatives, to which intellectuals alone can seriously address themselves: the task of recuperating history. History has been 'possessed' in recent years by the left establishment. Manning Clark writes as follows:

the fundamental issue (in Australia) has remained the same ever since the Great Strikes and the capitalist [note the word] crisis of 1890–1894, that issue being who should own the means of production, distribution and exchange, and what principle should determine how wealth should be divided amongst the members of society.

In such phrases Manning Clark does for Australia what historians like E. P. Thompson have done for England: he rewrites history in accordance with the half-baked notion that the course of events depends entirely upon the ownership of the means of 'production, distribution and exchange' (a trio of words that comes straight out of *Das Kapital*). We know perfectly well that history has little to do with the dispute about who should own what. The question of ownership and control arises only sometimes, and in response to particular and transitory grievances. True history is the evolving answer, not to the question who owns what, but rather to the question who owes allegiance to whom?

The answer to that question is normally implicit: it needs to be expressed and made consonant only in times of crisis. We have entered such a time, and the task of recuperation therefore lies before us. If people doubt their allegiance, politics – the true *process* of politics – is jeopardized. Only in the context of an acknowledged 'we' does it make sense to engage in political decision making. For it is *we* (through parliaments, through law, through public opinion) who make the choice. The breakdown of allegiance is the end of politics, and in its place the politicized world of the radical is revealed in all its violence: a world of life and death 'struggles' between opposing interests; a world of conflicts that can be resolved only by some 'irreversible shift' or 'final solution'; a world whose disorder is all the greater for the fervour with which it cries out for an abstract 'justice'. And at the root of that cry another and more sinister impulse is lurking: the desire for a totalitarian order in which conflicts will no longer exist, since opposition has been 'liquidated' – the desire for the 'post-political' society.

For us politics remains the guarantee of peace and freedom, the means of confining conflict within the courts and parliament, which are the instruments whereby we live with a thousand unsatisfiable claims. But this most rational of solutions to the problem of co-existence – the solution which teaches us to 'live with the problem' – is possible only because we recognize that we belong together, and are bound by a common allegiance. We must, then, recuperate the history of that allegiance. We must remind ourselves that, if we can feel the guilt which the radical urges upon us, it is because something – something momentous, fertile and good – has been created from the dust of human individuality, a true human 'we'. Our guilt refutes itself, by being *ours*.

From: *Quadrant*, November 1984.

27

THE LEFT
ESTABLISHMENT

During the run-up to the 1987 election, a survey of university and polytechnic teachers, conducted by the *Times Higher Education Supplement*, concluded that only 16% of academics would vote conservative; of the remainder, the majority would vote for the Labour Party, notwithstanding its move to the left, and its espousal of the fashionable causes of disaffection: unilateral disarmament, feminism, anti-racism, and the rights of sexual minorities. Some time previously, Mrs Thatcher had been proposed for an honorary doctorate at the University of Oxford, from which she had graduated some three decades before. The dons decided to make use of their vote and, mobilized by well-known leftists like Peter Pultzer and Steven Lukes, stampeded to the Court House to manifest their displeasure. Despite her historical importance as the first woman Prime Minister of our country, Mrs Thatcher was denied an honorary degree by her own *alma mater*. This fact should be set beside the ease with which honorary degrees are earned by left-wing politicians and heads of state. Robert Mugabe was recently honoured in this way by the University of Glasgow, and Mrs Ceausescu not only holds an honorary doctorate from the Polytechnic of Central London, but has also been granted – on the strength of her self-bestowed reputation as a chemist – an honorary fellowship of the Royal Institute of Chemists.

During the period in question, it became difficult for speakers judged to be 'right wing' to address university gatherings. Conservative politicians – especially those who could be characterized, on the usual makeshift evidence, as 'racists' – would be sometimes assaulted, usually denied a hearing, and always in need of police protection. An Oxford academic, David Selbourne, was ostracized by his students and colleagues, on account of having written for the *Times* (whose dispute with a trade union had been exalted into a 'noble struggle' for workers' rights). Selbourne was forced to resign; while a commission appointed to review the safeguards of academic freedom at his college made no censure of those who had provoked his resignation, and spoke of the need for lecturers to abide by the 'traditions' and 'sensibilities' of their institution, and to curb their tongues and their pens accordingly.

Other academics have been similarly abused: Professor Vincent was assaulted during his own lecture at the University of Bristol, on account of writing for the *Sun* newspaper (well known to students as the mouthpiece of the gutter Right); the author of this article has been threatened and shouted down – even when attempting to give a public lecture on the theme of 'Toleration' at the University of York – on account of the unsatisfactory ideological dossier which always precedes his arrival at a British university. Mr Honeyford (well-known for his contributions to the *Salisbury Review*) was lucky to escape from Liverpool University with his life, while anyone who offers to defend South Africa, the Nicaraguan Contras, or even Israel stands a serious risk of intimidation.

Of course the intolerance of the ultra-left does not meet with the approval of the majority of academics. Although the donnish classes lean to the left, they are relatively tolerant towards those who lean in another direction, looking on them as an endangered species, which ought to be preserved in captivity in numbers just large enough to breed. On the other hand, when someone is persecuted for views judged obnoxious by the left, the academic establishment will not put itself out to defend him. Left-liberals like Sir Isaiah Berlin, Bernard Williams, A. H. Halsey, Ronald Dworkin, and H. L. A. Hart spoke out, during the days when universities tried to discipline their revolutionary members, in order to justify the right of the individual to speak his mind, however offensively, assuming that this right was being curtailed by crusty old reactionaries for whom the dustheap of history lay prepared. On the other hand, those noble figures fall instantly silent, when the threat to freedom of speech and opinion comes from the left: either they do not perceive the threat, or else they regard it as a legitimate bridling of views which are too dangerous to be aired in public. We have even witnessed the strange spectacle of an amendment to a Parliamentary Bill, designed to guarantee freedom of speech on campus, being actually opposed by all those members of the House of Lords who are also Vice-Chancellors – on the recommendation, as a rule, of the impeccably liberal bodies over which they preside.

The incidents to which I have alluded are not isolated occurr-
ences: they are quite normal and run-of-the-mill. Nor are they
confined to universities. Ideological conformity has been rigor-
ously enforced in British schools, with local authorities and their
advisers often ensuring that promotion will not be offered to
those judged to be out of tune with the spirit of progress. Readers
of the *Salisbury Review* will be familiar with the 'anti-racist'
show-trial, as a weapon in the 'class struggle'. But it is only the
extreme point on a graduated scale of sanctions, which will
ensure, as a rule, that those who rise to the top in the educational
world are either on the left, or else liberal in the 'useful idiot'
manner.

A parallel development has taken place in the Church of England, once described as 'the Tory Party at prayer', and still counting far more Tories than socialists or social democrats among its
congregation. At their recent council, the Anglican bishops
made use of a standard piece of communist newspeak, in order
to express their sympathy for those engaged in 'armed struggle'
against oppressive regimes: meaning, of course, not the peoples
of Romania, Czechoslovakia or Poland (in whom Christianity
has largely cancelled the desire for violence), but those of South
Africa and Palestine. All recent reports issuing from the Church
of England (and especially those from its Board of Social Responsibility) have been of socialist persuasion, involving an attitude
of repudiation towards the history and institutions of England,
and a secular morality of 'social justice'.

I do not think that the case of Britain is in any way exceptional.
It would not be safe to defend the Contras, for example, in the
average American university, and the career of an academic
would be put seriously at risk if he were to become an outspoken
critic of homosexuality or feminism. The University of Stanford
– which offers degree courses in 'feminist studies', for which
ideological conformity is the *sine qua non* of success – is now
jettisoning its course in 'Western Civilization', not on the
grounds that the reading required for it is beyond the intellectual
capacity of many students (though this would be true) but on the
ground that such 'cultural imperialism' is unacceptable in a
university which has set its face against racism, élitism, and the
Eurocentric worldview. The formerly conservative Dartmouth
College has suspended right-wing students who have publicized the low academic standards and political bias of certain
courses; and once again the statistics – collected in this case by
the sociologist Seymour Martin Lipsett – indicate a preponder-
ance among American faculty members of left-liberal opinions.

Naturally labels like 'left' and 'right' are not very precise and always depend upon context for their interpretation. It is particularly difficult to see what they mean in the United States, where the person whom we in Britain should describe as 'on the left' is more normally designated as 'liberal'. Nevertheless, it is possible to give a rough sketch of what I mean by 'left' opinions that will be sufficient to identify the state of mind expressed in them:

The fundamental belief in human equality, accompanied by a hostility to all distinction, whether of class, race or gender.

The suspicion of 'power'; and the absence of any lively sense that the surrounding power might be legitimate, despite being in other hands than one's own.

The hostility to all that confers power: and especially to enterprise, business, and the market.

The 'critical' approach to society in which 'power' and 'conflict' are everywhere perceived and unmasked.

The paradoxical identification with the external enemies of power: especially with those states which pose a threat to the security of Western nations.

The willingness to believe the *bona fides* of those who speak the language of 'liberation' and 'struggle'.

Guilt towards one's country and its past – the attitude described in America as the 'liberal cringe': a form of embarrassment at one's ancestors, for having believed in their own superiority and having, through that belief, made themselves superior.

Anti-patriotism; usually accompanied by mockery towards patriotic sentiments in one's own nation – or an open war upon them as forms of 'militarism'.

Those opinions and attitudes form a coherent nexus, and ask for a single explanation: an explanation of how it is that the 'thinking intellectual' tends to repudiate the very social order which grants him the leisure to think, to teach and to agitate for change. It is not necessary to take sides in the underlying ideological conflict, in order to perceive that such an explanation ought to be forthcoming. In the days of McCarthyism, it was hardly puzzling that universities, schools and publications tended to manifest the same fears and bigotries as the surrounding world: such a fact does not cry out for special explanation. But when a seemingly immovable left-wing consensus emerges in the intellectual world at the very moment when the people as a whole are turning their backs on left-wing ways of thinking, we are faced with an interesting and in some ways surprising occurrence. We discover, for the first time in our history, a full-scale left establishment, at the very moment when the much sought-after constituency of the left – the industrial proletariat – has finally disappeared, not only from the real world, but also from the popular imagination.

Moreover, not only is the tide of popular opinion retreating from socialist ideas – at least from those which seem to legitimize the control of society by the state – these ideas are no longer put forward in a spirit of conviction even by those who claim to believe them. The only *strength* that attaches to them, is that of opposition to their enemy, whose evil, however, is so great as to endow them with a constantly renewable motivating power.

The case provides, I believe, a novel challenge to theories of ideology. How is this growth of a 'left establishment' to be explained, and what does it indicate about the social conditions of the 'capitalist' world? The first thing that will strike the student of Marx is that this ideology, which dominates churches, schools and academies, as well as much of the press and television, is not the ideology of a 'ruling class'. The case should be contrasted with the situation in the 'socialist countries', where ideology is expressly purveyed and maintained by the *nomenklatura*, even though neither the members of that (ruling) class, nor those who are subject to them, have the slightest tendency to believe in it. In the Western world, the 'ruling class' could mean one of two things: those who control the 'means of production', and those who control the instruments of political power. In Britain neither of those groups leans to the left, and both are scorned and ridiculed by the left establishment. So far as this aspect of the Marxian theory goes, therefore, it provides us with no explanation of the ruling ideology.

Before returning to Marx, I shall consider two alternatives. First, the 'indoctrination' theory. It might be said that an intellectual establishment owes its ideas primarily to what is taught in the schools and academies, and that this provides an opportunity for 'control from above' which no self-respecting activist of the left would fail to take. Anyone can conduct a 'movement of ideas' provided that there is no resistance, or that resistance comes only when it is too late. Once the crucial chairs are filled, the crucial bureaucrats installed, and the crucial textbooks written and made compulsory, the re-education of the intelligentsia follows as a matter of course.

David Marsland[1] has shown that this process has occurred in the discipline of British sociology, analysing all the major school textbooks in this subject, and demonstrating that they are so manifestly biased to the left, and so dismissive of the few 'right-wing' arguments that they consider, as to constitute little more than a sustained exercise in indoctrination. I shall illustrate with an example of my own, taken from the principal textbook currently used to teach school sociology:

> Inequality of power and advantage has been an extremely common, if not universal, feature of human societies, even if the degree of inequality has varied very greatly. It has almost always been the case that some group or groups have controlled or exploited other groups. At some points in the history of a given society people have rebelled and challenged this inequality; at other points they have meekly accepted their subordination.[2]

The passage introduces the discussion of inequality, in a book that openly professes the value of sociology as a catalyst of social change. Three conclusions are foregone in this paragraph, and throughout the ensuing discussion, and they are foregone in the interests of a political agenda: that inequality is tantamount to the existence of 'controlling' or 'exploiting' groups; that when people have rebelled against such groups it is in order to challenge 'inequality'; and that when they do not rebel it is because they 'meekly' accept 'subordination'. Now it is true that certain theories argue for those conclusions – the most important being Marxism. But Marxism is a theory with a political agenda, and people who neither accept the theory nor approve of the agenda will naturally not wish to see its conclusions being assumed throughout a discussion that ought to question them.

The political dispute concerning equality is wide-ranging. Nevertheless, there is a right-wing position which argues as follows: first that it is not inequality but equality that requires 'controlling groups' for its achievement; secondly, that exploitation occurs not in the social distribution of goods and advantages (however unequal that distribution might be) but in coercive relations between people – and hence that there may be exploitation even where there is equality; thirdly, that inequality is not what is resented or rebelled against, but tyranny – including the tyranny which has 'social equality' as its goal; finally that subordination occurs only where there is coercion, and not where economic relations are based – as in a market – on consent. That position is by no means uncommon or academically disreputable – unless you think Hayek and Nozick (both of whom have defended it) are academically disreputable. Yet it is not mentioned by the authors of the passage quoted, nor, so far as I have discovered, by *any other author of a school sociology textbook*. Nor is any attention paid to the thinker who has questioned egalitarian values most thoroughly – Nietzsche – whose account of the 'slave morality' (the morality typical of the left-establishment), quaint though it may appear to a philosopher, is a piece of genuine sociology. I do not say that those 'right-wing' ideas are correct: but they provide a case to answer, and the very language of the paragraph quoted shows a determination neither to answer, nor even to raise, the question that they pose.

I give the example in order to illustrate a process which can be witnessed not only in sociology, but in almost all subjects in the humanities (and especially those which touch on the concerns of those for whom the intellectual life is continuous with political action). A new kind of academic discourse has emerged, which is only superficially a discourse of enquiry, and which has the more urgent purpose of closing the mind around certain unexamined premises, and mobilizing the resources of the academy in the task of their legitimation. The practice is combined with another: that of ideological criticism, in which the texts and the assumptions of traditional subjects are exposed to a kind of third degree interrogation, in order to reveal the hidden premises in *them*. The very language of traditional literature is repudiated, on account of its 'patriarchal' or 'authoritarian' assumptions, and the texts themselves are examined less for what they say than for what is implied in the fact of saying it. Understanding and sympathy give way to what Paul Ricoeur has called a 'hermeneutics of suspicion': an obsessive hunt for the 'power' and 'oppression' which lie concealed in traditional discourse. As a result of these two practices, the humanities are open to total politicization, with the establishment left controlling the curriculum, the method, and the ideology of study.

Despite those practices, however, I do not think that we can accept the 'indoctrination theory'. To accept it is to commit one of the naïveties against which the history of Marxism should caution us. It is to attribute too great an influence to conscious planning, and not enough to the 'invisible hand'. What explains the growth of sociology in the first place, and the penetration of the schools by a subject that has no agreed discipline and which lends itself so easily to a political agenda? What explains the easy acceptance of such transparent indoctrination as I have described, or the widespread and simultaneous rise of 'ideological' criticism? And what explains the silence of academics themselves, faced with the flood of semi-literate and transparently political material which flows around them?

It is true that there is a penalty to be paid for criticizing the left establishment, and this provides a strong pressure to conformity. But this penalty is part of what needs to be explained. It may be useful at this point to consider an example and I hope I may be forgiven for describing experiences of my own. I recently published a series of essays, entitled *Thinkers of the New Left*, which originally appeared in the *Salisbury Review*. These essays argued, among other things, that the major authorities adopted in the teaching of humanities and social sciences are of no great intellectual significance, and owe their appeal to their ideological 'correctness'. The book was subjected to fierce abuse in the British press, and had the complement paid to it of appearing in *samizdat* editions in Czech and Polish. The response was typified by a letter to the publisher from Dr Michael Shortland, who teaches philosophy in the Department of External Studies at the University of Oxford. (Shortland is also reviews editor of *Radical Philosophy*, a journal devoted to the dissemination of socialist ideas.) 'I may say,' Dr Shortland wrote, 'that I have considered deeply the question [i.e. whether to review *Thinkers of the New Left*] with many colleagues in the Philosophy Faculty here [i.e. in Oxford]. Without exception, the feeling has been that this shabby, shoddy book deserves as little publicity as possible. You will by now have gauged the extremely unfavourable reviews generated by the book. But I may tell you with dismay that many colleagues here feel that the Longman imprint – a respected one – has been tarnished by association with Scruton's work.' The slightly menacing tone is repeated more emphatically later: 'I do hope that the negative reactions generated by this particular publishing venture may make Longman think more carefully about its policy in the future.'

At about the same time, I had been proposed for a personal chair at my own university, which honour can be conferred only on the recommendation of certain standing external advisers. The adviser first consulted (who is professor at a British university) responded with an interesting letter. He would have had no difficulty in recommending me, he wrote, before my articles began to appear in the *Times*, and on the strength of my academic work; but those articles were the real proof of my intellectual powers, and showed conclusively that I was unworthy of promotion. In other words, the adviser inferred intellectual incompetence from ideological unacceptability; and saw nothing strange in ignoring a candidate's academic work, and concentrating on his opinionated journalism, when assessing his fitness for an academic post.

I do not think my experiences are untypical; they have persuaded me that the penalty for outspoken criticism of the prevailing ideology – especially if it is criticism levelled from *within* the university – is more or less automatic, and spontaneously understood, by those who administer it, as a just retribution for intellectual error. This is how the idea of the conservative party as the 'stupid party' first arose: not because those who support it are actually stupid, but because their opponents are people who have *identified* their own position with the intellectual life.

When the pressure towards ideological conformity has acquired such an automatic character, we should not try to explain it as the outcome of a plan. We should look instead for an 'invisible hand' explanation, of the kind offered by the theorists of the market. This leads me to my second theory of the left establishment: the theory of 'public choice', as expounded by James Buchanan and the economists of the 'Virginia School'. According to this school of thought, the tendency of modern societies is to generate areas of advantage which are liberated from the constraints of the economic market, by the market in political power. For example, the services offered by the state are invariably secured from the possibility of bankruptcy, and their occupants made immune to economic competition. To secure a position in a state-controlled service industry is to acquire a life-interest in the social product, and a perpetual guarantee against disaster. A new opportunity is provided for what Buchanan calls 'rent-seeking': i.e., the process whereby an individual can claim a rent upon economic activities the risks of which he does not bear. People who have secured such rents form a natural 'interest group', whose principal concern will be to maximize the resources directed to their activity, and to ensure security of tenure for each of their members. Hence the law of bureaucratic expansion, discovered by Parkinson, and since universally confirmed.

Ideology performs two useful services to the rent-seeker. First, it maintains group coherence in the face of external threat. Ideological beliefs tend to declare a separation between 'us' and 'them': they offer a criterion of membership, which reinforces the unity of the group, while providing a barrier to intruders. An interest group united by an ideology has a much better chance of gaining control of a rent, for the reason that its members will be less likely to compete with each other in the pursuit of it, and more likely to lend support to each other against outside rivals.

Furthermore, the ideological test of membership has the effect of destroying rival criteria, in particular those which might re-introduce effective competition into the areas where rents can be obtained. For example, it would be normal to assume that offices in a public service – whether it be education, social work or medicine – should be 'open to the talents', and gained and lost on grounds of competence alone. In the sphere of education, this means that intellect and culture should be the principal qualifications for office. Now an ideology can *masquerade* as the sign of intellect and culture. It can provide an easily intelligible model of those virtues, and show exactly how to acquire them. Hence it permits the educational profession to erect a charade of competition, and to maintain a charade of standards, while in fact offering 'jobs for the boys'.

Left-wing ideology is particularly effective in this respect. For its ruling idea is that of equality. In its heart, it is a sustained attack on the concept of merit; while pretending to uphold standards it will, therefore, always end by undermining them. By its very nature, it tends to the gratifying conclusion that no criteria really matter, that all people are equal, and that discrimination is arbitrary and unjust. The only qualification that can be reconciled with conscience is that of ideology. The one who recognizes the injustice of privilege, therefore, is the one entitled to receive it.

In the context of rent-seeking, the interest group united by the ideology of the left has a great Darwinian advantage. It can put itself forward as qualified by the very criteria which determine the accepted framework of competition, while at the same time destroying that framework, in order to sit securely on the throne. It neutralizes all competition among its members, while effectively excluding its rivals on the very ground which they purport to respect.

This explains two very important facts: the vehemence with which the internal critic is condemned, and the language used to condemn him. The internal critic is an existential danger: unlike the one who has been successfully excluded, he is not a business rival, but a potential traitor to the cause of group cohesion. He needs to be exposed, denounced, and expelled from the fold. Usually he is condemned as an *elitist*: that is, someone who believes too seriously in the virtues of competition, in the scarcity of real achievement, and in the inequality of men. When the critic becomes too threatening, he must be cast out, perhaps with a show-trial, by wounded colleagues who protest at the 'atmosphere of intimidation' which he had created. (This atmosphere of intimidation was discerned by the critics of Mr Honeyford and Mr Savery; it was also noticed recently by the staff of the Open University, following an anonymous document prepared by students, criticizing the left-wing bias of certain courses. It was noticed too by the staff of Dartmouth College, who, in suspending the students responsible, rejoiced at the return of the 'academic freedoms' which the presence of those right-wing vigilantes had served to curtail.)

The 'public choice' theory of the left establishment has its merits, and can be interestingly compared with the classical Marxist theory of ideology. Like classical Marxism, the theory offers a *functional* explanation of ideology. But it rejects the distinctively Marxian claim that the beneficiary is a ruling class. The beneficiary, according to the 'public choice' explanation, is the believer himself, and the interest group of which he is a member.

Perhaps the most important merit of the theory, is that it can explain the otherwise rather puzzling posture of academic liberals. On the whole these too are maintained by rents derived from the welfare system. Their tolerance and open-mindedness are the virtues of people freed from the threat of disaster, eager to offer benefits which they can offer at no cost to themselves. Their position is safe, however, only so long as they gain the favour of the new rent-seekers, whose advance they protected by their very preparedness to speak for every viewpoint, and for the rights of every group. Once installed, the left establishment poses a potential threat to the liberal who helped it into power. He must take care not to be identified with those criteria of intellectual competence and rooted culture which the new barbarians fear. He is useful to the left, as the protector of the moral space in which ideology can flourish and fortify its positions. But let him step out of line – let him reveal his sympathy for the elitist, racist, sexist, or in any other way anti-egalitarian ideas which threaten the rights of conquest – and he too must take the consequences of enmity. Liberals are always at pains, therefore, to distance themselves from their right-wing colleagues and will tacitly cooperate with the left in excluding them from the rents available.

The 'public choice' theory explains the emergence of a left establishment within the state welfare system, or some other area of guaranteed rent. But does it explain the emergence of the very same establishment among the priesthood, membership of which involves a sacrifice and not a material gain? Or in the media, where fierce competition will always fragment any interest group sustained by ideological ties? It seems to me that it does not. In these cases, I suggest, we are dealing with a 'clerisy' – a class of people who identify themselves in relation to their fellow men as instructors, counsellors and guides. And it seems that there is something about this very role, in a world of declining faith, which turns its adherent in a left-wing direction.

The role of a clerk – whether priest or teacher – is to mediate. He transcribes and interprets for others the message of a higher authority. Such a role is dignified and ennobling, since it confers on the clerk some of the effulgence of authority. The traditions of learning, the body of knowledge, and the revelations of faith all make a distinction between those who possess them, and those who do not. The mediating role of the institute bestows authority on the clerk; in such circumstances, he will be sensible of merit and privilege, and endowed with a lively sense of the legitimacy of the powers which uphold his office.

Take away the belief in the higher authority – in God, civilization, or the given tradition of learning – and the role of mediator collapses. The clerk becomes foolish in his own eyes, as the interpreter of an authority in which he no longer believes. He is no longer elevated above the level of his pupil, and endeavours to negate all suggestion that his privilege and position are the sign of real inequality. The 'left establishment' attitude which I described emerges spontaneously among people subjected to this emotionally strenuous position.

If that is correct, however, it raises an interesting question concerning the idea of a university. To what extent is a 'liberal education', as it used to be called, really available in the modern world? When von Humboldt and Matthew Arnold mounted their defence of culture, and Cardinal Newman his vindication of the university, all took it for granted that freedom of thought could be as much a part of humane education as it was a necessary ingredient in scientific progress. None supposed that the results of this freedom could be known in advance: such a supposition is as much a contradiction in the humanities as it is in the natural sciences. And each imagined that a unifying culture could persist and be enriched through the process of enquiry, and passed on undiminished to future generations.

This manifestly has not happened. By the standards set by nineteenth-century academics, we have witnessed a decline, not only in the intellectual ability of academics, but also in their cultural standing and spiritual authority. Moreover, genuinely liberal teaching is everywhere in retreat.

Liberal education flourished only when it was possible to assume a belief in human excellence. It relied upon a long tradition of universalist thinking, with its roots in Greek philosophy, Christian religion and Roman law. Yet, as Alain Finkielkraut has mordantly demonstrated,[3] this universalist tradition has now been put in question, as the source of the very 'chauvinism' and 'racism' which liberalism has striven to eradicate. The liberal frame of mind is egalitarian, in that it offers equal respect to all persons. But it cannot survive the attempt to engineer some 'equality of outcome', or even 'equality of opportunity', which ignores the most fundamental differences between us: including the difference between those who are good at something, and those who are not. It is predicated on faith: faith in the civilizing process, in universal values, and – ultimately – in the God who is their guarantee. The priestly office is possible only so long as the clerk believes in the *authority* of his teachings, and in himself as the mediator between authority and ignorance.

The effect of the left establishment is therefore to endanger the liberal education which made it possible. Egalitarian ideology has a tendency to spread and settle. It is mild, and reassuring; it also serves, as I have argued, to neutralize the threat posed by talent. It is vindictive only towards its internal traitors, and occupies the seat of privilege quite benignly, so long as it is questioned from a point of view outside its chosen territory. It will continue to turn all education in its favoured direction, manufacturing 'subjects', 'authorities' and 'methods' which have nothing to recommend them besides their egalitarian assumptions. Gradually, however, as students perceive the futility of their studies, the universities will lose their following, just as the churches are losing theirs. Only the voice of authority can awaken the desire to learn, and a clerk without authority has nothing serious to teach.

From: *The Salisbury Review*, December 1988.

28
IN DEFENCE OF
THE NATION

It is neither polite nor politic for those brought up in the Western liberal tradition to defend the 'national idea' as the foundation of political order. Or rather, you can defend that idea on behalf of others – at least if they are engaged in some 'struggle for national liberation' – but not on behalf of your own community and kind. Indeed, you should be careful not to use words like 'kind', 'race', or 'kin'. Loyalties, if they are not universalist, must be expressed surreptitiously, in the self-deprecating language of one confessing to a private fault. In a recent publication, Professor Bikhu Parekh shows why there is a need for caution. He summarizes a nationalist view (which he attributes to various people, including myself), in 'four basic premises':

> First, a State is held together by a sense of nationality; that is, the unity of the State is grounded in the unity of the nation. Second, the sense of nationality is only possible among people of a common stock and sharing a feeling of kinship; that is, the unity of the nation is grounded in the unity of stock or kind. Third, the black communities in Britain are incapable of developing affection or loyalty for it and sharing a unity of sentiments with the whites. Fourth, the preservation of nationhood is a supreme moral value and justifies such morally repugnant deeds as their repatriation and forcible assimilation.[1]

The first of those 'premises' is something that I shall indeed defend – as a conclusion – in what follows. The second is familiar from the literature of nationalism, being proposed in one form by Herder, and in another by Fichte.[2] A century ago it would have been possible to discuss its truth with open mind and open heart, as did Renan and Acton.[3] And of course it was possible, even then, to perceive that the 'common stock' invoked in this 'premiss' is in part a metaphor, whose reality lies not only in descent, but also in language, proximity, faith and culture.

It is not for the sake of reviving that interesting debate that Parekh offers his analysis. The two further 'premisses' are the ones that have aroused his interest, as they naturally arouse the interest of all liberal readers. Are there really people prepared, in the modern world, to defend such things? And are they really permitted to retain academic positions? For the record, I should say that the peculiar belief that nationhood is a 'supreme moral value' is not one that *I* share. Nor do I think that repatriation or forcible assimilation are (unless perhaps *in extremis*) morally justifiable. Nor do I think the 'black communities' in Britain are incapable of developing loyalty to it – whatever 'it' may be. If I protest at the sentimentality which sees blacks always as members of 'communities' and never as individuals, it is not on grounds of 'liberal individualism' – for I am neither an individualist nor a liberal – but because the idea of 'community' here invoked runs counter to the national loyalty which it is my purpose to defend.

More interesting than Parekh's list of 'basic premisses' is the theory that he opposes to them. He argues that defenders of the four premisses fail to see that the modern state is founded in a new and autonomous principle of unity: a principle defined in purely *political* terms. The modern state, he writes, is

> not to subscribe to, let alone to enforce, a specific body of moral, religious or cultural beliefs, save those such as the rule of law which are inherent in its structure. Its job [is] to provide a framework of authority and a body of laws within which individuals and groups [are] at liberty to live the way they [want]; . . . to be its member is to acknowledge the structure of its authority and to bide by its laws.[4]

That 'structure of authority' is the only source of unity which a modern state has, or ought to have. To accept this structure is part of what is meant by *Sittlichkeit*, and those who argue for the primacy of *national* ideas in establishing political unity are in effect asking us to relate to our neighbours (or at least to those of them who do not belong to our 'kind' or 'nation'), through the more primitive, more entangled conceptions of *Moralität*, rather than as fellow citizens.

Parekh gives, as his single example of a 'modern state' constructed according to those enlightened principles, the United

States of America, which, he says, is composed of many different nations, and which self-evidently derives its unity and legitimacy from the system of authority erected and maintained by the Constitution. And, he implies, the more mature a state, the greater its capacity to develop real political unity out of religious and cultural diversity.

If I were to judge from Parekh's other writings – witness, for example, his critique of Oakeshott[5] – I should conclude that he is in fact a critic, and even a severe critic, of the abstract liberalism that he here seems to be defending. I suspect that the liberal theory of the state appeals to him on account of its polemical utility, rather than its truth. Nevertheless, there is undeniably something very attractive in the extreme liberal theory, as Parekh describes it. It sets before us a picture of the state constructed entirely according to the abstract principles of a pure political science, in which legitimacy is unpolluted by the messy claims of prescription. And while it always astonishes me that those who endorse it, and who give the United States as their principal example (it would be hard to find another one), are by no means uniformly pro-American – being often first in line to condemn the rootless, consumer-oriented chaos, as they see it, of 'capitalist democracy' – it is nevertheless true that no better theory has ever been devised with which to castigate obstinate reactionaries like myself, who freely admit to upholding Western institutions, Western values, and the features of political order which have been so powerfully realized in America.

The 'full liberal theory of the state' originated as an account of *legitimacy*. It is invoked by Parekh, however, as a theory of *unity*. (The tendency to answer the questions of unity and legitimacy in the same terms, and through a single theory, is a recurring feature of liberalism, and can also be seen in Sidgwick and Mill.[6]) I shall consider the unity of the body politic, rather than the legitimacy of the institutions used to govern it. The full liberal theory sees the state itself as the source of that unity, whereas, I shall argue, unity is, in the normal instance, social rather than political and ought also to be national.

The liberal theory has both a descriptive and a prescriptive version. It tells us sometimes that this is how things *are* in the modern world, sometimes that this is how things *ought* to be. As a prescriptive theory it commands widespread acceptance, defended by Spinoza, Locke and Kant, and perhaps even embodied, as Parekh suggests, in the US Constitution. A version has recently been advanced by John Gray, not in order to attack conservatism, but in order precisely to embody the insights of conservatism in a modified theory of the liberal state.[7] In all cases, however, an understandable concern for liberal ideas of legitimacy, has given rise to a quite untenable theory of political unity – and one which, if upheld as *realpolitik*, would almost certainly lead to the collapse of liberal jurisdiction.

Before considering the liberal theory of unity, however, it is useful to return to the theory of legitimacy from which it derives. The appeal of liberal theories lies in the ease with which they can be given a 'foundational' character, in terms which seem to presuppose no religious or metaphysical commitment on the part of those who subscribe to them. Two ideas have been particularly important in developing the 'deep' theory of the liberal state: the social contract, and the 'unconditioned rational chooser'. Defenders of the social contract argue that all obligation has its foundation in consent, and that we are under a political obligation only to the extent that we are bound by some contractual relation to comply with it. Those who base their liberalism on an idea of pure rational choice argue that a state is legitimate only to the extent that a rational being, consulting the principles of rational choice alone, and without reference to his distinguishing conditions, would choose to live within its jurisdiction. Sometimes the two theories are combined – as in Rawls, for whom, however, the second theory has gradually gained ascendancy. Both theories refuse to acknowledge 'prescriptive right' – that is, obligations which were never 'undertaken'. And both are founded on a conception of the human person that is psychologically, morally, and metaphysically highly questionable.

The objection to the 'liberal individualist' conception of the person has recently surfaced even in the literature of liberalism, usually distorted, as in Walzer, Sandel and Charles Taylor, so as to seem like a further move in a 'leftward' direction.[8] But its original proponent – Hegel, invoked by Parekh in the reference to *Sittlichkeit* and *Moralität* – was no left-winger. Indeed, in the matter under discussion, he was probably as reactionary as I. In Hegel's view, man owes his identity as a rational chooser to a process of development that implicates him inescapably in obligations which he did not choose. These obligations of piety are both pre-contractual and pre-political. (Hegel assigns them to the 'family', though, as his own argument shows, that is too narrow a designation.) The legitimacy of the state depends in part upon its ability to recuperate and articulate these non-political obligations, which form the original of its own non-contractual order.

The person who, on releasing himself into the freely contracting world of 'civil society', dishonours the pieties that nurtured him is not more, but less rational than the one who respects them. The blithe momentary Benthamite cuts away the ground from the rational choices that he pretends to be making, by depriving himself of every value other than his own pleasure – a commodity whose worth vanishes in the possession of it. He may, once he has risen to full autonomy, possess himself of another source of morality: the universalizing imperative of Kant, which derives its authority from reason alone. But the Kantian imperative sets a limit to goals, and does not provide them. Its capacity to become a *motive*, and so to be incorporated into the agent's acts and projects, depends upon what Hegel called a dialectical relation with those instincts, prejudices and pieties which it serves to qualify. Kant had imagined that reason could be its *own* motive: that the categorical imperative could be freed from all 'empirical determinations', and yet be sovereign. But in this he was wrong, for reasons which subsequent philosophers have made clear. Choice must start somewhere: and even if this starting point is later described, from the point of view of reason, as mere prejudice, this is not to condemn it, but on the contrary, to show the indispensability of prejudice in the make-up of a rational agent.

I mention those arguments only to remind the reader that the questions at issue are, at bottom, metaphysical, and that the assurance of liberals, that they have access to the truth of man's condition, ought to be set against the extreme implausibility of their metaphysical convictions. The same dubious metaphysics which informs the liberal theory of legitimacy motivates the liberal theory of unity. Every political order depends, and ought to depend, upon a non-political idea of membership. And to the extent that it emancipates itself from that idea, I claim, to that extent does it lose its motivating force, just as individuals lose their moral identity and will, to the extent that their prejudices, pieties and moral instincts are cancelled by the abstract imperatives of the 'pure rational chooser'. This is not to say that the full liberal theory of the state does not, in some sense, *describe* the society of the future. It prognosticates the death of political order, by its very ability to evaporate into abstract nothingness the prejudices upon which society depends. The result of this, I believe, will not be the birth of the liberal polity, but its final extinction. For as prejudice dwindles, tolerance is left unguarded by conviction, and falls prey to the ever-vigilant schemes of the fanatic.

Membership

It is often argued that the idea of the nation is a recent invention, coming to the fore either as a reaction to the Enlightenment,[9] or as part of the Enlightenment itself: the necessary replacement for an aristocratic entitlement and a dynastic crown.[10] Certainly there is a *doctrine* – 'nationalism' – which owes its being to the controversies of the late eighteenth century.[11] But an idea is not born with the doctrine that perverts it, nor does the fact wait attendance on our first conceiving it. Nations were realities by the time Shakespeare wrote his histories,[12] and the national idea is already luminous in those histories, even if detached from the bellicose doctrines that have polluted it in recent times. It was to the national idea that Cardinal Richelieu appealed in 1617, when he ruled that, in matters of state, no French Catholic should prefer a Spaniard to a French Protestant.[13] It was a nation, in some sense, which established its empire in South America. And, when the King James Bible has God say to Abraham 'And in thy seed shall all the nations of the earth be blessed' (Genesis 22:18), this is surely not so far from the national idea of recent history.

Nobody who defends the national idea is now likely to explain himself in terms of kinship or race: and not only through fear of the thought-police. The idea that mankind divides into biological 'races' has been put to such absurd use by the Gobinistes and their followers, and entangled itself with so much nonsense and pseudo-science, as to have lost all credibility.[14] Even if there were some element of truth in the theory, it could give no comfort to the nationalist, since races, if they exist, are not confined within national boundaries, and have no characteristic language, culture or history. Indeed biological races are defined without reference to history: there is no other justification for the concept. The idea therefore offers nothing to those searching for an historical identity, upon which to found a state which owes its legitimacy to birthright alone.

Nevertheless, it is difficult to avoid terms like 'race', not least because they accurately reflect *ways of conceiving* social unity. The Jewish self-identification as 'children of Israel' is an important instance. That the Jews form no homogeneous genetic entity is evident. Nevertheless, they identify themselves in terms of a common descent, and this is a feature of their pre-political unity which cannot be discarded without detriment to their cohesion. Our own terms for 'nation' also originate in ideas of common descent: *natio, patria, národ*, etc. German has as its normal term for pre-political unity, *Volk*, a word which is now neutral as to who begat whom, but which originally had connotations of family and tribe. Interesting, too, are the Arabic words for nation. One – *watan* – derives from *watana*, to dwell, and identifies a people purely in terms of its dwelling place. Another, *Umm*, the classical term still used in such phrases as *al-umam al-mutahidah* (The United Nations), derives from the same root as the words for 'source' and 'mother'. Yet another, *qawm* – the more usual term when it comes to questions of nationalism and national identity, and which means, in pre-political parlance, kinsfolk or fellow tribesmen – derives from the root *qāma*, meaning to stand up, to arise, to be proud, to attack, to be. In this root – which occurs in the description of God as *al-qayyum*, the Everlasting one – is condensed a whole philosophy of man's social nature, and one that should be borne in mind by the student of modern 'Arab nationalism'. For a *qawmah* is also an uprising, a 'revolution', and it is through such a 'standing up' against adversaries, the Arab nationalist believes, that a people is born.

In a loose sense, therefore, the term 'race' may still perform a function, even for those who have discarded the eugenic superstitions of the racists. It denotes a continuity across generations, based in kinship and intermarriage, but supported also by a consciousness of common descent. This common descent creates the obligation of inheritance: we must receive from our forefathers what we also pass to our children. Only the idea that the inheritance is entirely *biological*, rather than cultural, renders the concept suspect to those of open mind. The belief in racial inheritance, construed as an endlessly transferable set of benefits and burdens, is universally encountered, and not to be despised merely because it seems to conflict with the liberal conception of politics: the fault may lie, after all, with the liberal conception of politics. It would not be the first time that the conflict between liberalism and human nature had to be resolved in favour of humanity.

Concepts of race are kind-concepts. As is evident, we are not dealing with a natural kind, nor indeed with any other kind usually studied by contemporary philosophy. A race is an 'intentional' kind – one formed partly in obedience to a conception of itself.[15] And the simplest way to understand it is through the notion of membership, which I touched on above, in considering the relation between aesthetic experience and culture.[16]

The ceremony of membership has an important function, besides that of confirming rights and duties acquired by descent. It can be offered to strangers, and used to incorporate them, as limbs of the collective body, despite their lack of kinship. Of course, this privilege is a rare one, and all tribes are sensible of the dangers which ensue, when membership is offered on easy terms to those who have not proved their capacity for a lifetime's commitment. One way – maybe the principal way – in which membership is understood, is as a form of union with the unborn and the dead. Through membership I see the world as it will be seen by those who are yet to be. Hence I rise to an exalted perspective, a perspective above my own perishable being. Through the ceremonies of membership 'my eyes are opened', and I see the world no longer as an object of my own paltry needs and appetites, but as it really and eternally is (or, to be more philosophical, as it really and eternally seems). Through the ceremony of membership, therefore, the gods enter the world, and make themselves known. Hence 'immersive' membership, of the kind exemplified by the practice of initiation, is closely tied to religion. (Etymologically, a *religio* is a 'binding'.) Communities which experience immersive membership tend to define themselves, like the Jews, in religious terms. But the Jews also display the *revisionary* potential of religion. The gods themselves, once seriously believed in, have a tendency to detach themselves from the localities which gave birth to them, and to exert their sovereignty more extendedly, perhaps over all mankind. Indeed, when a religion is monotheistic, directed towards an all-wise and all-powerful creator, worship must be open to all who have the capacity for obedience. A people can be 'chosen', like the Jews, as the instruments of God's purpose or as a 'race of suppliants', but not as solely entitled to worship him. In such a case, therefore, the experience of membership, and the religious doctrine, have a tendency to separate, and to acquire independent histories.[17] It is one mark of a 'nation', in the modern sense, that this separation has occurred, so that membership can be defined without reference to religious obedience. (Cf. the injunction of Cardinal Richelieu, referred to above.)

At the opposite pole from tribal initiation stands the free contract of partnership, in which individuals meet on terms, and recognize no obligations that are not contained in the contract itself. In such cases association dissolves with the extinction of the mutual purpose. Such relations are only doubtfully described as relations of membership: for their character is entirely summarized by an agreement between individuals, who create no entity beyond themselves.

At the same time, however, there are associations, often verging on the contractual, which introduce new corporate entities, and which are rightly understood as forms of membership.

Clubs, corporations and trusts are treated by the law in special ways which reflect their corporate nature. Legal personality (which is sometimes accorded and sometimes withheld) is not a convenient fiction, but the transcription of a real and independent moral identity created by the ties of membership. Even when the law recognizes nothing but a contract (as in the 'unincorporated association'), the individuals may experience their relation as a form of corporate personality, with a common will and common goals. Contracts are means; membership is always at least partly an end in itself; and what begins in a contract (joining a club, for example) may outlast the dissolution of the contractual tie.

From such examples one can without too much difficulty envisage an axial ordering of associations. Some are purely contractual, others purely immersive. But contract and immersion exert their gravitational force over the entire field of human loyalty, and each association will involve its own particular synthesis of their contrasting vectors. Here sociologists might follow Tönnies, in distinguishing *Gemeinschaft* and *Gesellschaft*; or Weber, in contrasting 'traditional' with 'legal-rational' forms of authority. Others may take from Hegel the distinction between instrumental and constitutive relations, or borrow similar ideas from Oakeshott and Horkheimer. And it is worth bearing those discussions in mind, since they add a certain authority to an argument which I shall nevertheless develop without reference to them. More useful for my purpose is another and earlier attempt to describe the 'innocent' form of social unity – the form from which man drifts away into politics. In the *Muqaddimah*, Ibn Khaldūn (1332–1406) writes at length of *'asabiyah*, which denotes the 'binding force' of society. *'Asabiyah* results, in the normal case, from ties of blood and marriage, and involves a 'willingness to fight and die for each other'.[18] Its strength and value depend on the virtue of individuals, and its natural tendency is to create a sovereign authority (*malaka*), and thereby to transform itself into law. With law, however, comes indolence, luxury, and a false sense that the individual can stand alone, neither needing nor knowing his kind. *'Asabiyah* then disintegrates, and social life is at an end. (*'Asab* means sinew – and Ibn Khaldūn's imagery approximates to Homer's, as he describes the loosening of the sinews in death.)

Ibn Khaldūn was feeling his way, I believe, towards a very modern – even proto-Hegelian – conception of the mutual dependence of political and pre-political loyalties, and his belief that the concept of the citizen cancels, at last, the experience of membership is one that has been confirmed by modern history, even if not confirmed before.

Alienation

For there is no gainsaying that 'modernity' has involved an attempt to revise the experience of membership in a contractual direction. Yet there is no evidence that mankind has become happier (even if it has become more prosperous) as a result. The complaint against 'alienation' may, of course, be so much self-indulgence: after all, it issues from people who are 'not at home in the world'. Nevertheless, we ought for that very reason to take it seriously: when self-indulgence becomes the norm, something is wrong with the society that engenders it.

Two things are usually identified as the root of alienation: capitalism, and scientific thought (including the technology that springs from it). For the liberal there is a certain paradox here. For 'capitalism' is (by and large) a rude name for the sum of market relations – in other words, economic relations established by consent. And science is simply a name for the sum of propositions thought to be true, and believed for no other reason. Science and the market are the two fundamental forms of man's relation to an objective world: the two ways of recognizing the world's objectivity, either as thing (and therefore object of knowledge and use), or as person (and therefore subject of consent). It is perhaps a sign of original sin that these two indispensable links to an objective reality should be experienced as a 'fall' into something 'alien'.

One explanation of this 'fall' is provided by my discussion of membership. The relations established by a market, like those created by science, have a *universal* character. A contract requires no bond, no anterior attachment, between the parties, and its meaning is exhausted by its terms. Moreover, terms are dictated 'impersonally', by the rational self-interest of all who have access to the market. 'All' means everyone; defenders of the market are *ipso facto* defenders of free trade, wishing to multiply the benefits of a free economy through universal access. The alienating quality of the market consists partly in the fact that the 'alien' has utter equality with the friend. No *special* relationship exists to provide the meaning of the transaction, and I throw myself into the system only to set aside the claims of affection in the interests of agreement. There is a loneliness here, born of the very idea that consent is sovereign: the very same loneliness detected by de Tocqueville, at the heart of American democracy.

The desire for some new kind of economic relation is therefore invariably couched in terms of a 'communitarian' ideal – such as 'market socialism' – in which co-operatives, and the relations of trust and loyalty among their members, are proposed as antidote. This involves a move away from contract, towards economic relations which are 'bonded' and circumscribed by duties, in the manner of a feudal tenure. It is also a move in a particularist direction. The market offends by its universality: it pays no attention to people, but only to the abstract person, the 'rational economic man'. The communitarian economy 'restores man to himself' by recognizing his social nature, his *Gattungs-wesen*, his *membership*.[19]

Similarly with scientific thought. The categories of science arise directly from our rational interest in truth. Science is therefore *common* to all rational beings, and the peculiar possession of none of them. When I engage in scientific enquiry, I free my perception of the world from intentional concepts, and therefore from those categories whose sense derives from a particular community or particular way of life. I no longer see the world under the aspect of 'belonging'. I am not 'at home' in the world of science, for precisely the reason that I am just as much at home there, and just as little, as everyone else.

Two antidotes have been proposed to this condition: the search for a 'subjective' relation to the world (a search which begins in modern times with Kierkegaard, and which leads to Husserl, Heidegger and Patočka); and the search for a 'cultural' mode of knowledge, one that is formed in the image of membership. In the modern world, those two searches tend in a single direction. For the purely individualistic conception of 'subjectivity' again opens the way to solitude and alienation: it stands in need of 'redemption', and redemption either takes a religious form, as in the 'leap of faith' of Kierkegaard, or else involves a *Heimkehr* to the breast of some implied community – some Little Gidding of the imagination – as in the 'culture' of Arnold, Leavis and Eliot. In the opposition between science and culture, therefore, we find precisely the same contrast as that which exists between the free market and the 'moral economy' (to use E.P. Thompson's phrase): the contrast between a universalized relation to the world, and a relation circumscribed by some particular attachment. The same contrast galvanized and tormented the French Revolutionists, who could never decide whether the 'nation' which they had so unwisely deified consists of a contractual partnership of all-comers, or of a 'people', bound by destiny and by the unchosen ties of membership.

The contractual view of society is in one sense supremely rational: it recommends a negotiated solution to every conflict, and suggests a path to every goal. Of course, it does nothing to *provide* goals, which must be brought ready-made to the contractual encounter. It is silent about the meaning of life, and has nothing to offer to the lost and the disaffected. That, for the liberal, is its strength. To demand anything else from politics is to demand what cannot be obtained, except at enormous human cost – and perhaps not even then. Political institutions exist in order to mediate and adjudicate, not in order to mobilize and conscript.

Unfortunately, however, the political sphere cannot stand so serenely above the loyalties which feed it. The spirit of contract enters human relations, precisely in order that the liberal state should stand in judgement over them. Those relations are therefore voided of their residue of membership, and become provisional, rescindable, uncertain of themselves, with no authority beyond the transient 'sovereignty' of choice. Such is the celebrated transition from status to contract, described by Sir Henry Maine.[20]

The sanctity of human bonds is, however, inseparable from their reality as *bondage*. Rebuilt in contractual form they become profane, a system of façades, a Disneyland version of what was formerly dignified and monumental. What meaning they have no longer inheres in them as an objective and personal countenance, but merely shines momentarily, as we sweep the light of our desire across their disenchanted surfaces. Nobody, not even the liberal, is happy with this: only the crudest reformer actually *welcomes* what has happened to marriage, for example, in the wake of its desacralization. But the liberal sees no remedy to this misfortune: and for the true liberal there *is* none, besides some new habit of mind which enables us to live with the problem. Of course, there are those – Sandel, Walzer and Dworkin, for example[21] – who propose 'communitarian' ways of thinking, as a further move in the direction which a sophisticated liberalism requires. But none of them is prepared to accept the real price of community: which is sanctity, intolerance, exclusion, and a sense that life's meaning depends upon obedience, and also on vigilance against the enemy. Or at least, in so far as liberals have perceived this, they have deplored it, and tried to attribute these features to some *bad* form of community, in order to save the *good* form which is their heart's desire. If the 'nation' has often been identified as the *bad* form of social membership, this is partly because, in existing circumstances, loyalty to the nation is a real possibility. To fix one's desires on the irrecoverable enables one to persist in the liberal posture, of recommending nothing.

Nationalism

The experience of membership is precisely *not* political, but social. It arises, and ought to arise, independently of the state, and it should not be the state's concern either to impose or to forbid any particular form of it, or any particular experience of the sacred and the profane. So says the liberal, and the conservative partly agrees with him. Both are wary of the attempt to *achieve* social unity by political directives, even if they differ as to how it should be *safeguarded*. A core experience of membership, once lost, cannot be recovered by conscription. It is not for the state to manufacture the deeper forms of loyalty, and the attempt to do so is inherently totalitarian. It involves, and has always involved, the replacement of religion by ideology, of civil association by conscription and of law by conspiratorial power. This is so evident to us, in our time, as to go without saying. Nevertheless, the fault, I suggest, lies not in the national idea, but rather in the use that has been made of it. As an *ideology*, force-fed to the multitude, so as to enlist them in a new obedience, nationalism is the enemy of the liberal state. It is also the enemy of nationality, extinguishing, in its furious purposefulness, the purposeless bonding that holds men together in peace.

But the same is true of *every* ideology – including those universalist ideologies which are, in the modern world, set against the 'national idea'. As ideologies and instruments of conscription, 'equality' and 'liberation' have proved to be as much the enemies of freedom as the notion of a 'master race'. Indeed, it is only ignorance that could permit the belief that Soviet communism, founded on universalist principles, has involved less crime, less suffering, less insolence and indignity, than the particularist politics of the Nazis.

At the same time, there is little doubt that the ideology of nationalism has so formed contemporary perception of its leading idea, as to have made it difficult to separate the 'nation' from the tragi-comedy of pre-war Europe and of the present Middle East. Elie Kedourie and Kenneth Minogue have argued vigorously for the view that the ideology comes first, and has therefore given shape to the concept of nationhood. Minogue summarizes what is now a familiar liberal argument in the following words:

The point we have to emphasize about modern nationalism is that the politics comes first, and the national culture is constructed later. We have found nationalisms without nations, aspirations substituted for reality. Instead of a dog beginning to wag its political tail, we find political tails trying to wag dogs. The Irish government tries to promote an Irish culture, the Nigerian government tries to persuade Ibos, Hausa, Fulanis and Yorubas that they are part of a Nigerian or an African nation . . .

This amounts to saying that the concept of the nation is almost entirely empty of content, until a content is arbitrarily supplied from local circumstances . . .[22]

As we shall see, Minogue's last claim is untenable. Nevertheless, he is right to suggest that the national idea has been used to *conscript* people to nationhood: to impose a social unity by political means. In this respect, however, the full liberal theory of the state makes a comparable error. It too believes that there is, or ought to be, no source of political unity other than the political process itself: it differs in claiming that unity cannot be imposed, and that, in the right conditions, it emerges from, and expresses, an act of common consent. Until sustained by a national idea, however, the liberal state is, I believe, a solvent of unity and therefore contains the seeds of its own destruction.

Wandering and Settled Peoples

To establish that point, we need to make an important (although again not hard and fast) distinction, between wandering and settled peoples. Ideas of 'kind' are as important to the nomadic as to the sedate, perhaps more important. It was the nomadic Bedouin who provided Ibn Khaldūn with his paradigm of *'asabiyah*. Lacking territory, and lacking, after a time, even the common language that may have once united them, such people base their loyalty on ideas either of faith or of kinship, and usually on both. Kinship becomes, as for the Jews, a continuous and developing *story*, whose meaning is religious, and whose aspect is that of a homeless culture, based, however, in a consuming nostalgia for home. Religious conversion – whereby an outsider claims protection from the tribal gods – may be frowned upon, or (when not backed up by marriage, that is, by entry into the kinship relation) subjected to rigorous proofs. Thus, following the diaspora, and the birth of Judaism, Jews have less and less sought conversions, and more and more devoted themselves to safeguarding the faith among those required by birth to inherit it.

Nor are the Jews peculiar in this respect. Many of the 'confessional communities' of the Middle East have the character of peoples wandering or driven from their original pastures, holding on to their identity through ideas of membership which are gradually shorn of the transcendental convictions that once attached to them. The Druze are a particularly interesting case. In some frames of mind, they seem to believe that their membership has been fixed eternally, and can neither grow through conversion nor decline through apostasy.[23] According to certain of their authorities, every child born into a Druze family is the reincarnation of another Druze, and therefore stands in need of no further initiation. He does not need to discover the form or content of the faith to which his inheritance attaches him, for the simple reason that he can do nothing to lose it and is saved in any case. This belief is in fact extremely functional: the long-standing practice of *taqiyyah* (literally 'holiness', but in fact denoting the systematic concealment of doctrine for the sake of survival) seems to have resulted in a near-universal amnesia among the Druze as to what their religious doctrines are. The Druze are, in this instance, only an extreme case of a process that can also be witnessed among Maronites, Melkites and even Greek Orthodox in the region: the reduction of faith to ritual, and of ritual itself to a root relationship of kin. Such instances, while they show the vital importance of membership, also show again that it is quite different in kind from 'conscription to a cause', that is, from the *manufactured* loyalties of the ideological state.

So far I have given two examples of non-political unity: the tribal-racial and the religious. Both derive from a core experience of the sacred, in which membership is displayed as immersion (baptism). However, as I emphasized, religion and race may grow apart, and will tend to do so whenever God is one and infinite. Under favourable conditions, men advance towards the idea that this-worldly membership and other-worldly obedience are (*pace* the Druze and the Alawites) quite separate things. The way is open for a new kind of loyalty, one in which the individual is free to seek his god without consulting the gods of his neighbours. The way is open, too, to philosophy, theology and science: men can now *study* God and his works; they can put their beliefs to the test, since it is not on *belief* that political unity – and therefore peace and leisure – depends. This emancipation from dogma is one of the achievements of the *polis*, and causes liberals persistently to overlook the non-political loyalties upon which even the *polis* depends.

In a recent work Régis Debray has offered a powerful picture of religious doctrine (and its ideological substitutes, such as Marxism) as *formes a priori de la sociabilité (ou de l'existence*

politique).[24] Doctrine, he argues, is both necessary to the formation of a pre-political 'we', and also consequent upon it: *une
idéologie est un drapeau, mais on ne se rallie pas à un drapeau au vu
de ses couleurs, on adopte le drapeau parce qu'on s'incorpore à la
troupe.*[25] As Debray notices, this resuscitation of the Marxian
theory of ideology – not so as to criticize ideology, but rather so
as to endorse it, in terms similar to those used by Burkean
conservatives in defending 'prejudice' – has profoundly anti-
liberal implications. If it is true, then what hope do we have of
establishing the kind of polity esteemed by Parekh (and
defended by Rawls as uniquely conforming to a pre-philosophical
idea of justice), in which confession, doctrine and 'conceptions
of the good' are all required to vacate their thrones to the
sovereign rule of law?

But Debray's thesis is false: not because the foundation of
loyalty is, or can be, purely political, as the full liberal theory
requires, but because there are other forms of non-political unity
than those founded in doctrine. Race is one of them; nationality
another. *Pace* Kedourie and Minogue, there is a perfectly coherent
idea of membership based in those relations between people
which come from *occupying the same place*. People who are not,
like the Jews, 'strangers and sojourners' in the land, may have
things in common sufficient to constitute them as a 'kind'. The
most important of these is territory. People gathered in the same
place must accord to each other rights of occupation if they are to
live in peace. The network of those rights defines a portion of the
earth as 'ours'. Peoples from elsewhere are strangers to our
rights, uninterested in preserving them, and liable, in times of
war, to cancel them. There arises a common interest in defence,
which has territory as its object. Until territory is *ours*, there is no
real 'mine' or 'thine'.

If territory is to fall, in this way, under a common but divisible
right of ownership, there must be a content to the collective 'we',
which settles the terms and the boundaries of membership.
Certain factors, naturally associated with joint occupation, contribute to this 'we':[26]

(1) Shared language. There is no more dramatic mark of the
stranger than his inability to speak my language. My language is
not only mine. It is public, and shared, learned from and taught
to those who are dearest. My language is always *our* language;
the first thing that I inherit from my forefathers and the first that
I pass on to my child. Attachment to language is the root of
national culture, and, in favourable conditions, may be used to
define the boundaries of nationhood. (Cf. the history of Polish,
Turkish and especially Arab nationalism in our times.[27]) Lan-

guage may also be imposed, either to break down loyalties inimical to the political order (Bulgaria, the Soviet Union, the USA until recently), or in order to consolidate a political order that has been newly established (Israel, and also Ireland – in which the attempt met with failure).

(2) Shared associations. Settled people have more opportunity for association than those who wander. They can meet not only in family, festival, team and army, but also in places given to membership: churches, clubs, schools, localities of work and leisure. They have an opportunity for institution-building, and for attaching their institutions to the land. Their mutual ties lose the solemn and immersive nature of the ties formed by those who pass each other in the desert. They become looser, freer, and more 'civil', and at the same time fitted for corporate life. Societies differ, of course, as to which associations are permitted, and as to their ability to perpetuate themselves as institutions. The Hegelian idea of civil society is one of maximal association, under a rule of law which permits and encourages the incorporation of all lasting forms of membership. We can see a nation as partly constituted by the long-standing associations which are formed and inherited within it.

(3) Shared history. People united by language, association and territory triumph and suffer together. They have common friends and common enemies. An historical *narrative* is manifest in the very associations which serve to combine them, and the memory of it is attached to the landscape, the towns, the institutions and the climate by which they are surrounded.

(4) Common culture. There is both the desire and the need to consolidate community in the core experience of membership, as these are safeguarded and enhanced by faith, ritual and worship. For a wandering people this is the root of identity, and the sole durable source of a pre-political 'we'. In certain circumstances, however, membership can develop away from its 'angel infancy' and smile more inclusively, if also more coldly, on the surrounding world. The process – described by Spengler as a transition from 'culture' to 'civilization' – may perhaps foretell (as Spengler thought) the ruin of a people. Nevertheless it is the process that formed the nation states of Europe, and which conditions all that we have or hope for in the modern world. It is precisely this which permits the full loyalty of nationhood, and, with it, the moderating institutions of a liberal state.

A nation, like a race, is a kind formed through a conception of itself. The members of a nation do not merely share those four things (or some significant sub-set of them), but also *concede* them to each other as of right. Membership involves an acquiescence in the claims of others, and a recognition of a shared identity. Others of my nation have a right to the common territory, provided, at least, they are prepared to risk their life in defence of it. This self-consciousness of a nation is part of its moral character. It endows nations with a life of their own, a destiny, even a personality. People who think of themselves as a collective 'we' understand their successes and failures as 'ours', and apportion collective praise and blame for the common outcome. Hence there arises what Solzhenitsyn has called 'repentance and self-limitation in the life of nations':

> Those who set the highest value on the existence of the nation, who see in it not the ephemeral fruit of social formations but a complex, vivid, unrepeatable organism not invented by man, recognise that nations have a full spiritual life, that they can soar to the heights and plunge to the depths, run the whole gamut from saintliness to utter wickedness (although only individuals ever reach the extremes).[28]

There is something drastic in that utterance, as in the self-castigations which fill the Old Testament, and from which our forefathers acquired the idea of a collective and inherited guilt. But Solzhenitsyn's words correspond to a recurrent thought in the life of nations, one which reveals the force and the depth of every true non-political loyalty. Only when moderated by law, and by conceptions of corporate personality, do sentiments of such intensity become negotiable. And that is why the nation needs law as much as law needs the nation.

Home and Patriotism

What holds together the features that I have identified as part of nationhood? Why is the emergence of this new kind of loyalty not just a passing accident? To answer those questions is difficult, for it is always difficult to give what Kant called a 'deduction' of a non-natural kind. However, something can be said to awaken the reader to the importance of nationhood as I have described it. We need only reflect on the difference of predicament between a wandering and a settled people. What I have been defining is a special case of being *at home*, and of the attachment to home which is common to all people fortunate enough to have one. This attachment is sometimes referred to as patriotism, and has been so described and defended by one left-wing author, in terms which hearken back to, and indeed are largely taken from, Burke:

At its core, patriotism means love of one's homeplace, and of the familiar things and scenes associated with the homeplace. In this sense, patriotism is one of the basic human sentiments. If not a natural tendency in the species, it is at least a proclivity produced by realities basic to human life, for territoriality, along with family, has always been a primary associative bond. We become devoted to the people, places and ways that nurture us, and what is familiar and nurturing seems also natural and right. This is the root of patriotism. Furthermore, we are all subject to the immense power of habit, and patriotism has habit in its service.[29]

Hence 'the theme of homecoming is the central motif of patriotic discourse'.[30] John Scharr goes on to emphasize the importance of 'patrimony', meaning the inheritance of benefits and obligations which we cannot refuse without dishonour to ourselves and our children. This element of patrimony is, however, *common* to all forms of non-political loyalty, and not peculiar to the national idea. It implies that there will be a racial element in all national sentiment, an element of 'birthright' and 'birthduty'. In reminding the reader of this obvious fact, it is useful to be able to call on an established left-wing authority.

But this now brings me to the question of what we might actually mean by 'patriotism', and how, if at all, we might distinguish it from other forms of national loyalty. Because no particular use of words is forced on us, I shall make a proposal, in keeping with what I think are popular sentiments in the matter. I shall distinguish three 'moments' within non-political loyalties: attachment, patriotism, and ideology. The attachment is simply the relation of membership itself – the tribal, confessional, racial or national bond. National attachment defines a home; confessional attachment does not. Loyalty to the *polis* also defines a home, as is clear from the famous funeral oration of Pericles. Pericletian loyalty stands to the city state as national loyalty to the nation state: neither need be felt with any strength or deliberation and neither need be patriotic.

Patriotism consists in the extent to which the obligations of patrimony are *acted upon*. There is a patriotism of the 'little platoon', and a patriotism for every kind of membership, even those without a 'home'. Wandering peoples also have patriotism: the Jews more than any other. The manifestations of patriotism are many. First among them is the 'public spirit' which becomes an active force only when people live their lives in honourable recognition of the unborn and the dead. Throughout the middle ages the Jews gave to the *kuppah*, and to other

charitable works, a considerable part of all their earnings, and
offered shelter, employment and ransom to others of their kind.
They were right to do this then, and are right to do it now,
buying the oppressed members of their race from governments
degraded enough to sell them. Such charitable works are one
part of the public spirit which is the guarantee of national freedom. Another part is the willingness to die for the sake of the
group. That willingness depends upon a commitment to the
dead and the unborn; hence liberals have great difficulty in
seeing how it might be justified, the dead and the unborn being
excluded in the nature of things from the social contract among
the living.

The ideology of a pre-political attachment is a kind of
emergency measure, a response to external threat which should
not outlast the time of present danger. The ideology of the nation
is nationalism; that of the tribe is tribalism. Ideologies can be
used to conscript people to an artificial unity; but they are
neither substitutes for, nor friends of, the loyalties on which
they meditate.

Armed with those distinctions, we may return to the concept
of 'home', as this is advanced through the national idea. It is one
consequence of the analysis that I have given that there can be
'nested' nations – that is, nations which contain other nations as
parts. An example is Czechoslovakia, in which two nations, with
separate but related languages, customs and faiths, have merged
to form a single more comprehensive nation, whose sense of
identity, in the face of communist enslavement, is at least as
strong as the separate identities of the Czechs and the Slovaks. A
less clear example is the United Kingdom, in which separate but
vestigial nations have been merged into a union which used to
be called (in the eighteenth century) an 'empire'. This nesting of
national loyalties is the unsurprising consequence of the fact
that territories also nest within one another, and are captured or
defended together. The sentiment of 'ours' leaks easily across
the borders of Wales and England, or those of Moravia and
Slovakia, and people from one side of the border feel as much 'at
home' on the other.

It is impossible to separate the sense of home from that of
family. To acquire a family is to 'settle down'; and a person who
settles in a place wishes also (as a rule) to breed there. No settling
of territory can occur, therefore, without establishing family
bonds; the mingling of the two ensures that territorial loyalties
will be experienced in the patrimonial fashion that I have
described. Moreover, territory must be defended, and people
die in the defence of it: a sense of sacrifice therefore attaches to

the soil and to the memory of those who fought for it. A pro-
longed peace may erode this sense. But it is always renewed in a
time of crisis, and, when it ceases to be renewed, *'asabiyah* is at
an end, and the nation must die.

A nation may last, however, as long as the land provides a
'home' for it. Nations have an identity through time which is
distinct from that of the state, and independent of institutions,
even those dearest to its people. A nation can outlast the demise
of its system of government, and its ancestral laws, even though
it lives on, like the Russians and the Poles, in a state of deep
unhappiness. It is not right to attribute full moral personality to
nations, to regard them as Solzhenitsyn does in the passage
quoted earlier. Only in the political sphere does corporate personality emerge, and the non-political stands to the political as
the body to the soul. It is the source of life upon which rational
discourse is predicated. Nevertheless, the identity of a nation
through time has a clear moral aspect, and the reaffirmation of
this identity, through acts of pride and contrition, is a part of
belonging, and of living under immovable obligations.

The liberal state has no home, and generates no loyalty
towards generations which, being either dead or unborn, form
no part of the contract. Without such a loyalty there is neither
honourable accounting nor provision for the future, but only a
squandering of resources in the pursuit of present goals. The
liberal state must depend therefore upon some other loyalty than
loyalty to itself. More than any other system of government, the
liberal rule of law depends upon the renewal of public spirit, and
therefore on patriotism. Burke was wrong to speak of a *partnership* between the living, the unborn and the dead – for that is to
raise the feelings of piety from the realm of pre-political membership into the conscious light of politics, and so to make them
rescindable, defeasible and insecure. But he was right to suspect
that without loyalty to the dead, and to the land that houses
them, the whole project of liberal politics is endangered. For a
liberal state to be secure, the citizens must understand the
national interest as something other than the interest of the *state*.
Only the first can evoke in them the sacrificial spirit upon which
the second depends.

Loyalty and Jurisdiction

If we consult the standard works of liberal theory, we do not as a
rule find any discussion of social membership or social unity. It
is assumed that the principles which determine the legitimacy of

the ruling institutions will also settle the question as to who is governed by them. Advocates of the social contract, for example, suppose men to be gathered together by the very contract which settles their future obligations. But how were they gathered, and who did the gathering? On what basis are those unborn to be admitted to the contract? How do we distinguish those who are entitled to contract, from those who are 'barging in'? There is no satisfactory position for the contract theorist to take, short of universalism: if the contract is open to anyone, it is open to all. Anything short of world government is therefore tainted with illegitimacy. That is just another way of saying that, until moderated by a non-political loyalty, the contractarian view of the state is without application.

Similarly for democracy. When politicians address the people at an election (when they 'go to the country' as it is said in British parliamentary discourse), they ask a definite question: what do *we* want? The 'we' in question is the class of those entitled to vote. But how they acquired that entitlement, who conferred it and what justifies it, are questions whose answers are inseparable from the history of a nation.

Nor are liberals consistent in their repudiation of the national idea, as is shown by a characteristic liberal attitude to immigration, and to those like myself who wish to prevent or limit it. The argument is advanced that we have no right to close our doors against immigrants from our former colonies, since it was we who exploited them, or who reduced them to the state of economic and cultural dependence which ensures that their best – perhaps their only – prospects are now on British soil. If you examine the use of 'we' in that sentence, you will find a perfect instance of the national idea, as I have described it: the idea of a moral unity between people, based in territory, language, association, history and culture, and so bound up with the self-consciousness of those who are joined by it, as to make subsequent generations answerable for the sins of their forefathers, and entitled to the benefits which their ancestors forewent.

Supposing we accept the need for a non-political loyalty. Why should that loyalty be *national*? The answer is contained in the nature of the modern state. All law requires jurisdiction: that is, a principle for determining who is, and who is not, subject to its edicts. It is a peculiar feature of wandering peoples that they tend to be governed by laws which are co-terminous with their religious confessions, and which derive their authority from the same divine source. When the people are 'strangers and sojourners' this gives rise to an enormous problem of law-enforcement, as instanced by the Jews. (Consider the case of Noah Raphael da

Norsa in sixteenth-century Ferrara, which had to be tried innumerable times, all over the diaspora, before the culprit was forced by the pressure of public opinion, and the judgement of fifty rabbis, to yield.[31]) When a wandering people establishes an empire, and enforces its law over subject territories, the result is never a liberal *Rechtsstaat*. The *shari'a* of the Muslims, for instance, makes little provision for the legal rights of non-Muslims. Despite the ingenious arguments of the various schools of jurisprudence, it has never been decided whether the law really applies to non-Muslims, or whether their affairs are to be dealt with under treaties of pacification.[32] The name for the non-Muslim communities which enjoy protection is *dhimmi*, meaning those governed by treaty, as opposed to those governed by the holy law. (*Dhimma* = covenant, treaty, protection.) How to adjudicate a contract between a Muslim and a *dhimmi* is a question that still has no answer. There thus emerged the pattern, institutionalized under the Ottoman *millet* system, and still persisting (just) in modern Lebanon, whereby each confession governs its own relations of matrimony, family and inheritance, while one by one the transactions of civil society are removed from confessional adjudication and made subject to the secular law of the state. In modern Lebanon, legal order rests on appeals to Rome, to the Sunnite Mufti, to the Shi'ite *'ulema* and the Druze *'aql*. This undermines the idea of political unity, while establishing in the minds of the people the idea that those who do not share their religious beliefs and customs are in some important sense outside the law. Such an idea of jurisdiction is incompatible with the emergence of a state in which rights are offered regardless of confession. The emergence of a Jewish *Rechtsstaat* in Palestine was made possible partly by the fact that the law prevailing there is *not* Jewish law, but the law of the British mandate, established according to a territorial concept of jurisdiction.

The safety, continuity and stability necessary to a rule of law are unobtainable until territory is secure. And only a territorial idea of jurisdiction will permit the final separation of law from confessional attachment. Territorial jurisdiction exists in two forms: that of empire, and that of the sovereign state. The first is parasitic on the second, since only if there is a 'metropolitan power' can there be an empire. Empires provide the most striking examples that the world has known of trans-national rules of law: the Roman Empire, for example, the Russian Empire during the nineteenth century (especially in Finland and the Baltic states), and the British Empire in India and Africa. Even the Ottoman Empire, despite its disabilities and the imperfection of the *millet* system, made moves towards the rule of law, while the Austro-Hungarian Empire (to which I shall return) is the true paradigm for which Parekh is looking in the passage which I began by quoting, of a political unity which casts its mantle over many nations. There are two reasons, however, why liberals should be reluctant to countenance empire as their preferred form of jurisdiction. First, empires have now ceased to be founded on the rule of law: the Soviet Empire, for example, has persisted by *extinguishing* law and adjudication in all the territories which fall beneath its control. (Law is replaced by a Potemkin substitute, from which the sovereign Party is exempt, and to the extent that a rule of law can be reasserted – as in modern Hungary – to that extent is the Empire *threatened*.) Secondly, an empire *imposes* law on its subject peoples. The unity between them is an artificial unity, dependent upon the force exerted by the central power. This force in turn depends upon the cohesion of that power, and its territorial jurisdiction at home. And this depends upon a loyalty adapted to the defence of territory: in other words, on the persistence of something like a national idea. Hence the appeal to empire as the foundation of law may not, in the end, be distinct from the appeal to nationality. The collapse of the Roman Empire was caused precisely by the collapse of Rome, by the loosening of '*asabiyah* in the Empire's heart.

It is at this point, I think, that a liberal ought to bite the bullet, and confess to the advantages of the national idea. It establishes a social loyalty suited to territorial jurisdiction; and without territorial jurisdiction, there is no possibility of a liberal state. It is for this reason that the history of the *Rechtsstaat* and the history of the national idea are inseparable. In trying to understand this fact liberals have sometimes distinguished – as does Lord Acton in a famous essay – between nationality based in race and language, and nationality 'formed by the state', which is 'the only one to which we owe political duties . . . and the only one which has political rights'.[33] It seemed to Acton that the coincidence of national loyalty and legal obligation could be secured only if the nation were in some sense the creature of the law which governs it. (At the same time, he advocated empire, as the best guarantee of the freedom of nationalities, and therefore of the rights of individuals.) But the question is not which comes first – the law or the nation – but rather what determines the unity and durability of each. The national *Rechtsstaat* should be seen in terms of a continuing process of interaction, between a national loyalty and a territorial jurisdiction. The first is social rather than political, just like the loyalty of the Jews. Nationality and jurisdiction interpenetrate, and it is not absurd to envisage their relation in terms of that between body and soul (a special case, for Aristotle, of the relation between matter and form). To notice, as Acton does, their inseparability, is not to deny their distinctness. And to assign the unity of the body politic entirely to its legal part (as the liberal theory does), is as grave an error as to suppose, like Locke, that personal identity has nothing to do with the identity and continuity of the body.

Some Examples

This brings me to what is most objectionable in the standard liberal view of politics, namely, the refusal to perceive men and nations as they are: the refusal to clothe in flesh the abstract rational chooser who sits on the liberal chess-board. Consider, again, the all-important example put before us by Parekh. If the United States really is a multi-national state united by a single rule of law, whose authority is sufficient to establish political unity, then this would merely show that the United States is a peculiar exception among modern political systems. But of course, Parekh's description of the United States is a fantasy. Although it is true that the Constitution of the US has a unifying power, it owes this power to the fact that it draws upon, defines and upholds a national identity. Even though Abraham Lincoln declared the American 'nation' to be distinct from others, in being founded on a 'covenant', he did not mean to discard the national idea, but on the contrary to endorse it. Modern presidents and politicians make free use of this idea, and almost all children are inducted into citizenship by means of it. The most rebellious of leftist journals in the US calls itself *The Nation*, in order to emphasize the fact that the country has a *national* and not just a political interest, and that the left is its true custodian. As the United States now exists – the most stable liberal polity in the modern world – it has all the characteristics of nationhood, and actively renews itself from its own national consciousness. America is first of all a territory, possessed through a 'union' of states. It has a common language, common habits of association, common customs and a common Judaeo-Christian culture. It is intensely patriotic, and – in its healthy part – determined to defend its interests against the world. As all readers of Tocqueville know, the process of association is hyperactive in the United States, proliferating its 'little platoons' which add their fund of local loyalties to the larger loyalty upon which the political order depends. There is also a strong religious dimension to the American idea. A strange hybrid monotheism has grown from the thousand churches of America – Christian in form, Hebrew in content – and each new generation is absorbed into it by the process of national loyalty. And this loyalty has its own historical myths, its own 'dreams', its own sense of mission, its own powerful self-image, in which the American land is the last refuge of the dispossessed, and also the birthplace of a new and unfettered enterprise and will.

I do not say that the national loyalty is shared by *all* Americans. But whoever travels away from the universities (centres of disaffection in any state) will discover a process of nation-building that is second to none in the modern world. And those who stand *outside* the national loyalty – who attack their country's traditions and ridicule its culture, who scoff at its simplicity, despise its leaders and reject its God, who, in short, lack all vestige of American *'asabiyah* – who are they, in general, if not the liberals themselves, those inhabitants of ivory towers who wrinkle their noses at the surrounding swamp of moral bondage? And, by their single-minded attachment to the 'constitution' as the source of all political order, the liberals have changed this instrument of national government into an instrument of national interrogation: a means to question the legitimacy of American traditions, and to break down American culture. Only the amazing strength of the national idea has maintained unity (and therefore the rule of law) against a constitution now bent on destroying it. And it is partly because America exists so *manifestly* as a nation, in a world where national loyalties are failing or in disarray, that there is such hostility to America in the modern world.

Which brings me again to the example that Parekh should have chosen: the Austro-Hungarian Empire in Europe. On the surface this offers a paradigm case of the multi-national *Rechtsstaat*: where pre-political loyalty, such as it was, was owed not to a nation but to a *crown*. But the Empire was not always liberal: it became so during the eighteenth century, by virtue of the transformation which affected all of Europe, and which awoke the sleeping consciousness of nations. As the Empire moved in a liberal direction, so did its peoples begin to define their loyalty in territorial terms; and their whole conception of themselves was gradually turned upside down. For many years the national loyalties which grew in central Europe co-existed with the Habsburg obedience: but how long did it last, and how long was it likely to last? The Empire entered the First World War only to collapse in ruins. For the loyalties upon which it depended were by that time – thanks to the very liberal institutions which had been built on them – at variance with the imperial sovereignty. A similar collapse, accompanied by terrible civil war, followed the ending of the British Empire in India, peace being restored only when the rival confessions had formed themselves into separate states.

Why was the Ottoman Empire for so long the 'sick man of Europe'? Surely because its subject peoples, having (apart from the Turks and the Lebanese) no national but only a confessional loyalty, showed no disposition to defend their territory collectively, or to recognize a common jurisdiction over the people who resided there. At the collapse of the empire only two fragments of territory showed any lasting disposition to govern themselves by law and to permit the emergence of democratic institutions: Turkey and Lebanon, the two incipient nation states. In the case of Lebanon, however, national loyalty proved too fragile a thing, and gave way, in the face of external emergency, to confessional loyalties which have split the country and all but abolished its law.

Such examples remind us of the value of the national idea: not only as a source of unity, but also as a pre-condition of territorial defence. (It was his experience of the helplessness of Germany before the Napoleonic armies that inspired Fichte's nationalism: without an effective 'we', defined over territory, he realized, nothing can ever be defended.) In the modern world, it is precisely national loyalty that the liberal state requires, and national loyalty cannot emerge in a state where other, tighter, and fiercer loyalties compete with it. However, for Parekh, the liberal state is conceived as a staging post towards his real goal, which is the 'multi-cultural' society. In such a society the process of nation-building is impeded, or reversed, by the growth of loyalties of a non-national or anti-national kind. Experience ought to warn us against such a society: experience not only of Lebanon, but also of Cyprus, and India. If we really are interested in the survival of the liberal state, then we should be doing our best to preserve the loyalties which sustain the liberal jurisdiction.

Left Chauvinism

In a striking work, Alain Finkielkraut has pointed to the peculiar paradox of the 'multi-cultural' vision.[34] On the one hand it defends the universalist values of the Enlightenment, and recognizes the legitimacy of no exclusions, no loyalties, no claims of ancestral right. On the other hand it speaks out for minority cultures, defends their exclusivity and sense of inherited purpose, and makes space for them within the liberal state. To the question whether to be universalist or particularist, the multi-culturalist liberal has two incompatible answers, depending on who asks the question and why. He is universalist against Western loyalties, particularist for the loyalties of others. But this intellectual inconsistency hides a consistent purpose: which is to undermine the social loyalties of the Western states – the only loyalties which, in the modern world, have shown any tendency to sustain liberal (and universalist) jurisdictions.

Nor does this purpose go unperceived. The failure of the left in Western elections is the consequence of their perceived disloyalty. Parties which advocate the destruction of national defences, the surrender of national sovereignty, the relaxing of controls on immigration; which endorse the destruction of national culture, the liberalization of mores, and the dominance of urban élites; which show no attachment to the customs and ceremonies of the country, or to the religion that prevails in it – such parties naturally fail to capture a majority. If they were to do so, social loyalty would first have to disintegrate. And with it would disintegrate both the nation and the liberal state.

But this raises a deep question concerning liberal psychology. Why do the defenders of the liberal idea turn so angrily on those who oppose it? Why do these advocates of tolerance show so little tolerance of those who *really* disagree with them, and why are they prepared, like Parekh, to make false and damaging accusations against those with whom they most need to enter dialogue? The fact is that the advocates of the pure liberal theory are rarely satisfied by it. Just as much as the rest of us, they yearn after an original innocence, an experience of membership that will open the heart, and also close the mind. At a certain point the strain of living without an 'us' and a 'them' becomes intolerable. On the lonely heights of abstract choice nothing comforts and nothing consoles. The Kantian imperatives seem to blow more freezingly, and the unfed soul eventually flees from them, down into the fertile valleys of attachment. But where shall he rest? To whom will his loyalty be owed? What flock or herd or army can he join, who looks on all of them with the merely vicarious loyalty of the envious anthropologist? The answer is this: to find an enemy, to create a new kind of membership in the spirit of battle. The enemy is the one who believes what the liberal so tragically fails to believe – the one who feels the loyalties to which the liberal ought in conscience to attach himself but which his own thinking has destroyed. To turn on the conservative is, in a peculiar way, to partake of his conviction, just as the Huron Indian absorbs the courage of his vanquished enemy by eating his still unvanquished heart. This is the process of 'moral inversion'.[35] And it provides an interesting proof of our need for membership, in a world which – thanks to liberalism – is increasingly deprived of it.

Back to Hegel

This returns me, in conclusion, to the deepest question raised by Parekh in his article. The conservative view of nationhood, Parekh suggests, refuses to advance from *Moralität* to *Sittlichkeit*, in dealing with those who belong to other 'kinds'. The contrast drawn by Hegel was not, in fact, between *Sittlichkeit* and morality (which is a part of *Sittlichkeit*, and transcended in it), but between morality and abstract right. Morality consists in the sphere of particular obligations, arising among those who are brought together by the workings of history, destiny, and chance. It is a sphere of concrete duty and responsibility, in which our obligations are inseparable from the conditions of life as mortal and dependent creatures. Abstract right corresponds more closely to the idea of obligation that underlies the full liberal theory of the state. Right and duty are here defined universally, without reference to the historical circumstances of the individual agent. Nothing in the sphere of abstract right distinguishes me from you or you from your neighbour: like all abstract systems, Hegel suggests, this of right is purely formal, without content, offering no concrete answer to the question what to do. Content comes only when abstract right is *situated* in the sphere of morality, when its formal laws are 'determined' by reference to the circumstances of life.

The 'full liberal theory of the state' sees no necessity for that synthesis. It stays fixated in the idea of right, and in the purely abstract notion of the rational agent. It moves directly to the thought that government requires nothing else for its legitimacy. Its schemes for the regeneration of mankind make no reference to historical attachments or prescriptive obligations: government is legitimate only if it does not dirty itself with the messy particularities of the flesh. Abstract right, taken alone, points always away from the empirical world of politics, to the Kingdom of Ends. This phantom – appearing now as the 'just society' of the contractarians, now as the 'full communism' of Marx – poisons our attachment to the realities through which we might, in our fallen condition, live and find fulfilment.

For Hegel the reality of *Geist* – as we might say, of everything human – is acquired through a process of realization, in which the abstract is fixed in the concrete, and the universal disciplined by the particular. Reason, Hegel believed, will accomplish this transition of its own accord: out of the cold absolute of abstract right the urge to morality is born. But neither abstract right nor morality are fully real, he argued, until overcome in *Sittlichkeit*, which preserves in more conscious, more concrete form the distinguishing features of each. And *Sittlichkeit* in turn is sundered into three moments: the immediate and abstract, the mediated and concrete, and the final fulfilment of both in a self-conscious act of recuperation. These three moments are family, civil society and state. The legitimacy of the state depends upon its ability to overcome the separation inherent in civil society, and to recuperate in free and legal form the sense of belonging which surrounds us at birth, and nurtures our identity.

I would not defend the Hegelian picture in all its detail. But is it not a more plausible résumé of the interpenetration of the political and the social, and of the mutual dependence of political legitimacy and non-political unity, than we are offered by the full liberal theory of the state? To suppose that the national idea is somehow alien to the liberal state is to fail to perceive that our existence as political beings does not derive from the state, but from spheres of social loyalty, and that it is by means of such loyalty that the state persists.

From J. C. D. Clark (ed.), *Ideas and Politics in Modern Britain*, London, Macmillan, 1990.

NOTES

5 GIERKE AND THE CORPORATE PERSON

(1) Otto Gierke, *Political Theories of the Middle Ages*, trans. F. W. Maitland (Cambridge, 1900); Otto Gierke, *Natural Law and the Theory of Society 1500–1800*, trans. with an introduction by Sir Ernest Baker (Cambridge, 1934).
(2) *Das deutsche Genossenschaftsrecht*, vol. 3, p. 274.
(3) Compare Aristotle's distinction among the kinds of friendship in *Nicomachean Ethics*, book 8.
(4) J. N. Figgis, *Churches in the Modern State*, 2nd edn, London, 1914.
(5) Henri de Lubiac, S.J., *Catholicism, a Study of Dogma in Relation to the Corporate Destiny of Mankind* (London, 1950), pp.26–27.
(6) Gisbert Voet, *Politika ecclesiastica*, 4 vols, Amsterdam, 1663 et seq.
(7) Samuel von Pufendorf, *De Jure naturae et gentium* (1672), ch.1, sections 12–13.
(8) Wilhelm von Humboldt, *Ideen*, quoted by Gierke in *Political Theories*, p.127.
(9) F. W. Maitland, *Collected Papers*, ed. H. A. L. Fisher, Cambridge, 1911. See vol. 3, especially 'The Corporation Sole', 'The Unincorporate Body', 'Moral Personality and Legal Personality', 'Trust and Corporation'. Maitland's position is summarized in S. J. Stoljar, 'The Corporate Theories of F. W. Maitland', in *Legal Personality and Political Pluralism*, ed. Leicester C. Webb, Melbourne, 1958.
(10) Barker, in Gierke, *Natural Law*, lxxv.
(11) Barker, in Gierke, *Natural Law*, lxii.
(12) Barker, in Gierke, *Natural Law*, lxxiv.
(13) See the argument of Stable J, in *R. v. I.C.R. Haulage Ltd* 1944, K.B.551, and of Lord Caldecote, C.J., in *DPP v. Kent and Sussex Contractors* 1944, K.B. 146.
(14) Figgis, *Churches in the Modern State*, p.42. The grammatical oddity of the second sentence adds to, more than it detracts from, Figgis's natural vigour of style.
(15) Maurice Hauriou, *Précis de droit administratif*, 6th edn, Paris, 1907.
(16) Hauriou, *Précis de droit administratif*, p.34.
(17) Gierke, *Natural Law*, p.165.
(18) Quoted in Maitland, *Collected Papers*, vol.3, p.312.
(19) Auguste Cochin, *Les Sociétés de pensée et la Révolution en Bretagne*, Paris, 1925.
(20) See Timothy Ware, *The Orthodox Church*, London, 1963.

6 MASARYK, PATOČKA AND THE CAVE OF THE SOUL

(1) T. G. Masaryk, *Versuch einer concreten Logik*, Vienna, Carl Konegen, 1887.
(2) *Versuch*, p.206.
(3) Ibid., p.216.
(4) Ibid., p.58.
(5) Karel Čapek, *Hovory s T. G. Masarykem* (Prague, 1925), p.415.
(6) T. G. Masaryk, *Otázka sociální* (Prague , 1898–9), vol.1, p.71.
(7) Ibid., pp.202–3.
(8) T. G. Masaryk, *Světová revoluce* (Prague 1925), p.415.
(9) T. G. Masaryk, *The Spirit of Russia*, trans. E. & C. Paul, 2 vols., London, 1919.
(10) The letter, to F. Jančík, is reproduced in the afterword to the Czech edition of Husserl's *Cartesian Meditations*: Edmund Husserl, *Karteziánské meditace*, trans. M. Bayerov (Prague, 1968), pp.162–6. (This afterword is by Jan Patočka.) Some letters of Masaryk to Husserl, from the Louvain Husserl archive, have been published in Jan Patočka, *Masaryk* (a selection of papers, lectures and notes), issued in *samizdat* (Prague, 1979), pp.292–307.
(11) Karel Čapek, *Hovory*, p.194.
(12) Ibid., p.195.
(13) Cf. Erazim Kohák 'To Live in Truth', in Milič Čapek and Karel Hruby (eds.), *T. G. Masaryk in Perspective*, SVU Press, 1981.
(14) See T. G. Masaryk, *Ideály humanitní* (Prague, 1968), p.23f.
(15) *Hovory*, p.225; see also pp.300–301. Milan Machovec has noted how rarely Masaryk refers to *democracy* in his political writings (*T. G. Masaryk*, Prague, 1968 p.12). We should see this, however, not as a sign that he was unwilling to defend democracy, but rather as an indication of his reluctance to elaborate those aspects of his world-view which stood in need of a philosophical justification.
(16) *Ideály humanitní*, p.101.
(17) See Franz Brentano, *Vom Ursprung sittlicher Erkenntnis*, Leipzig, 1889.
(18) Husserl's work was issued by Martinus Nijhof at the Hague, 1974.
(19) The early work that is particularly important is *Přírození svět jako flosofický problém*, 1938, translated into French by Jaromír Daněk and Henri Decleve (*Le Monde naturel comme problème philosophique*, La Haye, 1976). The reference to the 'concretely lived world' is taken from Jan Patočka *Platón a Evropa* (*soukromé přednášky z roku 1973*; Prague, *samizdat*, 1979), p.53. These lectures have been translated into French by Erika Abrams (*Platon et l'Europe*, Paris, 1983).
(20) See Wittgenstein, *Philosophical Investigations*, esp. ss. 200–353.
(21) *Kacířské eseje*, Munich 1980, p.116. (Translated into French by Erika Abrams: *Essais hérétiques*, 1981.)
(22) *Dvě studie o Masarykovi*, Toronto, 1980.
(23) See note 19.
(24) *Platon a Evropa* p.61: Patočka speaks of *usilí, aby stát byl přece jenom pod světlem spravedlností a právdy, která neni z tohohle světa*.

(25) Ibid., pp. 155–6.
(26) See *Dvě studie o Masarykovi*, pp. 83 ff.
(27) See *Kacířské eseje*, ch.6.

7 ANALYTICAL PHILOSOPHY AND EMOTION

(1) Benedict de Spinoza, *Ethics: Demonstrated in Geometric Order*, Edwin Curley (ed.), *The Collected Works of Spinoza*, Vol. 1, Princeton, 1985.
(2) Ludwig Wittgenstein, *Philosophical Investigations*, tr. G. E. M. Anscombe (Oxford, 1978), Sections 243–363.
(3) See 'The meaning of meaning' in Hilary Putnam, *Mind, Language and Reality*, Philosophical Papers, Vol. 2, Cambridge, 1975.
(4) Saul Kripke, *Naming and Necessity*, Oxford, 1980.
(5) Thomas Nagel, *The View from Nowhere*, Oxford, 1986.
(6) J. P. Sartre, *Sketch for a Theory of the Emotions*, trans. Philip Mairet, London, 1971.
(7) Franz Brentano, *Psychologie vom empirischen Standpunkt*, Leipzig, 1874.
(8) Gottlob Frege, 'The thought' and 'On sense and reference', in *Collected Papers*, ed. P. T. Geach and M. Black, Oxford, 1984.
(9) See, for example, Max Scheler, *The Nature of Sympathy*, trans. P. Heath, London, 1954.
(10) Alfred Schutz, *Phenomenology of the Social World*, London, 1972.
(11) Edmund Husserl, *Die Krisis der europäischen Wissenschaften und die transcendentale Phänomenologie*, Belgrade, 1936.
(12) Roger Scruton, *Sexual Desire*, London, 1986.

8 MODERN PHILOSOPHY AND THE NEGLECT OF AESTHETICS

(1) H. Bloom et al., *Deconstruction and Criticism*, London, 1979.
(2) Nicholas Wolterstorff, *Works and Worlds of Art* (Oxford, 1980), p.9.
(3) 'Two Cultures? The Significance of Lord Snow', in F. R. Leavis, *Nor Shall My Sword*, London, 1972.
(4) See Edmund Husserl, *Die Krisis der europäischen Wissenschaften und die tranzendentale Phänomenologie*, ed. W. Biemal (The Hague, 1976). Part 2.
(5) See *Sexual Desire*, London, 1986. An application of the argument of that book can be found in 'Sexual morality and the liberal consensus', in this volume.
(6) See *The Aesthetics of Architecture*, London, 1979.

9 AESTHETIC EXPERIENCE AND CULTURE

(1) Though all praise to the valiant attempt by Mary Mothersill, in *Beauty Restored*, Oxford, 1985.

(2) For a subtle discussion of these distinctions, and their importance for aesthetic understanding, see Richard Wollheim, *The Thread of Life* (Cambridge, 1984), ch.3.

(3) *Art and Imagination*, 2nd edn, (London, 1981), part II.

(4) See 'Emotion and Common Culture', in *The Aesthetic Understanding*, London and Manchester, 1983.

(5) I have made an attempt to do so in 'The Politics of Culture', in *The Politics of Culture and Other Essays*, Manchester, 1981.

(6) On the traditionalist ideology of modern painters, see the illuminating discussion by Peter Fuller in *Theoria* (London, 1988), ch.15, 'The Spiritual in Art'.

(7) The change I have in mind is also described, in equally contentious terms, by Spengler, who, in *The Decline of the West*, makes much of an allegedly universal transition from 'culture', in which the religious experience is all, to 'civilization', in which the forms of a culture are ossified and rationalized in law and institutions. See pp.24–7 of this volume.

19 MAN'S SECOND DISOBEDIENCE

(1) Richard Cobb's views have been marvellously and meanderingly expressed in a variety of works, of which *The Police and the People: French Popular Protest 1789–1820* (London, 1970), and *Les armées révolutionnaires, instruments de la Terreur dans les départements* (2 vols., Paris and the Hague, 1961 and 1963), have been particularly influential. More important, from the interpretative point of view, however, are the essays in *Reactions to the French Revolution* (London, 1972), and *A Second Identity* (London, 1969).

(2) Hippolyte Adolphe Taine, *Les origines de la France contemporaine*, Paris, 1875. The relevant parts were translated by John Durand, as *The French Revolution*, New York, 1878, reprinted Gloucester, Mass. (Peter Smith) 1962.

(3) Edmund Burke, *Reflections on the Revolution in France*, in *Works*, vol. 3, Boston, Mass., 1865.

(4) Alexis, comte de Tocqueville, *L'Ancien régime et la Révolution*, eighth edition, Paris, 1877.

(5) François Furet, *Penser la Révolution Française*, Paris, 1978, revised edition 1983.

(6) Henry Thomas Buckle, *History of Civilization in England*, third edition, London, 1861, vol. 1, pp.425–433: a passage written with the author's usual verve and conviction.

(7) The point here is again also made by Burke, and is reaffirmed in a different context by Hannah Arendt who, taking her cue from Tocqueville, argues that anti-semitism reached its climax in Europe when Jews had lost their influence and power. (*The Origins of Totalitarianism*, new edition, New York, 1969, p.4.) Much more important, however, is Burke's observation: that the revolutionary hates something which he himself *constructs*, something which is a

'work of art' more than a reality (op. cit., p.415). Real power in the hands of the aristocrats would be as much an obstacle to revolutionary emotions as would real power in the hands of the mythologized 'bourgeoisie' of more recent revolutions.

(8) René Sedillot, *Le coût de la Révolution Française*, Paris, 1987.

(9) Alfred Cobban, 'The Myth of the French Revolution', in *Aspects of the French Revolution*, New York, 1968, pp.90–111. See also Colin Lucas, 'Nobles, Bourgeois and the Origins of the French Revolution', in *Past and Present*, no.60, August 1973, reprinted in Douglas Johnson, ed., *French Society and the Revolution*, Cambridge, 1976.

(10) See the monumental study by Augustin Cochin, *Les sociétés de pensée et la Révolution en Bretagne*, 2 vols, Paris, 1925.

(11) Daniel Mornet, *Les origines intéllectuels de la Révolution Française (1715–1787)*, Paris, 1947, p.393.

(12) Tocqueville, op. cit., pp.208, 303.

(13) V. I. Lenin, 'One Step Forward, Two Steps Back', in *Selected Works*, Moscow, 1963, p. 387. I have amended the translation. Lenin goes on interestingly to identify 'opportunism' with 'Girondism', and, in blocks of soul-less Newspeak to offer precisely the parallel between the two Revolutions that I wish to develop. Elsewhere Lenin compares the bolsheviks with 'the Jacobins of 1793': 'Enemies of the People', *Pravda*, June 1917, in R. C. Tucker (ed.), *The Lenin Anthology*, New York, 1975, p.305.

(14) Tocqueville, op. cit., p.7.

(15) Burke, op. cit., especially p.347 etc.

(16) L'Abbé Sieyès, *Qu'est-ce que le Tiers État?*, Paris 1789, translated as E. Sieyès, *What is the Third Estate?* by M. Blondel, ed. S. E. Finer, intro. by Peter Campbell, London 1963, p.124, 128.

(17) Cobban, 'The Enlightenment and the French Revolution', in *Aspects of the French Revolution, op. cit.*, p.24.

(18) Jules Michelet, *History of the French Revolution*, tr. Charles Cocks, ed. Gordon Wright, Chicago, 1967, p.444. Michelet's book is one of the first examples of a literary genre which became standard after the Russian Revolution: a panegyric, written half in Newspeak, half in a fairy-tale pastiche, in which deeds of heroism and fantastic protestations of commitment forge in unison the 'new society'.

(19) 'Civil Marriage' is as old as Roman Law, and probably already existed before the Twelve Tables; nevertheless it was not designed as a replacement for the sacred ceremonies, but only as a supplement, to cure deficiencies and confer legitimacy, in the absence of *confarreatio*. See Th. Mommsen, *The History of Rome*, tr. W. P. Dickson, 2nd edition, New York, 1868, vol. 1, pp.129–30.

(20) See Jean Robiquet, *Daily Life in the French Revolution*, translated James Kirkup, London, 1964, ch.IX.

(21) See, for example, *Reactions to the French Revolution*, op. cit., pp.5f, p.128.

(22) J. J. Rousseau, *Le Contrat Social*, Book 2, Chapter 4, note.

(23) Hannah Arendt, *On Revolution*, New York, 1963, p.69.

(24) György Lukács, *History and Class Consciousness, Studies in Marxist*

Dialectics, tr. R. Livingstone, London, 1971, p.74.

(25) Furet, *Penser la Révolution Française*, op. cit., p.76. Things have improved on the Left since the discovery that animals too are an oppressed class. Being dumb by nature, no animal can 'betray' the cause of his own liberation, not even those animals whose lives depend upon our eating them.

(26) This point has been brought home by a number of writers, Kolakowski, Havel and Zinoviev perhaps being the most important.

(27) Françoise Thom, *La langue de bois*, Paris, 1987.

(28) See note 13 above.

(29) F. A. Aulard, *La société des Jacobins, recueil de documents*, Paris 1897, 6 volumes.

(30) Petr Fidelius (pseud.), *Jazyk a moc*, ('Language and Power'), Munich 1983. Fidelius's book has been translated by Erika Abrams, as *L'esprit post-totalitaire*, Paris, 1985. See also the same author's 'Totalitarian Language', in *Salisbury Review*, vol.2 no.2, 1984, pp.33–5.

(31) But see further the analysis of Newspeak in Thom, op. cit.

(32) Quoted in James Logan Godfrey, *Revolutionary Justice*, Chapel Hill, University of North Carolina Press, 1951, p.71.

(33) Speech of 8 Ventôse (26 February 1894), to be found in Buchez and Roux, *Histoire parlementaire de la Révolution Française*, Paris 1834–38, vol.31, p.300.

(34) Speech of 25 June 1792 to the Jacobins, in Aulard, op. cit., vol.4.

(35) Cochin, op. cit., vol.1.

(36) That the Revolutionary Armies aimed to commit, and partly succeeded in committing, genocide against the rebellious people of La Vendée is clear from research summarized in Sedillot, op. cit., p.24f.

(37) Albert Mathiez, *La vie chère et le mouvement social sous la Terreur*, Paris, 1927.

(38) Donald Greer, *The Incidence of the Terror during the French Revolution*, Cambridge, Mass., 1935.

(39) Greer, op. cit., pp.96f.

(40) As in the Decree of 16 December 1793.

(41) Paul Mautouchet, *Le gouvernement révolutionnaire*, Paris, 1912, pp.158–71.

(42) See my '*Rechtsgefühl* and the Rule of Law', in J. C. Nyíri and Barry Smith, eds., *Practical Knowledge: Outline of a Theory of Traditions and Skills*, London, Sydney and New York, 1988, pp. 61–89.

(43) Louis Althusser, *Lenin and Philosophy and Other Essays*, tr. Ben Brewster, London, 1971, p.131. See my *Thinkers of the New Left*, London, 1985, Ch.9.

(44) Michel Foucault, *Power/Knowledge: Selected Interviews and Other Writings 1972–77*, ed. Colin Gordon, Brighton, 1980, p. 16.

(45) Tocqueville, op. cit., 296–7. Tocqueville adds that, in the French Revolution, it was not the process of justice, but the administrative *apparatus* that remained intact.

(46) Tocqueville, op. cit., pp.280–81.
(47) See Timothy Ware, *The Orthodox Church*, London, 1965, and Jane Ellis, *The Russian Orthodox Church: a Contemporary History*, Beckenham, 1986.
(48) Tocqueville, op. cit., pp.101–5.
(49) Sedillot, op. cit., pp.89–93.
(50) Saint-Just's education system is discussed in Robiquet, op. cit., p.83. Precisely similar proposals were put forward in the Soviet Union in 1918, with Zlata Lilina, director of education in Petrograd, demanding the 'nationalization' of all children. See Mikhail Heller and Aleksandr M. Nekrich, *Utopia in Power*, New York, 1986, p.61.
(51) See Robert Conquest, *The Harvest of Sorrow*, Oxford, 1986, and Myron Dolot, *Execution by Hunger*, New York, 1985.
(52) Václav Havel, 'The Power of the Powerless' in *Václav Havel or Living in Truth*, ed. Jan Vladislav, London, 1987, p.45.
(53) That this judgment is deserved is conclusively shown by Sedillot, op. cit., pp.117–47. And that the Revolution required the desecration of so many lovely things says something important about both the sacred and the beautiful.
(54) J-P Sartre, *Between Existentialism and Marxism*, tr. J. Matthews, London 1974, reissued 1983, p.109. I discuss Sartre's revolutionary mentality in *Thinkers of the New Left*, op. cit., ch.15.
(55) I have described this process in *Sexual Desire*, London, 1986.
(56) Cochin, op. cit., vol.1, pp.17–18.

24 IDEOLOGICALLY SPEAKING

(1) Sir Ernest Barker, introduction to Otto Gierke, *Natural Law and the Theory of Society 1500–1800*, trans. Barker (Cambridge, 1934), p.lxxi.
(2) D. Gauthier, *Morals by Agreement*, Oxford, 1985.
(3) Dale Spender, *Man-Made Language*, 2nd edn (London, 1985), p.149.
(4) Spender, *Man-Made Language*, pp.61, 63.
(5) Petr Fidelius, *Jazyk a Moc* ('Language and Power'; Munich, 1983), trans. by Erika Abrams as *L'Esprit post-totalitaire*, Paris, 1986; Françoise Thom, *La Langue de bois*, Paris, 1987; translated as *Newspeak*, London, 1984.
(6) Mikhail Gorbachev, *Perestroika: New Thinking for Our Country and the World* (London, 1987), p.126.
(7) Gorbachev, *Perestroika*, pp.127, 128.
(8) Gorbachev, *Perestroika*, p.128.
(9) Annette Kolodny, 'Dancing through the Minefield; Some Observations on the Theory, Practice and Politics of Feminist Literary Criticism', in Mary Eagleton (ed.), *Feminist Literary Theory: a Reader* (Oxford, 1986), p.186.

27 THE LEFT ESTABLISHMENT

(1) D. Marsland, *Seeds of Bankruptcy*, London, 1988.

(2) Tony Bilton et al., *Introducing Sociology*, London, 1981.
(3) Alain Finkielkraut, *The Undoing of Thought*, trans. Dennis O'Keeffe, London, 1988.

28 IN DEFENCE OF THE NATION

(1) Bikhu Parekh, 'The "New Right" and the Politics of Nationhood', in N. Deakin, ed., *The New Right: Image and Reality*, London, 1986.
(2) J. G. Herder, *J. G. Herder on Social and Political Culture*, tr. and ed., with an intro., by F. M. Barnard, Cambridge, 1969. J. G. Fichte, *Addresses to the German Nation*, tr. by F. R. Jones and G. H. Turnbull, London and Chicago, 1922.
(3) Ernest Renan, *'Qu'est ce qu'une Nation?'*; Lord Acton, 'Nationality' in *The History of Freedom and Other Essays*, ed. J. N. Figgis and R. V. Laurence, London, 1907.
(4) Parekh, op. cit., p. 39.
(5) See B. Parekh, *Contemporary Political Thinkers*, Oxford, 1982.
(6) See Henry Sidgwick, *Principles of Politics*, J. S. Mill, *On Liberty*.
(7) John Gray, 'The Politics of Culture Diversity,' *The Salisbury Review*, Vol.6, No.4,, July 1988.
(8) Michael Walzer, *Exodus and Revolution*, New York, 1985; Michael Sandel, *Liberalism and the Limits of Justice*, Cambridge, 1982; Charles Taylor, *Philosophy and the Human Sciences*, 2 vols., Cambridge, 1985.
(9) So argues, for example, Sir Isaiah Berlin, in 'Nationalism: Past Neglect and Present Power', in *Against the Current*, New York, 1980.
(10) Such, perhaps, is the nationalism of Sieyès and the Revolutionists.
(11) See Elie Kedourie, *Nationalism*, London, 1960.
(12) See R. A. D. Grant, 'Shakespeare as a Conservative Thinker', in R. Scruton, ed., *Conservative Thinkers*, London, 1988.
(13) See the commentary by H. T. Buckle, *History of Civilization in England*, third edition, London, vol.1, p.491.
(14) See the painstaking demolition by Jacques Barzun, *Race: a study in modern superstition*, London, 1938.
(15) On intentional kinds, see my *Sexual Desire*, London, 1986, Chapter 1.
(16) See above, chapter 6.
(17) The dilemma that this poses for the contemporary Jew is interestingly unfolded in Alan Montefiore, 'The Jewish Religion – Universal Truth and Particular Tradition', *Tel Aviv Review*, vol.1, 1988, pp.166–86.
(18) Ibn Khaldūn's *Muqaddimah*, tr. F. Rosenthal, 3 vols., New York, 1958. Chapter 2, sections 8, 19; Chapter 3, sections 1, 19, 24–26.
(19) In order to save Feuerbach and Marx from any suspicion of 'race thinking', *Gattungswesen* is normally translated as 'species-being' – which does little justice to the climate of opinion that gave birth to the term.
(20) Sir Henry Maine, *Ancient Law*, Cambridge, 1861.
(21) See note 7, and also R. Dworkin, *Law's Empire*, London, 1986.

(22) Kenneth Minogue, *Nationalism*, New York, 1967, p.154.

(23) I discuss the communities of Lebanon in more detail in *A Land Held Hostage*, London, 1987.

(24) Régis Debray, *Critique de la Raison Politique*, Paris, 1981, p.178.

(25) Ibid., p.208.

(26) The canonical Marxist theory of nationality acknowledges the same basic features as I do: 'The nation is a human community, stable and historically constituted, born from a common language, territory, economic life and psychological conditioning, which together are translated into a community of culture' – J. Stalin, *Communism and Russia*, 1913.

(27) See especially Albert Hourani, *Arabic Thought in the Liberal Age*, Oxford, 1962, in which the reader can clearly see the way in which liberal conceptions of law, and sovereignty, and national ideas of *'asabiyah*, have emerged simultaneously in the modern Arabic world, and stood always in a relation of mutual questioning and dependence.

(28) Alexander Solzhenitsyn, 'Repentance and Self-limitation in the Life of Nations', in *From Under the Rubble*, London, 1976.

(29) John H. Schaar, 'The Case for Patriotism', *American Review*, 17, May 1973, pp.62–3.

(30) Ibid., p.63.

(31) See Paul Johnson, *A History of the Jews*, London, 1987, p.238.

(32) See Antoine Fattal, *Le statut légal des non-musulmanes en pays d'Islam*, Beirut, 1958.

(33) Op. cit., p.294.

(34) Alain Finkielkraut, *La défaite de la pensée*, Paris, 1987.

(35) The term, but not the theory, comes from Michael Polanyi.

INDEX